COMMUNITY PARALEGALS AND THE PURSUIT OF JUSTICE

The United Nations estimates that 4 billion people worldwide live outside the protection of the law. These people can be driven from their land, intimidated by violence, and excluded from society. This Open Access book is about community paralegals – sometimes called barefoot lawyers – who demystify law and empower people to advocate for themselves. These paralegals date back to 1950s South Africa and are active today in many countries, but their role has largely been ignored by researchers. *Community Paralegals and the Pursuit of Justice* is the first book on the subject. Focusing on paralegal movements in six countries, Vivek Maru, Varun Gauri, and their coauthors have collected rich, vivid stories of paralegals helping people to take on injustice, from domestic violence to unlawful mining to denial of wages. From these stories emerges evidence of what works and how. The insights in this book will be of immense value in the global fight for universal justice.

Vivek Maru is the founder and chief executive officer of Namati, an organization dedicated to supporting legal empowerment around the world.

Varun Gauri is a senior economist in the Development Economics Vice Presidency of the World Bank.

"In the 2030 Sustainable Development Goals, world governments made a historic commitment to achieve 'access to justice for all.' This book is a must-read for anyone who, like me, believes in the urgency and vitality of that goal, and anyone who wants to understand how we go about achieving it. If 'access to justice' is an abstraction to you, it won't be once you read the stories in these pages of paralegals and clients seeking justice. Those stories are unforgettable. They hold lessons for all of us."
— Mary Robinson, former President of Ireland and former High Commissioner for Human Rights

"This book brings law to life in a thoroughly original way. It charts, with great empirical care, analytical acuity and historical sensitivity, the obstacles that lie in the path of making justice accessible to marginalized groups. It then addresses the question: to what extent can paralegals mitigate these obstacles? Through wonderful case studies of the incredibly innovative paralegal movement, it throws light on the toughest questions of our time: how can law become a site for an inclusionary imagination. Anyone interested in the future of law and justice will have to reckon with this book."
— Pratap Bhanu Mehta, Vice-Chancellor, Ashoka University

"This is a powerful guide to understanding one of the most promising emerging fields in the world today. Community paralegals are heroes on a daily basis. Each individual story is inspiring, and the global potential of this profession to change countless lives is thrilling."
— Ricken Patel, Founder and CEO, Avaaz - The World in Action

"Methodologically rigorous and deeply humane, this groundbreaking and hopeful book transports the reader to the frontlines of global community paralegal efforts to squeeze justice out of the most unlikely places. We bear witness to their successes as they champion the rights of individuals and communities against abuses of power by state actors, private corporations and dysfunctional justice systems. And through clear-eyed analysis of the challenges that community paralegals face, the book makes a convincing argument that only with sustainable financial resources, political will, and dedication to the cultivation of strong cadres of well-trained and supported grassroots advocates, can justice be a lived and long-lasting reality in the lives of the global masses."
— Chi Adanna Mgbako, Director of the Leitner International Human Rights Clinic, Fordham University School of Law

"For many people in the United States and worldwide, the law is a ruse for oppression. Frontline legal advocates can help people turn law into the guarantor of equality it is supposed to be. This book shows us how."
— Bryan Stevenson, Founder of Equal Justice Initiative and Macarthur Fellow

"This book consists of detailed and impressive studies of a worldwide program that might well constitute a revolution in the making: relying on ordinary citizens to use the power and majesty of the law to protect their rights."
— Owen Fiss, Sterling Professor, Yale Law School

"This compelling volume not only demonstrates the significance of "barefoot lawyering" in nations struggling for democracy. It contains important insights for the world wide effort to preserve and extend fundamental freedoms in the twenty-first century."
> – Bruce Ackerman, Sterling Professor of Law and Political Science, Yale University

"*Community Paralegals and the Pursuit of Justice* is a work of prodigious scholarship that represents a significant contribution to the development, human rights, and rule of law fields. Vivek Maru, Varun Gauri and contributing authors have evaluated paralegal organizations in six countries with scrupulous care and have drawn well-supported lessons for improving and expanding the model globally. *Community Paralegals and the Pursuit of Justice* provides welcome evidence that investment in paralegal organizations can not only pay significant dividends for the poor, but can improve the accessibility, capacity, and accountability of justice systems themselves."
> – Gary Haugen, Founder and CEO, International Justice Mission

Community Paralegals and the Pursuit of Justice

Edited by
VIVEK MARU
VARUN GAURI

CAMBRIDGE
UNIVERSITY PRESS

CAMBRIDGE
UNIVERSITY PRESS

University Printing House, Cambridge CB2 8BS, United Kingdom

One Liberty Plaza, 20th Floor, New York, NY 10006, USA

477 Williamstown Road, Port Melbourne, VIC 3207, Australia

314-321, 3rd Floor, Plot 3, Splendor Forum, Jasola District Centre, New Delhi - 110025, India

79 Anson Road, #06-04/06, Singapore 079906

Cambridge University Press is part of the University of Cambridge.

It furthers the University's mission by disseminating knowledge in the pursuit of education, learning and research at the highest international levels of excellence.

www.cambridge.org
Information on this title: www.cambridge.org/9781316612422
DOI: 10.1017/9781316671801

© Cambridge University Press 2018

This work is in copyright. It is subject to statutory exceptions
and to the provisions of relevant licensing agreements;
with the exception of the Creative Commons version the link for which is provided
below, no reproduction of any part of this work may take place without the written
permission of Cambridge University Press.

An online version of this work is published at http://dx.doi.org/10.1017/9781316671801 under
a Creative Commons Open Access license CC-BY-NC-ND 4.0 which permits re-use, distribution
and reproduction in any medium for non-commercial purposes providing appropriate credit to
the original work is given. You may not distribute derivative works without permission. To view
a copy of this license, visit https://creativecommons.org/licenses/by-nc-nd/4.0
All versions of this work may contain content reproduced under license from third parties.

Permission to reproduce this third-party content must be obtained from these third-parties directly.

When citing this work, please include a reference to the DOI 10.1017/9781316671801

First published 2018
First paperback edition 2020

A catalogue record for this publication is available from the British Library

Library of Congress Cataloging in Publication data
NAMES: Gauri, Varun, 1966– | Maru, Vivek.
TITLE: Community paralegals and the pursuit of justice / edited by Varun Gauri, The World Bank; Vivek Maru, The World Bank.
DESCRIPTION: Cambridge, United Kingdom ; New York, NY, USA : Cambridge University Press, 2018.
IDENTIFIERS: LCCN 2017050592 | ISBN 9781107159716 (hardback)
SUBJECTS: LCSH: Legal services – Developing countries. | Legal assistants – Developing countries. | BISAC: POLITICAL SCIENCE / Political Freedom & Security / Human Rights.
CLASSIFICATION: LCC K133 .C657 2018 | DDC 362.5/86–dc23
LC record available at https://lccn.loc.gov/2017050592

ISBN 978-1-107-15971-6 Hardback
ISBN 978-1-316-61242-2 Paperback

Cambridge University Press has no responsibility for the persistence or
accuracy of URLs for external or third-party internet websites referred to in
this publication, and does not guarantee that any content on such websites is,
or will remain, accurate or appropriate.

Contents

List of Figures		*page* viii
List of Contributors		ix
Acknowledgments		xiv

1. Paralegals in Comparative Perspective: What Have We Learned across These Six Countries?
   Vivek Maru and Varun Gauri — 1

2. "To whom do the people take their issues?": The Contribution of Community-Based Paralegals to Access to Justice in South Africa
   Jackie Dugard and Katherine Drage — 43

3. Community-Based Paralegalism in the Philippines: From Social Movements to Democratization
   Jennifer Franco, Hector Soliman, and Maria Roda Cisnero — 96

4. Paralegalism in Indonesia: Balancing Relationships in the Shadow of the Law
   Ward Berenschot and Taufik Rinaldi — 139

5. Kenya's Community-Based Paralegals: A Tradition of Grassroots Legal Activism
   H. Abigail Moy — 165

6. Squeezing Justice Out of a Broken System: Community Paralegals in Sierra Leone
   Vivek Maru, Lyttelton Braima, and Gibrill Jalloh — 210

7. The Contributions of Community-Based Paralegals in Delivering Access to Justice in Postwar Liberia
   Peter Chapman and Chelsea Payne — 241

Index — 264

Figures

1.1	Steps in solving justice problems	*page* 11
1.2	How sustainable is your funding situation for the coming year?	24
3.1	Incidence of paralegals by type of organization	109
3.2	Annex A: Anatomy of a typical paralegal training	135
3.3	Annex B: List of organizations participating in the study	136
4.1	Case handling by paralegals	151
4.2	Type of case	152
4.3	Cases reported by paralegals by date	155
6.1	Satisfaction with Timap, reporting versus non-reporting parties	214
6.2	Scaling up grassroots justice: Chiefdoms served by paralegals as of 2011	215
6.3	Common case types (2013)	216
6.4	Primary action taken by paralegals to resolve cases (2013)	217
6.5	Distribution of cases tracked	218
6.6	Who brought complaints?	219
6.7	Why did they choose the institution or organization they approached?	219
6.8	What kinds of cases?	220
6.9	What methods were used in addressing the case?	221
6.10	How did parties perceive the outcomes? (all interviewees)	221
6.11	Were participants aware of relevant law?	221
7.1	Successfully resolved cases: 2007–September 2012	252
7.2	Percentage of case type categories: 2007–September 2012	253

Contributors

Ward Berenschot is a postdoctoral researcher at KITLV researching local democracy, clientelism, and identity politics in India and Indonesia. Berenschot studied political science at the University of Amsterdam, where he also obtained his PhD cum laude with a dissertation on Hindu–Muslim violence in India. As a lecturer in conflict studies, he taught courses on political violence, ethnic conflict, and conflict transformation. He has managed a collaborative research project with the UNDP and the World Bank on access to justice in Indonesia, and he has worked with the Open Society Institute as well as Dutch development agencies on civil society building and legal aid. Berenschot is the author of *Riot Politics: India's Hindu–Muslim Violence and the Everyday Mediation of the State* (2011) and several other publications on ethnic violence, public service delivery, and access to justice. At KITLV Berenschot also coordinates the KNAW-SPIN research program "From Clients to Citizens? Emerging Citizenship in Democratizing Indonesia." His book on Indonesia's patronage democracy, *Democracy for Sale: Clientelism, Elections and the State in Indonesia* (coauthored with Edward Aspinall), will appear in the fall of 2018.

Lyttelton Braima is a Rotary World Peace Fellow from the Duke-UNC Rotary Peace Center. As a policy-oriented researcher, he has spent the past fifteen years on research and development practice, using research outcomes to advocate and effect public policy to improve the lives of marginalized communities. Before joining the World Bank Justice for the Poor program from 2008 to 2013, Braima worked for Care International's Rights-Based Approach (RBA) program in Sierra Leone, designing and implementing initiatives to rebuild community governance and justice systems after the civil conflict. His expertise includes participatory research methods and program evaluation. He is skilled in a number of key policy spheres, particularly governance, justice, health, mining, food security, and social accountability.

Peter Chapman is a senior policy officer working on law and development with the Open Society Justice Initiative. He has a particular focus on legal empowerment and community-based justice services. Prior to joining the Justice Initiative, Chapman worked on governance and justice reform in East Asia and Africa with the World Bank's Justice for the Poor program, with the Carter Center in Liberia, and with the Public International Law and Policy Group in Uganda and Washington, DC. He has authored publications on law and development for a variety of audiences. Chapman holds a JD from the Washington College of Law, American University; an MA in international affairs from the School of International Service, American University; and a BA in political science and peace studies from Colgate University.

Maria Roda Cisnero is the Asia Foundations Philippines project officer for the Law and Human Rights Unit. In her role for the Child Protection against Online Sexual Abuse and Exploitation Project, she supports the implementation of the two-year project with the Australian Embassy and UNICEF. An alternative lawyer by vocation, Cisnero is honing her expertise on computer-facilitated crimes against children, child protection, and policy reform. Cisnero served as a national advocacy director of International Justice Mission Philippines (IJM) from 2011 until joining the Foundation in 2015. Prior to her work at IJM, she worked for the Legal Assistance Center for Indigenous Filipinos and Tanggol Kalikasan. She is a product of the developmental law internship program of the Ateneo Human Rights Center, LRC KsK Friends of the Earth Philippines and Environmental Legal Assistance Center (ELAC). Cisnero received her BA in broadcast communication from the University of the Philippines, Diliman; her JD from Ateneo De Manila University; and her MA in development studies, social justice perspectives from Erasmus University–ISS.

Katherine Drage is a qualifying attorney with Withers LLP (London) where she has a broad civil litigation practice and serves as the firm's pro bono coordinator for the UK Solicitors Pro Bono Group. Drage was a litigation and research intern at SERI from July 2010 to July 2011. She has a diverse interest in international human rights law, and especially in education and the promotion of access to justice and the uptake of rights-based litigation. She holds a master of arts degree in English from Cambridge University; a bachelor of laws degree (First) from BPP Law School, London; and an LLM degree from the University of Pennsylvania. Drage has completed her Legal Practitioner's Course with distinction and received her Solicitor's Training Contract.

Jackie Dugard is an associate professor at the School of Law, University of the Witwatersrand (Johannesburg), where she teaches property law and jurisprudence. In January 2010 Dugard cofounded and (between January 2010 and December 2012) was the first executive director of the Socio-Economic Rights Institute of South Africa (SERI), where she is now the chairperson of SERI's board of directors. Prior to founding SERI, between 2004 and 2009, she was a senior researcher at the Centre for Applied Legal Studies (CALS) at the University of the Witwatersrand. In February 2014 Dugard established the Gender Equity Office (GEO) at the

University of the Witwatersrand to deal holistically with gender-based harm, which she directed until December 2016. Dugard's areas of expertise are socioeconomic rights, socio-legal studies, land and property rights, and access to basic services and justice for the poor. She has a BA (Hons) in African politics and an LLB from the University of the Witwatersrand, an MPhil in the sociology and politics of development and a PhD in social and political sciences from the University of Cambridge, and an LLM in international human rights law from the University of Essex.

Jennifer Franco is a senior researcher at the Transnational Institute (TNI) based in Amsterdam, where she is part of the Agrarian and Environmental Justice team and the Myanmar in Focus team. Her research interests are mainly in the realm of action research with rural social movements and grassroots organizations in relation to claiming rights to land and territory. Prior to joining TNI she worked with local peasants' movements in the Philippines in support of their struggles for right to land and territory, human rights, and social justice. She received a PhD in politics from Brandeis University in the late 1990s and wrote a doctoral dissertation on the impact of less-than-democratic elections on regime transition and democratization in the Philippines. Since 2012 she has been working with local civil society organizations and communities in Myanmar in support of democratization of land access and control.

Varun Gauri is a senior economist in the Development Economics Vice Presidency of the World Bank. He co-leads the Mind, Behavior, and Development Unit (eMBeD), which integrates behavioral science into the design of antipoverty policies worldwide. He serves on the editorial board of the journals *Behavioral Public Policy* and *Health and Human Rights*, and is a member of the World Economic Forum Council on Behavior, the advisory board of Academics Stand against Poverty, and the board of the Behavioral Economics Action Research Centre at the University of Toronto. His research has appeared in journals spanning the fields of economics, philosophy, political science, and law, and has been covered in the *New York Times*, the *Economist*, the *Washington Post*, *Forbes*, the *Hindu*, and *Frontline*, among many media outlets. He has published three books: *Courting Social Justice*, *School Choice in Chile*, and *Bringing Law to Life*. His current research is investigating the influence of social norms on women's economic decision-making, compliance with judicial human rights orders, and the influence of cooperation and identity on ideas of distributive justice. He has a BA from the University of Chicago and a PhD from Princeton University, and has held positions as a visiting lecturer in public and international affairs at Princeton University, the Withrow Chair at Deep Springs College, and a visiting professor in the Department of Economics at ILADES in Santiago, Chile.

Gibrill Jalloh is a 2014 Mason Fellow at the Harvard Kennedy School of Government, Ash Center for Democratic Governance and Innovation. He worked for the World Bank Justice for the Poor program in Sierra Leone from 2006 to 2013. His work was focused on understanding "context" in the design and execution of development interventions. His work has used social accountability and legal empowerment approaches to advance local-level justice and improve social service delivery outcomes in suburban and rural Sierra Leone; this involves researching, designing, testing, evaluating, and informing mainstream development interventions. He is also a pioneer of the case-tracking method in the evaluation of social justice interventions. Prior to joining the World Bank, he was an environmental advocate and worked with a consortium of environmental NGOs to preserve protected areas in Sierra Leone and across the border. He holds an MA in public administration from the Kennedy School of Government, Harvard, and a BSc in environment science from Njala University.

Vivek Maru started Namati in 2011 to grow the movement for legal empowerment around the world. Namati and its partners have built cadres of grassroots legal advocates – also known as "community paralegals" – in eight countries. The advocates have worked with more than 65,000 people to protect community lands, enforce environmental law, and secure basic rights to health care and citizenship. Namati convenes the Global Legal Empowerment Network, made up of more than 1,500 groups from 130 countries who are learning from one another and collaborating on common challenges. Vivek was named a Social Entrepreneur of the Year by the World Economic Forum, a "legal rebel" by the American Bar Association, and an Ashoka Fellow. He, Namati, and the Global Legal Empowerment Network received the Skoll Award for Social Entrepreneurship in 2016.

H. Abigail Moy is the director of the Global Legal Empowerment Network, convened by Namati. Since Namati's earliest days, she has led efforts to build a thriving global movement for legal empowerment, one capable of innovating boldly and collectively tackling the greatest justice challenges of our time. The Global Legal Empowerment Network works to achieve this vision by connecting, strengthening, and expanding the number of community paralegals around the world. Prior to joining Namati, Abigail worked with access to justice programs in Africa, Latin America, and South Asia, in cooperation with the World Bank, the Asia Foundation, Fundacion Soros-Guatemala, and Timap for Justice. She previously clerked for the Hon. David H. Coar in the Northern District of Illinois, served in the Office of the Legal Adviser at the US Department of State, and worked in the New York office of White & Case, LLP. Moy was awarded a Fulbright Fellowship, graduated cum laude from Harvard Law School, and holds a master's degree in law and development from the Fletcher School of Law and Diplomacy.

Chelsea Payne was the country representative of the Carter Center in Liberia (2010–12) where she led the access to justice program. At the time of writing,

Payne was a rule of law officer in the United Nations Rule of Law Unit in the Executive Office of the Secretary-General. Payne has a bachelor of civil laws (BCL) degree and a master of science degree in African studies from the University of Oxford, where she studied on a Rhodes Scholarship.

Taufik Rinaldi is an expert in the field of community development and legal aid in Indonesia. He initiated the Justice for the Poor program (the World Bank) and has conducted various studies in the field of access to justice to the poor, good governance, and anti-corruption. In addition to research and program management, Rinaldi is involved in drafting the National Strategy on Access to Justice in Indonesia (2010) and the Road Map Sustainability Community Empowerment in Indonesia (2014). Currently he is working as a freelance consultant who provides strategic policy advice to governments and donor agencies in Indonesia.

Hector Soliman acted as a team leader/project director for eight years in various multiyear access to justice and judicial reform projects, managing an intercultural staff to deliver results in court-annexed ADR, justice reform advocacy, and community legal services (legal advice, community meditation, litigation services, and referral to justice institutions). Soliman worked as a senior government official (Assistant Secretary and Undersecretary) managing the legal affairs of the Department of Agrarian Reform, including adjudication of agrarian disputes, community-level mediation programs for farmers, and internal matters such as contract review, procurement, promotions, and personnel discipline. He also acted as chief legal advisor to the Secretary of Agriculture. Soliman consulted for the ADB, the UNDP, the JBIC, the CIDA, the World Bank, the Global Fund, WHO, the Ford Foundation, and the Asia Foundation on various legal reform issues such as strengthening the administrative and financial systems of the judiciary, improving the criminal justice system and the national prosecution service, community paralegals, and others. He has been active in the legal service NGO sector for at least ten years, working closely in the fields of agrarian reform law and environmental law; facilitated the formation of a network of legal service organizations in the Philippines that eventually evolved into the Alternative Law Groups; and provided support to the network, as well as individual legal NGOs that work in the public interest. Soliman remains active in the practice of law intermittently in his career as partner or advisor of a law firm that works with, among others, alternative energy companies in the setting up of their operations in the Philippines.

Acknowledgments

This book has been a long time coming. To everyone involved: thank you for bearing with us.

Thank you to our twelve coauthors, who span research and practice and many corners of the globe. You taught us so much. We're already wondering: how can we get the band back together? We want to keep learning with you.

Thank you to the terrific team at Cambridge University Press, including John Berger, Rebecca Jackaman, Anubam Vijayakrishanan, and Ami Naramor.

Thank you to two anonymous peer reviewers. Your feedback made this book better.

A generous grant from the World Bank Netherlands Partnership Program supported most of the field research, though the findings and views expressed in this book do not necessarily represent the views of the World Bank or its Executive Directors. Thank you to World Bank colleagues past and present who gave us their time and insight, including Nick Menzies, Rick Messick, Adrian Di Giovanni, Caroline Sage, Christina Biebesheimer, and Michael Woolcock.

Thank you to the entire extraordinary team at Namati. Deyla Curtis has been a caring steward for years now. Jinyoung Lee and Alice Goldenberg were indefatigable researchers, organizers, cheerleaders, and problem solvers. They were the community paralegals of this project in its final stage. Without them it may not have crossed the finish line.

Thank you to the Open Society Foundations. We dreamed that this book could be available for free to legal empowerment practitioners worldwide. OSF made that possible. OSF also supported completion of the project. Zaza Namarodze has backed the work this book describes with passion, persistence, and an ethic of quiet service for fifteen years. He's just getting started.

Thank you to participants in the Legal Empowerment Leadership Course at Central European University. Their feedback – drawn from hard-won experience – was precious.

Thank you to our families: Tania, Ayesha, Yasmeen, Sharif, Safya, Luka, Sajan, and the Maru, James, Gauri, and Khan clans.

Thank you to the members of the Global Legal Empowerment Network. There are thousands of us now, from 150 countries, working to put the power of law in people's hands.

Our greatest debt is to the communities and paralegals who shared their stories with us. We honor your struggles for justice. We dedicate this book to you.

1

Paralegals in Comparative Perspective

What Have We Learned across These Six Countries?

Vivek Maru and Varun Gauri

I. INTRODUCTION

In Mbiuni, a town in a dry region of eastern Kenya, sand miners from Nairobi nearly destroyed the only local sources of drinking water. Sand retains water – removing it in vast quantities causes the water table to drop. A prominent woman from Mbiuni, Mary M., said simply: "The water catchment was on the verge of drying up . . . Water is very precious here. Without it we will all be dead."

Mary and several other community members approached the police, the district officer, and the local chief to complain. Every one of those officials claimed he lacked the authority to act against the miners. Desperate, some people set fire to a truck that came to pick up sand. Police arrested and imprisoned two of the demonstrators. The mining continued.

Where were the people of Mbiuni supposed to go? Kenya adopted national guidelines on sand harvesting in 2007. According to the guidelines, no one can mine sand outside of sites approved by district-level sand-harvesting committees. The committees are supposed to designate sites only after considering social and environmental risks.[1]

The mine in Mbiuni was not in an approved site. Mary and others in Mbiuni hadn't seen the guidelines and didn't know approval was required. The district officer didn't mention the guidelines when they approached him. Mary suspected that he and other officials were receiving a cut of the revenue from the mine.

The situation of the Mbiuni residents is not uncommon. For perhaps a majority of human beings – 4 billion people as estimated by the UN Commission on Legal Empowerment – the promises of law and government are often unmet.[2] Many people have never heard of laws that are supposed to protect them. Others cannot avail themselves of nominally good rules and systems because of cost, dysfunction,

---

[1] National Environment Management Authority (NEMA), Kenya National Sand Harvesting Guidelines, 2007, Section 4.

[2] See Commission on Legal Empowerment of the Poor, UN Development Programme, *Making the Law Work for Everyone: Report of the Commission on Legal Empowerment*, vol. 1 (New York: United Nations, 2008), 1.

corruption, or abuse of power. In many other cases, the law itself is unjust. As a result, people are denied even basic rights to dignity, safety, and livelihood.

Advancing justice requires at least three elements. First, people need to conceive of themselves as bearers of rights, as agents capable of action. In other words, they must undergo that transformation of outlook in which, as Hannah Pitkin puts it, "I want" becomes "I am entitled to."[3] Second, state institutions – administrative agencies, legislatures, the courts – need to be fair, effective, and responsive to their citizens. Much of political science is about how to make governments more so. Third, in our view, there is a need for intermediary institutions that assist citizens in exercising their rights.[4] In other words, there needs to be, as Gauri and Brinks describe it, a "legal support structure appropriate to the claims being brought, in light of the institutional requirements" in any given context.[5]

There are many kinds of intermediary institutions. Political parties and unions, for example, serve as intermediaries for electoral politics and workplaces respectively. Public interest lawyers help people access formal courts. Ombudsman offices serve as intermediaries for citizens seeking to resolve grievances against the state. In this book, we aim to characterize and assess a lesser-known intermediate institution – the community paralegal.

According to the 2012 Kampala Declaration on Community Paralegals, community paralegals "use knowledge of law and government and tools like mediation, organizing, education, and advocacy to [help people] seek concrete solutions to instances of injustice."[6]

While conventional paralegals typically serve as back-office assistants to lawyers, *community* paralegals – also known as community legal workers, or barefoot lawyers – work directly with people affected by injustice. Because these community

---

[3] Hanna F. Pitkin, "Justice: On Relating Public and Private," *Political Theory* 9, no. 3 (1981): 347, www.jstor.org/stable/191093. On this transformation of outlook, *see also* Lynn Hunt, *Inventing Human Rights: A History*, for a history of how Europeans and Americans came to believe in universal rights. Lynn A. Hunt, *Inventing Human Rights: A History* (New York: W. W. Norton & Co., 2007). *See also* Arjun Appadurai, "The Capacity to Aspire: Culture and the Terms of Recognition," in *Culture and Public Action*, ed. Vijayendra Rao and Michael Walton (Stanford, CA: Stanford University Press, 2004), 59–84.

[4] *See, for example*, Daniel Brinks and Sarah Botero, "Inequality and Rule of Law: Ineffective Rights in Latin American Democracies" (paper presented at the American Political Science Association Annual Meeting, Washington, DC, September 2–5, 2010), 11. Brinks and Botero emphasize the importance of what they call "lateral support," which they describe as a "dense network ... of ancillary rules, and of third party facilitators and controllers" that promotes rule enforcement. This network helps close the gap between de jure rule regimes and de facto practice.

[5] Varun Gauri and Daniel M. Brinks, "Introduction: The Elements of Legalization and the Triangular Shape of Social and Economic Rights," in *Courting Social Justice: Judicial Enforcement of Social and Economic Rights in the Developing World*, ed. Varun Gauri and Daniel M. Brinks (Cambridge: Cambridge University Press, 2008), 1–37.

[6] "Kampala Declaration on Community Paralegals," Kampala, Uganda, July 26, 2012, www.namati.org/news/newsfeed/kampala-declaration/. The Declaration was adopted in 2012 by more than fifty paralegal organizations from more than twenty African countries. Full disclosure – one of us, Vivek, helped draft the Kampala Declaration.

paralegals help people to understand and use the law themselves, their work is often referred to as "legal empowerment."

Stephen Golub, who coined the phrase "legal empowerment" in the early 2000s, distinguishes legal empowerment from what he calls the "rule of law orthodoxy." Golub describes rule of law orthodoxy as "a 'top-down,' state-centered approach [that] concentrates on law reform and government institutions, particularly judiciaries, to build business-friendly legal systems that presumably spur poverty alleviation." In contrast, legal empowerment focuses on placing the power of law in the hands of ordinary people.[7]

Throughout this volume, when we use the term "paralegal," we are referring to community paralegals rather than conventional paralegals unless we specify otherwise.

Community paralegals and their clients[8] typically address three kinds of problems: disputes among people, grievances by people against state institutions, and disputes between people and private firms. Sometimes these cases involve individuals seeking justice; often they involve groups or entire communities.

Paralegals aim to help people achieve practical remedies: a group of workers wins unpaid back wages from their employer; a fishing community secures environmental enforcement against a factory releasing illegal effluents into the sea; a mother receives support for her children from a derelict father.

Like community health workers – who have an established place in health care delivery systems around the world[9] – community paralegals are close to the communities in which they work and deploy a flexible set of tools. Also like community health workers, paralegals work in tandem with a strong, typically well-organized profession. While community health workers refer difficult cases to doctors and the formal medical system, community paralegals are typically connected to lawyers who can engage in litigation or high-level advocacy if the paralegals' frontline methods fail.

---

[7] Stephen Golub, "Beyond Rule of Law Orthodoxy: The Legal Empowerment Alternative," *Carnegie Endowment for International Peace Working Papers* 41 (October 2003), 3, 33–37.

[8] In this book, we often use the term "clients" to refer to the people whom paralegals serve. We borrow that term from the legal profession. It's a convenient but imperfect shorthand. "Client" can connote dependency, whereas paralegals aim to equip people to advocate for themselves. Many legal empowerment groups do not use the term for that reason. Paralegals working with the organization Natural Justice in Kenya, for example, call the people they serve "community partners."

[9] Community health workers were a central part of the vision of primary health care endorsed by 134 countries at Alma-Ata in 1978. See "Declaration of Alma-Ata," International Convention on Primary Health Care, Alma-Alta, USSR, September 6–12, 1978, art. 7, sec. 3.7. Today they are a front line for health care delivery systems around the world, and a key focus of the global public health movement. See Anne Liu, Sarah Sullivan, Mohammed Khan, Sonia Sachs, and Prabhjot Singh, "Community Health Workers in Global Health: Scale and Scalability," *Mt. Sinai Journal of Medicine* 78 (2011): 419–35. *See also* Prabhjot Singh and Jeffrey D. Sachs, "1 Million Community Health Workers in Sub-Saharan Africa by 2015," *The Lancet* 382, no. 9889 (2013): 363–65, doi: 10.1016/S0140-6736(12)62002-9.

In Mbiuni, after local authorities refused to take action, and public demonstrations led to violence and arrests but no progress, Mary and others approached a pair of community paralegals. The paralegals organized two public meetings, attended by 400 people each, in which they suggested the community use the law. The paralegals explained the sand-harvesting guidelines and other regulations related to natural resources.

The chief and assistant chief objected to the gatherings, but the paralegals urged the community not to be afraid. The paralegals helped community members draft a written petition to several agencies, including the National Environmental Management Authority (NEMA), which issued the sand harvesting guidelines. NEMA responded: it ordered the operation to close, and requested the provincial administration to enforce its order.

The mining stopped. According to Mary, "now there is enough water." She said, "the paralegals cooled tempers, educated us and even told [people involved in mining] the legal provisions on sand harvesting ... The law says water catchment areas belong to the community ... We have said no to sand mining forever."

Mary could be overestimating the victory. Sand-mining cartels are very powerful in Kenya, as they are in many countries.[10] The profits at stake are often enough to overcome legal prohibitions and the officials who are supposed to enforce them. It's hard to say how long the "no" from the community will hold. But those two paralegals helped Mary and others bend a hopeless situation in the direction of justice.

Community paralegals of different kinds exist throughout the world,[11] and date back to at least the 1950s, when Black Sash and other organizations deployed paralegals to help nonwhite South Africans navigate and defend themselves against apartheid. Community paralegals are recognized by legislation in Afghanistan, Indonesia, Kenya, Malawi, Moldova, Mongolia, New Zealand, Nigeria, Sierra Leone, Uganda, England and Wales, and Ontario and British Columbia in Canada.[12]

---

[10] *See, for example*, Shadrack Kavilu, "Kenya's Illegal Sand Miners Destroy Farms to Plunder Scarce Resource," *Reuters*, October 6, 2016, www.reuters.com/article/us-kenya-landrights-sand-mining/ken yas-illegal-sand-miners-destroy-farms-to-plunder-scarce-resource-idUSKCN126116.

[11] *See, for example*, Vivek Maru, "Between Law and Society: Paralegals and Provision of Justice Services in Sierra Leone and Worldwide," *The Yale Journal of International Law* 31 (2006), 427–76; Mary McClymont and Stephen Golub, eds., *Many Roads to Justice: The Law-Related Work of Ford Foundation Grantees around the World* (New York: The Ford Foundation, 2000); Stephen Golub and Kim McQuay, eds., "Legal Empowerment: Advancing Good Governance and Poverty Reduction," in *Law and Policy Reform at the Asian Development Bank* (Asian Development Bank, 2001), 7–164.

[12] Legal Aid Regulation, OFFICIAL GAZETTE No. 950 (2008) §§ 2, 15 (Afghanistan); Law Concerning Legal Aid, No. 16/2011 §§ 1, 4, 7–10 (Indonesia); The Legal Aid Act, No. 6 (2016), KENYA GAZETTE SUPPLEMENT No. 56 § 68; Legal Aid Act No. 7 of 2011 (Malawi); Law on State Guaranteed Legal Aid, Law No. 1988-XVI, of July 26, 2007 (Moldova); National Program on Legal Aid to Indigent Citizens 2006 (Mongolia); Legal Services Act 2011 (N.Z.), cls 3, 69, 75, 93–94; Legal Aid Act, 2011 §§ 17, 24 (Nigeria); The Legal Aid Act, No. 6 (2012), SUPPLEMENT TO THE SIERRA LEONE GAZETTE Vol. CXLIII, No. 42; The Advocates Act, Cap. 267 (Uganda); Access to Justice Act 1999 art. 4 ¶ 8 (England and

The NGO BRAC has one of the largest paralegal efforts in the world – it deploys more than 6,000 paralegals or "barefoot lawyers" and has addressed more than 2 million complaints through its legal aid clinics.[13] Community paralegals have attracted increasing attention from international organizations, including the UN Commission on Legal Empowerment.[14]

Proponents of the paralegal approach have suggested the following four advantages, among others:

- **Empowerment.** A conventional legal aid approach tends to treat people as victims requiring a technical service. In contrast, paralegals aspire to cultivate the knowledge and power of the people with whom they work. Not "I will solve this problem for you," but "We will solve it together, and in the process we will both grow."
- **Mixed methods.** Community paralegals combine several strategies: advocacy, mediation, organizing, monitoring, and education. This allows them to pursue creative and constructive solutions to justice problems. Paralegals can tailor their approach in any given case to the wishes of the communities with whom they work.
- **Creative about institutions.** Community paralegals don't focus on the judiciary alone. They pursue remedies everywhere: administrative agencies, local governments, accountability bodies like ombudsmen and human rights commissions, parliaments, customary justice institutions, and others.
- **Cost-effectiveness and scale.** Lawyers are the conventional providers of legal services, but lawyers are often costly and difficult to access. In many countries, one finds a few ad hoc legal aid centers, often in capital cities, and no serious attempt to reach those in the countryside. The paralegal approach poses a more plausible model for delivering primary justice services to all.[15]

On the other hand, a paralegal approach has several potential problems and limitations. For example:

- **Limits on effectiveness.** Paralegal involvement in local, intra-community disputes can be redundant with existing institutions. In conflicts with the

---

Wales); and in Canada the Province of Ontario Legal Aid Services Act, S.O. 1998, c. 26 (Can.) and the Legal Services Society Act, S.B.C. 2002, c. 30 (Can.).

[13] BRAC, "Human Rights and Legal Aid Services Programme: Figure up to September 2013," BRAC, September 2013, http://hrls.brac.net/images/pdf/HRLS-Sept-2013.pdf.
[14] *See* Commission on Legal Empowerment of the Poor, UN Development Programme, *Making the Law Work for Everyone*, 24 (*see* n. 2) (stating "paralegals are critically important to improving legal service delivery to poor communities").
[15] *See* Vivek Maru, "Allies Unknown: Social Accountability and Legal Empowerment," *Health and Human Rights* 12, no. 1 (2010): 85; *See also* Maru, "Between Law and Society," 468–70 (*see* n. 11).

state or with private firms, on the other hand, paralegals and their clients may not be able to win against powerful interests.
- **Consistency and quality.** Without rigorous training, supervision, and support, paralegal efforts can be of inconsistent quality.
- **Risk of abuse.** Paralegals can use their knowledge and status to take advantage of others.
- **Sustainability.** Funding from donors, development agencies, and governments can prove inadequate and unreliable.

There has been relatively little systematic study of the workings of paralegal programs. In "Nonlawyers as Legal Resources for Their Communities," Stephen Golub describes Ford Foundation grantees deploying paralegals in Asia, Latin America, and Africa.[16] In "Legal Empowerment: Advancing Good Governance and Poverty Reduction," Golub and Kim McQuay document paralegal work in several Asian countries.

One of us (Vivek) offered an overview of paralegal efforts around the world in a 2006 article that was primarily about the methodology of the Sierra Leonean program Timap for Justice.[17] Another of us (Varun) has presented theoretical accounts of the kind of "legality" that paralegals engage with, and of the pathways through which paralegals can promote economic and social outcomes for poor individuals.[18]

A 2017 review of evidence on civil society efforts at legal empowerment, which considered academic articles as well as "grey" literature like organizational reports and conference papers, turned up twenty-nine pieces that deal with paralegals, not including the ones in this book.[19] The majority was published in the past decade. Most of these pieces are case studies of individual programs; some involved research on impact.

For example, Jacobs, Saggers, and Namy studied a pilot program in Lowero District, Uganda that deployed paralegals to educate people about women's land rights and to address individual disputes. The authors drew on surveys, interviews with clients and paralegals, and the program's internal monitoring data. They found that paralegals were able to resolve many cases quickly – 17 percent of the cases

---

[16] Stephen Golub, "Nonlawyers as Legal Resources for Their Communities," in *Many Roads to Justice: The Law-Related Work of Ford Foundation Grantees around the World*, ed. Mary McClymont and Stephen Golub (New York: Ford Foundation, 2000), 297–314.

[17] Maru, "Between Law and Society" (see n. 11).

[18] Varun Gauri, "The Publicity 'Defect' of Customary Law," in *Legal Pluralism and Development: Scholars and Practitioners in Dialogue*, ed. Caroline Sage, Brian Z. Tamanaha, and Michael Woolcock (Cambridge: Cambridge University Press, 2013), 215–27; Varun Gauri, "Customary Law and Economic Outcomes in Indonesia," *Hague Journal on the Rule of Law* 2, no. 1 (2010): 75–94.

[19] Laura Goodwin and Vivek Maru, "What Do We Know about Legal Empowerment? Mapping the Evidence," *Hague Journal on the Rule of Law* 9, no. 1 (2017): 157, doi: 10.1007/s40803-016-0047-5. The review gathered evidence from 2013 and earlier, 199 studies in total.

brought to paralegals resulted in mediation agreements between disputing parties. For another 33 percent of cases, paralegals referred people to institutions like the local council or the local council court. In general clients praised paralegals for being accessible and responsive, in contrast to formal institutions that they found expensive, slow, and hard to reach.[20]

Sunil Kumar narrates the experience of a government-sponsored program in Andhra Pradesh, India, which also sought to improve access to land rights for poor rural women. The Society for Elimination of Rural Poverty in the state's Rural Development Department trained community-based paralegals and community-based surveyors to work with women's self-help groups. The program was piloted in 2004 and extended to all twenty-two districts of the state in 2006.

Between 2006 and 2010, paralegals and community surveyors identified land problems of 610,000 rural poor people involving 1.18 million acres of land. Of those, the paralegals and community surveyors helped to resolve the problems of 430,000 people, which involved 870,000 acres of land. The National Rural Livelihoods Mission committed to scale up this approach to several more states throughout the country.[21]

Rachael Knight and her coauthors conducted a two-year randomized controlled trial in Liberia, Mozambique, and Uganda that compared the effectiveness of paralegals with two other ways of protecting community land rights. Organizations in all three countries supported communities to document customary land claims, resolve boundary disputes, and strengthen the rules and structures for governing community lands.

Knight and her colleagues found that paralegals were more effective than both a full legal services approach, in which communities had direct assistance from lawyers, and a pared-down rights education approach, in which information was provided and little else. They observed that communities receiving full legal services tended to place their hopes with the outside professionals, while communities with paralegals tended to take greater ownership over the process.[22]

Scholars have conducted two evaluations of the Sierra Leonean legal empowerment group Timap for Justice.[23] In one study by Pamela Dale, researchers selected forty-two cases from Timap's docket and interviewed all parties involved. Dale

[20] Krista Jacobs, Meredith Saggers, and Sophie Namy, *How Do Community-Based Legal Programs Work? Understanding the Process and Benefits of a Pilot Program to Advance Women's Property Rights in Uganda* (Washington, DC: International Center for Research on Women, 2011), 2.

[21] M. Sunil Kumar, "A Systems Approach for Providing Legal Aid for Land" (paper presented at the Annual World Bank Conference on Land and Poverty, Washington, DC, April 8–11, 2013), 15. *See also* Robert Mitchell and Tim Hanstad, *Innovative Approaches to Reducing Rural Landlessness in Andhra Pradesh: A Report on the Experience of the IKP Land Activities* (Seattle, WA: Rural Development Institute, 2008).

[22] Rachael Knight, Judy Adoko, Teresa Aluma, Ali Kaba, Alda Salomao, Silas Siakor, and Issufo Tankar, *Protecting Community Land and Resources: Evidence from Liberia, Mozambique, and Uganda* (Rome: International Development Law Organization/Washington, DC: Namati, 2012).

[23] One of us, Vivek, cofounded Timap for Justice and served as co-director from 2004 to 2007.

reports that respondents were "overwhelmingly positive" about their experiences with Timap paralegals. Respondents "praised Timap's effectiveness in resolving difficult disputes, particularly those that confront institutions or power relationships."[24]

A second evaluation focused on a newer program, in which Timap trains paralegals to work in police stations and prisons. The paralegals educate detainees and remand prisoners about criminal law and assist them with basic procedures like bail petitions. This initiative was modeled in part on the Paralegal Advisory Service in Malawi, which has deployed paralegals in prisons since 2000.

Justin Sandefur, Bilal Siddiqui, and Alaina Varvaloucas used a difference-in-difference approach to compare prisons in which Timap paralegals were working with other prisons where there were no paralegals. They found that the paralegal intervention led to a 13 percent increase in the share of detainees receiving bail and a 20 percent decrease in the share of prisoners held without trial or conviction.[25]

The evidence on paralegal approaches is not limited to the developing world. Jay Wiggan and Colin Talbot review literature on citizen advocates in the United Kingdom who help people to understand and access basic welfare benefits. Wiggan and Talbot find that "welfare rights advisors" increase participation in public entitlements and improve the living standards and mental health of their clients.[26]

Rebecca Sandefur and Thomas Clarke studied the work of non-lawyer "access to justice navigators" who assist self-represented litigants in housing and civil courts in New York City. The navigators help people to understand the legal process and to prepare basic documents, like a tenant's "answer" to a landlord's petition for nonpayment of rent.

Normally, one in nine nonpayment of rent cases in New York City leads to eviction. Many of the evictions result from imbalances of power between landlords and tenants. Sandefur and Clarke found that navigators could narrow those imbalances considerably, at a very low cost. Out of 150 cases handled by one set of navigators in the borough of Brooklyn, Sandefur and Clarke found no evictions at all.[27]

Together, these studies suggest that community paralegals succeed in advancing justice in some circumstances, and that the advantages posited earlier in this

---

[24] Pamela Dale, *Delivering Justice to Sierra Leone's Poor: An Analysis of the Work of Timap for Justice*, Justice for the Poor Research Report, no. 1 (Washington, DC: World Bank, 2009), iv.

[25] Justin Sandefur, Bilal Siddiqi, and Alaina Varvaloucas, *Timap for Justice Criminal Justice Pilot: Impact Evaluation Report* (Oxford: Center for the Study of African Economies, Oxford University, 2012), 9, 72.

[26] Jay Wiggan and Colin Talbot, *The Benefits of Welfare Rights Advice: A Review of the Literature* (Manchester: National Association of Welfare Rights Advisors, 2006), 6–7.

[27] Rebecca L. Sandefur and Thomas M. Clarke, "Roles beyond Lawyers: Summary, Recommendations, and Research Report of an Evaluation of the New York City Court Navigators Program and Its Three Pilot Projects" (American Bar Foundation, National Center for State Courts, Public Welfare Foundation, December 2016), 5. *See also* Matthew Desmond, *Evicted: Poverty and Profit in the American City* (New York: Crown Publishers, 2016). Desmond provides an in-depth account of how housing courts in the United States are biased against poor tenants.

chapter – empowerment, mixed methods, institutional creativity, cost-effectiveness – do apply, at least in some cases. There is very little existing research, however, on the factors that shape paralegal work, and the way paralegals interact with political and social context. We pay particular attention to those questions here.

This is the first book on the subject, and the first effort to bring together original empirical work on multiple paralegal programs from several countries, using a structured and explicitly comparative approach. By taking a comparative approach, we are able to venture more generalized conclusions, which extend beyond a particular program in a particular place.

In the next section, we describe the scope and methods of our research. After that we discuss the methodology of paralegals themselves, in particular the six approaches we found them using in their work. We then explore how three sets of factors shape community paralegal efforts: government institutions, culture, and paralegal organizations. We close with a summary of our findings and a reflection on the role of paralegals in deepening democracy.

II. METHODS AND SCOPE

This book considers community paralegals in six countries. We chose to study South Africa and the Philippines because they have some of the oldest and richest experience with paralegals, dating back to the 1950s and 1970s, respectively. In the other four countries – Indonesia, Kenya, Sierra Leone, and Liberia – community paralegals are more recent but are now serving significant portions of the population, and are the subject of current national policy debate. In Indonesia, Kenya, and Sierra Leone, recent legal aid laws recognize the role paralegals play and call for expansion of paralegal services.[28] We have organized the chapters by the longevity of the paralegal movements, with South Africa first and Liberia – where paralegals began to operate in 2007 – last.

In five of the countries (all but Liberia) we adopted an explicitly comparative approach in advance. The research teams first met in Washington, DC, in 2010 to discuss a shared methodology and approach. The core elements were (a) to study paralegal programs empirically, using case-tracking methods and a counterfactual where possible; and (b) to examine the factors – institutional, cultural, and organizational – that affect the nature and the effectiveness of paralegal efforts. Having developed this common approach, each of the country teams was free to adapt the methods in light of its specific circumstances.

---

[28] See The Legal Aid Act, No. 6 (2012), SUPPLEMENT TO THE SIERRA LEONE GAZETTE Vol. CXLIII, No. 42 § 36(1) (stating "The Board shall ensure that at least one legal assistant or accredited paralegal is appointed in a neutral office in every chiefdom ... in order to provide legal advice and assistance to such chief, his officials and inhabitants of such chiefdom"); The Law of the Republic of Indonesia Concerning Legal Aid No. 16/2011 (Official Translation), available at www.namati.org/tools/legal-aid-bill-indonesia/; Legal Aid Act No. 6 (2016), KENYA GAZETTE SUPPLEMENT No. 56 §§ 7(1)(h), 7(1)(o), and 68(1).

All six research teams conducted interviews with paralegal organizations, including paralegals themselves, lawyers, and other program staff. The teams reviewed organization documents, including data on cases when they were available. All teams also interviewed key stakeholders in executive and judicial branches of government, as well as in the private bar.

Everywhere except the Philippines, the teams undertook some form of case tracking: selecting a sample of cases handled by paralegals and interviewing clients and others involved in those cases. The teams in Indonesia and Sierra Leone followed the same case-tracking process in similar areas where paralegals were not operating, in order to establish a basis for comparison. Researchers identified cases in those non-paralegal areas by interviewing chiefs and other leaders who commonly address disputes.

The Liberia chapter draws on interviews with stakeholders conducted by the chapter authors as well as a randomized controlled trial led by two other researchers, Justin Sandefur and Bilal Siddiqui.[29] The randomized controlled trial compared people who had help from a paralegal with people who had requested help but not yet received it.

The findings in the South Africa, Philippines, and Kenya chapters are largely qualitative, while the Indonesia, Sierra Leone, and Liberia chapters blend qualitative and quantitative analysis. Some variations in methodology were due to local circumstances, others to time and resource constraints. Despite the variation, we believe there is enough commonality across the six studies to yield meaningful comparative insight.

III. MODES OF ACTION: HOW PARALEGALS WORK

What exactly do community paralegals do? In our research we found paralegals using six broad approaches: (1) education, (2) mediation, (3) organizing, (4) advocacy, (5) monitoring, and, with the help of lawyers, (6) litigation. Most of these approaches appear, for example, in the diagram that follows, from the Timap for Justice paralegal manual, on the steps Timap paralegals take to address a case.

Paralegals try to demystify law – to transform it from something abstract and intimidating into something that people can understand, use, and shape. In all six countries, paralegals dedicate significant time to educating communities about laws that affect them. In Indonesia, paralegals conduct village-level discussions on topics like contract law, corruption, the rights of criminal suspects, and a 2004 law on domestic violence. Similar meetings in Liberia often address women's rights, land rights, and labor rights.

In the two countries where we quantified comparisons between those receiving paralegal services and "control" populations – Sierra Leone and Liberia – we found

[29] Justin Sandefur and Bilal Siddiqi, "Delivering Justice to the Poor: Theory and Experimental Evidence from Liberia" (paper presented at the World Bank Workshop on African Political Economy, Washington, DC, May 2013).

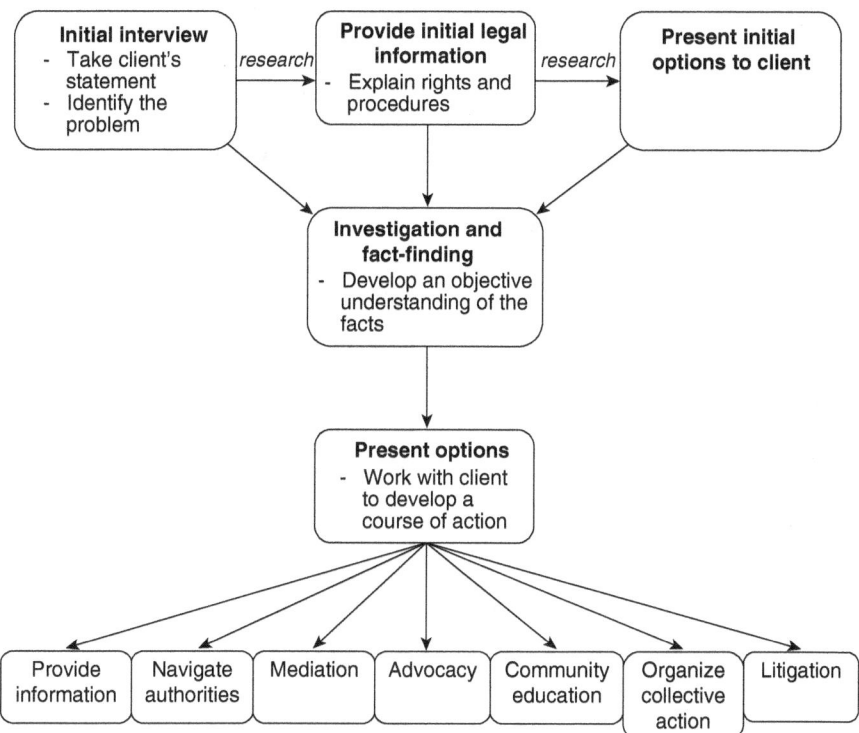

FIGURE 1.1 Steps in solving justice problems
Source: Timap for Justice, *Paralegal Manual 2012: A Practitioner's Guide to Providing Basic Justice Services in Sierra Leone* (Freetown: Timap for Justice, 2012), 5; also printed in Open Society Foundations, *Community Based Paralegals: A Practitioner's Guide* (New York: Open Society Institute, 2010), 94.

that parties in cases handled by paralegals were significantly more likely than their counterparts to have knowledge of relevant national law.

But raising legal awareness by itself is usually not enough. Paralegals go further: they walk with clients toward a solution. In citizen versus citizen disputes, paralegals often attempt mediation. In Northwest Province of South Africa, for example, members of a burial society approached a paralegal at the Lethabong community advice office, whom they heard about from workers on neighboring farms. Two members of their society had failed to make the agreed financial contributions, and the rest of the membership had to bear the burden. The paralegal conducted a three-hour mediation – in the end, the two defaulters acknowledged their debt and agreed to pay it off in monthly installments. In Sierra Leone and Liberia, mediation was the approach paralegals used most often.

Paralegal mediations tend to differ from those conducted by other local dispute resolvers – a village chief, say, or a religious elder – in that paralegals inject information about the law, and are willing to assist a wronged party to pursue a remedy if mediation fails. This is one of the ways that paralegals "enlarge," as Berenschot and Rinaldi write in the Indonesia chapter, "the shadow of the law."

A common step beyond mediation is organizing community members for collective action.[30] After mediating between the burial society and its defaulting members, the paralegal from Lethabong helped the society draft a constitution and formal membership agreement, so that the rules would be clearer and more easily enforced in the future.

In cases involving government or private firms, paralegals often combine organizing and advocacy. The sand-mining case from Kenya with which we opened the chapter involved both organizing and advocacy. So too a case from Indonesia, in which a nationwide fund for village-level infrastructure projects called PNPM (Program Nasional Pemberdayaan Mandiri) allocated resources for only half of the village of Bandung Baru in Lampung Province.

A paralegal named Ulhaidi educated people from the neglected half of the village about the policies governing PNPM. He then organized them to demonstrate outside the village headman's house. They demanded that the headman request PNPM officials to provide resources for the entire village; the headman made the request, and the PNPM officials complied.

Paralegals do not always wait for community members to approach them with problems; in some cases, they actively monitor for possible rights violations. In the Philippines, for example, some paralegals supported by the Alternative Law Groups take water samples to examine the impact of tailings from mines on community water supply. When they identify violations, paralegals and communities use the evidence to lodge complaints with the Department of Environment and Natural Resources.

When both mediation and advocacy fail, paralegals sometimes turn to lawyers to litigate. In 2014 in the Nimiyama chiefdom of Sierra Leone, seventy families woke up to find poles erected on the land they have farmed for generations. Their paramount chief had sold 1,400 acres to a Chinese rubber company without asking them.

Blocked from entering their land, some of them moved to neighboring chiefdoms to find work as laborers. Some stayed, hoping to challenge the sale. The ones who stayed connected with two paralegals working in the region, Hassan Sesay and Fatmata Kanu.

[30] Paralegals are part of a broader tradition of combining organizing with the use of law. In *Suburban Sweatshops*, for example, Jennifer Gordon describes how undocumented immigrants on Long Island in the United States came together to demand just treatment in their workplaces – restaurants, construction sites, and private homes where they cooked and cleaned. Gordon reflects on how the group she founded, The Workplace Project, combined legal services to solve specific cases with community organizing to build courage and power within a population that has been historically powerless. Jennifer Gordon, *Suburban Sweatshops: The Fight for Immigrant Rights* (Cambridge, MA: Harvard University Press, 2007).

Hassan and Fatmata explained that the deal between the chief and the rubber company was illegal. At most the chief could have leased farmland – outright sale of customary land is prohibited by law – but even that would have required the consent of the families who have customary rights to it.

The paralegals helped the families try for redress – they approached the chief and the company directly, and they engaged the ministries of land and agriculture. But in this case, the firm and the chief were intransigent, and the ministries were unresponsive. So the families and paralegals partnered with a single Sierra Leonean lawyer, Sonkita Conteh, to bring a case in the High Court.

After a long litigation, the High Court ordered in February 2016 that the company return the land and pay reparations for the damage that was done.[31] The families were able to return to their farms in time for planting season. Fanta Nyanda, one of the women whose land it was, said at the courthouse the day the judgment came out: "We now know the law is for us."[32]

A successful court judgment – like a positive new law or regulation – offers a lever paralegals and communities can use in the future. Paralegals in Sierra Leone have educated people about the Nimiyama judgment via radio and community meetings, with the aim of stopping land grabs before they happen.

Community paralegals are not the only ones who apply these various approaches. Governments and many civic organizations provide education about the law. Respected members of society – customary authorities, religious leaders, family elders – often mediate local disputes. For grievances with the state or with private firms, those same leaders, as well as members of political, social, or trade associations, sometimes organize collective action and advocate for remedies. The private bar engages in litigation, as do some public interest lawyers who are not connected to community paralegals.

What distinguishes community paralegals is the way they combine these various approaches. They do not stop at educating people about the law; they actively seek remedies. When voluntary mediation does not result in an agreement in an intra-community dispute, they assist the wronged party to pursue other channels of redress. Their organizing and advocacy are informed by their understanding of law and government, and are bolstered by their connection to lawyers and the possibility of litigation.

Some social workers, trade unionists, and community organizers may indeed combine these six approaches in ways very similar to that of paralegals, without referring to themselves as such. The findings in this book may have relevance for those other actors as well, irrespective of which term they use.

---

[31] Edna Smalle, "Namati Wins Land Case ... Chinese Company to Restore 1,486 Acres of Land," Awoko, March 1, 2016. http://awoko.org/2016/03/01/sierra-leone-news-namati-wins-land-case-chinese-company-to-restore-1486-acres-of-land/. This case took place after our case-tracking research was complete.

[32] This is according to Sonkita Conteh, the lawyer who represented the families. Sonkita Conteh (director of Namati Sierra Leone), interview, March 5, 2016.

IV. FACTORS THAT SHAPE PARALEGAL EFFORTS: INSTITUTIONS, CULTURE, AND ORGANIZATIONS

We found evidence of paralegal effectiveness in all six countries. In Liberia, people who had worked with paralegals demonstrated significantly greater knowledge of law than people who hadn't. Paralegal clients were also 35 percent more likely to think that the outcome of their case was fair and 37 percent more likely to be satisfied with the outcome.[33] In the other countries, findings on effectiveness were qualitative rather than quantitative, but thematically similar. We heard repeatedly that help from a paralegal increased people's understanding of law and government, increased their confidence to take action, and allowed them to achieve at least a partial solution to an injustice they would have otherwise had to bear.[34]

But the specific nature of paralegal work varied greatly: the types of cases paralegals take on, for example, or the institutions they engage, or the kinds of remedies they're able to achieve, or the scale at which they operate, or the extent to which governments are responsive to their efforts. We saw variation across countries, across organizations, and across individual paralegals.

In the remainder of this chapter we draw conclusions about the factors that shape the nature of paralegal efforts. We divide our findings according to three kinds of factors: institutional (the nature of a legal system and government), social (norms and culture), and organizational (the way a program is run). This typology of factors emerged from the collaborative workshop we held with research teams, and it serves as the general explanatory framework in each of the chapters in this book, though variously adapted to match the data available in each country context. Our interpretations in this comparative chapter grow directly from the country-level empirical work, though in some cases, our views may not be identical to those of the country study authors.

V. POLITICAL AND LEGAL INSTITUTIONS

A. *Paralegals in the Justice Landscape*

1. From Resisting Repressive Regimes to Realizing the Promises of Democracy, and Back Again

The kinds of injustices paralegals take on and their chances of winning are shaped by the legal and governance climate in which paralegals work. In three countries in our study, paralegals at first helped people to navigate and survive repressive regimes. In South Africa, community paralegals emerged in the 1950s, during apartheid.

---

[33] Sandefur and Siddiqi, "Delivering Justice to the Poor: Experimental Evidence from Liberia," 32–37 (see n. 29).

[34] The Philippines is the only country in which researchers did not speak with clients. There, accounts of effectiveness came from institutional actors, organizational staff, and the paralegals themselves.

Some were based in African National Congress offices, some worked from the homes of community leaders, and others were supported by the NGO Black Sash. Paralegals assisted people of color to defend themselves against repressive laws, in particular pass laws and others that restricted movement. They also monitored and publicized the conditions of people who were forcibly displaced.

In the 1970s in the Philippines, during the dictatorship of President Marcos, the Free Legal Assistance Group began training paralegals to provide "first aid legal aid," often for people accused of violating martial law. During the New Order in Indonesia, two legal aid movements emerged, both deploying paralegals: *bantuan hukum structural* – structural legal aid – in the 1970s and *pendidikan hukum kritis* – critical legal education – in the 1990s. Paralegals in both movements supported communities to pursue women's rights and rights related to land, natural resources, and labor. *Pendidikan hukum kritis* placed particular emphasis on customary legal regimes as alternatives to inherently repressive official law.

In all three of these repressive regimes – apartheid South Africa, the Philippines under Marcos, and New Order Indonesia – paralegals sought to mobilize communities to change laws and government structures, though many of those efforts were thwarted and paralegals themselves were often subject to repression.

As these countries underwent transitions toward democracy, the paralegals in each one devoted more time to the realization of newly codified legal rights. The combination of progressive, pro-poor legislation with massive gaps in the state's capacity to deliver (the existence of "big policies in small states"[35]) creates an opportunity for paralegals.[36] Paralegals can help citizens hold the state accountable to its new promises. South African paralegals, for example, now focus their efforts on assisting clients to access state provisions like social security, pension, and health care, or on enforcing new protections for women and workers.

Paralegals in the Philippines have played a central role in the implementation of post-Marcos laws on environment, agrarian reform, and labor – they educate communities about the laws, monitor compliance, and help clients to seek enforcement. Paralegals can provide representation in agrarian reform and labor tribunals, and some are deputized as community-based coast and forest guards. In some cases, paralegals were involved in lobbying for the laws they now help to implement.

In a review of literature on the relationship between citizen action and state services, Ringold and colleagues conclude that asymmetries in information and

---

[35] Gauri and Brinks, "Introduction," 27 (*see* n. 5).
[36] *See, for example*, Daniel M. Brinks and Varun Gauri, "A New Policy Landscape: Legalizing Social and Economic Rights in the Developing World," in *Courting Social Justice: Judicial Enforcement of Social and Economic Rights in the Developing World*, ed. Varun Gauri and Daniel M. Brinks (New York: Cambridge University Press, 2008), 318. Brinks and Gauri argue that remedies tend to follow rather than create detailed and comprehensive policy frameworks.

power are key barriers that limit citizen capacity to hold the state accountable to its positive commitments.[37] Paralegals aim to reduce both kinds of asymmetry.

Unfortunately, the journey from extractive to inclusive institutions is not linear. South Africa, the Philippines, Kenya, and Sierra Leone have all arguably zigzagged in recent years.[38] Paralegal groups have adapted their work accordingly. In the Philippines, in response to President Duterte's "War on Drugs," paralegals with the organization SALIGAN have re-focused their community education efforts on laws governing police searches and arrests.

Paralegals with the coalition Alternative Law Groups are planning to train communities on how to document extra-judicial killings, to collect evidence in the hope of future efforts to hold public and private actors accountable. Marlon Manuel, National Coordinator of Alternative Law Groups, said "we are more prepared to resist repression now because of our experience in the days of Marcos and what we learned from that period."[39]

2. Variation in Impact across Case Types, and the Relationship between Grassroots Experience and Systemic Change

The kind of value paralegals add varies across different types of cases. When people have disputes with other community members, rather than with the state or private firms, they generally have a wider choice of forums, including customary authorities like traditional courts and chiefs, state institutions like the police, and other actors who will mediate or arbitrate, like a religious leader or a school principal. Paralegals sometimes help community members to engage these various forums; in other cases, they mediate the disputes themselves.

The more functional and fair the existing forums are, it seems, the less important is the role of paralegals in cases that would go before them. In the Philippines, the local *barangay* justice system, which is a hybrid structure that combines traditional and formal elements – is reasonably accessible and accepted.[40] Likely as a result of

---

[37] Dena Ringold et al., *Citizens and Service Delivery: Assessing the Use of Social Accountability Approaches in Human Development* (Washington, DC: International Bank for Reconstruction and Development, World Bank, 2012), 93–95.

[38] See, for example, Benjamin Fogel and Sean Jacobs, "Getting Rid of Zuma Isn't a Panacea for All South Africa's Ills," *The Guardian*, April 5, 2017, www.theguardian.com/commentisfree/2017/apr/05/getting-rid-jacob-zuma-not-panacea-south-africa-problems; Felipe Villamor, "President Rodrigo Duterte of Philippines Criticized over Martial Law Warning," *New York Times*, January 16, 2017, www.nytimes.com/2017/01/16/world/asia/philippines-duterte-martial-law.html; Jina Moore, "Kenya's About-Face: Fear for Democracy as Dissent Is Muzzled," *New York Times*, February 4, 2018, www.nytimes.com/2018/02/04/world/africa/kenya-political-repression-kenyatta-odinga.html;

Cooper Inveen, "President's Iron-Fist Methods Raise Fears for Future of Democracy in Sierra Leone," *The Guardian*, October 20, 2017, www.theguardian.com/global-development/2017/oct/20/president-ernest-bai-koroma-iron-fist-methods-raise-fears-for-future-of-democracy-in-sierra-leone-march-election.

[39] Manuel Marlon (National Coordinator, Alternative Law Groups [ALG]), interview. January 23, 2018.

[40] Surveys suggest that the *barangay* system is highly regarded by past users and by the general population. Between 1999 and 2005, the *barangay* system successfully mediated 75 to 85 percent of

this, paralegals in the Philippines focus comparatively less on intra-community disputes and more on efforts to hold government and private firms accountable.

In Indonesia, village heads resolve most intra-community disputes. Paralegals often advise people who are going before these village leaders. Berenshcot and Rinaldi tracked some cases in which advice from paralegals strengthened the ability of poor parties to argue for themselves, and to invoke the law in doing so. But in many other cases resolved by village heads, the paralegals seemed to have minimal impact, perhaps at best boosting a poor person's confidence. In Indonesia, like in the Philippines, paralegals' significance in intra-community disputes seemed to be lower when village heads were functioning well.

Paralegal intervention can be very valuable in intra-community disputes, on the other hand, when local institutions are likely to be systematically unfair. The rights of women is a prime example. There are paralegals who help women exercise their rights in relation to family and community members in every country we studied.

In Sierra Leone, child support, alimony, child custody, wife neglect, and rape/sexual abuse made up 43 percent of all cases handled by paralegals, but less than 10 percent of the cases we encountered in non-paralegal sites. All of these cases involved complaints by women against men. The Sierra Leone chapter infers that "women are bringing these cases more often to paralegals and less often to local authorities because of the bias of existing institutions."

For cases that do not involve a serious crime, paralegals will often attempt mediation with the aim of reaching an agreement that respects women's rights under law. If mediation fails, or if a violation is too serious for mediation to be appropriate (e.g., rape), paralegals help women seek a fair result from existing institutions.

In Liberia, a paralegal (locally called a community justice advisor), assisted a woman, Musu, whose boyfriend threw acid on her, severely burning her face and torso. The man was initially arrested, but the state dropped his case and released him, which led Musu to fear for her life. A paralegal educated Musu about criminal procedure and accompanied her in a meeting with the county attorney. Together they pressed for prosecution, and Musu offered to serve as a witness. The county attorney complied, and the man was re-apprehended and convicted. Chapman and Payne conclude in the Liberia chapter that "without the [paralegal's] intervention, the case would likely have been forgotten, [and] Musu's justice denied."

---

the cases it received. Carol Mercado, "*Barangay* Justice System: Model of Citizen-Driven Justice System" (paper prepared for National Workshop on Local Justice, Dhaka, May 11–12, 2008). On the other hand, another study shows that when the parties to the mediation have a huge power imbalance, then the disputants are less likely to come before the *barangay* justice system. Jennifer C. Franco, "Peripheral Justice? Rethinking Justice Sector Reform in the Philippines," *World Development* 36, no. 10 (2008): 1864, doi: 10.1016/j.worlddev.3007.10.011.

The forward-looking implication of our findings on intra-community disputes is this: paralegals should avoid redundancy with existing institutions by focusing their work with respect to intra-community disputes on areas, like women's rights, for which existing institutions are likely to be systematically unfair.

Researchers in all six countries found that paralegals have some of their greatest impact when dealing with disputes between people and the state, as in the infrastructure fund case we described from Indonesia, or disputes between people and private firms, as with the sand mining case from Kenya with which we opened the book. The Indonesia, Kenya, and Sierra Leone chapters recommend that paralegals in those countries place greater emphasis on such cases.

The stakes in state and corporate accountability cases are typically high, and the imbalance of power is great. Resolving them frequently involves engaging administrative institutions (like the PNPM administration in Indonesia, or the National Environmental Management Authority in Kenya), which do not require a lawyer but which are often opaque, intimidating, or corrupt. A paralegal can help people to understand the terrain, identify favorable laws and regulations, and find their way to a remedy.[41]

Paralegals and their clients do not always win when they take on tough cases of any type. The solutions they do achieve are usually partial victories. By and large this is to be expected – if the cases are too easy, then paralegals wouldn't be adding much value. But it is important that they can make enough progress to inspire hope. If remedies are completely out of reach, Franco, Soliman, and Cisnero point out in the Philippines chapter, "the cumulative effects" on communities "can be demoralization, demobilization, or a turn toward violence."

In all three categories of cases – disputes with the state, disputes with firms, and disputes between citizens – paralegal casework provides a detailed picture of how people experience the law in practice. Organizations and the communities they serve can draw on that information to identify and advocate for systemic changes. In the Philippines, after a decade of working to implement the agrarian reform passed in 1988, paralegals and their clients were crucial in advocating for two extensions of the law – first for another ten years until 1998, and then again until 2014. Franco, Soliman, and Cisnero explain that "[t]he work of paralegals was instrumental in providing the much-needed evidence of the weaknesses and shortcomings of the law as crafted. For example, landowners in the coconut-producing areas used criminal statutes in order to circumvent the intent of the law, and this practice was corrected in subsequent legislation."

[41] *See, for example,* Paralegals for Environmental Justice, a practice guide that describes how paralegals and communities can seek administrative remedies to social and environmental harms arising from development projects. The guide is based on the work of a team of paralegals focused on environmental justice in India. Manju Menon, Meenakshi Kapoor, Vivek Maru, and Kanchi Kohli, *Paralegals for Environmental Justice* (New Delhi: Center for Policy Research – Namati Environmental Justice Program, 2017), https://namati.org/wp-content/uploads/2017/12/Practice-Guide-for-Environmental-Justice-Paralegals.pdf.

By translating grassroots experience into nuanced calls for reform, paralegals and their clients can help shape the institutional landscapes they inhabit.

B. Recognition and Regulation

1. Paralegal Groups Have Sought, and Sometimes Won, Recognition within National Legal Aid Systems

In all six countries, as paralegal movements have matured, they have raised the question of their status vis-à-vis the state. Paralegals and paralegal organizations seek formal recognition for three reasons. First, recognition can bring greater legitimacy, and thereby make government officials and private actors more responsive to advocacy by paralegals.

Second, recognition can lead to public financing. Third, standards for who qualifies as a paralegal may improve the consistency of paralegal services and guard against fraud and abuse. On the other hand, state recognition and regulation also pose risks: too much state involvement might replace dynamism with rigidity[42] and curtail paralegals' ability to hold the state accountable.[43]

Segments of the private bar, meanwhile, often oppose recognition of community paralegals. These lawyers are typically concerned with maintaining their monopoly over legal services; as a result, they often only welcome paralegals who work as lawyers' assistants. Legal empowerment groups respond that there is almost no overlap between the two spheres of practice because community paralegal clients are too poor to access lawyers.

Chapman and Payne write that "objections from many members of the bar miss a fundamental reality confronting many in Liberia: most individuals simply cannot engage lawyers for advice or assistance or access formal courts with legal and administrative issues. The fees and geographic factors are prohibitive." Moreover, several of the methods community paralegals deploy, including mediation, organizing, and navigating administrative and traditional institutions, are outside lawyers' core competence.

In Indonesia, Kenya, and Sierra Leone, legal empowerment organizations have overcome opposition from the bar and successfully advocated for legal aid

---

[42] Billings, Meinzen-Dick, and Mueller caution, for example, that a proposed legal aid bill in Tanzania could reduce the reach of legal aid programs in remote areas. The bill requires that paralegals have at least a Form III education. Billings and colleagues point out that this could make it difficult to recruit paralegals in areas with lower education levels, and that the requirement may overshadow other recruitment priorities, like achieving gender balance and selecting people with a demonstrated commitment to public service. Lucy Billings, Ruth Meinzen-Dick, and Valerie Mueller, *Implications of Community-Based Legal Aid Regulation on Women's Land Rights*, IFPRI Research Brief (Washington, DC: International Food Policy Research Institute, 2014), 1–2.

[43] The 2012 Kampala Declaration on Community Paralegals articulates similar principles: the organizations (1) commit to improving the quality and consistency of paralegal efforts; (2) call for governments to recognize the role paralegals play; (3) ask governments and other institutions to invest in the scale up of paralegal services; and (4) call on governments to respect paralegals' independence. *See* "Kampala Declaration on Community Paralegals" (*see* n. 6).

legislation that recognizes community paralegals. The 2012 Sierra Leone Legal Aid Law establishes an independent Legal Aid Board and authorizes the Board to accredit legal aid providers, including civil society organizations and paralegals. The law calls for a paralegal in every chiefdom of the country.[44]

The 2011 Indonesia Law on Legal Assistance also recognizes community paralegals. The law does not set up a separate board; rather, it mandates the Ministry of Law and Human Rights to directly accredit legal aid providers.[45] Paralegal proponents in Indonesia have therefore expressed concern as to whether accredited paralegals will be able to maintain their independence from government.[46]

The 2016 Kenya Legal Aid Act recognizes paralegals, including community paralegals, so long as they are supervised by an advocate or an accredited legal aid organization. The Act establishes a national Legal Aid Service responsible, among other things, for coordinating, monitoring, and evaluating paralegals. The governing board for the Service includes a reserved seat for a representative elected by a joint forum of civil society legal aid providers. The Act establishes a legal aid fund to "meet the expenses incurred by legal aid providers,"[47] although details on how the fund will work in practice are still being negotiated as of this writing.

In South Africa, two bills that would have recognized paralegals – the Legal Practice Bill of 2002 and the Legal Services Charter of 2007 – stalled in parliament, in part because of opposition to paralegal recognition by the private bar.[48] The bar was particularly resistant to provisions that would have allowed paralegals to collect fees and to represent clients in low-level administrative courts. Dugard and Drage point out in the South Africa chapter that the lack of recognition, and in particular the failure to integrate community advice offices more fully with Legal Aid South Africa, creates challenges for sustainability and quality control.

In March 2015, South Africa established a Legal Practice Council through a new law, the Legal Aid South Africa Act. The Act requires the Council to make recommendations, within two years of its creation, regarding the statutory recognition of community paralegals.[49] Two national coalitions dedicated to community paralegals – the Association of Community Advice Offices in South Africa (ACAOSA) and the National Alliance for the Development of Community Advice Offices (NADCAO) – applauded the passage of the Act.[50]

[44] The Legal Aid Act, No. 6 (2012), SUPPLEMENT TO THE SIERRA LEONE GAZETTE Vol. CXLIII, No. 42 § 36(1).
[45] Republic of Indonesia, Draft: Indonesia Law No. 16 Concerning Legal Aid (2011), https://namati.org/wp-content/uploads/2012/01/Uli_Legal_Aid_Bill.pdf, Article 9, 7(1)(b), 7(2). *See also* Michael Otto, "Indonesia – Community Paralegal Research Brief," 5 (on file with author).
[46] Uli Sibombing (Indonesia Legal Resource Center), interview, July 2012, Kampala.
[47] The Legal Aid Act No. 6 (2016), *Kenya Gazette* Supplement No. 56 § 30(c).
[48] David McQuoid-Mason (Center of Socio-legal Studies, University of KwaZulu-Natal), interview, November 2010, Geneva.
[49] Legal Practice Act 28 of 2014 § 34(9) (S. Afr.).
[50] *See, for example,* "Legal Practice Bill Assented," NADCAO, May 14, 2015, http://nadcao.org.za/legal-practice-bill-assented/.

Where legal empowerment groups have managed to secure legislative recognition for community paralegals, they have tended to work in coalitions like NADCAO and ACAOSA, rather than as lone organizations acting in isolation. They have also cultivated champions within government. Advocates in Sierra Leone reached a turning point when they persuaded the attorney general to change his position from opposing paralegal recognition to embracing it. In Kenya, the Parliamentary Human Rights Association proved to be a vital ally. Immediately after a meeting with legal empowerment groups in 2015, association members reintroduced the legal aid bill that had been stuck since 2013. The bill passed by the end of the session.

2. The Challenges of Recognition within Legal Aid Systems, and Two Alternatives: Sectoral Departments and Local Governments

There are drawbacks to seeking recognition from national legal aid schemes. Because legal aid is traditionally the domain of lawyers, this avenue of recognition often runs directly into opposition from the bar.

Recognition within a legal aid scheme also poses budgetary challenges. Legal aid systems often lack the resources to meet their constitutional obligations to provide a defense counsel to people facing serious criminal charges.[51] Asking cash-strapped institutions to broaden their mandate can be like trying to squeeze juice out of dry limes.[52]

As a result, some paralegal movements have sought recognition on a sector-specific basis, as a complement or an alternative to recognition by a national legal aid system. In the Philippines, for example, the Supreme Court objected to a component of an access to justice project that involved training community paralegals. The Court found that the project would constitute unlawful practice of law.

But despite this rejection by the judiciary, community paralegals have gained recognition from several sectoral departments. Paralegals can provide representation in agrarian reform tribunals (through the Department of Agrarian Reform Adjudication Board) and labor disputes (through the National Labor Relations Commission). Some are deputized as community-based forest guards (by the Department of the Environment and Natural Resources). The Department of Agrarian Reform has also provided financial support for the training of farmer

---

[51] *See, for example,* "Legal Aid in Europe: Minimum Requirements under International Law," Open Society Foundation (April 2015), www.opensocietyfoundations.org/sites/default/files/ee-legal-aid-standards-20150427.pdf, 2, 13; "Access to Legal Aid in Criminal Justice Systems in Africa: Survey Report," *United Nations Office on Drugs and Crime* (2011), www.un.org/ruleoflaw/files/Access_to_Legal_Aid_in_Criminal_Justice_Systems_in_Africa.pdf, vii–viii, 11, 18–19.

[52] Legal Aid South Africa, for example, does have a broad mandate that includes both civil and criminal issues. But criminal defense is a constitutional obligation and takes up 93 percent of LASA's docket. Community advice offices focus largely on civil issues, so without increased allocations, any support to community paralegals would have to come out of the remaining 7 percent of LASA's budget. *See, for example,* Annual Report: Legal Aid South Africa 2009/2010, www.legal-aid.co.za/wp-content/uploads/2012/04/Legal-Aid-SA-Annual-Report-2009-10.pdf, 26.

paralegals.[53] Community paralegals are not part of a national legal aid scheme to date. But Supreme Court opposition did not crush the paralegal movement, in part because the movement found recognition elsewhere.

Paralegal groups have secured a sector-specific form of recognition in Sierra Leone as well. Government there was slow to constitute the Legal Aid Board after passage of the Legal Aid Law. As of this writing, the Board has not recognized or funded community paralegals, with the exception of a small pilot focused on pretrial detainees. In the meantime, legal empowerment groups have successfully advocated for recognition in the new National Land Policy for the role of paralegals in supporting communities in relation to investors.

The policy requires firms interested in leasing land to pay into a basket fund that will finance legal support via paralegals for landowning communities.[54] If implemented, this provision will create revenue for an urgent need. The Sierra Leone government is aggressively courting large-scale agriculture and mining investments as a way of restarting the economy after the Ebola epidemic. The investments often lead to gross exploitation, as with the case from Nimiyama that we described earlier. With basic legal support communities can defend themselves against outright land grabs, negotiate equitable terms if they do choose to welcome investment, and seek enforcement if those terms are violated.[55]

In addition to sectoral recognition, another alternative to the national legal aid route is to make inroads with government at a local level. In South Africa, the Zola municipal government in Gauteng Province pays rent and utilities for its local community advice office; the Mpola municipality in Kwa Zulu Natal provides its local advice office with free space in the town hall. Other paralegals in South Africa have recognition from local traditional authorities: fifteen community advice offices in Kwa Zulu Natal are located in the offices of traditional courts.

In the Philippines some *barangay* (village-level) governments have similarly provided community paralegals with office space and operational expenses. Good relations with *barangay* officials can be of great value to paralegals, especially for addressing the rights of women and children. In those matters, *barangay* officials carry significant authority, including the power to issue protection orders.

But paralegal informants in the Philippines identified risks with this local government approach as well. Paralegals can become associated with the *barangay* officials

---

[53] *See, for example*, Republic of the Philippines, Department of Agrarian Reform, DAR Memorandum Circular No. 15-04, "Reaffirming the Vital Role of Farmer-Paralegals in Facilitating the Delivery of Agrarian Justice and Providing for the Creation of Agrarian Justice Paralegal Support Fund," August 6, 2014, http://lis.dar.gov.ph/documents/1547#.

[54] The Government of Sierra Leone, Ministry of Lands, Country Planning and the Environment, *National Land Policy of Sierra Leone*, October 2016, § 6.4.

[55] South Africa offers another example of sector-specific financing. There, the labor department is "a reliable funder" of community advice offices working with farmworkers, for the role of paralegals in raising awareness of the Compensation for Occupational Injuries and Diseases Act. Debbie Budlender, *Developing a Model for Funding of Community Advice Offices in South Africa*, draft as of 2017 on file with authors.

that support them, and therefore go out of favor when those officials lose elections. While the supportive officials are in power, paralegals may find it difficult to oppose them in the event that they act illegally or unjustly.

Whether recognition flows from a national legal aid scheme, a sector-specific department like land or labor, or a local government, it is always a double-edged sword: the state can provide legitimacy and possibly resources, but it can also potentially constrain the autonomy of paralegal organizations.

There might be greater mission alignment with ombudsman offices and human rights commissions, both of which are explicitly designed to help citizens hold the state accountable. We did not observe affiliations between paralegal groups and such national accountability institutions in any of the six countries we studied, but it may be an avenue worth exploring. Overall, our impression is that community paralegals are not likely to ever outgrow the need to dance delicately between recognition and independence.

C. Funding

Community paralegal efforts cost money. Paralegals who work full time require a salary; those who serve their own village or their own membership association as volunteers require support from lawyers or more senior paralegals who earn a salary. There are also costs associated with training, office space, materials, transportation to reach clients and government offices, and litigation for a small percentage of cases.

The costs tend to be low. In Sierra Leone, the legal empowerment group Namati[56] estimates that it would cost US$2 million per year to provide paralegal services throughout the country. That figure includes a small corps of lawyers to provide paralegals with supervision and support. To put that figure into context, US $2 million is three-tenths of a percent of the total 2013 national budget and 3 percent of what the Sierra Leone government allocated to health care that year.[57] Law and Development Partnership estimated costs for nationwide delivery of seventeen basic legal services programs, most of which included paralegals. The estimates ranged from US$0.1 to US$1.3 per capita in less developed countries, and from US$3 to US$6 per capita in highly developed countries.[58]

Despite relatively modest costs, paralegal groups in every country identified unstable funding as a key constraint.[59] This is consistent with data from the Global Legal Empowerment Network. When asked "How sustainable is your

[56] One of us, Vivek, is CEO of Namati.
[57] The Government of Sierra Leone, Ministry of Finance and Economic Development, "Budget Profile for FY 2011-2015," annex I, http://mofed.gov.sl/speeches/profile%202013-15.pdf.
[58] Law and Development Partnership, *Developing a Portfolio of Financially Sustainable, Scalable Basic Legal Service Models: Briefing Paper* (London: The Law and Development Partnership, Ltd., 2016), 8.
[59] See Vivek Maru, "Only the Law Can Restrain Trump," *Foreign Policy*, March 9, 2017, http://foreignpolicy.com/2017/03/09/only-the-law-can-restrain-trump-legal-aid-barefoot-lawyers/. Maru offers four principles for overcoming the persistent challenge of financing access to justice.

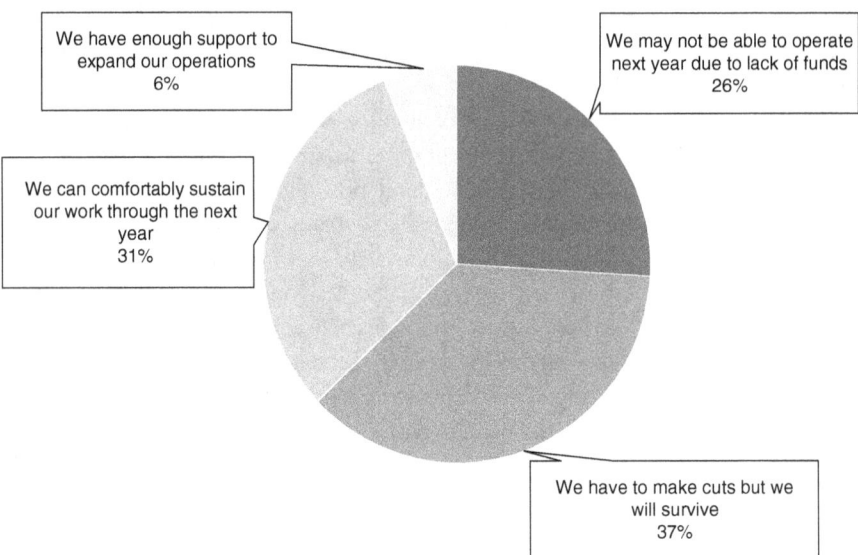

FIGURE 1.2 How sustainable is your funding situation for the coming year?
Source: Michael Otto, "5 Key Takeaways from Our Annual Network Survey," Namati, May 12, 2017, https://namati.org/news/5-key-takeaways-annual-network-survey-2016/.

funding situation for the coming year?" in a 2017 member survey, 63 percent of respondents said either "we have to make cuts but we will survive" or "we may not be able to operate next year due to lack of funds."[60]

The bulk of the funding that does exist in all six countries comes from international donors: foundations like the Atlantic Philanthropies and the Open Society Foundation, bilateral development agencies like Britain's Department for International Development, and multilateral institutions like the UN Development Programme.

1. Seeking a Greater Share of International Development Assistance

Paralegal groups are keen to expand investment from development agencies. Official development assistance amounts to more than US$130 billion per year.[61] Only a small share of that is dedicated to governance and the rule of law,[62] and the vast majority of

---

[60] Michael Otto, "5 Key Takeaways from Our Annual Network Survey," Namati, May 12, 2017, https://namati.org/news/5-key-takeaways-annual-network-survey-2016/.
[61] See OECD Data, "Net ODA," Organization for Economic Cooperation and Development. doi: 10.1787/33346549-en; See also, "Net Official Development Assistance and Official Aid Received," The World Bank. http://data.worldbank.org/indicator/DT.ODA.ALLD.CD.
[62] Law and Development Partnership, Developing a Portfolio of Financially Sustainable, Scalable Basic Legal Service Models, 2 (see n. 58) ("[F]or the period 2005–2013 justice sector funding comprised only 1.8% of total aid flows."). See also, Organization for Economic Cooperation and Development, "Detailed Aid Statistics: Official Bilateral Commitments by Sector," OECD International Development Statistics., doi: 10.1787/data-00073-en.

what is invested in those areas goes to support state institutions rather than civil society organizations.[63] The Millennium Development Goals, which were adopted in 2000 and were influential on development spending and policy, did not mention justice, fairness, or accountability at all.

Many paralegal groups campaigned for incorporation of access to justice in the 2030 Sustainable Goals, which were adopted in 2015 after the Millennium Development Goals expired. They argued that legal empowerment is essential to the mission of poverty alleviation – people cannot improve their lives if they cannot exercise basic rights.[64]

Despite significant opposition from countries inclined to define development in exclusively technical, economic terms, that campaign was ultimately successful: Goal 16 in the new framework commits to "access to justice for all."[65] Legal empowerment groups now hope to translate that nominal commitment into increased financing.[66]

2. Efforts to Diversify Revenue: Domestic Government, Social Enterprise, and Community Contributions

Sole reliance on development aid, or any other single source, leaves paralegal efforts vulnerable to interference or political whim. A resilient, independent paralegal movement requires diverse support. As discussed earlier, groups in all six countries in the study are seeking some degree of financing from domestic governments, via national legal aid schemes, sectoral departments like land and labor, or local governments.

In addition to those, social enterprise and community contributions offer two other channels for diversifying revenue. The NGO BRAC, for example, earns more than 60 percent of its revenue from microfinance and from social enterprises like

---

[63] *See, for example*, Rachel Kleinfeld, *How to Advance the Rule of Law Abroad* (Washington, DC: Carnegie Endowment for International Peace, 2013), 4, http://carnegieendowment.org/files/Kleinfeld-PO-web.pdf; Thomas Carothers and Saskia Brechenmacher, *Closing Space: Democracy and Human Rights Support under Fire* (Washington, DC: Carnegie Endowment for International Peace, 2014), 20.

[64] "Justice 2015 – Appeal to the Member States of the United Nations: Justice Should Be Included in the Post-2015 Development Goals," Namati, Open Society Foundations, November 2014. https://namati.org/wp-content/uploads/2014/11/Justice2015Appeal1.pdf.

[65] United Nations, "Sustainable Development Goals – Goal 16: Promote Just, Peaceful and Inclusive Societies." www.un.org/sustainabledevelopment/peace-justice/. *See also*, "Justice in the Development Goals – We Won!" *Namati*, October 6, 2015. https://namati.org/news/justice-in-the-global-development-goals-we-won/.

[66] *See, for example*, Stacey Cram, Sumaiya Islam, Temitayo O. Peters, Jennifer Tsai, and Betsy Walters, *Advocacy: Justice and the SDGs – How to Translate International Justice Commitments into National Reform* (New York: Transparency, Accountability, and Participation Network, 2017). This guide explains how civil society groups can use Goal 16 to advocate for domestic access to justice reforms. *See also* Global Legal Empowerment Network Community Discussions Page, "Upcoming Global Campaign: Where We Are At, the Details, and Are You In?" January 10, 2018, https://community.namati.org/t/upcoming-global-campaign-where-we-are-at-the-details-and-are-you-in/40848.

rural computer learning centers.[67] The work of BRAC's 6,000 "barefoot lawyers" is primarily donor-funded, but BRAC's business revenue does subsidize the legal empowerment efforts, in part by sustaining programs if there is a gap between grants. On a smaller scale, one community paralegal office in Orange Farm Township, South Africa, pays its staff with revenue from a recycling business that it runs.[68]

Community contributions can be in cash or in kind. Some legal aid laws, including the ones in Kenya and Sierra Leone, prohibit charging fees for paralegal services.[69] But none bars collective contributions or voluntary individual donations. In Sierra Leone, all the chiefdoms where the legal empowerment group Timap for Justice works have offered land where Timap can build permanent offices. In the Philippines and Indonesia, some trade unions and farmers' associations use membership dues to defray paralegal expenses.

Many paralegal offices in South Africa hold community fundraisers like fish barbecues and car washes. The Social Change Assistance Trust incentivizes this local fundraising by providing five rand of donor funding for every rand raised from the community. By itself, community financing is often able to cover only a small proportion of the total cost. But it has the additional benefit of increasing the accountability of paralegals to their constituents.

Overall, the challenge of securing diverse revenue is an existential one for paralegal movements – large-scale, long-term impact is difficult to achieve without it.

VI. SOCIETY AND CULTURE

Social dynamics – of power and inequality, of cohesion and conflict – shape paralegal efforts as much as public institutions.

A. Paralegal Groups Both Respond to Demand and Try to Stimulate It

Social conditions shape the demand for paralegal services. The civil wars in Sierra Leone and Liberia, for example, caused severe disruption: some people fought, some fled, and some stayed behind; some people survived and some did not. That disruption, along with poverty, urbanization, and other factors, has led to particularly unstable family arrangements.[70] Instability in the family, in turn, may be part of

---

[67] See, for example, Ernst & Young, S. F. Ahmed & Co., *Audited Financial Statements of BRAC in Bangladesh: For the Year Ended December 2014* (Dhaka: BRAC, 2015), 78.

[68] Mustafa Mahmoud, "Funding Projects with Trash," *Namati News* (blog), June 14, 2016, https://namati.org/news/funding_with_trash/.

[69] The Legal Aid Act, No. 6 (2012), SUPPLEMENT TO THE SIERRA LEONE GAZETTE Vol. CXLIII, No. 42, § 37(1); The Legal Aid Act No. 6 (2016), KENYA GAZETTE SUPPLEMENT No. 56 § 68(2).

[70] See, for example, Patricia Justino, *Women Working for Recovery: The Impact of Female Employment on Family and Community Welfare after Conflict* (New York: UN Women, 2011), 3 (hypothesizing that one will find "higher shares of separated, divorced and/or widowed women, of female-headed households, and of dependency ratios in conflict-affected areas, in relation to areas less affected").

why child support cases make up a large proportion of paralegal dockets in both places.

In South Africa, Dugard and Drage find that the most common issues paralegals address are domestic violence and access to social grants. They observe that the prevalence of those cases flows naturally from central features of contemporary South African society. "These areas of work relate to two of the most serious remaining fault lines in South Africa: endemic violence in the home and structural unemployment, meaning that a very high proportion of South Africans relies on social grants to survive."

But express demand may not reflect perfectly the actual experience of injustice across society. For many people in Sierra Leone and Liberia the state is a remote presence, one that has not offered much over the years. Rural people in those countries often conceive of state failures as facts of life rather than rights violations for which a remedy is worth pursuing.[71]

Berenschot and Rinaldi note a related tendency, associated with the repressive New Order regime but lingering among many Indonesians still, to eschew confrontation with authorities, to make polite requests but avoid formal channels for redress.

Given the way culture can limit people's ability to conceive of and act on breaches of rights, some paralegal groups depart from the tradition of taking priorities from the cases people bring. Instead, these organizations adopt a more proactive stance toward the kinds of injustices their constituents might not conceive of as such, like failures in the delivery of state services.[72] The paralegals educate people about state policies, and proactively encourage them to take action against violations. Berenschot and Rinaldi observe – cautiously, for their sample of relevant cases was small – that the presence of paralegals can lead people to complain about problems they might otherwise ignore, and to "press authorities in a more straightforward manner."

B. Paralegals and Social Movements

When demand for change does gain momentum, and paralegals are a part of larger social movements, they are more likely to succeed in having an impact on not just

---

[71] See, for example, Deborah H. Isser, Stephen C. Lubkemann, and Saah N'Tow, *Looking for Justice: Liberian Experiences with and Perceptions of Local Justice Options* (Washington, DC: United States Institute of Peace – Peaceworks, 2009), www.usip.org/sites/default/files/PW63-Looking%20for%20Justice-Liberian%20Experiences%20with%20and%20Perceptions%20of%20Local%20Justice%20Options.pdf, 3–4.

[72] One of us argues elsewhere that legal empowerment efforts could gain from using "social accountability" approaches that gather information on public services and use that information to catalyze action. Maru, "Allies Unknown" (*see* n. 15). Feinglass, Gomes, and Maru describe the results of an effort to help people protect rights to basic health care using a combination of legal empowerment and social accountability approaches in "Transforming Policy into Justice." Ellie Feinglass, Nadja Gomes, and Vivek Maru, "Transforming Policy into Justice: The Role of Health Advocates in Mozambique," *Health and Human Rights* 18, no. 2 (December 2016): 233–46.

local state actors but large-scale policy as well. Paralegals in the Philippines, for example, were not alone in pushing for implementation and extension of agrarian reform legislation. They were part of a broad coalition of peasant organizations and public interest lawyers.

In South Africa, paralegals were intimately tied to the antiapartheid movement. After the transition to democracy, individual advice offices were no longer united by a single national struggle. NADCAO and ACAOSA were founded in part as a response to fragmentation. Those coalitions aim to build greater unity among community advice offices, and to connect paralegals with broader movements for justice. The coalition of organizations scaling up paralegal services in Sierra Leone has similar aspirations.

VII. PARALEGAL ORGANIZATIONS

The success of paralegal efforts turns in large part on the skill and commitment of individual paralegals. The best paralegals we observed were able to help clients make improbable strides toward justice, even when state institutions were brutal or dysfunctional.

But not all paralegals are the same. In the worst case scenario, paralegals could use their knowledge and status to exploit others. We did encounter one example of abuse in our six studies. A paralegal in Kenya collected money from clients, saying he needed to pay an attorney to help with their dispute. Instead he kept the money for himself. Another paralegal discovered what happened and confronted him, but the offending paralegal refused to return the money until he was arrested and summoned to court.

There are many shades between the dynamism of the best paralegals and the outright corruption of that paralegal in Kenya. Paralegal organizations have a vital role in preventing abuse, ensuring consistent quality, and nurturing excellence. We begin this section by describing five qualities we observed in effective paralegals. We then discuss five ways in which organizations try to foster those qualities in the paralegal cadres with whom they work.

A. *Five Qualities of Effective Paralegals*

1. Trusted by Constituents

Successful paralegals earn the trust of the communities they serve. Dugard and Drage take the title of their chapter from Greg Erasmus, former coordinator of NADCAO, who said, "Simply ask where and to whom do the people take their issues? That person is the paralegal." Erasmus' definition holds when communities have confidence in a paralegal's character and ability. Without that trust a paralegal will not have work.

2. Focus on Empowerment

At the outset of our research, we identified an emphasis on empowerment as one of the key potential advantages of paralegals over a conventional legal aid approach. Not all the paralegals we observed demonstrated this value. Dugard and Drage found that some paralegals "failed to explain each step of the process to the client, meaning that the client would probably have to come to the paralegal if the same or similar problem arose again."

But the most effective paralegals served as educators, demystifying law and equipping people to advocate for themselves. In Sierra Leone and Liberia, as mentioned earlier, we found that paralegal clients had greater knowledge of national law than those who had not worked with paralegals.

At their best, paralegals help people journey from powerlessness to hope. In Kenya, a community leader in Western Province said that since paralegals had begun to operate, "Women now know their rights ... the paralegals have encouraged them to embrace and live these rights." A man who received help from a paralegal in Indonesia spoke of what he learned from his case this way: "Our neighbors were surprised that we could win against powerful people. We are an example for poor people. If we are enlightened, we do not always have to be the victim; we can fight."

3. Dogged, Creative Problem Solving

To help their clients win against powerful interests, and to achieve fair results from dysfunctional institutions, paralegals need to be persistent and resourceful. Berenschot and Rinaldi describe the best paralegals they observed in Indonesia as possessing "savoir faire," and as pragmatically blending legal action with mediation, advocacy, and community organizing in order to reach a solution. Dugard and Drage observed in paralegals "an extraordinary capacity to go the extra mile for clients" and a commitment to "creating authentic, lived solutions at the grassroots level."

4. Strong Relationships with Local Institutions

Success in problem solving depends in turn on constructive relationships with local authorities. Moy finds in the Kenya chapter that "[t]he success of paralegal efforts often hinged on the quality of their relationships with principal institutional actors and local leaders, including police, local administrative and other government officials, prison authorities, councilors, and chiefs."

She quotes a local official in Eastern Province of Kenya, who said that "[t]he fact that the [paralegal] office is next to mine should tell you more about our relationship. Us delegating peace and reconciliation to them speaks volumes ... It is the biggest resource center in the district ... They have the legal knowledge while we have the administrative capability. We even seek advice there."

In South Africa, officials similarly demonstrate confidence in paralegals by referring cases to them. In 2010, 38 percent of cases handled by paralegals with the Center for Criminal Justice came from state institutions like the police and the social welfare department.

Paralegals sometimes need to challenge local officials or hold them accountable for abuse, and so the relationships are not straightforward.[73] But the best paralegals find spaces for constructive engagement.

5. Connected to a Vertical Network

Not all problems can be solved locally. The most effective paralegals are embedded in vertical networks that can help them engage higher levels of authority when necessary – state, national, and sometimes international. With the help of a network, paralegals can engage strategically across a wide range of institutions, including administrative agencies, parliaments, ombudsman offices, courts, and corporations.[74]

When paralegals and their clients achieved (partial) redress for abuses by mining companies in Sierra Leone, for example, progress was due in part to key moments in which the lawyer who supervised the paralegals helped advocate with either the Ministry of Mines in Freetown or the mining company directly.

Berenschot and Rinaldi observe that links to farmers' associations and labor unions are useful, and that "support from city-based lawyers signals to possible clients that a paralegal might actually succeed in bringing a case to court." Some informants told Franco, Soliman, and Cisnero that in the Philippines, "without lawyers to train and guide paralegals, there can be no paralegal movement."

Not only do paralegals need a vertical network to succeed in specific tough cases, it is through a network that paralegals and clients can come together to advocate for

---

[73] Indeed, if paralegals are not working to hold officials accountable, there is a risk that they are merely serving as substitutes for the state's responsibility to adjudicate disputes. We offer the quote from Eastern Province, Kenya as an example of a paralegal earning trust from local officials. But taken too far, "delegating peace and reconciliation" could imply that paralegals are doing the job of local courts without receiving any of the public revenue dedicated to that function. This is a common risk with civil society in general. In the section on institutional factors, we conclude that paralegals add less value with respect to intra-community disputes when existing institutions are functioning effectively and fairly. Putting it more sharply, we might say: if paralegals don't focus on systemic injustice, they risk serving as substitutes for the state.

[74] This resonates with work by Jonathan Fox and others that highlights integrated approaches to accountability, which span vertical levels of authority (local, provincial, and national) and engage horizontally across public institutions. Jonathan Fox, "Social Accountability: What Does the Evidence Really Say?," *World Development* 72 (August 2015): 346–61, doi: 10.1016/j.worlddev.2015.03.011. *See also*, Jonathan Fox and Brendan Halloran, eds., "Connecting the Dots for Accountability: Civil Society Policy Monitoring and Advocacy Strategies" (report from international workshop, June 18–20, 2015, Washington, DC, London: Transparency and Accountability Initiative, School of International Service, American University, International Budget Partnership, Government Watch, SIMLab, 2016): 5–6; Jashodhara Dasgupta, "Ten Years of Negotiating Rights around Maternal Health in Uttar Pradesh, India," *BMC International Health and Human Rights* 11, no. S3 (2011): 2–4, doi: 10.1186/1472-698X-11-S3-S4.

large-scale systemic changes, like extension of agrarian reform in the Philippines or improvements to land policy in Sierra Leone.

B. Five Organizational Approaches to Ensure Effectiveness

Organizational choices shape whether, and how much, a paralegal cadre attains the dimensions of excellence we've just described. Looking across the studies in this volume, five aspects of organizational practice stand out as most important.

1. Recruitment and Selection

As with most endeavors, choosing the right people for the job is crucial. In Indonesia, organizations selected paralegals using three criteria: "a) trusted by the community; b) actively involved in community organization or activities; [and] c) having organizational, advocacy or legal aid experience." The coalition of paralegal groups in Sierra Leone goes a bit further, by applying four criteria: (a) trusted by the community; (b) demonstrated commitment to the common good; (c) decent writing skills; and (d) strong analytical and problem-solving ability.

Sierra Leonean groups assess the first two – which are akin to the criteria from Indonesia – through interviews and reference checks. They assess the latter two through a written exercise, often along the lines of "here is an example of an actual justice problem – how would you go about helping your clients?"

An environmental justice paralegal in the Philippines emphasized another specific quality – he said that a paralegal must have "the courage to defend the rights of the people."

Some paralegals in South Africa and Liberia are elected by the communities they serve. This method has the benefit of establishing the direct accountability of paralegals to their constituents; it is most feasible when the paralegal is serving a relatively small population. Organizations can combine meritocratic and democratic selection by asking the community to elect several candidates who then apply in a competitive process, or by doing the reverse – selecting finalists through a competitive process and then subjecting those finalists to a community vote.

Overall, based on qualitative findings across the studies, we believe that greater stringency in paralegal selection would help to address the weaknesses identified in paralegal performance.

2. Payment

On the surface, it seemed there was a split among the countries we studied with respect to payment. In the Philippines, Indonesia, and Kenya, the majority of paralegals are volunteers who have other occupations. They typically receive stipends for their transport costs and other expenses but not salaries. In South Africa, Sierra Leone, and Liberia, most paralegals work full time and are paid modest salaries.

But this difference turns out to stem in large part from the way the term *paralegal* is applied. The paid paralegals in South Africa, Sierra Leone, and Liberia tend to serve larger populations – a chiefdom in Sierra Leone, a district in Liberia – and they often interact with village-level liaisons who are volunteers. The volunteers referred to as paralegals in the Philippines, Indonesia, and Kenya, on the other hand, often serve a single village or a small membership group (e.g., a local farmers' association). The volunteers are typically supported in turn by paid NGO staff who cover a larger area, like the *"posko* facilitators" in Indonesia. Indonesian *posko* facilitators play a similar role to that of paralegals in Sierra Leone. The staff structure can be roughly similar, then, with the term *paralegal* applied to different rungs.

Moy reports that in Kenya, "most interviewees felt that truly effective and sustainable paralegal work requires financial support in some form." Dugard and Drage conclude that "community-based paralegals are undoubtedly underpaid for their work" and that low salaries increase "the turnover in staff, leading to a brain drain in the [paralegal] sector and the loss of capacity as paralegals look for employment elsewhere to mitigate their own hardship."

Looking across the six studies, we agree with Moy, Dugard, and Drage. Local-level volunteers play a crucial role in paralegal efforts everywhere. But high-quality, rigorous paralegal work that takes on complex injustices requires a layer of staff who earn a living wage. Whether the volunteers or the paid staff or both are given the name *paralegals* may not matter intrinsically – that choice is likely shaped in part by organizational practice and in part by regulation. Given limited resources, in a trade-off between a smaller number of people receiving a living wage and a larger number receiving significantly less, our qualitative findings suggest the former is preferable.[75]

3. Support, Supervision, and the Importance of Case Data

All organizations we examined provide training to paralegals at the outset. But the studies suggest that paralegal effectiveness depends less on the initial orientation and more on the provision of ongoing supervision and support. It is through a continuous relationship with paralegals that organizations can ensure consistent quality, learn and improve over time, and integrate paralegals into a vertical network for taking on powerful interests.

---

[75] The public health community grapples with an analogous question with respect to the payment of community health workers. A panel convened by Prime Minister Hailemariam Dessalegn of Ethiopia and Raymond Chambers, UN Special Envoy for Financing the Health Millennium Development Goals, found that "some of the highest-performing Community Health Worker systems [are] ones in which CHWs are formalized, paid, and given other appropriate incentives." As with paralegal efforts, many primary health care systems combine a layer of paid community health workers with a layer of volunteers. Bernice Dahn, Assis Tamire Woldemariam, Henry Perry et al., *Strengthening Primary Health Care through Community Health Workers: Investment Case and Financing Recommendations* (New York: Office of the UN Secretary-General's Special Envoy for Health in Agenda 2030 and for Malaria, 2015), 2.

Support and supervision are structured differently in different places. In the Philippines, the most common arrangement is for paralegals to be members of grassroots organizations, often labor unions or farmers' associations. National or regional legal empowerment groups, like Saligan, which focuses on labor rights, and Kaisahan, which focuses on agrarian issues, provide paralegals with ongoing training and support. In South Africa, most community advice offices are independent organizations in and of themselves. The paralegals receive support from umbrella networks they belong to, such as ACAOSA, NADCAO, and the Community Law and Rural Development Center in Kwazulu Natal.

In Sierra Leone and Liberia, the paralegals, "lead paralegals," and at least one lawyer often work in the same organization, like Timap for Justice in Sierra Leone and the Catholic Justice and Peace Commission in Liberia. In Kenya, Moy identifies a range of approaches and concludes that "greater levels of legal support will on the whole strengthen the long-term morale, commitment, and performance of paralegals."

Rigorous tracking of case information is essential for effective supervision and support. If paralegals keep good case records, senior staff can review how a case is handled, learn from the paralegal's work, and provide feedback or suggestions on how to take a case forward. The aggregation of case-level data into a central database, moreover, allows for learning across the cadre. Organizations can draw on aggregate information to identify common problems that are arising, or innovations worth replicating, or specific paralegals who are having trouble.

Aggregate data from cases also provides nuanced evidence from which to identify and advocate for reforms to laws and institutions. Without it, organizations may miss the opportunity to translate their grassroots experience into proposals for systemic change.

Not all the organizations we studied had systems for tracking and aggregating case data. Even the ones that did – in South Africa, Indonesia, Kenya, Sierra Leone, and Liberia – reported challenges in operating these systems smoothly. Paralegals make errors or omissions in filling case-tracking forms, for example, and there are often delays in data entry, aggregation, and analysis.

This challenge is reflective of a larger dynamic with paralegal efforts. Most paralegal organizations grew organically out of social movements, like people power in the Philippines and the antiapartheid movement in South Africa. Many paralegals conceive of their work more as activism than service delivery. They often focus on responding to immediate crises rather than building organizations. But if paralegal groups are to reach their full potential, they need to invest in the systems that make consistent excellence possible.

4. Accountability to Communities

Paralegals regularly make subjective judgments about justice in the course of their work. They choose which cases to take on and, for citizen versus citizen cases, they often take the side of one community member in a dispute against another.

How do we know those choices will be judicious and that the community's trust will not be abused? In many places, there is a class of people who offer themselves as legal intermediaries – in the Philippines, they are called *abogadillos*, literally "small lawyers," in Indonesia, *makelar kasus*, in Sierra Leone, *blackman lawya*. These intermediaries often charge exploitative fees for their services. A paralegal from Quezon Province in the Philippines told of an *abogadillo* charging 5,000 pesos (around US$120) to secure a document from the Department of Agrarian Reform that was officially available for free.

There is a risk that paralegals similarly use their knowledge and reputation to exploit others, as with the one example we observed of a paralegal defrauding clients in Kenya. Support and supervision from paralegal organizations is crucial for preventing abuse, as we've just discussed.

Equally important is the accountability of paralegals to the people they serve. Dugard and Drage argue that "embeddedness in communities," the fact that paralegals live among their clients, is one of the strongest virtues of South African community advice offices. This was a common observation across all six studies and indeed is one of the key arguments in favor of a paralegal approach. But as the phenomenon of *abogadillos* and their counterparts suggests, embeddedness does not guarantee an alignment with the interests of community members.[76]

Many organizations seek to establish formal structures to ensure accountability. The Social Change Assistance Trust in South Africa requires advice offices it supports to be governed by management committees that include community representatives. The committees in turn must regularly hold open community meetings to review performance. In the Philippines, paralegals who are a part of membership organizations like farmers' associations and trade unions are answerable to their fellow members. In Sierra Leone, Timap for Justice has community oversight boards in every chiefdom; the boards are charged with ensuring that the paralegals are serving the constituent community effectively.[77]

In addition to providing a channel for accountability, these structures resonate with the ideal of empowerment. Ultimately the work of exercising rights – and the paralegal who can help – are in the people's hands.

5. Specialization and Coordination across Paralegal Efforts

Some paralegals are holistic in their scope – they attempt to take on whatever problems community members bring them. But many others focus on specific justice issues, like

---

[76] Ghazala Mansuri and Vijayendra Rao, for example, review a large body of evidence on participatory approaches to development, and find that abuse of authority by local elites and power brokers is a common problem. Ghazala Mansuri and Vijayendra Rao, *Localizing Development: Does Participation Work?* (Washington, DC: World Bank, 2013), 97–98, 108–09.

[77] Simeon Koroma, "Paralegals and the Experience of Community Oversight Boards in Sierra Leone," in *Legal Empowerment in Practice: Using Legal Tools to Secure Land Rights in Africa*, ed. Lorenzo Cotula and Paul Matheiu (London: International Institute for Environment and Development, 2008).

gender-based violence or land and environmental rights. When paralegal groups specialize, they tend to choose persistent, systemic injustices of great importance to their constituents. They typically conclude that paralegals will not be effective with respect to the chosen problem – including learning the relevant laws and developing strong relationships with relevant authorities – unless they focus their efforts.

The fact of specialization, and the larger reality that the need for legal support dwarfs the availability of paralegals in every country we studied, present a challenge: how to coordinate services across issues and across the population so as to maximize the impact of limited resources?

Where autonomous public bodies like legal aid boards or ombudsman offices recognize paralegals, as discussed earlier, those bodies could be a useful hub for coordination among paralegal organizations. Coalitions made up of paralegal organizations themselves, like the Alternative Law Groups in the Philippines, NADCAO and ACAOSA in South Africa, and the Paralegal Support Network in Kenya, can also play that role.

The pursuit of scale, across pressing issues and across geography, is a long-run challenge in all the countries we studied. In the meanwhile, it is important that paralegal movements make the most of what they have.

VIII. SUMMARY AND CONCLUSION

For many people around the world, law is an abstraction, if not also a threat. Community paralegals have the potential to turn law into something people can understand, use, and shape. In the six countries where this research took place, we found paralegals applying a combination of six broad approaches to help people exercise their rights: (1) education, (2) mediation, (3) organizing, (4) advocacy, (5) monitoring, and, with the help of lawyers, (6) litigation.

Here and in the chapters that follow, we have considered how this work of paralegals is shaped by institutional, cultural, and organizational factors.

In South Africa, the Philippines, and Indonesia, paralegal movements began by helping people to defend themselves against repressive regimes. Once those countries transitioned toward democracy, paralegals shifted their focus to the realization of newly enshrined rights. Paralegal groups emerged in Kenya after the return of multiparty elections in the early 1990s, and in Sierra Leone and Liberia after democratic transitions from protracted conflict, and so paralegals in those three countries placed substantial emphasis on legal enforcement and implementation from the start.

As aspects of the rule of law have grown weaker in some of these countries in recent years, paralegals have adapted their work accordingly. In the Philippines, for example, some legal empowerment groups are invoking once again the techniques of resistance with which they began.

Across all six countries, we observed paralegals having the greatest impact in cases where there are significant imbalances of power and information. These conditions are prevalent – and we observed paralegals playing a particularly vital role – in disputes between citizens and the state, as when an Indonesian infrastructure fund ignored half of a village it was meant to serve. The same is true in disputes between citizens and private firms, as when a community in Kenya sought to stop a sand mine from exhausting local water supply.

In citizen versus citizen disputes, we found paralegals are most useful when existing local forums are systematically unfair – as with women's rights under family law in Sierra Leone and Liberia. But the more functional and fair the existing institutions were with respect to citizen versus citizen disputes, the less value we saw in paralegal involvement.

In aggregate, paralegal casework creates a map of how laws are working in practice. Paralegal movements have used that information to advocate for systematic reforms, like a more progressive land policy in Sierra Leone or the extension of agrarian reform in the Philippines.

In Indonesia, Kenya, and Sierra Leone, paralegal movements have successfully advocated for legislative recognition of paralegals as legal aid providers (in South Africa, the parliament has taken an intermediate step in this direction). Paralegal groups seek recognition to gain legitimacy and government financing; they aim to reap those benefits while at the same time protecting their independence.

Because recognition under legal aid legislation can invoke opposition from the private bar, and because the lion's share of legal aid funding is dedicated to criminal defense, paralegal groups sometimes seek recognition from sector-specific institutions or from local governments. In the Philippines, for example, paralegals are opposed by the Supreme Court but recognized by national departments for labor, agrarian reform, and environment, as well as some *barangay* (village-level) governments.

Lack of sustainable funding is a major challenge faced by paralegal groups in all six countries. Most of the financing that does exist comes from international donors – either foundations or development agencies like the UK Department for International Development and the UN Development Programme. Legal empowerment groups successfully campaigned for inclusion of access to justice in the 2030 Sustainable Development Goals, and organizations now hope to translate that nominal commitment into increased financing.

Sole reliance on any single source leaves paralegal groups vulnerable to interference or political whim. Paralegal movements will be more resilient if they are able to secure a diverse mix of revenue that includes foreign and domestic philanthropy, development assistance, domestic government financing, profits from social enterprises, and community contributions.

Cultural dynamics shape the kinds of cases paralegals address: in South Africa, for example, domestic violence is common and therefore makes up a large portion of paralegal dockets. But culture can mask injustice as well. Low expectations in Sierra Leone and Liberia about what the state owes its people, or a tendency to avoid confrontation in Indonesia, may prevent people from taking action on the gravest violations of their rights.

For this reason, paralegal groups sometimes proactively focus on specific forms of injustice – rights to land and environment, for example, and rights to basic services like health care – that communities may not raise themselves without education and encouragement.

Although paralegal groups often aim to counteract cultural complacency, on the other hand they seem most likely to achieve large-scale systemic changes when they are a part of broader social movements for change. Extension of agrarian reform in the Philippines, for example, was in response to not just legal empowerment groups but a national movement of farmers.

In addition to institutions and culture, the work of paralegals is shaped substantially by the practices of the organizations to which they belong. We identified five features that characterize effective paralegals: they are trusted by the communities they serve; they are dedicated to educating and empowering their clients; they are dogged and creative problem solvers; they cultivate strong relationships with local institutions; and they are connected to a vertical network that can help them take on powerful interests.

The extent to which paralegal cadres attain these characteristics depends in significant part on organizational choices. First, it is crucial that organizations choose people who have the character and the aptitude necessary for the job. Greater rigor in paralegal selection can help address the weaknesses and inconsistencies that we observed. Second, although all paralegal efforts involve volunteers, it is crucial that there is a layer of staff who are paid a living wage. Paid staff can sustain a high level of effort and grow in ability and sophistication over time.

Third, and far more important than the initial training paralegals receive, organizations need to provide paralegals with ongoing support and supervision. Continuous relationships with paralegals allow organizations to ensure consistent quality, to learn and improve, and to integrate paralegals into a vertical network for taking on powerful interests.

Fourth, organizations have found value in developing mechanisms by which paralegals are accountable to the communities they serve. Last, organizations can usefully coordinate among themselves – via national coalitions like the Alternative Law Groups in the Philippines, or in conjunction with a public body like an Ombudsman's Office – so as to make the most of limited paralegal resources across geographies and issues.

As authoritarian, nationalist politicians have gained traction in many parts of the world, some have wondered about democracy itself. Are electoral democratic structures able to fulfill the ideal of enlightened self-rule? Or are the structures we have overly prone to concentration of power and manipulation by demagogues? The work of paralegals points to a deeper version of democracy – where people not only cast ballots periodically, they actively take part in the rules and institutions that tie them together.

But the intermediary space paralegals occupy is fragile. On the one hand, without sustainable revenue and rigorous organization, paralegal efforts are likely to remain marginal. On the other hand, too much involvement from the state could diminish paralegals' independence and dynamism. If these intermediaries are to play an important role in deepening modern democracies, they will need to find firm middle ground.

REFERENCES

"Access to Legal Aid in Criminal Justice Systems in Africa: Survey Report." *United Nations Office on Drugs and Crime* (2011). www.un.org/ruleoflaw/files/Access_to_Legal_Aid_in_Criminal_Justice_Systems_in_Africa.pdf.

The Advocates Act, Cap. 267 (Uganda); Access to Justice Act 1999 art. 4 ¶ 8 (England and Wales)

Appadurai, Arjun. "The Capacity to Aspire: Culture and the Terms of Recognition." In *Culture and Public Action*, edited by Vijayendra Rao and Michael Walton, 59–84. Stanford, CA: Stanford University Press, 2004.

Billings, Lucy, Ruth Meinzen-Dick, and Valeria Mueller. *Implications of Community-Based Legal Aid Regulation on Women's Land Rights*. IFPRI Research Brief. Washington, DC: International Food Policy Research Institute, 2014.

BRAC. "Human Rights and Legal Aid Services Programme: Figure up to September 2013." BRAC, September 2013. http://hrls.brac.net/images/pdf/HRLS-Sept-2013.pdf.

Brinks, Daniel and Sarah Botero. "Inequality and the Rule of Law: Ineffective Rights in Latin American Democracies." Paper presented at the American Political Science Association Annual Meeting, Washington, DC, September 2–5, 2010.

Brinks, Daniel M. and Varun Gauri. "A New Policy Landscape: Legalizing Social and Economic Rights in the Developing World." In *Courting Social Justice: Judicial Enforcement of Social and Economic Rights in the Developing World*, edited by Varun Gauri and Daniel M. Brinks. New York: Cambridge University Press, 2008.

Budlender, Debbie. "Developing a Model for Funding of Community Advice Offices in South Africa." Draft as of 2017 on file with authors.

Carothers, Thomas and Saskia Brechenmacher. *Closing Space: Democracy and Human Rights Support under Fire*. Washington, DC: Carnegie Endowment for International Peace, 2014.

Commission on Legal Empowerment of the Poor and United Nations Development Programme. Vol. 1 of *Making the Law Work for Everyone: Report of the Commission on Legal Empowerment*. New York: United Nations, 2008.

Cram, Stacey, Sumaiya Islam, Temitayo O. Peters, Jennifer Tsai, and Betsy Walters. *Advocacy: Justice and the SDGs – How to Translate International Justice Commitments into National Reform*. New York: Transparency, Accountability, & Participation Network, 2017.

Dahn, Bernice, Assis Tamire Woldemariam, Henry Perry, et al. *Strengthening Primary Health Care through Community Health Workers: Investment Case and Financing Recommendations*. New York: Office of the UN Secretary-General's Special Envoy for Health in Agenda 2030 and for Malaria, 2015.

Dale, Pamela. *Delivering Justice to Sierra Leone's Poor: An Analysis of the Work of Timap for Justice*. Justice for the Poor Research Report, no. 1. Washington, DC: World Bank, 2009.

Dasgupta, Jashodhara. "Ten Years of Negotiating Rights around Maternal Health in Uttar Pradesh, India." *BMC International Health and Human Rights* 11, no. S3 (2011): 1–11. doi: 10.1186/1472-698X-11-S3-S4.

David McQuoid-Mason (Center of Socio-legal Studies, University of KwaZulu-Natal), interview, November 2010, Geneva.

"Declaration of Alma-Ata." International Convention on Primary Health Care, Alma-Alta, USSR, September 6–12, 1978.

Desmond, Matthew. *Evicted: Poverty and Profit in the American City*. New York: Crown Publishers, 2016.

Ernst & Young, S. F. Ahmed & Co. *Audited Financial Statements of BRAC in Bangladesh: For the Year Ended December 2014*. Dhaka: BRAC, 2015.

Feinglass, Ellie, Nadia Gomes, and Vivek Maru. "Transforming Policy into Justice: The Role of Heath Advocates in Mozambique." *Health and Human Rights* 18, no. 2 (December 2016): 233–46.

Franco, Jennifer C. "Peripheral Justice? Rethinking Justice Sector Reform in the Philippines." *World Development* 36, no. 10 (2008): 1858–73. doi: 10.1016/j.worlddev.2007.10.011.

Fogel, Benjamin and Sean Jacobs. "Getting Rid of Zuma Isn't a Panacea for All South Africa's Ills." *The Guardian*, April 2017. www.theguardian.com/commentisfree/2017/apr/05/getting-rid-jacob-zuma-not-panacea-south-africa-problems.

Fox, Jonathan. "Social Accountability: What Does the Evidence Really Say?," *World Development* 72 (August 2015): 346–61. doi: 10.1016/j.worlddev.2015.03.011.

Fox, Jonathan and Brendan Halloran, eds., with Anna Levy, Joy Aceron, and Albert van Zyl. "Connecting the Dots for Accountability: Civil Society Policy Monitoring and Advocacy Strategies." Report from an international workshop, June 18–20, 2015. Washington, DC, and London: Transparency and Accountability Initiative, School of International Service, American University, International Budget Partnership, Government Watch, SIMLab, 2016.

Gauri, Varun. "Customary Law and Economic Outcomes in Indonesia." *Hague Journal on the Rule of Law* 2, no. 1 (2010): 75–94.

"The Publicity 'Defect' of Customary Law." In *Legal Pluralism and Development: Scholars and Practitioners in Dialogue*, edited by Caroline Sage, Brian Z. Tamanaha, and Michael Woolcock, 215–27. Cambridge: Cambridge University Press, 2013.

Gauri, Varun and Daniel M. Brinks. "Introduction: The Elements of Legalization and the Triangular Shape of Social and Economic Rights." In *Courting Social Justice: Judicial Enforcement of Social and Economic Rights in the Developing World*, edited by Varun Gauri and Daniel M. Brinks, 1–37. Cambridge: Cambridge University Press, 2008.

Global Legal Empowerment Network Community Discussions Page. "Upcoming Global Campaign: Where We Are At, the Details, and Are You In?" January 10, 2018. https://community.namati.org/t/upcoming-global-campaign-where-we-are-at-the-details-and-are-you-in/40848.

Golub, Stephen. "Beyond Rule of Law Orthodoxy: The Legal Empowerment Alternative." *Carnegie Endowment for International Peace Working Papers* 41, 2003.

"Nonlawyers as Legal Resources for Their Communities." In *Many Roads to Justice: The Law-Related Work of Ford Foundation Grantees around the World*, edited by Mary McClymont and Stephen Golub, 297–314. New York: Ford Foundation, 2000.

Golub, Stephen and Kim McQuay, eds. "Legal Empowerment: Advancing Good Governance and Poverty Reduction." In *Law and Policy Reform at the Asian Development Bank*, 7–164. Manila: Asian Development Bank, 2001.

Goodwin, Laura and Vivek Maru. "What Do We Know about Legal Empowerment? Mapping the Evidence." *Hague Journal on the Rule of Law* 9, no. 1 (2017): 157–94. doi: 10.1007/s40803-016-0047-5.

Gordon, Jennifer. *Suburban Sweatshops: The Fight for Immigrant Rights*. Cambridge, MA: Harvard University Press, 2007.

Government of Sierra Leone, Ministry of Finance and Economic Development. "Budget Profile for FY 2011–2015." Annex I. http://mofed.gov.sl/speeches/profile%202013-15.pdf.

Government of Sierra Leone, Ministry of Lands Country Planning and the Environment. *National Land Policy of Sierra Leone*, October 2016.

Hunt, Lynn A. *Inventing Human Rights: A History*. New York: W. W. Norton & Co., 2007.

Inveen, Cooper. "President's Iron-Fist Methods Raise Fears for Future of Democracy in Sierra Leone." *The Guardian*, October 2017. www.theguardian.com/global-development/2017/oct/20/president-ernest-bai-koroma-iron-fist-methods-raise-fears-for-future-of-democracy-in-sierra-leone-march-election.

Isser, Deborah H., Stephen C. Lubkemann, and Saah N'Tow. *Looking for Justice: Liberian Experiences with and Perceptions of Local Justice Options* (Washington, DC: United States Institute of Peace – Peaceworks, 2009), www.usip.org/sites/default/files/PW63-Looking%20for%20Justice-Liberian%20Experiences%20with%20and%20Perceptions%20of%20Local%20Justice%20Options.pdf, 3–4.

Jacobs, Krista, Meredith Saggers, and Sophie Namy. *How Do Community-Based Legal Programs Work? Understanding the Process and Benefits of a Pilot Program to Advance Women's Property Rights in Uganda*. Washington, DC: International Center for Research on Women, 2011.

"Justice 2015 – Appeal to the Member States of the United Nations: Justice Should Be Included in the Post-2015 Development Goals." Namati, Open Society Foundations. November 2014. https://namati.org/wp-content/uploads/2014/11/Justice2015Appeal1.pdf.

"Justice in the Development Goals – We Won!" Namati. October 6, 2015. https://namati.org/news/justice-in-the-global-development-goals-we-won/.

Justino, Patricia. *Women Working for Recovery: The Impact of Female Employment on Family and Community Welfare after Conflict*. New York: UN Women, 2011.

Kavilu, Shadrack. "Kenya's Illegal Sand Miners Destroy Farms to Plunder Scarce Resource." *Reuters*, October 6, 2016. www.reuters.com/article/us-kenya-landrights-sand-mining/kenyas-illegal-sand-miners-destroy-farms-to-plunder-scarce-resource-idUSKCN126116.

"Kampala Declaration on Community Paralegals." Kampala, Uganda, July 26, 2012. www.namati.org/news/newsfeed/kampala-declaration/.

Kleinfeld, Rachel. "How to Advance the Rule of Law Abroad." Policy Outlook, Carnegie Endowment for International Peace. September 2013. http://carnegieendowment.org/files/Kleinfeld-PO-web.pdf.

Knight, Rachael, Judy Adoko, Teresa Aluma, Ali Kaba, Alda Salomao, Silas Siakor, and Issufo Tankar. *Protecting Community Land and Resources: Evidence from Liberia, Mozambique, and Uganda*. Rome: International Development Law Organization/Washington, DC: Namati, 2012.

Koroma, Simeon. "Paralegals and the Experience of Community Oversight Boards in Sierra Leone." In *Legal Empowerment in Practice: Using Legal Tools to Secure Land Rights in Africa*, edited by Lorenzo Cotula and Paul Matheiu. London: International Institute for Environment and Development, 2008.

Kumar, M. Sunil. "A Systems Approach for Providing Legal Aid for Land." Paper presented at the Annual World Bank Conference on Land and Poverty, Washington, DC, April 8–11, 2013.

Law Concerning Legal Aid, No. 16/2011 §§ 1, 4, 7–10 (Indonesia)

Law and Development Partnership. *Developing a Portfolio of Financially Sustainable, Scalable Basic Legal Service Models: Briefing Paper*. London: The Law and Development Partnership, Ltd., 2016.

The Law of the Republic of Indoneisa Concerning Legal Aid No. 16/2011 (Official Translation)

Law on State Guaranteed Legal Aid, Law No. 1988-XVI, of July 26, 2007 (Moldova)
The Legal Aid Act, No. 6 (2012), SUPPLEMENT TO THE SIERRA LEONE GAZETTE Vol. CXLIII, No. 42
Legal Aid Act No. 6 (2016), *Kenya Gazette* Supplement No. 56.
Legal Aid Act No. 7 of 2011 (Malawi)
Legal Aid in Europe: Minimum Requirements under International Law." Open Society Foundation (April 2015). www.opensocietyfoundations.org/sites/default/files/ee-legal-aid-standards-20150427.pdf.
Legal Aid Regulation, OFFICIAL GAZETTE No. 950 (2008) §§ 2, 15 (Afghanistan)
Legal Aid South Africa (LASA). *Annual Report: Legal Aid South Africa 2009/2010*. www.legal-aid.co.za/wp-content/uploads/2012/04/Legal-Aid-SA-Annual-Report-2009-10.pdf.
Legal Practice Act 28 of 2014 § 34(9) (S. Afr.).
"Legal Practice Bill Assented." NADCAO. May 14, 2015. http://nadcao.org.za/legal-practice-bill-assented/.
Legal Services Act 2011 (N.Z.), cls 3, 69, 75, 93–94; Legal Aid Act, 2011 §§ 17, 24 (Nigeria)
Liu, Anne, Sarah Sullivan, Mohammed Khan, Sonia Sachs, and Prabhjot Singh. "Community Health Workers in Global Health: Scale and Scalability." *Mt. Sinai Journal of Medicine* 78 (2011): 419–35.
Mahmoud, Mustafa. "Funding Projects with Trash." *Namati News* (blog). June 14, 2016. https://namati.org/news/funding_with_trash/.
Mansuri, Ghazala and Vijayendra Rao. *Localizing Development: Does Participation Work?* Washington, DC: World Bank, 2013.
Manuel, Marlon (National Coordinator, Alternative Law Groups [ALG]), interview. January 23, 2018.
Maru, Vivek. "Allies Unknown: Social Accountability and Legal Empowerment." *Harvard Journal of Health and Human Rights* 12, no. 1 (2012): 83–93.
"Between Law and Society: Paralegals and Provision of Justice Services in Sierra Leone and Worldwide." *The Yale Journal of International Law* 31, no. 2 (2006): 427–76.
"Only the Law Can Restrain Trump." *Foreign Policy*. March 9, 2017. http://foreignpolicy.com/2017/03/09/only-the-law-can-restrain-trump-legal-aid-barefoot-lawyers/.
McClymont, Mary and Stephen Golub. *Many Roads to Justice: The Law-Related Work of Ford Foundation Grantees around the World*. New York: The Ford Foundation, 2000.
Menon, Manju, Meenakshi Kapoor, Vivek Maru, and Kanchi Kohli, *Paralegals for Environmental Justice* (New Delhi: Center for Policy Research – Namati Environmental Justice Program, 2017), https://namati.org/wp-content/uploads/2017/12/Practice-Guide-for-Environmental-Justice-Paralegals.pdf.
Mercado, Carol. Barangay Justice System: Model of Citizen-Driven Justice System. Paper prepared for National Workshop on Local Justice. Dhaka, May 11–12, 2008.
Mitchell, Robert and Tim Hanstad. *Innovative Approaches to Reducing Rural Landlessness in Andhra Pradesh: A Report on the Experience of the IKP Land Activities*. Seattle, WA: Rural Development Institute, 2008.
Moore, Jina. "Kenya's About-Face: Fear for Democracy as Dissent Is Muzzled." *New York Times*, February 4, 2018. www.nytimes.com/2018/02/04/world/africa/kenya-political-repression-kenyatta-odinga.html.
National Environment Management Authority (NEMA). Kenya National Sand Harvesting Guidelines, 2007.
National Program on Legal Aid to Indigent Citizens 2006 (Mongolia)
Organization for Economic Cooperation and Development (OECD). "Detailed Aid Statistics: Official Bilateral Commitments by Sector." OECD International Development Statistics. doi: 10.1787/data-00073-en.

OECD Data. "Net ODA." OECD International Development Statistics. doi: 10.1787/33346549-en.

Otto, Michael. "5 Key Takeaways from Our Annual Network Survey." *Namati*. May 12, 2017. https://namati.org/news/5-key-takeaways-annual-network-survey–2016/.

Otto, Michael. "Indonesia – Community Paralegal Research Brief." Draft as of 2017 on file with author.

Pitkin, Hanna F. "Justice: On Relating Public and Private." *Political Theory* 9, no. 3 (1981): 327–52. www.jstor.org/stable/191093.

Province of Ontario Legal Aid Services Act, S.O. 1998, c. 26 (Can.) and the Legal Services Society Act, S.B.C. 2002, c. 30 (Can.).

Republic of Indonesia. Draft: Indonesia Law No. 16 Concerning Legal Aid. 2011. https://namati.org/wp-content/uploads/2012/01/Uli_Legal_Aid_Bill.pdf.

Republic of the Philippines, Department of Agrarian Reform. DAR Memorandum Circular No. 15–04. "Reaffirming the Vital Role of Farmer-Paralegals in Facilitating the Delivery of Agrarian Justice and Providing the Creation of Agrarian Justice Paralegal Support Fund." August 6, 2014. http://lis.dar.gov.ph/documents/1547#.

Ringold, Dena, Alaka Holla, Margaret Koziol, and Santhosh Srinivasan. *Citizens and Service Delivery: Assessing the Use of Social Accountability Approaches in the Human Development Sectors*. Washington, DC: International Bank for Reconstruction and Development, World Bank, 2012.

Sage, Caroline, Brian Z. Tamanaha, and Michael Woolcock (Cambridge: Cambridge University Press, 2013), 215–27.

Sandefur, Justin and Bilal Siddiqi. "Delivering Justice to the Poor: Theory and Experimental Evidence from Liberia." Paper presented at the World Bank Workshop on African Political Economy, Washington, DC, May 2013.

Sandefur, Justin, Bilal Siddiqi, and Alaina Varvaloucas. *Timap for Justice Criminal Justice Pilot: Impact Evaluation Report*. Oxford: Center for the Study of African Economies, Oxford University, 2012.

Sandefur, Rebecca L. and Thomas M. Clarke. "Roles beyond Lawyers: Summary, Recommendations, and Research Report of an Evaluation of the New York City Court Navigators Program and Its Three Pilot Projects." American Bar Foundation, National Center for State Courts, Public Welfare Foundation, December 2016.

Singh, Prabhjot and Jeffrey D. Sachs. "1 Million Community Health Workers in Sub-Saharan Africa by 2015." *The Lancet* 382, no. 9889 (2013): 363–65. doi: 10.1016/S0140-6736(12)62002-9.

Smalle, Edna. "Namati Wins Land Case … Chines Company to Restore 1,486 Acres of Land. *Awoko*. March 1, 2016. http://awoko.org/2016/03/01/sierra-leone-news-namati-wins-land-case-chinese-company-to-restore-1486-acres-of-land/.

Sonkita Conteh (director of Namati Sierra Leone), interview, March 5, 2016

Uli Sibombing (Indonesia Legal Resource Center), interview, July 2012, Kampala.

United Nations. "Sustainable Development Goals – Goal 16: Promote Just, Peaceful and Inclusive Societies." www.un.org/sustainabledevelopment/peace-justice/.

Villamor, Felipe. "President Rodrigo Duterte of Philippines Criticized over Martial Law Warning." *New York Times*, January 2017. www.nytimes.com/2017/01/16/world/asia/philippines-duterte-martial-law.html.

Wiggan, Jay and Colin Talbot. *The Benefits of Welfare Rights Advice: A Review of the Literature*. Manchester: National Association of Welfare Rights Advisors, 2006.

World Bank. "Net Official Development Assistance and Official Aid Received." http://data.worldbank.org/indicator/DT.ODA.ALLD.CD.

2

"To whom do the people take their issues?"

The Contribution of Community-Based Paralegals to Access to Justice in South Africa

Jackie Dugard and Katherine Drage

1. INTRODUCTION

It was a routine home visit to Ntabamnyana village at Inkomba Farm in Greytown by Margaret, the paralegal at the Mooi River Community Advice Office (CAO).[1] Margaret had heard that an elderly woman in the community, Agnes, was having trouble accessing her social grant and therefore could not get a wheelchair. Leaving the Advice Office car by the side of road, Margaret walked for two hours to the remote mountain village in the heart of the KwaZulu-Natal midlands. When she reached her client's homestead, she began to help Agnes to complete the identity documentation forms required so that she would be able to apply for a grant. Living with Agnes were her daughter, Lindiwe, and granddaughter, Grace, a seventeen-year-old girl with obvious learning difficulties. During Margaret's consultation, she heard Grace complain to her mother that something had "fallen out again," and that she was in pain. Margaret then witnessed an apparently common event in the household, whereby Lindiwe covered her hand with an empty plastic bag and pushed Grace's prolapsed uterus back inside her.

Speaking with the family, Margaret learned that the injury had been sustained from years of rape and sexual abuse inflicted by Grace's father and uncle, and that Lindiwe and Grace had moved to Agnes' homestead for Grace's safety. Seeing the extreme risk to the child's health, Margaret took Grace to the closest hospital in her car and pleaded with officials for the next twelve hours in order to get appropriate medical attention, explaining the process and developments to Grace's family at each stage. Proper examination revealed that Grace's reproductive organs were severely infected and would have to be removed. Grace stayed in the hospital for

---

[1] The quote within the chapter title comes from a description of a paralegal by Greg Erasmus. Greg Erasmus (former national coordinator of the National Alliance for the Development of Community Advice Offices [NADCAO]), interview, Johannesburg, January 25, 2011. The research for this chapter was undertaken in 2011 and the chapter was written in 2012 and revised in 2013. Since then there have been significant changes to the paralegal structures and frameworks.

four months to recover from the infection before surgery. However, tragically, when she was finally operated on, she did not wake up from the anesthesia. There was no money for Grace's funeral, so Margaret organized donations from the hospital staff and the CAO community outreach to bury her. Margaret discussed with the family the idea of laying criminal charges against the father and uncle. Having their agreement, she referred the matter to attorneys at the Centre for Criminal Justice, where a case is being mounted.[2]

South African paralegals occupy a critical, albeit as yet under-formalized space within South Africa's legal and welfare structures. Unregulated and largely undefined, paralegals nonetheless constitute an essential component of the justice and social security systems as they assist poor people in translating hard-fought constitutional rights into accessible and tangible benefits. Often embedded in the frequently far-flung communities they serve and undertaking a wide range of complementary services to help their clients achieve the best resolution to their problems, paralegals regularly operate beyond the capacity, locality, or comfort of the legal profession. Indeed, it is unlikely that a lawyer would even be in the kind of situation Margaret encountered, let alone know how to address it.

Legal assistance remains a vital component of accessing justice in South Africa. This is particularly so in light of both the relatively recent transition from apartheid rule and the often conflicted legal system that takes account of common and traditional law alongside constitutional law. Yet the country's current judicial system is fragmented and lacks the consistency required for effective cooperation between legal service providers and the efficient use of resources. There are 17,000 lawyers in South Africa, serving 45 million people. But the figure of 17,000 in fact vastly overstates the number of accessible lawyers, particularly given the divided bar, which means that 2,000 of these lawyers are advocates (barristers) who rarely have direct interaction with clients – especially poor ones. Moreover, the legal fees charged by both attorneys and advocates are much too high for the majority of South Africans,[3] and in any case, the vast majority of law firms are situated in the larger towns and cities, with few if any lawyers in small towns or rural areas. Thus the cost and distance required to physically access lawyers make pursuing litigation an overwhelmingly impractical option.

Another issue is that although structurally the judicial system is well placed to uphold the promise of the Bill of Rights, there is a disproportionate emphasis on state-oriented institutions and formal legal traditions.[4] However, much of the hard

---

[2] This is a true case study of the intervention of a community-based paralegal, as recounted by Winnie Kubayi. Names have been changed to protect anonymity. Winnie Kubayi (director, Centre for Community Justice [CCJ]), interview, Pietermaritzburg, October 13, 2010.

[3] The Socio-Economic Rights Institute of South Africa's (SERI) own experience of offering free legal assistance is that clients with a monthly income of R 600 (around US$67) are frequently charged fees in the region of R 1,500 (US$168) just for an initial consultation.

[4] South Africans have recourse to the Small Claims Court, Consumer Court, Land Claims Court, the Commission for Conciliation, Mediation and Arbitration (CCMA), and the Labour Court, as well as

work of advancing access to social justice is performed by paralegals, who function as much more than merely an adjunct to formal legal aid institutions. This is for two main reasons. First, whereas most lawyers live in urban areas, paralegals live in communities scattered across the country and as such, are well located geographically to respond to community issues. Second, on the whole, lawyers are less equipped than paralegals to deal appropriately with some of the more complex social issues that arise in poor communities, and especially to tackle these through non-adversarial dispute resolution.

It is clear from anecdotes such as Grace's story that South African paralegals play a substantive role in helping especially rural poor communities to realize their rights, whether through increasing access to justice or through directly resolving problems. Yet there has been little in the way of qualitative research into the functioning, value, and challenges faced by the paralegal sector. This chapter begins to fill this gap by providing an overview analysis of the sector's contribution to democratic consolidation in South Africa in the context of the historical development of paralegal work between 1948 and 2011. It is based mainly on primary research interviews conducted between September and November 2010 with sixteen organizations working in the paralegal sector, as well as an evaluation of the work of six CAOs between January and March 2011 that assessed the contribution of community-based paralegals by tracking specific resolved and unresolved cases.[5]

Section II of this chapter provides an overview of the genesis of South African paralegals, from their origins under the apartheid system until 2013, showing how their role has changed since the transition to democracy in 1994. The contemporary paralegal sector is mapped out in Section III, which describes where and how paralegals currently operate and outlines the current governance, funding, and support structures. Having mapped this diverse sector, the remainder of the examination focuses on CAOs, as they have played the most unique role from a community-based perspective. Thus Sections IV through VI investigate the work of CAOs, evaluating their impact on clients and communities and assessing how various factors either facilitate or hinder their capacity to fulfill their potential in South Africa. In Section IV, the results of the case-tracking exercise are presented, pulling out the critical factors in the successes or failures of each case, and Sections V and VI provide an analysis of CAO functions, both at the institutional (Section V)

---

the criminal and civil courts at various levels. In parallel, disputes are resolved within chiefs' courts in rural areas. Complaints can also be submitted to the Public Protector, the Commission for Gender Equality, the South African Human Rights Commission, and the Commission for the Promotion and Protection of the Rights of Cultural, Religious and Linguistic Communities. However, regarding these Chapter 9 institutions, most are weak, dysfunctional, and/or fractured by infighting, and they do not offer a real option for most poor people in addressing problems. Recently, though, there have been some signs that the Public Protector's office has been energized by the appointment of Thuli Madonsela as Public Protector in 2009.

[5] In order to safeguard anonymity, we have not identified individual clients or paralegals that we observed during the case-tracking exercise. Those paralegals we interviewed outside case-tracking who were happy to speak on record have been quoted directly.

and the organizational (Section VI) levels, that are reflected in the cases and research more generally. Conclusions are drawn in Section VII.

II. HISTORICAL OVERVIEW

The South African paralegal movement has a long history that is intimately linked to, first, the historical context of the apartheid legal order and, subsequently, the ongoing struggle to consolidate democracy in South Africa. The majority of South African CAOs were established between the 1960s and the 1980s in response to the increasingly oppressive apartheid state, buttressed by a racist legal order oriented toward the political and economic dominance of the white minority.

A. The Apartheid Era: 1948–1990

Between 1948 and 1990, the apartheid government's unfettered adherence to the doctrine of parliamentary supremacy created an "omnipotent law-making machine" that was "able to ride roughshod over individual liberty without fear of judicial obstruction."[6] This debasement of the legal system endorsed a carefully constructed legal order based on racial separation in which a host of legislation governed the personal, social, economic, and political status of the black person, based on an elaborate racial classification scheme whereby "Coloured" or "Bantu" classification meant automatic relegation to an inferior racial stratum with lesser rights.[7]

Under the apartheid system, black people were allocated separate facilities and interracial relations were illegal.[8] A series of "pass laws" confined black people to tribal homelands, forcing removal of thousands of people from white areas and resettlement on land frequently at a great distance from sources of employment and lacking proper amenities. The "dom pass," an identity book that had to be produced on demand, was an apartheid tool that gave rise to the most arbitrary and pernicious administration of the law. Additionally, the best-paid skilled jobs were reserved for whites, and black children received inferior education, with just R 39.53 per capita expenditure for black students in primary and secondary schools compared to R 605 spent on each white child.[9] Various statutes (known as "influx control") controlled both the number of black people allowed into urban areas and their behavior when they were there.[10] The holding of any meeting or social gathering attended by a black person in an urban area could be prohibited by the authorities, whether on public or

---

[6] This section draws on a seminal book about the apartheid legal order, *Human Rights and the South African Legal Order*, as well as interviews with all the paralegal organizations and experts examined in this study. See John Dugard, *Human Rights and the South African Legal Order* (Princeton, NJ: Princeton University Press, 1978), 35.

[7] Ibid., 55–62.   [8] By the term *black* we refer inclusively to all nonwhite people.

[9] Dugard, *Human Rights*, 84 (see n. 6). This equates to US$5.99 and US$91.73, respectively.

[10] Some of the most notable of these include the Bantu Land Act (1913), which designated 13 percent of South African land as "reserves" or black homelands; the Bantu (Urban Areas) Consolidation Act

private property. State agents also had the power to attend any such gathering when they believed internal security was being threatened. Beyond this institutional structure were the widespread manifestations of informal repression, such as arbitrary arrest, solitary confinement, torture, and extrajudicial killings – quite apart from the high rate of lawful executions of political opponents by the state.

1. The Emergence of Antiapartheid Movements

It was against this backdrop of exclusion, injustice, and repression that antiapartheid movements and organizations were established.[11] Similarly, CAOs were formed by community members out of the need for a space in which to mobilize against the apartheid regime, as well as out of a profound distrust of a judicial system that endorsed racially exclusive legal structures. For blacks, the law was not "a body of rules which their elected representatives [had] conceived in Parliament, but a repressing system imposed without consultation and enforced by an array of instruments of coercion – the army, the police, and the legal administration machine."[12] Some CAOs were, in fact, initially conceived as African National Congress (ANC) constituency offices,[13] helping to address the specific injustices of the time, such as the problems of being politically associated, the dom pass, and the consequences of forced removals.

Alongside the CAOs, Legal Aid South Africa (LASA) was founded in 1969 as a state-funded independent statutory body (established under the Legal Aid Act [1969]) particularly to provide means-tested free legal assistance via a judicare system for defendants in political trials. It was established because the government had received criticism following the banning of the South African Defence and Aid Fund for conducting such trials.[14] However, the LASA scheme was largely ineffective until the new democratic government widely extended its budget. In 1975 and 1976, only 810 applications were approved for legal aid in criminal cases.[15] Thus for the most part, black South Africans relied on CAOs and those

---

(1945), which established strict controls over how long and the purpose for which a black person could be present in an urban area; and the Group Areas Act (1950), which demarcated separate race areas in towns and cities. Bantu Land Act No. 27 (1913); Bantu Urban Areas Consolidation Act No. 25 (1945); Group Areas Act No. 41 (1950).

[11] These include the Pan Africanist Congress of Azania (PAC), established in 1959, and the Black Consciousness Movement founded in the mid-1960s in the context of the banning of the African National Congress (ANC) and the PAC on April 8, 1960 (following the Sharpeville massacre of civilians by police).

[12] Dugard, *Human Rights*, 391 (see n. 6).

[13] The ANC was formed in 1912 as a political organization (albeit unable to become a political party) for black people. Banned in 1960, it continued to operate underground and in exile until its legal recognition in 1991.

[14] The South African Defence and Aid Fund was established in 1956 (then called Christian Action) to assist political activists and their families by paying for legal representation for accused persons in political trials, as well as providing financial assistance to the families. After being banned in South Africa, it continued as the International Defence and Aid Fund based in London.

[15] Dugard, *Human Rights*, 246 (see n. 6).

limited elements of progressive white legal society that offered legal representation to blacks. During the late 1970s, the latter opportunities were consolidated into a few human rights legal organizations – such as the Centre for Applied Legal Studies (CALS) (1978) at the University of the Witwatersrand, the Legal Resources Centre (LRC) (1979), and Lawyers for Human Rights (LHR) (1979) – which took on mainly civil and political rights cases to advance social justice in South Africa.

During the late 1970s (and throughout the 1980s and early 1990s), CAOs worked collaboratively with organizations such as the CALS, the LRC, and the LHR in their attempt to advance what few rights they could on behalf of black people.[16] Collectively, they attempted to rally covertly with other civil society organizations at a time when such community activities were viewed with hostility by the state, and in response, CAO staff were frequently subjected to harassment and generally operated in a toxic environment.[17]

One of the most important organizations that networked with and supported the work of CAOs in the apartheid era was the Black Sash, which was founded just seven years after the formal advent of apartheid and, as elaborated on in Section III, is still playing an important role as a community-based paralegal, state monitoring, and advocacy organization today. The Black Sash was established in 1955 by six white women as a membership-based (and membership-funded), volunteer, antiapartheid activist organization. The name refers to the black sash that the activists wore across their chests during protests. Initially, the group's advocacy work centered on advancing a nonracial, morality-based vision within white society that questioned the validity of several pieces of apartheid legislation by holding mass meetings and vigils and launching petitions. From 1956 to the early 1960s, the Black Sash approach shifted to public education twinned with protest action. At the same time, the Black Sash set up CAOs in urban areas to assist black people who contravened the apartheid laws, particularly those that restricted freedom of movement. The CAOs provided support and free paralegal services, addressing concerns around housing, unemployment, pensions, influx control, and detention without trial. Between the 1960s and the 1980s, Black Sash CAOs flourished, and provided evidence with which the group informed its public protests and its monitoring of government policy, legislation, and action, as well as court activities. Through the CAO network, the Black Sash also monitored and recorded protests, rallies, arrests, detentions, and deaths.

[16] Further civil society organizations were established in the late 1980s, including the Institute for a Democratic Alternative in South Africa (IDASA) (1987), Earthlife Africa (1988), and People Opposing Women's Abuse (POWA) (1989).

[17] For instance, in 1989, the Langa and Nyanga (townships in Cape Town) branches of the Western Cape Hostel Dwellers Associations were firebombed and rebuilt. The offices of funding partners such as the Social Change Assistance Trust (SCAT), established in 1984 and overviewed in Section III, were also vandalized and subject to arson attacks.

2. Intensified Antiapartheid Efforts in the 1980s

During the 1980s, as political opposition mounted and insurrectionary fervor escalated in the wake of successive declarations by the government of states of emergency (1985–89), CAOs sprang up across the country in the homes of community leaders. These CAOs tackled immediate manifestations of apartheid rule such as forced evictions. For example, in 1986, the Logra CAO in the Western Cape was established to assist residents who had been forcibly removed from urban areas in Cape Town to the Cape Flats, to monitor unrest in the area, and to support the families of political detainees and those on trial. The Bhongolethu CAO in Oudtshoorn was also set up that year to assist community members with claims against the minister of law and order regarding farm evictions, as there was no legislation to protect workers. At the same time, the George Civic Association organized residents in opposition to forced removals, and CAOs such as the Grahamstown Rural Committee investigated and publicized the conditions of resettled communities through a newsletter and sympathetic media contacts. Over and above dealing with crisis interventions, CAOs focused more broadly on the end goal of ending the apartheid system. Notwithstanding the dangers of being allied to antiapartheid forces, CAOs networked with political organizations such as the South African National Civic Organisation (SANCO) and the United Democratic Front (UDF).[18]

The range of problems black people faced as a result of apartheid conditions exposed community-based paralegals to a diverse set of problems and allowed them to acquire a wide skill set, including the ability to provide therapy, trauma counseling, and resource procurement. For example, in 1988, the Woodstock CAO in Cape Town initiated an anti–Group Areas organization in the area (the 1950 Group Areas Act stipulated separate race areas in towns and cities), and the office provided counseling to residents under threat of removal. There were further distinct problems in rural areas; a great deal of suffering stemmed from the breakdown of family structures, which was in turn caused by the migrant labor system, as women and children were left in rural areas while men went to the cities for work.[19] Organizations such as the Community Law and Rural Development Centre (CLRDC) were established at this time to help rural populations access the scant resources available to them from the Bantu or homeland administrations. In 1989,

---

[18] SANCO was established in 1992 to represent affiliated organized community groupings around the country. It aimed to advance political and socioeconomic change for black communities in South Africa. The UDF was formed in 1983 under the shadow of the banned ANC, as a progressive front of community groupings and organizations united under the banner of forging a nonracial, nonsexist, and democratic South Africa. It ceased operating when the ANC was legally recognized in 1991. *See, for example*, "UDF Definition," Padraig O'Malley, Nelson Mandela Centre of Memory, last modified May 1996, www.nelsonmandela.org/omalley/index.php/site/q/03lv02424/04lv02730/05lv03176/06lv03184.htm.

[19] In 1985, the migrant labor system was at its highest, with 1,833,636 South Africans classed as migrants. Migrant mineworkers were also the first group of heterosexual men to test HIV positive in large numbers.

when the CLRDC was founded, it began providing access to information and social justice services to about 1 million people living in Natal and the Eastern Cape.[20]

The CAO movement gained an important avenue for funding through the establishment of the Social Change Assistance Trust (SCAT) in 1984. Drawing funds from the Norwegian government channeled through Norwegian Church Aid, SCAT initially provided funding to the Citizens Advice Forum, then extended its operations in the late 1980s to fund individual CAOs. By 1986, SCAT funded twenty-six CAOs and rural development organizations in the Cape and Natal. By 1990 – and despite some diluted reforms instituted by the apartheid regime to try to quell the rising tide of resistance – the combined weight of community mobilization and international economic disinvestment had forced the government into a stalemate, as a result of which it initiated a transitional period of negotiations toward democratic change. (Information about these and other organizations mentioned can be found in Section III.)

B. The Transitional Period: 1990–1994

The transitional period was defined by heightened political jostling as the old apartheid order conceded political power but sought to consolidate economic leverage, while the ANC struggled to gain political control.[21] It was a time of unrest, intense political violence, and police brutality. At the same time, it brought a new surge of civil society organizations, including paralegal organizations, which were set up to support the transitional process. For example, the Centre for Criminal Justice (CCJ), which was established in 1989 as a research unit affiliated to the Faculty of Law at the University of KwaZulu-Natal (UKZN), focused on investigating the role of criminal justice for those charged with political violence under the apartheid regime. Newly formed individual CAOs also had landmark cases. For instance, the Berlin CAO in the Eastern Cape was formed in 1991 when the head of the Ciskei government (Ciskei is a black homeland in the southeast region of the country) decided that the old and sick would no longer receive social grants, and community leaders formed a CAO to fight the ruling. They mounted litigation, and with the help of the Grahamstown LRC, they took the Ciskei government to the Supreme Court and won their case, resulting in the reinstatement of monthly grants for more than 3,000 people.

In response to the changing environment, paralegal organizations began to shift their focus, for the first time looking to a more democratic future with a more forward-looking approach. The Black Sash, for example, monitored the Convention for a Democratic South Africa negotiations and pushed for a new constitution. They

---

[20] Statistics courtesy of SCAT records. Margie Orford, *Rural Voice: The Social Change Assistance Trust 1984–2004: Working in South Africa* (Cape Town: David Phillip Publishers, 2004).

[21] Hein Marais, *South Africa: Pushed to the Limit: The Political Economy of Change* (Claremont: UCT Press, 2011).

also formed LegiWatch, a group of women who monitored legislation in Parliament. In addition, throughout the CAO network, the Black Sash provided voter training for the first democratic elections in 1994. The CLRDC also shifted its strategy to one of legal training and education, trying to bridge the divide between the Amakhosi, tribal authorities who have no formal legal training but who implement customary law, and the local magistrates, helping the traditional leaders to better understand the common law system, especially in the context of newly emerging humans rights standards and the advent of formal democracy.

C. Democratic Consolidation: 1994 to Today

"We don't really taste the new South Africa yet. We can see it, but we don't taste it."[22]
– Gideon Lottering, chairperson of the Prince Albert Advice Office, Western Cape

The historic democratic election in April 1994 ushered in an as yet unfinished period defined by three linked formal processes: first, a wholesale project of law reform, which worked to repeal and replace apartheid legal frameworks and institutions with democratic ones; second, the Truth and Reconciliation Commission (TRC), which sought to settle past human rights abuses; third, the related mission to advance the civil and political, as well as socioeconomic, incorporation of the majority of South Africans into the mainstream state, economy, and society.[23] These processes and their objectives have enjoyed varying degrees of success.

The first process of legal and institutional reform has been relatively successful. There has been wide-ranging reform of laws, policies, and institutions to bring them in line with the democratic, rights-based dispensation. The final constitution was adopted in 1996,[24] and is considered one of the most progressive constitutions in the world (not least for prohibiting unfair discrimination based on a wide range of listed grounds, including sexual orientation),[25] and government departments were established that acknowledged their human rights mandate. One of the founding

---

[22] Orford, *Rural Voice*, 56 (see n. 21).
[23] Apartheid's socioeconomic legacy was one where two worlds existed in one country. A rich, overwhelmingly white realm, with first world services and amenities, and a poor, black world characterized by poverty, un- or underemployment, and economic marginalization. Thus, in 1994, while virtually all white people had adequate access to water and sanitation, approximately 12 million black people did not have access to clean drinking water and 21 million black people did not have adequate sanitation. As recognized by the 1994 Reconstruction and Development Programme (the postapartheid government's first economic development policy), "access to water resources is dominated by a privileged minority while the majority of the population enjoy little or no water security." African National Congress (ANC), *The Reconstruction and Development Programme* (Johannesburg: Umanyano Publishers, 1994), § 2.6.1.
[24] *Constitution of the Republic of South Africa*, Act 108 (1996).
[25] Section 9(4) of the constitution outlaws direct or indirect unfair discrimination based on "one or more grounds, including race, gender, sex, pregnancy, marital status, ethnic or social origin, colour, sexual orientation, age, disability, religion, conscience, belief, culture, language and birth." Ibid., § 9(4).

objectives of the constitution is the espousing of "human dignity, the achievement of equality and the advancement of human rights and freedoms."[26] The constitution also entrenches the right of access to courts by guaranteeing everyone's right "to have any dispute that can be resolved by the application of law decided in a fair public hearing before a court or, where appropriate, another independent and impartial tribunal or forum."[27] It additionally goes some way toward recognizing a right to legal assistance at state expense by establishing that every detained, arrested, or sentenced prisoner has the right "to have a legal practitioner assigned to the detained person by the state and at state expenses, if substantial injustice would otherwise result."[28] Moreover, it provides for a form of legal aid (outlined in section 3.1), mainly for criminal issues.

But the second two processes have been less successful. The TRC has been criticized for not achieving reconciliation between whites and blacks, and it has been suggested that the TRC process actually exacerbated race relations, without promoting the kind of soul-searching and apologies expected from whites. If it was additionally hoped that the TRC might contribute to a safer, more secure society, such hopes have been dashed in that South Africa remains one of the most violent and unequal societies in the world, pointing to structural shortcomings of the third process. Indeed, it is increasingly clear that deep social and economic fractures remain and, in some instances, have worsened.

1. Deteriorating Socioeconomic Conditions

Gender-based violence is currently widespread in South Africa,[29] and socioeconomic inequality is increasing. Approximately 50 percent of South Africa's population of 49.9 million live below the poverty line. Unemployment is estimated at 25 percent of the economically active population;[30] 51 percent of South Africans aged between fifteen and twenty-four are unemployed,[31] and this is highest among black women (63 percent). The fact that black youth have not been properly incorporated into the productive economy is clear from the fact that 30 percent of the population currently receives social grants. While expansion of social security provides a vital safety net for those in dire need, this extent of grant dependence is financially unsustainable; at the local level, for instance, in towns such as Lady Frere in Eastern Cape, the entire population of 5,000 people and eighty-five surrounding villages depends on social grants.[32] The creeping sense of disillusionment with the liberation government has now also, after years of nondelivery in public service, firmly taken root. The ANC's

[26] Ibid., § 1(a).   [27] Ibid., § 34.   [28] Ibid., § 35(c).
[29] A Medical Research Council study recently found that 50 percent of all women who are murdered in South Africa are killed by men with whom they have an intimate relationship.
[30] South African Institute of Race Relations (SAIRR), "South Africa Survey 2008/2009" (Johannesburg: SAIRR, 2009), 193.
[31] See "Institute of Race Relations," The South African Institute of Race Relations. http://sairr.org.za/. In contrast, only 21 percent of white youth are unemployed.
[32] Orford, Rural Voice, 37 (see n. 21).

failure to deliver on socioeconomic rights in the terms of the constitution has dashed hopes of ameliorating long-standing problems of inadequate housing, electricity, and water and sanitation services, as well as education, health care, and social security, an accountable police force, and decent work opportunities.

Moreover, notwithstanding the formal legal and policy frameworks, there has been a gradual erosion of human rights principles over the past decade, in the form of HIV/AIDS denialism, a preoccupation with cost recovery for basic services, and a general lethargy in state institutions regarding the fulfillment of human rights obligations. At the sharper end of this retreat from the promise of the early "rainbow" days were the government's proposals during 2010 to pass protection of information legislation that would have undermined public access to information and established a tribunal to regulate the media.

2. New NGOs Confront the New Problems

This somewhat conflicting context of formal spaces and conducive frameworks on the one hand, and entrenched structural barriers alongside increasing failures of governance and service delivery on the other, has led to a burgeoning of civil society organizations. These include nongovernmental organizations (NGOs), trade unions, and social movements such as the Anti-Privatisation Forum, the Informal Settlements Network, the Landless People's Movement, and the Abahlali base Mjondolo (shack dwellers' movement). There has also been an increased demand for legal advice, training, and representation within the new democratic dispensation. After 1994, although all South Africans technically had all sorts of rights (civil and political, as well as socioeconomic), it remained difficult to actually access them, providing a new role for paralegals to attempt to translate the new Bill of Rights into reality. Indeed, as people gradually become aware of their rights (in no small part due to the educational work of paralegals), there has been an ever-growing need for paralegal assistance in claiming them.

While access to justice has significantly improved with the augmentation of LASA, which has expanded as one of the institutional pillars of the new constitutional order, the access has not expanded to meet the vast legal and quasi-legal needs of the majority poor, particularly in rural areas and generally with regard to civil claims.[33] It is in this context that CAOs have redefined their role as pioneers of development, as translators of the Bill of Rights, and most particularly as conduits of justice for people in far-flung rural areas. At the same time, probably in response to operating in the more nuanced post-1994 context when the (ANC-dominated) government was sometimes part of the problem for people in poor communities, many CAOs also began to distance themselves from the ANC and to become more politically neutral – or at least to portray themselves as such.

---

[33] Civil claims, by which the vast majority of socioeconomic rights issues are administered, still make up only 7 percent of LASA's caseload.

In addition, there have been structural changes in the paralegal sector during this period. For example, to optimize reach and efficacy, from 1994 to 1996 the National Community Based Paralegal Association (NCBPA) was established as a national CAO network, thereby increasing knowledge sharing and communication among paralegals on the ground.[34] The Black Sash also evolved during this time, in form and function. Between 1994 and 1999, the Black Sash helped to draft legislation and contributed to parliamentary standing committees looking at legal reform. It eventually became a professional NGO rather than a membership organization, with full-time paid staff and a board of trustees.[35] As discussed in Section III.B, the Black Sash has developed its own human rights programs, implemented them through rights education and advocacy, and monitored the impact of legislation through its regional centers.

Organizations such as CCJ also adopted a new operating structure after the end of apartheid, shifting their focus from the treatment of political prisoners to becoming protectors and defenders of rights, particularly with respect to violence against women and children.[36] CCJ realized that a new approach was required, and that the South African Police Service was struggling to grapple with such crimes.[37] CCJ thus began a pilot scheme to train civilians as paralegals, with specific focus on how to take statements from and counsel someone who has suffered a trauma in a confidential, private space, teaching the victim about his or her rights at each stage, and arranging follow-up support. At the end of the first month of this scheme, the first paralegal trained had been involved in thirty-five cases, and by the end of six months, this figure was 100. This collaborative model led to an influx of reporting, and established an iterative program between CCJ, police, magistrates' courts, and traditional and community leaders.[38] SCAT also shifted to focus solely on rural areas and to phase out its funding of urban-based service organizations, on the basis that rural people's exclusion from wealth and power would likely be perpetuated unless actively challenged, and that the positive changes following the democratic election would come more slowly to rural than urban areas.[39]

---

[34] The national coordination facilitated by the NCBPA was lost when the organization folded in 2003. However, a new CAO network agency, the National Alliance for the Development of Community Advice Offices (NADCAO), was set up in 2007 and is profiled in detail in Section III.C.

[35] Tim Lebert and Umhlaba Associates, *Holding Government to Account: Advocacy in an Emerging Democracy: The Story of the Black Sash* (New York: The Atlantic Philanthropies, 2009). Similarly, by 1999, increasing numbers of CAO staff and volunteers did not come from an activist background of working for the struggle and instead demanded a living wage and benefits.

[36] Kubayi, interview (see n. 2).

[37] The police failure to tackle violent crime and particularly domestic/gender crime relates generally to problems with transforming the service from an apartheid security apparatus to a public safety service, and also to poor investigative, detection, and reporting capacity. But it also relates to the specific and universal difficulties of policing domestic and gender-based crimes because of victims' reluctance to report.

[38] Kubayi, interview (see n. 2).   [39] Orford, *Rural Voice*, 13 (see n. 21).

III. MAPPING THE PARALEGAL SECTOR TODAY

In South Africa, paralegals are not as strictly or formally defined as they are in many other countries. Occupying a variety of terrains, some work as unpaid volunteers, others on a salaried basis; some work closely with lawyers, while others operate totally independently; and some hold tertiary education paralegal qualifications, while others learn on the job, building experience through years in community activism and service. The trait they share is their direct legal and quasi-legal interface with the clients and communities they serve. Given their largely amorphous character, paralegals are here defined as people who attempt to resolve individual matters for their clients. It is also useful, as a broad-brush definition, to look at the clients' perspective of paralegals. In the words of Greg Erasmus, "Simply ask where and to whom do the people take their issues? That person is the paralegal."[40]

Looking generally at the things paralegals do, what sets them apart from many other service providers is how they seek to resolve a multitude of wide-ranging community issues, straddling the legal (criminal and civil) and social welfare systems. As Vivek Maru identifies, "[t]he substantive directions of the program are determined by the specific problems that clients and community members bring to our offices."[41] In terms of techniques, paralegals commonly use alternative dispute resolution (ADR) techniques of mediation and negotiation to establish a holistic approach to help solve people's problems within families, and with traditional and state authorities. Paralegals investigate cases that require representation by an advocate, and connect people in their communities to trained lawyers who may be able to help them in this capacity, smoothing the litigation process by helping to draft witness statements. Where necessary, paralegals will also refer people to other sources of assistance, whether local government departments, health clinics, or welfare agencies. They create a network of information providers and referral systems for their communities, often with NGOs and other paralegal organizations. As well as responding to individual and community problems, paralegals take an active stance to improve local people's legal literacy, engaging in peer-to-peer education techniques to better rights education, legislation, and legal processes. They also mobilize people around pressing community issues to lobby for changes to be made by state powers.

To carry out these tasks, paralegals hone skills in counseling, administration, monitoring, communications, and networking, as well as the practical legal skills of drafting letters and gathering evidence. They also develop a knowledge of basic laws and procedures relating to civil actions, arrest, detention, and bail. Paralegals operate in this vein in South Africa within a variety of organizations, as well as independently. Thematically, while covering a wide variety of justice-related work,

---

[40] Erasmus, interview (see n. 1).
[41] Vivek Maru, "Between Law and Society: Paralegals and the Provision of Justice Services in Sierra Leone and Worldwide," *The Yale Journal of International Law* 31, no. 2 (2006): 442.

South African paralegals primarily deal with concerns involving domestic violence and access to social grants. As outlined earlier, these areas of work relate to two of the most serious remaining fault lines in South Africa: endemic violence in the home and structural unemployment, meaning that a very high proportion of South Africans relies on social grants to survive.[42] It is thus no coincidence that these are the most common cases dealt with by paralegals.

This chapter distinguishes between four categories of paralegals. First is the most formalized category, found specifically in private law firms, trade unions, or government departments, where they service the needs of the agency they work for rather than the general public. Although private law firms tend to utilize candidate attorneys rather than paralegals, there are still a few paralegals working in these offices, where they carry out initial consultations, take statements, and make referrals to other organizations. Trade unions also employ paralegals in lawyerly roles, where they use ADR techniques of mediation and negotiation to resolve labor law matters. Additionally, many paralegals are absorbed into municipal government structures, where they may continue to provide primary legal advice to citizens on behalf of the government, but most probably not in a solely paralegal capacity. This chapter does not address this more formal and recognizable category of paralegals.

The second category is those paralegals who serve the public through their work in legal structures (other than private law firms, trade unions, or government departments) where they provide valuable client interface and support services to public lawyers. Notable setups here are the paralegals who work within litigating NGOs and branches of LASA, whose operations are described in Section III.A. The third category is the paralegals who work for the Black Sash, an NGO that operates *sui generis* in the South African landscape to advance social security on a quasi-legal frontier and overwhelmingly relies on paralegals. Its paralegal work is outlined in Section III.B.

Finally, there are those paralegals who work more autonomously in organizations or arrangements that are primarily about paralegal services per se and wherein paralegals take up and resolve matters themselves, referring to lawyers only as a last resort when litigation is necessary. It is here in the CAOs that paralegals contribute the most broadly to the promotion and enforcement of access to justice across South Africa, both through their wide geographic range and the fact that they

---

[42] According to government statistics, for the years 2011–2012, there were 15.3 million social grant beneficiaries (out of a total South African population of approximately 49 million), including children, people with disabilities, and the elderly (these are the main social grants). See Francis Hweshe, "More to Benefit from Social Grants," *BuaNews*, April 15, 2011, www.southafrica.info/about/social/436302.htm. Indeed, in South Africa, there are approximately three times more social grant recipients than taxpayers (there are 5 million registered individual taxpayers in South Africa). Notwithstanding the official statistics, there are serious problems with the administration of the social grant system, with systemic corruption and maladministration resulting in social grants being unlawfully terminated or delayed, etc., and precipitating the relatively high number of social grant cases brought by paralegals.

are often the only legal or quasi-legal option within far-flung rural communities. This category of paralegals is the research focus of this chapter, and it is examined in Section III.C.[43]

A. Paralegals in Lawyer-Support Roles: Litigating NGOs and Legal Aid South Africa (LASA)

In South Africa, NGOs that undertake public interest litigation quite commonly employ paralegals to work on the front line of community relations, as the initial client contact, and subsequently in support of the NGO's attorneys as cases progress. The LRC is one such NGO that, as mentioned earlier, has incorporated paralegals into its work since its inception. Currently, the LRC employs seven paralegals in each of its four offices across the country, all except one having worked at the LRC for more than a decade. Their time is split between the front desk of the office, where each morning paralegals consult with walk-in clients, and in the litigation department. LRC paralegals are typical of others working in this type of environment in that their training is incorporated into the wider legal training of the organization's staff, giving them the opportunity to be up-skilled and better resourced across the LRC's broad areas of focus. Paralegals in litigating NGOs can therefore provide a high-quality level of service, and paralegals at the LRC build up an expertise over their careers such that their initial consultation with clients is often sufficient to resolve the matter. However, more complicated issues are handed over to the attorneys. Paralegals generally do not direct the outcome of a case, but rather facilitate the court process by serving and filing papers, commissioning affidavits, and giving feedback and explanations to clients. Paralegals in the LRC also join their colleagues in giving community training workshops based on emergent trends or the NGO's strategic focus issues.

LASA is the largest employer of paralegals in the country, with 185 paralegals working across its various branches. Funded by the Ministry of Justice, with a R 900 million budget for 2010,[44] LASA has its national headquarters in Johannesburg and six regional head offices. LASA operates through sixty-four justice centers, where legal aid applicants go for legal assistance as they would to a law firm, and it is staffed by attorneys, candidate attorneys, and paralegals, with fifty-five satellite offices, including sub-offices in rural areas that are too remote to be serviced by the nearest justice center. One hundred fifty paralegals work within the justice centers and satellite offices; these vary in size, with sometimes two or three paralegals in each. LASA employs twelve paralegals to consult with prisoners awaiting trial, a case

---

[43] Note that, for logistical reasons, we did not examine the multitude of paralegals and CAOs operating outside of any structure or umbrella organization, in terms of which, typically, one- or two-person outfits spring up in local communities and provide assistance with common community problems, often for a small direct fee.

[44] A budget equivalent to around US$1.1 million.

flow management project aimed at reducing overcrowding in prisons by providing legal representation to people who cannot afford it, and thus formalizing the case so that it can proceed in court. Nine paralegals work within the LASA high court unit, assisting at the administrative level with post-sentence prisoners who want to appeal or file petitions about their case.

Finally, fourteen paralegals work in the LASA call center, launched in June 2010 to overcome the barrier to access to justice due to onerous long-distance transport costs by providing legal advice over the phone with subsequent allocation to the nearest justice center or satellite office if necessary. This last group of LASA paralegals is the most highly qualified and received two months of intensive training before the center opened. The training, remuneration, and evaluation of paralegals at LASA is formalized in their performance contracts, by which they must undertake a certain number of hours of training per year, and according to which they are evaluated every quarter against a specific set of criteria. Entry-level paralegals earn approximately R 8,000 (US$980) per month.

The presence of paralegals at LASA enables the organization to resolve more client problems than if the office consisted only of qualified lawyers. Walk-in clients to justice centers and satellite offices often require only initial advice from paralegal staff, a testament to the value of and need for providing a general legal advice service in South Africa. The call center advice line has been very successful in this respect, with a 93 percent rate of internal resolution between August and October 2010. Nevertheless, the paralegals' role remains limited beyond undertaking an initial consultation and client means tests. As soon as the application for a legal aid lawyer has been approved, paralegals are not involved in the case file except for evidence gathering and follow-ups with the client. This makes their role more rigid than that of the paralegals in the Black Sash and CAOs, and it restrains their ability to have a deeper impact. This is coupled with the fact that LASA admits that the organization has limited capacity to render civil legal aid services, with civil matters accounting for just 7 percent of LASA's caseload:

> The lack of funding for civil legal aid services has resulted in limited capacity to render civil legal aid services, impacting negatively on the number of clients assisted in civil legal matters as evident from the decline in the number of persons assisted in civil matters. This limited capacity to undertake civil legal aid also results in a limited presence in rural areas making it difficult for clients in rural areas to access legal aid.[45]

LASA acknowledges the negative impact that this dearth in capacity has on access to justice in rural areas. However, the answer probably does not lie in opening more LASA satellite offices, as the expense of opening a fully fledged office cannot be

---

[45] Legal Aid South Africa (LASA), *Annual Report: Legal Aid South Africa 2009/2010*: 11. www.legal-aid.co.za/wp-content/uploads/2012/04/Legal-Aid-SA-Annual-Report-2009-10.pdf.

justified for the relatively slight quantity of work that will arise from small remote communities; instead, it would make more sense financially for LASA to use its budget to pay for the setup and training of paralegals in a CAO.[46]

B. The Black Sash

Emerging from a long history of antiapartheid activism, today the Black Sash offers human rights advice to communities, predominately using paralegals. There are currently seven Black Sash regional offices around the country, in Cape Town, Knysna, Port Elizabeth, Grahamstown, Durban, Pietermaritzburg, and Johannesburg, as well as a national office near Parliament in Cape Town. There are also three Black Sash satellite offices that run two or three times per month in rural locations, enabling clients far from a regional center to speak to Black Sash paralegals about their issues. Donor-funded by the Charles Stewart Mott Foundation and the Atlantic Philanthropies, with additional funding from the Foundation for Human Rights and the European Union on a project basis, the Black Sash employs fifteen paralegals, two in each regional office apart from Johannesburg, which has three. All paralegals have the paralegal diploma certificate,[47] are part of the way through an LLB degree, or have other such experience; for example, Thandiwe Zulu, director of the Johannesburg regional office, is a qualified social worker and psychologist. The Black Sash stipulates quite high qualifications as part of its recruitment criteria after an upgrade in 2001 in the quality of service being provided, due to the high number of applications it was receiving from younger-generation career paralegals for relatively few positions. The organization also pays relatively well for the sector, with entry-level salaries of around R 10,000 increasing to R 17,000 per month (US$1,200–US$2,100).

The Black Sash's work is split between providing free legal advice and paralegal support, conducting rights education campaigns to help people access their socio-economic rights as outlined in the constitution, and advocating for legislative and policy reform. Broadly speaking, the organization's interventions range across four thematic areas: social security, consumer protection, access to basic services, and

---

[46] David Mcquoid-Mason (professor of law, University of KwaZulu/Natal), interview, Durban, October 11, 2010.

[47] Two national qualifications for paralegals are currently registered with the South African Qualifications Authority: a one-year National Paralegal Certificate and a three-year Diploma in Paralegal Studies. According to course provider websites, the materials are drawn up in consultation with the South African Institute of Legal Training. The Certificate/Diploma is available as per other South African tertiary qualifications, upon enrollment and payment of fees. The South African Law School and South African School of Paralegal Studies run courses, as does the University of Johannesburg. The fact that this is an expensive course, often geared toward a more corporate angle, confirms the value of the training for community-based paralegals provided by CLRDC/CCJ through the University of Kwa-Zulu Natal (UKZN). "Paralegal Practice," South African Law School. http://lawschool.co.za/courses/paralegal-practice/; "Home," The South African School of Paralegal Studies. www.paralegal.za.org/.

access to decent work. The first of these is their largest program and covers social assistance grants (such as child support and disability grants), and social insurance grants (such as pensions and maintenance grants) owed to people by the Department of Social Development (DSD).

The group also runs advocacy campaigns to make social protection measures more inclusive, for instance, for children aged fifteen to eighteen and the unemployed, and to make social insurance cover those employed in the informal sector as well as part-time and domestic workers. It also helps clients exercise their consumer rights and promotes credit record access to build a fairer consumer environment. The Black Sash is assessing the impact of the National Credit Act (2005), which, along with the new Consumer Protection Act (2011), aims to protect the public from overzealous banks and credit facilities by creating stringent conditions for banks and other institutions providing credit and thereby to advance consumer-related rights. Access to basic services is a new area, focused mainly on municipal indigent policies.[48]

1. Mandate to Report on Service Delivery

More generally in terms of this new mandate, the Black Sash has a memorandum of understanding with the Department of Home Affairs, DSD, and the South African Social Security Agency (SASSA) to carry out monitoring and report back at a local level on service delivery.[49] The project, known as the Community Monitoring and Advocacy Programme (CMAP), commenced in November 2009 and is run jointly by the Black Sash and the Social Change Assistance Trust (SCAT), which together coordinate volunteers nominated by 270 CAOs and community-based organizations to record their observations at service delivery points across all nine provinces over an eighteen-month period.[50] When the reports come in, these observations are used to access and report on government service delivery in specified state departments as experienced by beneficiaries. Finally, the Black Sash is starting to look at labor advocacy, which currently makes up around 25 percent of its cases. In this regard, it is investigating how to work with unions, as the majority of clients' labor matters relate to union–member disputes.

Across offices and projects, the Black Sash paralegals work in a particular way. They capture trends and feedback from their casework that are entered in a database held at each regional office. These statistics show the prevalence and location of certain issues, as well as the turnover of cases handled. The Black Sash's advocacy strategy is informed by analyzing these case logs, using hard evidence as proof of

---

[48] Indigent policies are a common means through which municipalities allocate free basic services to low-income households. They are a targeted, means-tested social grant at the local government level.

[49] This manages quality social security services (social grants and pensions) to eligible and potential beneficiaries.

[50] Drawn from networks within NADCAO, the South African Council of Churches, and the National Welfare, Social Service and Development Forum, which are monitoring partners in this project.

what the paralegals witnessed on a daily basis rather than relying on rough notebooks. The database is used to identify emerging trends and developments in regard to which the group then lobbies for policy implementation or reform.

Through its case management system, the Black Sash is able to analyze trends and mount strategic interventions in a way that most CAOs (discussed later in this chapter) are not. For example, the Black Sash is currently advocating that the qualifying age for a child support grant be raised to eighteen years rather than the current fifteen years. An analysis of regional trends can also give rise to a class action, although the Black Sash makes clear that litigation is used only as an absolute last resort, after all avenues of cooperative engagement are exhausted and no solutions are forthcoming.[51] The organization has, however, had important successes gathering evidence from regional case data with which to mount a case, most frequently partnering with the LRC in line with the two organizations' long history of collaboration.

In 2000, the regional director of the Grahamstown Regional Office noticed that an overwhelming number of clients were having problems getting their social grants approved on time, and that when finally approved, they did not receive any back pay from the date of application. Case logs from the Black Sash database showed clients waiting from nine months to three years for approval of their grants. Given that Regulation 11 of the Social Assistance Act (1992) limited back payments to ninety days from date of approval, the long wait was having a serious impact on the lives of poor people while the Eastern Cape government saved money by allowing such long delays. The Grahamstown Regional Office monitored the issue for a year before taking it to the Black Sash National Advocacy manager for assistance. When other Black Sash regional offices showed similar patterns, the Black Sash referred the evidence to the LRC, which found grounds for a legal case against the National DSD and Eastern Cape DSD on the ground that Regulation 11, in relation to back pay, was unconstitutional.[52]

A settlement was eventually reached one day before trial, the Regulation was set aside, and an order was issued giving people the right to back pay from the date of application. An amount of R 2.1 million (roughly US$260,000) was made available for back pay to all who had been affected by the offending regulation. The Black Sash then went back to the grassroots level where the problem had been detected to make sure that the benefit of this order was felt by the thousands of people who had been affected. Paralegals communicated with DSD, requested a list of all entitled applicants, and lobbied for DSD to create pamphlets informing people of the court order and how to access their back pay. Individual CAOs then took on the task of finding people entitled to back pay and taking them to pay points with the necessary

---

[51] Only 15 percent of individual cases are referred to litigation if the matter cannot be resolved by discussion and negotiation.
[52] *Njongi v. Member of the Executive Council*, Department of Welfare, Eastern Cape (CCT 37/07) [2008] ZACC 4; 2008 (6) BCLR 571 (CC); 2008 (4) SA 237 (CC); 2011 (7) BCLR 651 (CC) (March 28, 2008).

documents. More recently, in January 2011, the Black Sash won a case against the Eastern Cape DSD, compelling it to hear disability grant appeals and clear the backlog in which around 65,000 South Africans are currently trapped. In both cases, from start to finish, the Black Sash paralegals were the impetus and enforcement of the progressive realization of the right to social security, and helped secure administrative justice for poor and vulnerable people without the means to access other legal help to uphold their rights.

2. Providing Education about Rights

More generally, paralegals working within the Black Sash see themselves as legal facilitators, informing people of the right channels to take and unblocking any obstacles they encounter. Rights education is the Black Sash's priority, and information captured from casework helps to develop rights education programs through targeted media channels. In the Johannesburg regional office, the paralegals worked with three local community radio stations as well as one national radio station in 2010, talking on air about rights associated with their focus areas.[53] In all their offices, Black Sash paralegals do a substantial amount of community and peer training, from queue education for walk-in clients waiting in the office reception for consultation, to running workshops on social security in conjunction with the National Welfare Forum.[54] They also train people to open new CAOs;[55] indeed, it was paralegals at the Black Sash who trained the LASA paralegals working in the new LASA call center. Finally, through its paralegal guides and manuals,[56] produced annually to update CAO paralegals on new legislation and policies, the Black Sash also extends its impact beyond the urban centers that are its primary focus, keeping in touch with the CAOs with which they were so strongly connected as an activist organization under apartheid.

C. Community Advice Offices (CAOs)

South Africa's approximately 350 CAOs are small, nonprofit organizations staffed by paralegals and administrative coordinators who work to address the social ills caused by the continuing economic, social, and spatial legacy of apartheid.

---

[53] In these radio talk show programs, hosted on Mteta, Alex, Gasi, and Mholbo FM community radio stations, Black Sash paralegals discuss issues relating to the labor system, particularly surrounding retrenchment and injuries in the workplace, as well as consumer issues and what to do if your social grant is delayed or denied.

[54] The National Welfare Forum is a coordinating body fostering dialog and human rights advocacy with regard to social welfare. National Welfare Social Service and Development Forum, www.forum.org.za/.

[55] The paralegals in the Johannesburg regional office are currently assisting prospective paralegals to establish an advice office at Khanya Community College.

[56] One such guide, *Social Assistance: A Reference Guide for Paralegals*, is in use at the Lethabong Advice Office in the North West Province, a rural area without the physical presence of the Black Sash but that is still benefiting from its resources. The Black Sash, *Social Assistance: A Reference Guide for Paralegals* (Mowbray: The Black Sash, 2010).

CAOs provide free basic legal and human rights information to poor communities in peri-urban areas, rural villages, urban townships, and informal settlements, and form a central hub for local economic development and improvement in social welfare. A CAO paralegal's casework might involve negotiations with relevant governmental departments, ADR, or engagement with lawyers via a referral network. They might also engage in human rights- and livelihood-related education.[57] In addition, many CAOs take an active role in advocating for improvement in government policies and practices, and to this end form working partnerships with other civil society organizations to advocate and mobilize around relevant issues such as the back-pay matter raised by the Black Sash and the LRC discussed earlier. Thematically, CAOs work on a wide range of issues involving both the resolution of private disputes and matters concerning state accountability, but generally tend to tailor their interventions and focus to the specific environment and needs of the local communities they serve. Whether in a remedial or advocacy capacity, CAOs occupy central territory in terms of community development and legal empowerment of the poor by working to erase the detrimental legacy of apartheid and the current conditions of poverty experienced by many South Africans.

CAOs currently run without formal regulation, and there are no prescribed minimum standards of operation or regulatory authority to ensure compliance. The majority of South African CAOs (most with only one paralegal and sometimes one coordinator per office) are founded on the impetus of a community leader or other community-based organization, or on the suggestion of a neighboring CAO if it is clear that a nearby community has need for such an office. Once established and running with some form of community management in place, CAOs frequently align themselves under umbrella networks or within advice office clusters to maximize their efficacy and sustainability, particularly in the context of insecure funding. Outlined next are the structures through which affiliated CAOs operate at both the national and regional levels.

1. National Alliance for the Development of Community Advice Offices (NADCAO)

The National Alliance for the Development of Community Advice Offices (NADCAO) is an affiliation agency that seeks to facilitate the operations of the 230 CAOs that have joined the alliance.[58] It was set up in 2007 to fill the lacunae left

---

[57] Our research focused on case tracking and, as such, we did not monitor any human rights awareness training. Critically, as elaborated on in Sections V, VI, and VII, while CAOs undertake human rights awareness/education training, the ones we observed do not seem to convert their paralegal case resolution experience into strategic lessons/training for the communities they serve.

[58] It is notable that not all CAOs have affiliated with NADCAO, which is working to incorporate these organizations and extend its network, although a certain degree of formal establishment is required for affiliation. When we spoke to Greg Erasmus (former national coordinator of NADCAO) in Johannesburg on January 25, 2011, he explained that NADCAO was in the process of establishing

by the closure of the NCBPA four years earlier.[59] During this time the sector lost much of its coordination and knowledge-sharing capacity, and without communication at the national level, the larger players in the sector (which later became NADCAO's founders) lost much of their footprint in terms of trend analysis across the country, while individual CAOs became increasingly isolated and unsupported.[60] NADCAO was founded by a steering committee of seven founding members, including influential bodies in the paralegal sector such as the Black Sash Trust (in whose Cape Town offices NADCAO is based), the CLRDC, the Association of University Legal Advice Institutions (AULAI) Trust, and SCAT. It is neither a membership,[61] nor a funding organization (centralized funding is channeled to the sector through other umbrella organizations, namely SCAT, CLRDC, CCJ, and AULAI as described later in this chapter),[62] but sees its role as providing strategic support and an advocacy platform to the community-based paralegal sector, helping it to consolidate a national footprint, position itself within national legal and institutional frameworks, and increase the capacity and sustainability of individual affiliated CAOs.

Funded by the Atlantic Philanthropies, the Charles Stewart Mott Foundation, and the Joseph Rowntree Charitable Trust, NADCAO plays a strong advocacy role and envisions an organized, institutionalized, and regulated sector, while recognizing the supporting role played by civil society organizations, with the goal that every community in South Africa will have walking-distance access to a functioning, well-resourced CAO. NADCAO's main functions are to increase communication and knowledge sharing among CAOs; to broker partnerships between CAOs and

minimum operating criteria for a CAO to join the alliance. Erasmus, interview (see n. 1). To maximize research efficiency, in this project we focused on affiliated CAOs as, without the assistance of a network structure, the unaffiliated CAOs are more difficult to identify and reach (indeed, most do not have Internet or good telecommunications access). Using NADCAO as the entry point also enabled access to hundreds of CAOs across the country, so we were able to include a range of CAOs in different localities.

[59] The NCBPA was established in 1996 as an umbrella organization for CAOs across South Africa, funded through a R 150 million grant for ten years from the International Commission of Jurists. It aimed to uphold and develop CAOs and influence governmental bodies to improve working conditions for paralegals as well as implement national training schemes. Primarily the NCBPA worked as a membership organization providing funding to its members. The NCBPA's subsidiary project, the National Paralegal Institute (NPI), focused on developing a unified training system, and specifically it developed the Paralegal Diploma registered with the South African Qualifications Authority (SAQA). At its peak in 2001, the NCBPA represented 312 CAOs across all nine provinces. After management and finance problems, both organizations were no longer operational from 2003.

[60] Schalk Meyer (director, AULAI Trust), interview, Potchestroom, October 25, 2010. In Meyer's words, "it is a pity that the NCBPA collapsed, as it was on its way somewhere, doing good work. The advice offices too were working well at the time as they were being funded, and didn't have the frustration that is occurring now."

[61] This was the structure and modus of the NCBPA and NPI. However, issues of poor governance, fundraising, and long-term sustainability experienced within those organizations led to NADCAO's decision to create an alliance of CAOs with ownership placed within the CAOs themselves.

[62] However, one of NADCAO's functions is to try to secure long-term funding for the sector as a whole.

community stakeholders in government, civil society, and the private sector to garner financial support; to provide paralegal training; and more generally, to strengthen the efficacy and sustainability of CAOs.

Out of the 230 CAOs belonging to the alliance, former NADCAO national coordinator Greg Erasmus estimates that there are currently 150 "good" offices, in terms of governance, accountability, and quality of service.[63] For Erasmus, the "good" CAOs are characterized by effective internal governance and accountability within the communities they serve. In the "not so good" CAOs, there are problems related to handling budgets,[64] practicing good governance,[65] and being unresponsive to local communities or simply not performing paralegal duties for community members. Such problems mainly stem from a lack of regulation and management and, in response, NADCAO is encouraging the forums to establish minimum standards for CAO governing bodies (management committees), and mandatory training in human resources and finance that is tailored to the CAO management committees.[66] At the time of this writing, however, this had not yet occurred.

NADCAO has been instrumental in advocating a role and institutional framework for paralegals in the Legal Practice Bill (discussed under Section V) and otherwise acting as a mouthpiece for the sector's attempts to gain further formal recognition and public funding. Generally speaking, the paralegal sector appears to have welcomed NADCAO as a countrywide organizational tool and national voice after a long period of fragmentation brought about when the NCBPA shut down. Under NADCAO, CAOs are also organized according to smaller specialist affiliation networks or clusters run by organizations on the NADCAO steering committee board.[67] Thus, at the regional level, CAOs are affiliated with SCAT (predominantly a centralized funding source) in the Northern, Western, and Eastern Capes, and the CLRDC and CCJ (providing training and funding) in KwaZulu-Natal (KZN). CAOs are also clustered by AULAI (providing mainly case referral support, as well as some training and a little funding) around university legal clinics. While NADCAO is formally independent of these support organizations, their directors

[63] Erasmus, interview (see n. 1).
[64] In 2010, Erasmus purposefully tested whether the coordinators could effectively distribute R 20,000 from NADCAO for activities within their provinces. The majority handed the lump sum back to NADCAO, preferring instead to draw down the money on an ad hoc basis in response to demand.
[65] Typical governance-related problems include absence of a management board, lack of transparency regarding finances, poor labor or working practices, and nonperformance of duties. John Moerane (provincial coordinator of the Northwest Paralegal Advice Officers Cluster), interview, Lethabong, February 14, 2011.
[66] For example, Bheki Shange, coordinator of the Gauteng forum, is supervised by NADCAO to train CAO management committees across the forum on governance, finance, recruitment, and fundraising initiatives.
[67] While this might, at first glance, appear to be a strange structure, NADCAO provides a national presence and mouthpiece for the sector, while the other umbrella organizations described later provide specific assistance within regional contexts, including funding. It is possible that if NADCAO succeeds in achieving a more professional, better-resourced CAO sector, NADCAO itself might no longer be needed.

are on the NADCAO steering committee board. The following sections examine the ethos and operations of these various organizations.

2. Social Changes Assistance Trust (SCAT)

With twenty-seven years of involvement in the CAO sector, today, SCAT's vision is to make CAOs institutional centers of democracy within communities that empower the rural poor and strengthen civil society in remote areas of the Eastern, Western, and Northern Capes. It does so primarily through channeling start-up funding to CAOs,[68] raised primarily from international donors.[69] SCAT currently funds forty-five CAOs (all NADCAO affiliates),[70] managed by elected community members and mentored by a SCAT fieldworker who has the indigenous knowledge to pick up on community dynamics and issues.

SCAT shares NADCAO's belief that community control is an essential component of civil society and accountable governance, a belief that directly shapes SCAT's funding policy requirement that the CAO is community based, rural, and collectively owned. More particularly, SCAT requires a CAO to have management committee annual general meetings (AGMs), a committee constitution, and regular committee meetings with the community that include a report from the CAO. Financially, the CAO needs to produce an audited financial statement within two years and then annually, as well as monthly or quarterly reports to SCAT. The CAO must be nonpartisan both politically and religiously, and membership and access must be open to all (a strategy aimed particularly at preventing xenophobia). Within two years of receiving SCAT funds, a CAO also needs to show a meaningful form of participation by women, either at the governance level within the CAO management committee or as paralegals or coordinators, or it must be able to show 50 percent female representation at all CAO workshops.[71] This is part of SCAT's belief that the key to social justice lies in actively involving women and other marginalized groups in all levels of decision-making, and that gender empowerment in rural communities can be achieved by giving women a space in which they can claim expertise, power, and ownership.

As SCAT is primarily a start-up funding conduit, one of its main functions is to assist affiliated CAOs in becoming self-financing. This model obviously assumes that CAOs

[68] The SCAT model is to provide initial funding and to try to move CAOs as expeditiously as possible into a self-sufficiency mode in terms of which the CAO finds alternative sources of financial support, such as small contributions or levies from the community, as well as private sector involvement and local government service contracts on a project-by-project basis where possible.

[69] SCAT itself is funded by twenty-two donors. "Donor Partners," Social Change Assistance Trust. www.scat.org.za/partners/donor-partners.

[70] Referred to by the organization as Local Development Agencies. At one time SCAT funded eighty-eight CAOs, but a shortage in its own resources has meant a restriction in the number of CAOs it can support. Joanne Harding (executive director of SCAT) and Anthea Davids-Thomas (training coordinator of SCAT), interview, Cape Town, October 5, 2010.

[71] SCAT funding will cease for CAOs where men refuse to involve women in community affairs, although SCAT will intervene with a series of gender sensitivity strategies before this occurs.

can attract funding elsewhere, though this is far from evident,[72] and there is some anxiety among CAOs related to future sustainability.[73] Nevertheless, SCAT remains committed to preparing CAOs for self-sufficiency and to this end, facilitates a platform for alternative funding models. The most influential, and arguably most successful part of SCAT's exit strategy is the Fund-Raising Incentive Scheme (FRIS). FRIS was launched by SCAT in 1996 as a grant-making mechanism that rewards CAOs for raising money in their communities, as through every R 1 raised through a local event, SCAT rewards the CAO with R 5. Around 80 percent of SCAT-affiliated CAOs participate in this scheme, through which they can claim up to R 25,000 per annum (US$3,000), or up to R 100,000 (US$12,000) if a CAO is not using its core grant of R $4,000 (just under US$500) per month. The intention of the scheme is to foster a CAO's independence, reducing its reliance on grant funding and enabling it to access resources from local government and other community stakeholders.

According to the observations of SCAT's fieldworkers,[74] FRIS raises the status of the CAO within the community by promoting community networking and participation. The average FRIS event involves between 160 and 200 community participants and raises about R 2,000 (US$250), although in 2009, the Prince Albert CAO fish barbeque raised R 50,000 (US$6,150), and the Thusa CAO taxi wash raised R 25,000 (US$3,000). The money is much needed and used to keep the CAO running on a daily basis, providing transport to service surrounding villages, starting community development projects, purchasing stationary stock, paying electricity bills, or increasing staff salaries. SCAT's incentive scheme to encourage a CAO to raise funds through its own efforts promotes a sense of responsibility, develops the CAO's financial skills, and promotes planning, budgeting, and transparency.

Since 2001, SCAT has also run HIV/AIDS awareness programs on an incentive basis, providing funding of up to R 50,000 for a good HIV/AIDS program by a CAO. Thus far SCAT has funded thirty-eight CAOs through this system, although specific funding for HIV/AIDS programs is currently being substituted in favor of funding related to health-systems strengthening. CAOs are also encouraged to apply to tap SCAT's Development Fund for training staff and volunteers,[75] again, with an

---

[72] There is currently a similar trend with NGO funders in South Africa, which are attempting to "wean" many of their grantees off funding, even in the face of no other sources of funding becoming available. This is partially a consequence of the global economic recession, which has adversely affected many of the Western donors. But it is also a result of a generalized sentiment that funding should be decreased to South Africa because it is a middle-income country and has already benefited from large amounts of donor funding.

[73] According to Joanne Harding, when SCAT starts to decrease support (as part of its exit strategy), CAOs sometimes feel they are being punished for bad behavior. Joanne Harding (executive director of SCAT), interview, Cape Town, October 5, 2010.

[74] Colleen Alexander (regional coordinator of fieldworkers in the Western and Northern Capes, SCAT), interview, Ceres, October 6, 2011.

[75] SCAT uses the South African Law School for paralegal qualifications, most usually the one-year correspondence course that can be completed on site. Details available at "Paralegal Practice," South African Law School. http://lawschool.co.za/courses/paralegal-practice/.

emphasis on self-starting and self-policing, CAOs have to meet certain criteria for a budgetary allocation to be claimed as needed.

Notwithstanding concerns over longer-term financial sustainability, SCAT's support to CAOs appears to work well at the developmental stage, putting in systems to build strong institutions that are attractive to donors. SCAT fieldworkers, who usually have a background in social sciences, complete a developmental practice course on how to work progressively with communities, and receive training on specific issues such as HIV/AIDS awareness and testing and local economic development initiatives. The fieldworkers assess how the management committees and coordinators of CAOs are building the capacity of the institution; they also provide on-site support to CAOs and play a brokerage role with the municipality, frequently auditing the organizations' management and technical skills and giving advice on project management and budgeting.

3. Community Law and Rural Development Centre (CLRDC) and Centre for Criminal Justice (CCJ)

The CLRDC and CCJ are based in KZN and work closely together on research, training, monitoring, and funding proposals to advocate for the recognition and regulation of paralegals, particularly those who service rural areas. In total, the two organizations cover forty-five advice offices (CCJ has fifteen and CLRDC has thirty affiliated CAOs) with fifty-four paralegals, accounting for more than 80 percent of the CAOs in KZN. The CLRDC and CCJ mainly provide funding, training, and capacity-building support to their affiliated CAOs, which also have access to two in-house attorneys based at CCJ for back-up legal advice. Although the substance of the work of their CAO branches is similar, as parent organizations, CLRDC focuses more on management support and performance monitoring, while CCJ is more responsible for training, capacity building, documentation, and research.[76] They also operate in different contexts. For the past twenty years, the CLRDC has been operating in communities governed by customary law and tribal authorities, and more than half of CLRDC's thirty branch CAOs are located within traditional court office buildings rather than municipal structures. Meanwhile, CCJ supports fifteen CAOs,[77] operating in more "modern" settings, such as police stations or magistrates' courts.

Together, CCJ and CLRDC are working on a five-year strategic plan for each of their branch CAOs to be independent NADCAO affiliates, without requiring funding by the CLRDC or CCJ, and instead creating localized programs and raising

---

[76] CCJ operates from the UKZN in Pietermaritzburg and is affiliated with the Law Department. CCJ runs two programs: its outreach program, which involves twenty paralegals in fourteen CAOs, and a research program, which maintains a library and database of 65,000 cases for the benefit of UKZN law students.

[77] Referred to by the organization as "support centers."

their own resources.⁷⁸ Similar to SCAT's exit strategy, CLRDC and CCJ are currently identifying and building the prerequisite capacities of CAO management committees and paralegal staff to take full responsibility for running their organizations.⁷⁹ Both CLRDC and CCJ are funded by the Atlantic Philanthropies, with CLRDC also receiving funding from the Joseph Rowntree Charitable Trust and CCJ from the Ford Foundation. Although the organizations would like to pay paralegals a salary of at least R 5,000 per month, in 2010, salaries had to be cut to around R 2,500 per person per month due to a shortage of funds.

CLRDC and CCJ paralegals operate mainly in rural and peri-urban areas in KZN,⁸⁰ and handle client matters similar to the SCAT-affiliated CAOs. The paralegals' jurisdiction is wide given the remote locations in which they work; one CCJ CAO, for instance, services a population of 1.2 million. On average, CCJ CAOs handle eighty cases per month; however, it is notable that 50 percent of cases handled by CCJ CAOs are related to domestic and sexual violence.⁸¹ CCJ-affiliated CAOs receive around 9,000 such complaints per year, a high figure that Winnie Kubayi, director of CCJ since 1997, believes is inextricably linked to living in rural areas, where rights education is weakest and the patriarchal Zulu community makes the solutions typical in cities more difficult to attain.⁸² It is also worth noting that CCJ only employs women as paralegals as part of its policy of gender empowerment in rural areas. CCJ identifies cases by working alongside the police and making home visits within communities, which helps to bring to light cases of a sensitive nature and encourages victims to report crimes. Physical proximity to the police station is the best place for the CAO to ensure that clients' issues are handled appropriately, affording them safety, confidentiality, and access to medical treatment. It also places the CAO strategically in the best position to play a watchdog role over the police, aiming to decrease abuse and increase the accountability of the criminal justice system.

---

78 The attempt to build the capacity of CAOs is out of the belief that doing so will ensure their long-term sustainability. This is certainly closely related to the funding crisis within CCJ and CLRDC themselves. At one stage, CLRDC had sixty-seven offices, with a footprint in every corner of the province and frequent meetings with Amakhosi; by 2005, this was reduced by nearly half, due to cash flow issues and the new demarcation of the province leading to a necessary reshuffle of offices around various districts. CLRDC itself cut its head office staff from twenty to two. Once CLRDC and CCJ have built up the capacity of their branch CAOs in order to make them financially independent, CLRDC and CCJ intend for the CAOs to maintain a strong affiliation with them in terms of mentorship, collaborations on areas of mutual interest, and paralegal training programs.

79 A joint infrastructural assessment and skills audit of the forty-five CAOs affiliated to CLRDC and CCJ, conducted between February and April 2010, confirmed that 95 percent of paralegals have the National Diploma in Paralegal Studies, but only 50 percent of CAOs have the basic infrastructure required for autonomy.

80 This is due to the presence of the Black Sash, LASA, and the UKZN law clinics in the KZN urban centers of Durban and Pietermaritzburg.

81 See "Cases," University of Kwazulu-Natal, Centre for Criminal Justice. http://ccj.ukzn.ac.za/Cases/CasesOverview.aspx. CAOs do not actually resolve criminal matters, but rather assist claimants to go to the police station to lay charges and also provide support to victims of violence.

82 Kubayi, interview (see n. 2).

CLRDC and CCJ paralegals are also active community educators, mandated by their parent organizations to run two workshops and make four school visits per month. They make weekly presentations at medical clinics, church groups, or community development meetings, and hold focus group workshops every quarter, where a group of former clients will gather to discuss common concerns.

4. The Access to Justice Cluster (AJC) Program of the Association of University Legal Aid Institutions (AULAI) Trust

The remaining organizational structure for CAOs is the Access to Justice Cluster (AJC) program run by the AULAI Trust. The AULAI Trust, which developed out of the AULAI that was established in 1982 as a kind of trade union for all university law clinics, was founded in 1998 with a once-off grant from the Ford Foundation. The Trust acts as a funding agency to South Africa's eighteen university law clinics and their associated projects, one of which is the AJC program, which operates through eight AJC clusters attached to eight of the university law clinics.[83]

These eight AJC clusters consist of the cooperative body of university law clinics, LASA justice centers,[84] NGOs, CAOs, community-based and faith-based organizational networks, and private practitioners working together to provide access to justice and services to poor and marginalized people in rural and remote areas, informal settlements, and squatter camps.[85] South Africa's eight clusters provide training and back-up legal services to approximately 100 CAOs across the country, enabling qualified lawyers to support paralegals without prescribing or restricting their broad scope of work.[86] For example, within the Northwest AJC (NWAJC), an attorney from the university law clinic at Potchestroom visits eight CAOs in the province on a monthly basis. This attorney visits each CAO in the cluster to pick up cases that are beyond the capacity of the paralegal to assist. At the time of this research, the NWAJC attorney had 500 live cluster case files on her desk, which did not account for the extent of legal advice provided ad hoc on the day of her monthly visit in consultation with walk-in clients. The CAOs within NWAJC stockpile cases in advance of the attorney visit, or call the university law clinic if advice is required more urgently.

A key benefit for CAOs within a cluster network is the level of training provided by the university law clinic. Again the training focus is institution building as well as legal literacy. The NWAJC on-site training manual for office administration hosted in 2010 includes information on following banking procedures, maintaining efficient filing systems, making funding proposals, and writing notices and agendas of

---

[83] Operating from the Universities of the Western Cape, Free State, Northwest (Potchestroom and Mafeking), Limpopo, Rhodes, and Stellenbosch.

[84] As mentioned earlier, the access to justice clusters have a cooperation agreement with LASA, with which they have been working since 1993.

[85] Meyer, interview (see n. 61).

[86] In a similar way to the CAOs affiliated with SCAT, most CAOs within the cluster networks are part of NADCAO's provincial structures.

meetings, as well as information on how to take statements, draft a letter of demand, make checklists of documents required for civil claims, and complete client interview intake forms. Formal legal training is also provided with differing areas of focus. For instance, the training given to paralegals in NWAJC in November 2010 focused on domestic violence and the law with regard to seeking a protection order, as well as consumer law and issues around breach of contract and malfunctioning goods. Less frequently, AJCs provide funding to CAOs within their clusters if they can prove that the office has a functioning management committee, is registered as an nonprofit organization, has a constitution, takes minutes from general meetings, possesses an operational bank account, and has been running for at least two years. For the past three years, the AULAI Trust has provided some funding on this basis to qualifying CAOs, with each CAO normally receiving R 2,000–3,000 (US$245–US$370) per month.

IV. EVALUATING THE IMPACT OF CAOS ON CLIENTS AND COMMUNITIES

Evaluating the impact of human rights work is notoriously difficult. Moreover, as hard as it is for NGOs to demonstrate impact, it is usually much harder for CAOs, which inevitably have fewer and less-skilled staff members to undertake the kinds of record keeping, case management, and follow-through necessary for effective impact analysis. Indeed, many CAOs find themselves in a vicious cycle of not having the skills and personnel to properly monitor and report on their work, which inhibits attempts to raise the requisite funding and thereby limits the scope and value of their work with communities.

At the same time, human rights practitioners, including paralegals, realistically understand donors' needs to show progress and value for funding. Indeed, funders' requirements are not only about form, and there is obviously much benefit from being able to evaluate the value of interventions in some form or other. For organizations such as the Black Sash, which keeps a case log database, it is more possible to measure the impact of paralegal case resolutions and to see, for instance, that Black Sash clients access more than R 1 million in social grants and private pensions each month due to their interventions. Likewise, where they exist, past funding proposals yield hard data from which a quantitative impact can be assessed.

For example, the CLRDC 2009 report to the Charles Stewart Mott Foundation collated CAO available statistics and showed that approximately R 3 million (US$370,000) was recovered for clients and more than 300 community education workshops attended by more than 15,000 participants took place in 2008–2009. However, although such figures, when available, do provide an insight into the impact of community-based paralegal work, they do not properly give a sense of how paralegals address specific problems within their communities, how appropriate their techniques are to local dynamics and sensitivities, or what obstacles hinder their work. We have therefore attempted, on a very modest scale, to provide some qualitative data on the kinds of cases being taken up by paralegals and the ways these impact the clients and communities.

Drawing from the broader case studies of eight CAOs, our evaluation is based primarily on twelve case-tracking interviews (using a semi-structured questionnaire), with current and former clients at six CAOs – four in KZN,[87] and two in the North West Province.[88] Access to the CAOs was provided by CLRDC and CCJ in KZN, and NWAJC in the North West Province.[89] The emerging themes were surprisingly consistent, suggesting that there are systemic challenges and opportunities within the sector. In what follows, we present an empirically rich impressionistic picture of the impact of CAO work on clients and communities drawn directly from our case-tracking exercise. We then analyze the seemingly generalized features as either facilitating or hindering institutional and organizational determinants in Sections V and VI. Given the nuanced, contextual, and very detailed nature of this work, it is worthwhile to present the case studies in their entirety before integrating the salient fault lines into the analysis.

A. Twelve Cases from Six CAOs

At a relatively late stage in our research, we added a case-based evaluation component in an attempt to better analyze the role and work of CAOs. However, due to time and budgetary constraints, we were unable to conduct an extremely intensive, long-term case-tracking exercise. Instead, we opted to parachute into the exercise through the entry point of the umbrella organizations outlined earlier, specifically CLRDC and CCJ in KZN and NWAJC in the North West Province.

In KZN, we asked CCJ and CLRDC CAO paralegals to identify relevant cases (we asked to have access to "successful/resolved" as well as "unsuccessful/unresolved" cases on a range of issues) and also asked willing clients to stop at the CAO during our visit. We also observed walk-in clients. In the North West Province, we accompanied NWAJC attorneys on their monthly visits to the CAOs, observed paralegals dealing with cases, and interviewed the clients present at the CAO if they were willing to discuss their issue.

---

[87] Elotheni, Mpopomeni, Impendle, and Kwa-Qiko.   [88] Phokeng and Lethabong.
[89] We concede that some bias might have crept in as a result of using the umbrella affiliates as entry points to the clients and cases, but this was the most effective way to identify sources given our time constraint. However, we did attempt to mitigate any bias by speaking to clients directly and wherever possible without a translator or paralegal. Moreover, by asking to have access to "losing" cases and through meeting clients with live cases at the offices, we were able to gain a relatively realistic snapshot of CAO work. We should point out, however, that we found it almost impossible to assess the counterfactual. For example, when we asked clients "what would you have done if the paralegal was not here to help?" the overwhelming responses were "I don't know" or "I would have given up." One client answered that she would have "had a heart attack from stress." We have therefore focused rather on why each case went well or did not go well.

CASE 1: PENSION CLAIM (STATE)

Location: Elotheni CAO (CLRDC Branch), Kwa-Sani, KZN
Date: February 8, 2011

In the first case, which concerned an elderly woman whose pension was suddenly and inexplicably stopped, the paralegal became involved only when the client's relationship with DSD had turned sour: "It was very painful when my pension stopped, as for five months I had nothing to support myself or my grandchildren." The paralegal was able to use her contacts in DSD to investigate what had happened. She also contacted a fellow CLRDC paralegal to inquire how to elevate the matter to a Member of the Executive Council (MEC) for Social Development. After writing to MEC, the client's pension was restarted and she was awarded back pay of more than R 9,000 (US$1,100). Here it was apparent that the close working relationship between the state and the CAO was an advantage, as it made possible a swift and effective resolution of the matter. As the client explained regarding the paralegal:

> Lerato is experienced in helping people with these things and she knows what to do. The DSD people were hostile to me but they work together with her as she knows what she is doing. It helps that she is a local person so she knows us but also knows the protocol of working with the municipality. She knows what doors to knock on.

It was also clear that being able to call on the knowledge and experience of other community-based paralegals was very useful, as the paralegal relied on the network of advice offices within the CLRDC. However, when we asked, the client was not clear about the details of how her case was resolved and it was evident that the paralegal had not explained the process or the content of the phone calls and letters. Should a similar problem occur, it is likely that the client will not be able to resolve it independently, although it was clearly a simple administrative error. Indeed, the client told us that many people in the community face the same problem, yet the CAO had not attempted to empower the community collectively to tackle the issue. When we asked the paralegal whether the problem was too difficult to explain to people, she told us that such cases are common and very easy for her to resolve. To us it seemed that an educational opportunity that might free up paralegals for other, more complex cases was being missed. It is possible that the paralegal was guarding her territory for fear of being seen as superfluous, or she simply was not thinking more strategically.

CASE 2: UNEMPLOYMENT BENEFIT CLAIM (STATE)

Location: Elotheni CAO (CLRDC Branch), Kwa-Sani, KZN
Date: February 8, 2011

In this case, the CAO was attempting to assist a client in accessing unemployment benefits from his former employer in Johannesburg. The paralegal had previously helped the client complete the official forms to apply for the benefit, but this had not been successful. The case had remained unresolved for some time and evidently the paralegal did not feel confident about how to proceed unaided. At the time of our observation, the paralegal was telephoning CRLDC for advice on taking the matter to the Financial Services Board.

Although pointing to the importance of the relationship with umbrella clusters such as CRLDC, this "unresolved" case reflects a level of disempowerment or incapacity among CAO staff. While this particular paralegal knew how to complete forms, he was not able to take the matter further without assistance, involving a long and expensive telephone call (which the paralegal had to pay for, using his own cell phone), as well as delays (given that CLRDC's staff has fallen from twenty to two). With enhanced legal advice and better knowledge sharing between paralegals, the paralegal at this CAO probably could have resolved the matter more efficiently. This case also highlighted the problem of insufficient funding for CAOs, as it was evident that paralegals often have to put their own meager earnings into the project to pay for such basics as telephone calls.

CASE 3: CHILD CUSTODY DISPUTE (FAMILY)

Location: Impendle CAO (CCJ Branch), Ingwe, KZN
Date: February 8, 2011

Here, the client was the mother of four young children staying with their paternal grandparents while she worked in Pietermaritzburg. Traditional custom dictates that children born to unmarried parents belong to the father's family and that a child can be brought into the house in exchange for cattle. After receiving some financial support from the father's family, the client was refused access to her children for two years, during which time she realized they were being forced to work for the family: "they were being treated like slaves, going out into the forests far away to look for [lost] cattle, and doing all the cooking and cleaning in the house." Relationships within the family had broken down by the time the client sought the help of the advice office. She

CASE 3: (Cont.)

turned to the paralegal for help, as she knew her already as a person in the community who could assist in such matters.

To assist her client to regain custody, the paralegal drew on her connections with the police and the traditional court. First, the paralegal discussed with the tribal court elder how traditional custom had been distorted in this case and that paying money within families was leading to a form of trafficking. Having gained the support of the traditional court authority, she went to the house with the client and a police escort, and was able to retrieve the children. She then began the process of assisting her client in applying for child grants.

This case demonstrates the value of the paralegal's position of straddling plural legal systems. It also shows the importance of being embedded within the community and being able to forge ongoing relationships with key stakeholders. In this case, the client approached the paralegal as an external but trusted source of help, and she told us that she particularly appreciated the patience and sensitivity with which the paralegal handled the matter.

CASE 4: FAMILIAL DISPUTE OVER PROVIDENT FUND BENEFIT (FAMILY)

Location: Impendle CAO (CCJ Branch), Ingwe, KZN
Date: February 8, 2011

This case involved a familial dispute around claims to access the provident fund of the client's estranged late husband. The matter was referred from the estates office next door to the CAO within the Impendle Magistrate's Court. Relationships within the family had broken down when the client's in-laws did not recognize her legitimate claim to the money. The client had difficulty completing the necessary application forms and applying for a letter of authority in order to access the provident fund. As she explained:

> I could not sort out the complexities of this problem. I'm not clued up about these things and I wouldn't have known where to go to get help. I'm an elderly person and I was going to give up as my husband had never told his employers he had a wife and so I faced a lot of difficulties.

The paralegal was able to resolve the issue by accompanying the client to the Impendle Magistrate's Court and explaining to the rest of the family the

CASE 4: (Cont.)

legal implications, including that the client was a beneficiary. The client eventually received a benefit of R 207,000 (US$25,500). In the client's words: "Sipho (the paralegal) took the stress from me and handled the problem much quicker than I could have. At the time I was very poor, but Sipho swallowed all the costs, using her car to get to court and make family visits."

This case exemplifies how paralegal intervention is often a hand-holding exercise for clients made vulnerable due to their lack of legal literacy and confidence in approaching state or judicial institutions. It also shows the value of being linked to umbrella clusters such as CCJ.

CASE 5: ACCESS TO HEALTH CARE AND SOCIAL SECURITY (STATE)

Location: Mpopomene CAO, KZN
Date: February 9, 2011

In this case, the intervention by the CAO was wide-ranging. The paralegal became involved after hearing reports that the client's eleven-year-old daughter was frequently absent from school. On visiting the family, the paralegal found that the girl was caring for her sick mother and three-year-old brother, rather than going to school. The paralegal deduced that the client was suffering with HIV/AIDS and was no longer able to work. Moreover, the family did not have enough food, as the client's disability grant had been terminated. The client told us that the paralegal's intervention saved her life. The paralegal organized food parcels to be delivered to the family, and applied for the client's disability grant to be restarted. She referred the matter to an NGO providing home-based care so that the elder child could return to school, and she also enrolled the younger child in a nursery school. The client has since regained her strength and is healthy enough to return to work.

This case points to the special role that paralegals play by virtue of being embedded in a community and attuned to people's problems, as well as operating on the nexus between legal and social work, so that they are able to simultaneously meet needs for legal assistance and social care.

CASE 6: SOCIAL SECURITY GRANT FOR MIGRANTS (STATE)

Location: Mpopomene CAO, KZN
Date: February 9, 2011

This client was a permanent resident, originally from Lesotho. He had misplaced his South African identity document, a prerequisite for a social grant application. His family was struggling to survive, and the client wanted to apply for child support grants for his three children. He had repeatedly been frustrated in his attempts to sort out the problem at the municipal Department of Home Affairs, and was advised by the local police station to go to the CAO. The paralegal contacted the Department to report the missing identity document. She then had the creative idea of asking the client's neighbor to stand in as a named adult recipient to receive the grant on the children's behalf. Having organized this, she took the client to SASSA and made a successful application. The whole process took about six weeks and alleviated some of the family's financial struggles. In the client's words:

> I was about to give up as I had tried everything. If a minister had been here I would have thrown myself at his feet. I did not know what else I could do and we were desperate as I have found it hard to find work since my wife died three years ago. Lebo (the paralegal) thinks of ways around problems that are less obvious, and she knows the people to talk to. Getting the grant has meant I can stay here with my children and look for work here rather than leave them to go to the city.

This case highlights how a good working relationship with state departments, along with the use of ingenious tactics, enables paralegals to find solutions for clients who believe they have exhausted all options.

CASE 7: ACCESS TO HOUSING (STATE)

Location: Mpopomene CAO, KZN
Date: February 9, 2011

The client in this matter was disputing the ownership of a Reconstruction and Development Programme (RDP) house that had been occupied by her late cousin.[90] At the time of our research, the matter was unresolved, as the paralegal's attempts to mediate between different family members had broken

---

[90] RDP houses are small houses transferred to poor households by the state. They are usually on the urban periphery and often in areas that have limited transport connections and job opportunities. They have thus been criticized by many human rights activists as not constituting the kind of convenient and useful social housing found in the central business district areas in some cities.

CASE 7: (Cont.)

down due to the hostility of the parties. The paralegal subsequently tried to refer the matter to LASA, which did not have the capacity to assist, and then managed to refer the matter to the in-house attorney at CCJ (we were unable to ascertain whether any progress had been made). The client appeared remarkably philosophical about the case, accepting the limits of the paralegal's intervention and telling us that a paralegal "can only go so far."

Nevertheless, it seemed to us that a hindering factor in this case was the unavailability of LASA assistance and public interest lawyers, especially in rural areas, to assist in a case that, ultimately, had to be resolved in court.

CASE 8: DISABILITY GRANT (STATE)

Location: Qiko CAO (CLRDC Affiliate), KZN
Date: February 10, 2011

In this case, the paralegal assisted a client whose disability grant was terminated without explanation or medical examination. The client had claimed the disability grant since suffering a stroke in 2002. Apparently, the grant had been erroneously cut as part of DSD's campaign to stop people from fraudulently claiming disability benefits. The client, through family members, had been repeatedly told by DSD that she had been declared healthy, despite the fact that no medical examination had taken place. The client took the matter to the CAO, and the paralegal wrote to DSD and secured a medical assessment on behalf of the client to prove she was entitled to the benefit. The process took three years, but the client was able to restart her disability grant and received more than R 40,000 (US$5,000) in back pay.

This case illustrated again the critical role for paralegals in sorting out systemic problems with DSD/SASSA and the administration of social welfare grants. It also highlighted the need for greater knowledge sharing and a strategic approach to such generalized problems. Clearly, the same issues within the state bodies occur repeatedly – of grants being refused, cut, or administered with long delays. The know-how regarding resolution of such issues exists within the paralegal network, but tapping into this would require a better case management system, better communication between CAOs, and the willingness or capacity to think more strategically about systemic problems and their resolution.

CASE 9: CONTRACTUAL DISPUTE (PRIVATE)

Location: Phokeng CAO (within AULAI's NWAJC), North West Province
Date: February 14, 2011

This case involved a breach of contract on the part of a gravestone manufacturer and shop outlet. The client paid R 10,400 (nearly US$1,300) for a gravestone that was never delivered, and on visiting the premises, she found the business had closed down. The police could not assist her, and the LASA satellite office in Rustenburg was not taking on civil cases at the time. The client therefore approached the CAO, which consulted with her before referring the matter to the AJC attorneys. In this case, the client was unhappy, as following the referral, the attorneys had not been in touch with her or the paralegal for several months and she had no idea what progress, if any, had been made on her case.

This case highlights how, notwithstanding the importance of links with umbrella clusters such as AJC and its lawyers, a key quality of the relationship with paralegals and clients can become lost when the matter is referred to lawyers. It is likely that with more resources and better case management, the paralegal might be able to dedicate more time and energy into keeping up communications between the lawyer and the client. However, as things stood in this case, once the matter was referred, it was effectively removed from the paralegal's desk, to the frustration of the client.

CASE 10: DEBT CLAIM (PRIVATE)

Location: Lethabong CAO (within AULAI's NWAJC), North West Province
Date: February 15, 2011

This dispute involved a breach of agreement by two members of a burial society who failed to make the agreed contributions, resulting in a financial loss for all the other members. The clients – aggrieved members of the burial society – lived in a remote area, and had heard about the CAO office from workers on neighboring farms. Once the matter was brought to the CAO, the paralegal mediated between the parties in a three-hour session, which culminated in the debtors signing an acknowledgment of debt to be paid off in monthly installments. In addition, the paralegal advised the burial society on the benefits of making formal, more easily enforceable agreements, and helped the society draw up a constitution.

CASE 10: (Cont.)

Here, the paralegal was able to take the case further than the resolution of the matter at hand, by assisting the farmworkers to draw up formal documentation for the burial society. As explained by the paralegal: "Local people often do not enter into formal agreements and relations go sour. They do not have the financial or administration knowledge to be able to protect their investment in community enterprises. We try to educate people about how to enter into formal agreements, and encourage them to visit the CAO for advice."

The case also showcased the value of mediation as an ADR technique that was able to resolve the issue without the expense of lawyers, and how it was particularly appropriate for the people involved in the context of rural society and culture. In the paralegal's words:

> Mediation brings peace. These people live in the same village and they need each other. It does not help community participation in development when people who live close together are warring with each other.

CASE 11: INHERITANCE (FAMILY)

**Location: Lethabong CAO (within AULAI's NWAJC), North West Province
Date: February 15, 2011**

The client in this matter was a legitimate beneficiary of her late husband's estate but was being prevented by her husband's family from accessing the resources to which she and the children from her marriage were entitled. Despite having a letter of authority from the Magistrate's Court naming her as a beneficiary of his estate, her husband's family refused to acknowledge that the couple was married.

The paralegal did the groundwork on this case before referring it to attorneys at NWAJC, who were able to deal with the issue and enforce her claim to the estate. Neither paralegal nor client was involved in this process and the attorneys did not, in that sense, up-skill the paralegal, pointing again to the complexities of referral to lawyers. While this is as much a criticism of lawyers as of paralegals, it is likely that better resourcing and better case management would improve paralegals' proactive ability to learn from lawyers.

> CASE 12: DEBT CLAIM (PRIVATE)
>
> **Location: Lethabong CAO (within AULAI's NWAJC), North West Province**
> **Date: February 15, 2011**
>
> The client in this case was a traditional healer who was owed R 600 (US$75) for a service he performed for another community member who refused to pay. The client approached the advice office because there is no chief's office in the area and the small claims court is far away and expensive to get to. The paralegal had been trained in mediation techniques by NWAJC, and after sending a letter of demand, approached both parties to participate in a mediation session. The client appreciated the authority and objectivity that came with the intervention of the advice office. He told us that he also appreciated that the paralegal did not enforce a solution on the parties, and how this led them to shake hands. This was important to the client, as the two men are neighbors and it is essential to remain on good terms.
>
> At the end of the mediation, the parties made an oral agreement that the debt would be repaid within one month in two installments, receipted for at the CAO. The client told us that using the services of the advice office was an "eye opener" for him, as he had no means of otherwise recovering the debt. The benefit of having a trained mediator in the community was very clear in this case, where a mutually acceptable and speedy resolution was achieved without either the cost or damage to community relations that litigation would have caused.

V. INSTITUTIONAL DETERMINANTS FOR CAOS

From the case studies it appears that there are several facilitating as well as hindering determinants that can be broadly defined as institutional, that is determinants that relate to formal institutions of the state. Relationships with the state and with traditional authorities have been analyzed as facilitating and hindering determinants, an unclear regulatory environment, insecure and insufficient funding (which was included here for reasons outlined in what follows, but it obviously also impacts organizational capacity, etc.), and a reliance on remote lawyers and LASA.

A. *Facilitating Determinants*

1. Relationships with the State

State institutions are some of the most important stakeholders within the community-based paralegal sector. The ultimate resolution of the many problems facing their clients often depends upon these institutions, and nurturing state relations is crucial if CAOs are to become stronger organizations and embed themselves into the fabric of society. The generalist nature of the work of community-based paralegals means that they foster relationships with a wide range of state bodies and government departments at the municipal, provincial, and national levels. Based on their common individual client matters, South African paralegals deal most frequently with DSD for social security concerns, the Department of Home Affairs for identity documentation issues, the Department of Health for issues relating to the rights of people with HIV/AIDS, the Department of Labour for employment concerns, and the police for family and gender-based matters.

For the most part, it seems there is substantial (nonmaterial) support for CAOs from the state, based on the state's appreciation of the role paralegals play in smoothing the process of service delivery.[91] This good working relationship, as explained by a paralegal at the Mpopomene CAO, is because "[the municipality] could not serve the community properly but now, knowing that the advice office is there, they are working better on the people's behalf and making more effort, for instance with the provision of free funeral services and food parcels."[92] The state has acknowledged its support for community-based paralegals in very practical, valuable ways, for example, in the way that CCJ branch CAOs have been able to physically mainstream their advice offices within state criminal justice institutions. This affiliation with the police has made their watchdog role easier, given the paralegals' greater influence in community affairs, and allowed them to share resources in terms of rental and utility payments and transport costs. Similarly, the municipality shows its approval of the work of the Zola CAO by paying the cost of rent, electricity, and water for its base at the Jabulani Youth Club, and for the Mpola CAO by providing an office free of charge within the town hall.

This somewhat strange symbiotic relationship, which helps CAOs resolve community problems such as the mistaken termination of social grants and so forth, in essence means that CAOs often do "the government's job." Interestingly, there does not seem to be much animosity on the part of state officials toward paralegals for effectively showing them up, and this is possibly related to the non-adversarial way

---

[91] Using CCJ as an example of the mutual reliance of the two parties, in 2010, 38 percent of referrals to CCJ (totaling 2,157 cases) were made by government service departments, the most common being the Police and Social Welfare Department, as well as referrals from hospitals and health clinics. Pointing to the reciprocal relationship between community-based paralegals and the state, in the same year, CCJ's support centers referred 27 percent of cases (1,548 cases in total) to other service providers, with the police, hospitals, and social welfare agencies the most frequent partners. "Working with Police," University of Kwazulu-Natal, Centre for Criminal Justice. http://ccj.ukzn.ac.za/WorkingwithPartners/Police.aspx; "Working with Hospitals and Clinics," University of Kwazulu-Natal, Centre for Criminal Justice. http://ccj.ukzn.ac.za/WorkingwithPartners/HospitalsandClinics.aspx; "Social Welfare," University of Kwazulu-Natal, Centre for Criminal Justice. http://ccj.ukzn.ac.za/WorkingwithPartners/SocialWelfare.aspx. Many of these referrals were followed by negotiations with service providers on behalf of a client, and by a monitoring of the service given.

[92] Lucky Mkhize (Mpopomene), interview, KwaZulu/Natal, February 9, 2011.

CAO paralegals work, as elaborated on in Section VI. More research is required to examine the dynamic between state officials and CAOs more fully. Most importantly, the clients and communities clearly benefit significantly from these solid relationships with state institutions as reflected in cases 1, 3, 6, and 8, in which problems relating to the state's nonperformance were resolved by CAOs through their good relationships with state bodies (specifically, DSD/SASSA and the police in these cases).

2. Relationships with Traditional Authorities

Traditional authorities operate within a dualist system of government in seven of South Africa's nine provinces, most notably in the rural areas of KZN and the Northwest and Eastern Capes, and the constitution recognizes customary law that is upheld and acknowledged within common law courts.[93] Paralegals in rural areas under chieftain leadership play an important role in reconciling the interpretation of common law with respect for cultural values and practices. Being part of the community, these paralegals are well placed to straddle South Africa's dualist legal system, as they have the training to translate the Bill of Rights and so can supplement the role and function of the chiefs' offices and tribal courts. For example, during our research, we were told about a chief asking the paralegal to conduct the proceedings in his court so as to ensure the parties in dispute were aware of their legal rights and options.[94] Indeed, according to our observations, community-based paralegals in these areas have good working relationships with the chiefs' offices, as highlighted in case 3. There are more formal manifestations of the close working relationship between CAOs and traditional authorities. For example, in KZN, fifteen CLRDC CAOs are located in traditional court office buildings, and it is also tribal headmen who usually approach the CLRDC to say that their community needs a CAO and to suggest candidate paralegals for training.

Msomi, a paralegal at the Mpola CAO in KZN, explained that it is important for her to maintain good connections with the traditional leaders in her community if she is to conduct effective mediation strategies, given that it is the norm for people to consult with the headmen when disputes arise as well as with the CAO.[95] To this end, paralegals work hard to ensure cooperation between the CAO and the chief's office. John Moerane, provincial coordinator of the Northwest Paralegal Advice Office Cluster, for example, drew support from the South African Human Rights Commission (SAHRC) and the Department of Judicial Affairs and Constitutional Development (DJCD) to come and talk to traditional leaders in the Northwest Cape about the Bill of Rights and its ramifications. As a result, a new CAO is being opened at Letlhakane within the chief's office, following the CLRDC model, which

---

[93] This determinant obviously overlaps and intersects with what we viewed as the social determinant of CAOs' embeddedness in communities.
[94] Kubayi, interview (see n. 2).
[95] Msomi (paralegal, Mpola Advice Office), interview, Mpola-Durban, October 12, 2010.

Moerane hopes will set a precedent of common engagement between CAOs and tribal authorities in the province. CAOs also involve the traditional authorities in their ongoing community education programs. As Sophia Tumelo, paralegal at the Phokeng CAO, recounted, before approaching the community, she goes to the nearby chiefs' offices at Bethani, Motlhabe, and Lema and asks to participate in their workshops. This approach often leads to profitable collaboration; for example, the Phokeng CAO is currently working with Chief Legwale at Siga Village on a poverty alleviation campaign.[96]

B. Hindering Determinants

1. Unclear Regulatory Environment

Although not apparent from our case-tracking exercise per se, a more overarching problem in the sector is the unclear regulatory environment within which CAOs operate. With no formal requirements and no mandatory regulatory oversight, CAOs operate largely unregulated apart from their relationship, where they have one, with the umbrella structures discussed earlier. There are undoubted advantages to this system, such as allowing a large number of unique, locally specific, and dynamic CAOs to spring up (and flourish or sink). However, the downside is that there is no comprehensive quality assurance or control, meaning that communities are vulnerable to fly-by-night CAOs (although we saw no evidence of this, probably because we primarily observed CAOs affiliated to NADCAO structures). It also undoubtedly impacts negatively on the availability of funding, which is discussed later in this chapter.

The issue of formal regulation has been extensively debated within the sector. While there are many opponents, including some CAOs and umbrella structures that fear regulation might lead to an over-restrictive definition of paralegal work, other CAOs support such recognition because of its funding implications. NADCAO, for example, lobbied for many years for the participation of CAOs in the process surrounding the Legal Practice Bill (LPB). This bill, which was stalled for many years seemingly due to hostility from a legal profession that is skeptical about the role and standing of CAOs, was resuscitated at the end of 2012. Among the main objectives of the LPB are more affordable legal services and a restructuring of the legal profession. Notwithstanding NADCAO's calls for CAOs to be incorporated into the legal profession and regulated by legislation,[97] when it was ultimately passed in 2014 the Legal Practice Act 28 of 2014 did not encompass CAOs.

---

[96] Sophia Tumelo (paralegal, Phokeng Advice Office), interview, Phokeng-Rustenburg, February 14, 2011.

[97] *See* Joint Submission to the South African Parliamentary Portfolio Committee on Justice and Constitutional Development on the Legal Practice Bill, http://nadcao.org.za/wp-content/uploads/2013/08/Joint-Submission-to-Parly-on-Legal-Practice-Bill.pdf.

Another regulatory option would be to formally draw CAOs into the LASA structures. This model could enhance sustainability and professionalism within the CAO sector, as is the case, for example, with the Ceres CAO in the Western Cape, which maintains a very close relationship with the Stellenbosch LASA Justice Centre, seeking and receiving regular advice on client matters.

Some paralegals expressed skepticism about this model, complaining about a lack of financial cooperation and the frequent unreliability of the LASA centers. Yet, from our interviews and observations, it seems there is scope for developing the model and, in particular, for improved knowledge sharing in the sector, which could be enhanced through the integration of NADCAO and LASA structures. This not only could have the potential to support the greater professionalism of CAOs but might be the most cost-effective way for LASA to increase its national footprint and its number of civil cases. For University of KwaZulu professor of law David McQuoid-Mason, who supports this model of cooperation between CAOs and LASA, such a relationship should be formalized for the sake of the sustainability of the paralegal sector. For him, "ideally, community-based paralegal services should be funded by the state and integrated into the national Legal Aid scheme via contractual agreements that stipulate that the CAOs provide preliminary advice at the grassroots level."[98]

Agreeing with McQuoid-Mason, CLRDC Director Langa Mtshali advocates apportioning some of LASA's annual budget to CAOs, pointing out to the Socio-Economic Rights Institute of South Africa (SERI) that it would cost only 1 percent of the DJCD annual budget (R 1.4 billion for the year 2009–10, of which LASA received R 900 million) to run 230 CAOs for a year.[99] While there are clear concerns regarding the absorption of CAOs by the state administration, integration with LASA, which remains structurally autonomous from government, would provide CAOs with an assured referral mechanism for representation of potential litigants. It would have the additional benefit for LASA of lifting the burden of rights education and thus reducing the number of walk-in clients seeking very basic advice. However, notwithstanding such ideas about how to regularize the sector, with no clear regulatory nirvana in sight, CAOs continue to triumph or flounder in an unregulated environment.

2. Insecure and Insufficient Funding

A further hindering factor across the sector – again, more apparent from interviews than from the case-tracking exercise – is that there is currently a funding crisis among CAOs in South Africa.[100] The vast majority do not receive financing from the

---

[98] David McQuoid-Mason (professor of law, University of KwaZulu-Natal), interview, KwaZulu-Natal, October 11, 2010.
[99] Langa Mtshali (director, CLRDC), interview, Durban, October 12, 2010.
[100] This determinant is arguably at least partly related to organizational weaknesses in the sector (specifically, the sector's generally poor management). However, in our view, the absence of funding sits more accurately as a hindering institutional feature that itself impacts negatively the ability of CAOs to function optimally. In other words, we see the primary causal relationship being that the managerial failures of CAOs are caused by the absence of necessary funding, rather than the other

government for the day-to-day running of their offices and since their inception have relied heavily on international donors. However, the donor environment has changed, as donors are increasingly placing their money elsewhere on the continent on the basis that South Africa is now a middle-income country. While arguably understandable, this trend ignores the fundamental structural problem that remains (and indeed is intensifying) in South Africa, namely the enormous and growing divide between rich and poor. It also overlooks the fact that this divide is racially defined, and is as damaging as legislated apartheid. As SCAT executive director Joanne Harding explains, "the overt 'political' injustice of apartheid attracted foreign interest but in global contexts, economic apartheid under a democratic state is neither attractive nor compelling."[101]

Nevertheless, the exodus of international donors has affected CAOs predominantly as it has dried up funds for their parent and affiliate organizations such as AULAI, SCAT, CLRDC, and CCJ. These organizations also find South African donors reluctant to engage with them, as they prefer to focus on charity rather than social justice. Funding is therefore more erratic, short term, and insecure. SCAT, for instance, currently has twenty funders, but these bring in less income than ten years ago when there were just six donors. Attaining multiyear funding is a huge challenge, requiring new grant applications every year for grants that tend to support specific projects rather than the day-to-day running of CAOs.

Indeed, many CAOs have had to close due to lack of funds (for example, SCAT has cut support for forty-three CAOs and CLRDC for thirty-seven CAOs), while others operate with minimal resources. CAOs currently generate an income from a variety of sources – local grants, income from community-based projects, donations from community members, government subsidies – some more successfully than others. However, given that CAOs operate in poor communities, they struggle to sustain their operations solely from donations and local income generation. This has led to fragmentation within the sector and a breakdown in information sharing. Moreover, scant resources also mean that CAOs are restricted in their work; the Ceres CAO receives an income of R 6,000 per month (US$750 – R 2,000 from SCAT and R 4,000 from the Office of Consumer Protection within the Department of Economic Affairs. For this latter sum, the office has to see eight clients and hold one workshop per month, and run campaigns to raise awareness of consumer affairs.[102]

Lack of funding also means a cut in paralegal salaries. Community-based paralegals are undoubtedly underpaid for their work, as evidenced by the broader extent of their mandate and significantly lower remuneration in comparison to paralegals employed by LASA and litigating NGOs. In addition, salary cuts increase the

> way around (that the managerial failures drive the insufficient funding). However, both determinants obviously interact with each other, with negative results.
[101] Harding, interview (see n. 74).
[102] Typically, one such workshop would cost in the region of R 4,000 (US$500).

turnover in staff, leading to a brain drain in the CAO sector and the loss of capacity as paralegals look for employment elsewhere to mitigate their own hardship. Although the pattern of paralegals using CAO work to springboard political careers has lessened, absorption into state structures is still a threat, given paralegals' suitable skill set and the draw of better remuneration. Such loss of personnel will create a deficit in the fabric of democracy, with widening gaps in coverage by paralegals and their capacity to build democracy at the local level. While the South African paralegal sector is characterized by passionate and committed community developers,[103] Vivek Maru's comment about the need for remuneration for the sector globally – that "most paralegal programs which are serious about providing a sophisticated service pay their staff" – remains true in South Africa.[104]

In this context, one of NADCAO's main current objectives is to attempt to establish a funding mechanism to support the basic operating costs of at least one CAO per municipality (with additional or satellite CAOs if required in the most remote villages). As NADCAO explains, "in order for people in poor and marginalized communities in South Africa to have access to reliable and effective CAOs, the sector requires a sustained and comprehensive national funding mechanism that would support local efforts by the community advice offices themselves to sustain their operations."[105] Greg Erasmus points to NADCAO's overarching vision for the sustainability of CAOs as the ultimate manifestation of community self-help,[106] whereby a CAO is hooked in to a mutually supportive framework, including the municipality and local businesses, leading to engagement with provincial stakeholders such as the Law Society, regional government departments, and major provincial industry bodies (for instance, the Consumer Protection Office, Life Assurance Office, or Banking Counsel).[107] The CAO could then enter into service agreements with the relevant organization to secure funds for specific campaigns that would advance the goals of the funder.[108]

In the meantime, though, CAOs face a constant struggle to access secure and sufficient funding, which undoubtedly impairs the reach and quality of their

---

[103] In the words of John Moerane, "I do this job because of having passion, commitment, and trust in the community. It's not about me, it's about 50,000 people." John Moerane (provincial coordinator of the Northwest Paralegal Advice Officers Cluster and Lead Paralegal of the Lethabong CAO), interview, Lethabong-Rustenburg, February 14, 2011.

[104] Maru, "Between Law and Society" (see n. 42).

[105] "About Us," National Alliance for the Development of Community Advice Offices. http://nadcao.org.za/overview/.

[106] Erasmus, interview (see n. 1).

[107] It would be here that a centralized structure such as NADCAO would act as a guiding force, identifying suitable stakeholders and providing access to appropriate provincial and national institutions.

[108] Ten advice offices in the Cape recently collaborated to form the Save the Advice Offices campaign, lobbying the Office of Consumer Protection (OCP) for recognition of the value of the services they provide in connection with the OCP's work. The support of their communities alone raised funds of R 1.2 million.

interventions. This is so not least because it means that most CAO offices are one-person ventures, which places substantial strain on the paralegal to cover all the program work, as well as to manage and administer the office. In many cases, the paralegal has to also fund at least part of the work himself/herself, as was evident in case 2, where the paralegal had to use his own cell phone credit to make the required telephone calls to resolve a matter. These circumstances contribute to a firefighting approach and in all likelihood underlie the generalized lack of proactive or systemic problem solving we observed during case-tracking, which we expand on in the next section.

3. Reliance on Remote Urban-Based Lawyers (including LASA)

While formalistic legal solutions, and in particular the adversarial approach of lawyers, are not always appropriate, our research indicates that a CAO's ability to fully resolve all disputes often relies on the availability of an effective lawyer referral network for cases requiring more adversarial efforts, such as in cases 7, 9, and 11. Indeed, for the most part, community-based paralegals lack the legal qualifications necessary to represent clients in court should their matters require litigation. Their legal skills are usually acquired informally on the job and, while often precisely tailored for their clients' needs (see later in this chapter), there are obvious limitations, especially with respect to formal litigation in the court system. Thus, in order to go beyond civil matters and provide access to justice for clients facing criminal charges, paralegals are reliant on effective referral mechanisms to qualified attorneys. The CAOs within AJC networks are well served in this regard, given the formal system by which visits to the rural offices are conducted and case files taken on. Paralegals at the Black Sash and in CAOs operating in urban areas also have more options in terms of recourse to litigating NGOs and pro bono lawyers. Generally speaking, where these relationships are well established, they are often successful; referrals from community-based paralegals inform the public interest litigation focus of NGOs,[109] while law firms that mandate their fee earners to commit to a certain amount of pro bono work have a ready caseload.[110]

However, these relationships are more precarious when paralegals serve remote, rural communities where sympathetic private lawyers are few and far between and

---

[109] For this reason, NGOs such as the LRC have an open-door policy for the CAOs in Johannesburg's townships, from whom they frequently accept referrals and whom they offer advice and include in LRC training workshops when possible. Conversely, community-based paralegals can be negatively impacted by NGOs' strategic litigation approach. NGOs are also affected by the mandates of their funders and are therefore restricted, for instance, in their capacity to take on every unremarkable eviction matter. Nomfundo Gobodo (regional director, LRC), interview, Johannesburg, September 28, 2010.

[110] Probono.org is an NGO that facilitates the placement of matters with private lawyers in South African firms. With a presence mainly in Johannesburg and Mpumalanga, and soon to be collaborating with CAOs in Limpopo and the Northwest Cape, probono.org operates as a clearinghouse for clients who warrant free legal representation, fielding out such cases to attorneys and advocates within private practice with whom they have cooperation agreements. See Probono.org, www.probono.org.za/.

the CAOs lack support structures such as that provided to the AJCs. Frustration occurs when paralegals do not find adequate support from LASA justice centers, leaving their clients no option but to scrape together funds, if they can, to seek out legal advice in the nearest town,[111] despite their growing mistrust of local practitioners who, in the words of one CAO, provide a slapdash service for extortionate fees.[112] The lack of an effective referral system remains an obvious disadvantage for those with matters requiring administrative action,[113] and represents the South African justice system's failure to fulfill Sections 33 and 34 of the constitution enshrining every person's rights to just administrative action and access to the courts system.

Nevertheless, as illustrated in cases 7, 9, and 11, even where CAOs are effectively linked to lawyers, a disconnect can occur when a matter leaves the immediate setting, effectively distancing the client to the point where he or she loses touch with the case. While this does point to a critique of some lawyers' inadequate efforts to remain in regular communication with clients, it also indicates a greater problem among CAOs: that of ineffective case management and the tendency to deal with anything other than the first, immediate stage of a matter, which is expanded on in Section VI.B.

VI. ORGANIZATIONAL DETERMINANTS FOR CAOS

There are also several facilitating and hindering organizational determinants, meaning determinants that relate to the way CAOs are organized, operate, and work. We have analyzed as facilitating determinants support of umbrella clusters, as well as social embeddedness and appropriate techniques, and as hindering determinants limited strategic capacity and weak management systems.

A. Facilitating Determinants

1. Support of Umbrella Clusters

One of the defining features of the South African CAO network is the structure of umbrella clusters. It is clear that organizations such as NADCAO, CCJ, and CLRDC provide much support to the sector, especially in terms of fund-raising and lobbying for formal recognition. In many instances, as observed in cases 1, 2, 4, 9,

---

[111] According to Schalk Meyer, director of the AULAI Trust, for many indigent people this is simply not feasible, while for other communities the distances to travel are too great with scant means of transport. One community near Madike in the Northern Cape has a population of 1,000 people, with one taxi and two cars to share among them. Meyer, interview (see n. 61).

[112] Opinion of Albert Makwela (provincial coordinator, Limpopo Community Advice Office Consortium), interview, Tzaneen, October 4, 2010.

[113] All such claims are processed through a singular court system.

and 11, the support structure also facilitates a referral system for matters that paralegals are not able to resolve on their own. This is critical, especially in the multitude of single-person CAOs across the country. However, it is possible that reliance on this very support and referral structure might ultimately contribute to the lack of proactiveness that we encountered in some of the CAOs, which we elaborate on in what follows. More generally, the precise nature, effect, and value of affiliations to umbrella structures is worthy of closer examination than our study afforded, especially in terms of comparing affiliated with nonaffiliated CAOs, which our study did not do.

2. Social Embeddedness and Appropriate Techniques

Overwhelmingly, we found that embeddedness in communities was one of the most facilitating of all determinants with respect to South African CAOs. We understand this to cover many of the more "soft" skills of paralegals that we believe derive from living in the community served by paralegal work. Indeed, we did not witness any negative aspect arising from the proximate location of paralegals to their work – as hypothesized in this project's overall rubric. Rather, we saw ample evidence of the overwhelmingly positive impact of this close social location, which resulted in attuned sensitivity to local issues combined with an extraordinary capacity to go the extra mile for clients.

In many of the cases we tracked, as well as from our broader interviews, we experienced and were told about paralegals who combined the skills of psychologist, social worker, public servant, and paralegal. We are convinced that this holistic approach is facilitated by the similar and proximate living conditions and spaces between paralegals and clients (even where the geographic distances might be relatively wide), which promotes empathy and enables paralegals to go beyond formal methodologies, as illustrated in the case study set out at the beginning of this chapter, as well as in cases 4 and 5. Evidently, living within the community (or having lived in such circumstances) facilitates an understanding of the dynamics of that community and the value of social harmony in a way that remote lawyering does not. Whatever formal incorporation and/or regulation occurs within the sector, we hope that it is not to the detriment of this somewhat intangible but overwhelmingly positive feature of paralegal assistance.

Social embeddedness, as well, of course, as not being trained and entitled to act as registered lawyers, means that paralegals frequently use mediation techniques. When compared with litigation, mediation is a more informal legal procedure that is often most appropriate for intercommunity disputes, as evidenced in cases 10 and 12. Particularly in rural CAOs, paralegals resolve disputes by negotiating with both parties until a settlement is agreed, and only then going to the magistrate to set down the agreement. This type of settlement is often a more durable solution than the court could implement by itself, and magistrates frequently ask paralegals to mediate in advance to make the system work more smoothly.[114]

The paralegals we interviewed recognized the intrinsic value of creating authentic, lived solutions at the grassroots level within their communities, and not simply referring matters to lawyers for litigation. Indeed, Bheki Shange, a coordinator at one paralegal office, explained to SERI that he wanted the case referral figure to be as low as possible, given that "the nature of the case may not be appropriate for an attorney, the clients may prefer to use a paralegal as a go-between, and in any case, mediation is the best tool for conflict resolution as it allows people to decide the matter for themselves rather than having an imposed solution." It is for this reason that community-based paralegals have a good relationship with the courts, as mediation as a precursor to litigation promotes harmonious reconciliation, and means that clients often go to court with a ready settlement agreement.[115] In this way, paralegals within CAOs work to painstakingly build the democratic capacity of their communities brick by brick and question by question.

B. Hindering Determinants

1. Limited Strategic Capacity

One of the most notable observations from our research is the limited capacity of CAOs to abstract or strategize beyond an immediate firefighting approach to routine cases. As such, the paralegals we monitored appeared unable, unwilling, or uninterested in seeking systemic solutions to everyday problems. Rather, they relied on rolling out the same solutions to frequently occurring problems, such as the wrongful termination of social security benefits, which often involve a mere phone call or the completion of a form. Thus, we were struck, especially through the experiences of cases 1, 2, and 8, by the fact that the paralegals had not considered engaging in information sharing or workshops with the communities they serve in order to educate the public about how to resolve such simple cases, and thereby to lessen their load. A related feature of this nonstrategic approach was the paralegals' more generalized failure to explain each step of the process to the client, meaning that the client would probably have to come back to the paralegal if the same or similar problem arose again.

In addition, alongside this vacuum with respect to empowering the public to deal with matters themselves, we noticed a certain disempowerment in some of the paralegals in terms of taking matters beyond the first phase of telephone calls or

---

[114] Kubayi, interview (see n. 2).
[115] Bheki Shange (provincial coordinator, Gauteng Paralegal Advice Office Forum), interview, Soweto, October 19, 2010 (discussing his experiences in the maintenance court, part of the magistrates' courts' jurisdiction); John Moerane (provincial coordinator, Northwest Paralegal Advice Office Cluster), interview, Lethabong, February 14, 2011 (explaining to SERI how at Lethabong CAO, the paralegals help women complete protection order claims, ensuring that clients understand the process before going to the domestic violence court at the Rustenburg Magistrate's Court).

form completion. For example, in case 2 concerning unemployment benefits, the matter was significantly delayed because the paralegal did not know how to escalate the issue without external assistance. Here, we saw a role for better information sharing and education from the umbrella clusters. Further research is necessary to delve into these issues, but it is possible that the degree of passivity we witnessed might relate to paralegals' attempt to safeguard their position by not sharing knowledge. Alternatively, it might relate more structurally to limited funding (outlined earlier) and/or a weakness in the existing management training programs offered by NADCAO and the other umbrella structures.

2. Weak Management Systems

Our research interviews indicate that there is a generalized weakness in management systems across the sector, which means that individual CAOs, especially the smaller ones in rural areas, struggle with the technical requirements of external donors. The big foreign donors in particular have onerous proposal and reporting requirements that can be crippling to small, understaffed organizations. Typically, the proposals require access to technology, good written English, and the ability to draw up comprehensive budgets. The reports also require constant monitoring, evaluation, and considerable capacity. Such reporting requirements are made more burdensome by the fact that many CAOs do not yet have an effective case log system, making it difficult for paralegals with a waiting room full of clients each day to properly document every client, issue, and resolution. For example, CCJ is six years behind in its reporting, purely due to time restraints, and told us that it has had to accept anecdotal reporting to make the task less onerous for its paralegals.[116] Concerns over funding also mean that CAO paralegals spend too much of their time preoccupied with raising enough money to cover their operating costs. A vicious cycle thus ensues, whereby CAOs' lack of funds inhibits their chance of sourcing funding in the future and limits their productivity.

Institutionalization, in this sense, is certainly an aspiration for community-based paralegals working with CAOs. However, as CLRDC director Langa Mtshali explains, enormous infrastructure and capacity-building needs are required for CAOs to be able to cope with the demands of "independence."[117] Msomi, paralegal at the Mpola CAO, agreed, stating that CAOs need better knowledge of fundraising, management, and drawing up constitutions and cooperation agreements before making that leap.[118] To this end, training for community-based paralegals needs to be more consistent across the board, and more frequent. According to Joanne Harding, "we need to move away from the idea that informal training is enough and increase the professionalism of the sector."[119] More uniform training would

---

[116] Together with the CLRDC, CCJ wants to document its work, properly measuring the impact of a case resolution on a family or community by recording the number of people involved.
[117] Mtshali, interview (see n. 100). [118] Msomi, interview (see n. 96).
[119] Harding, interview (see n. 74).

prevent CAOs from being so reliant on their individual staff members, and limit the damage caused by personnel changes.

In terms of increased knowledge sharing, an effective case management system would also be of substantial benefit for CAOs. Just as the Black Sash database captures trends from its casework and feedback on best practice techniques, a case log system accessible by the NADCAO CAO network would be an invaluable training resource and cross-regional research tool by which to identify patterns in socioeconomic problems to create advocacy campaigns. It would also provide the quantitative data required for funding proposals. Such a case management system has been put in place by NADCAO and trialed in certain CAOs. NADCAO's Central Case Management System is Internet-based; paralegals input data onto a computer and later upload it onto the Internet to be accessed by the centralized data capturer. However, with very low information technology connectivity and limited access to computers in most rural CAOs, the roll-out of the system has had limited success, and NADCAO is exploring ways to circumvent the connectivity challenges.

VII. CONCLUSION

In many respects, South Africa represents a triumph of form over content. The institutional frameworks for access to justice could not be more favorable. There is a right of access to courts and a right to legal assistance at state expense in criminal matters when "substantial injustice would otherwise result," and there are certain institutional options for legal aid as well as NGOs and the like.[120]

Yet, as our research has highlighted, beyond law and policy, there are real problems related to the need for and the (un)availability of legal assistance, especially in rural areas. The formal justice system clearly cannot provide the kind of assistance required by poor people to fully realize their human rights without the support of community-based paralegals. This is particularly the case in rural areas, where non-lawyers remain the only conduit for indigent and marginalized communities to afford equal access to justice.

This study has highlighted the critical contribution that South African paralegals make in advancing access to justice. This is done in ways that straddle not only different pluralities between modernity and tradition but also different modes, with paralegals taking on a quasi-welfare and community-sensitive role in dispute resolution, as well as acting as a critical bridge between state and society in assisting communities to access services and goods. As such, paralegals are contributing substantially to attempts to consolidate South Africa's fledgling democracy.

However, beyond the facilitating support from umbrella organizations and the high degree of relevance and appropriateness of CAOs to local contexts, the sector is

---

[120] *Constitution of the Republic of South Africa* (1996), §§ 35(2)(c), 35(3)(g).

struggling with real problems. Without formal regulation or recognition, CAOs face the twin problems of insufficient funding and inadequate training, which in turn, often prevent paralegals from taking on more strategic, proactive empowerment on behalf of the communities they serve. To realize their potential, it is imperative that CAOs receive further financial and training support and that the issue of their regulation is speedily settled. Continued failure to resolve these issues will squander the sector's contributions that have been built up through decades of struggling for better conditions, and thus undermine the very fabric of South Africa's democratic project.

REFERENCES

African National Congress (ANC). *The Reconstruction and Development Programme.* Johannesburg: Umanyano Publishers, 1994.

Alexander, Colleen (Regional coordinator of fieldworkers in the Western and Northern Capes, SCAT). Interview, Ceres, October 6, 2011.

Bantu Land Act No. 27 (1913).

Bantu Urban Areas Consolidation Act No. 25 (1945).

The Black Sash. *Social Assistance: A Reference Guide for Paralegals.* Mowbray: The Black Sash, 2010.

Constitution of the Republic of South Africa (1996).

Dugard, John. *Human Rights and the South African Legal Order.* Princeton, NJ: Princeton University Press, 1978.

Erasmus, Greg (Former national coordinator of the National Alliance for the Development of Community Advice Offices [NADCAO]). Interview, Johannesburg, January 25, 2011.

Gobodo, Nomfundo (Regional director, LRC). Interview, Johannesburg, September 28, 2010.

Group Areas Act No. 41 (1950).

Harding, Joanne (Executive director of SCAT). Interview, Cape Town, October 5, 2010.

Harding, Joanne (Executive director of SCAT) and Anthea Davids-Thomas (Training coordinator of SCAT). Interview, Cape Town, October 5, 2010.

Hweshe, Francis. "More to Benefit from Social Grants." *BuaNews*, April 15, 2011. www.southafrica.info/about/social/436302.htm.

Kubayi, Winnie (Director, Centre for Community Justice [CCJ]). Interview, Pietermaritzburg, October 13, 2010.

Lebert, Tim and Umhlaba Associates. *Holding Government to Account: Advocacy in an Emerging Democracy: The Story of the Black Sash.* New York: The Atlantic Philanthropies, 2009.

Legal Aid South Africa (LASA). *Annual Report: Legal Aid South Africa 2009/2010.* www.legal-aid.co.za/wp-content/uploads/2012/04/Legal-Aid-SA-Annual-Report-2009-10.pdf.

Makwela, Albert (Provincial coordinator, Limpopo Community Advice Office Consortium). Interview, Tzaneen, October 4, 2010.

Marais, Hein. *South Africa: Pushed to the Limit: The Political Economy of Change.* Claremont: UCT Press, 2011.

Maru, Vivek. "Between Law and Society: Paralegals and the Provision of Justice Services in Sierra Leone and Worldwide." *The Yale Journal of International Law* 31, no. 427 (2006): 428–76.

Mcquoid-Mason, David (Professor of law, University of KwaZulu/Natal). Interview, Durban, October 11, 2010.
Meyer, Schalk (Director, AULAI Trust). Interview, Potchestroom, October 25, 2010.
Mkhize, Lucky (Mpopomene). Interview, KwaZulu/Natal, February 9, 2011.
Moerane, John (Provincial coordinator of the Northwest Paralegal Advice Officers Cluster). Interview, Lethabong, February 14, 2011.
Msomi (Paralegal, Mpola Advice Office). Interview, Mpola-Durban, October 12, 2010.
Mtshali, Langa (Director, CLRDC). Interview, Durban, October 12, 2010.
National Alliance for the Development of Community Advice Offices. "About Us." http://nadcao.org.za/overview/.
Njongi v. Member of the Executive Council, Department of Welfare, Eastern Cape (CCT 37/07) [2008] ZACC 4; 2008 (6) BCLR 571 (CC); 2008 (4) SA 237 (CC); 2011 (7) BCLR 651 (CC) (March 28, 2008).
O'Malley, Padraid. Nelson Mandela Centre of Memory. "UDF Definition." Last modified May 1996. www.nelsonmandela.org/omalley/index.php/site/q/03lv02424/04lv02730/05lv03176/06lv03184.htm.
Orford, Margie. *Rural Voice: The Social Change Assistance Trust 1984–2004: Working in South Africa.* Cape Town: David Phillip Publishers, 2004.
Republic of South Africa. *Constitution of the Republic of South Africa.* Pretoria: Government Printer, 1996.
Shange, Bheki (Provincial coordinator, Gauteng Paralegal Advice Office Forum). Interview, Soweto, October 19, 2010.
Social Change Assistance Trust. "Donor Partners." www.scat.org.za/partners/donor-partners.
South African Institute of Race Relations (SAIRR). "South Africa Survey 2008/2009." Johannesburg: SAIRR, 2009.
"Institute of Race Relations." http://sairr.org.za/.
South African Law School. "Paralegal Practice." http://lawschool.co.za/courses/paralegal-practice/.
South African School of Paralegal Studies. "Home." www.paralegal.za.org/.
Tumelo, Sophia (Paralegal, Phokeng Advice Office). Interview, Phokeng-Rustenburg, February 14, 2011.
University of Kwazulu-Natal, Centre for Criminal Justice. "Cases." http://ccj.ukzn.ac.za/Cases/CasesOverview.aspx.
"Social Welfare." http://ccj.ukzn.ac.za/WorkingwithPartners/SocialWelfare.aspx.
"Working with Hospitals and Clinics." http://ccj.ukzn.ac.za/WorkingwithPartners/HospitalsandClinics.aspx.
"Working with Police." http://ccj.ukzn.ac.za/WorkingwithPartners/Police.aspx.

3

Community-Based Paralegalism in the Philippines

From Social Movements to Democratization

Jennifer Franco, Hector Soliman, and Maria Roda Cisnero

1. INTRODUCTION

In recent years, the challenge of expanding access to justice for the poor has received increasing attention from the international development community. Promoting justice in settings where state legal and judicial institutions and the rule of law are weak or compromised is a difficult proposition. Today, many societies, despite formal recognition of the legal rights of poorer citizens, fall short of full and effective realization of those rights in practice. In many countries, civil society spaces and organizations oriented toward legal empowerment of the poor may also be inadequate or nonexistent, and thus still limited in their potential contribution to expanding access to justice for the poor.

Deepening interest in the problem of access to justice has emerged within a broader emphasis on judicial and rule of law reform as a necessary prerequisite to development more generally. Efforts to address weak state legal and judicial institutions have often focused on interventions defined in terms of creating and/or reforming the relevant rules and procedures, often based on idealized understandings of what constitutes a well-functioning system of law and justice. At the same time, more attention is being paid to increasing legal assistance to the poor in order to increase their capacity to effectively use state law and institutions in the pursuit of justice.[1] Legal assistance has involved diverse interpretations ranging from "legal aid" to "legal empowerment."[2] Taken together, such efforts reflect changing understandings of the processes and obstacles involved as citizens attempt to get their justice concerns met. It is no longer enough to address formal legal institutions

---

[1] Another type of response has involved revaluing and drawing on more localized, "non-state" types of indigenous and customary practices in social regulation and in determining and dispensing justice as an additional means to expand access to justice for the poor. However, this type of innovation is not the subject of the present study.

[2] Legal aid usually focuses on the state's obligation to provide legal services for the poor, while legal empowerment stresses the process by which the poor use the law to make a claim on their entitlements and hold governments more accountable to their rights.

(such as the judiciary and ministries of justice) alone; as important are: (i) how formal legal institutions actually operate in real societies, (ii) whether and how different members of a given society experience and use law in their pursuit of justice, and (iii) which strategies and practices have what effects in terms of law reform and justice.

One strategy involves community-based paralegals. In the Philippines, community-based paralegals have existed for decades,[3] with a practice that spans a variety of local circumstances and is largely assumed to contribute to poor people "getting justice." The conditions under which community-based paralegals emerge and operate in the Philippines and the impacts they may have remain unclear, not least because although community paralegals are often cited as important, in fact, "there has been little systematic study of the workings of paralegal programs" in that country.[4] The question thus remains whether and to what extent community-based paralegalism is a socially relevant and empowering innovation for Filipino society.

II. METHODOLOGY

To begin addressing this question, a broad scan was taken of the Philippines' contemporary paralegal movement. Because the country has a long and extensive experience in using state law to defend and deepen people's rights – an approach Filipino activists refer to as "developmental legal aid" or "alternative law"[5] – this study involved casting the net wide and deep to gather insights from a diversity of actors working in the field. The analytical approach used can be described as *historical, institutional,* and *process oriented.*

The approach is *historical* in order to capture changes that affect the practice or direction of community-based paralegalism over time, including, among other factors: (i) the nature of the overall political-legal framework that may either recognize community-based paralegalism or not; (ii) the degree of the presence and reach of alternative lawyering networks that can facilitate the growth of community-based paralegalism; and (iii) the degree of attention given by key actors involved in cultivating paralegalism to assessing the social and political impacts of their work.

The approach is *institutional* in that it gives attention to how formal and informal institutions shape the power and activity of paralegals over time, as well as other

---

[3] Paralegals are understood here as community-based in the broad sense of being based in or catering to a grassroots-level organization, whether workplace, neighborhood, parish, school, or some other basic social-institutional setting. This concept is elaborated in Section 4.1.
[4] Vivek Maru and Varun Gauri, "BNPP Concept Note," World Bank Justice for the Poor Program, December 2009.
[5] The terms *developmental legal aid, alternative lawyering,* and *public interest lawyering* are all used interchangeably. They all denote the use of the law by the poor with the assistance of legal service nongovernmental organizations (NGOs) or lawyers, so that the ends of justice may be fully served and the poor's rights and entitlements fully realized. See Box 3.1 for a definition of "developmental legal aid."

actors that may affect their activity and practice. For example, the state judicial and quasi-judicial dispute tribunals (such as agrarian adjudication boards or labor relations tribunals) can affect paralegal practice and activity and the standing of individual practitioners by according formal recognition (or not).[6] Entrenched political patronage networks can also influence and constrain community paralegals both inside the courtroom and in the differentiated and stratified communities where they work.

But institutions alone do not determine outcomes, and thus the approach used here is also *process oriented*, emphasizing human actors and their actions and interactions in order to better detect the role of perception, interpretation, and choice regarding particular laws or legal provisions in relevant interactions over time and in specific situations.

The main analytical point is that no law, policy, program, or project is "self-implementing"; rather, laws and policies are interpreted and implemented by real people.[7] Oftentimes this involves conflicting parties with different political and/or legal standing and the need to bring different interpretative frames to bear in interactions. The implementation of laws and policies is therefore to a certain extent open ended and contingent upon the actions and interactions of numerous competing actors embedded in diverse power relations and structures. Many of the actors involved in making law *in a broader sociological sense* – that is, beyond the mere formal legal processes of making and implementing laws and policies to include the more fundamental processes of making laws and policies actually *authoritative in society* – are themselves embedded in social structures that are not necessarily coterminous with the state. This includes an array of actors from municipal judges, public attorneys, and local police commanders who may be part of broader local kinship or regional political networks, to private lawyers, corporations, landlords, public interest attorneys, civil rights advocates and rights advocacy networks, and social and political change activists – each with his or her own organizational interests and sources of authority.

A. Study Participants

The study included a variety of actors operationalizing diverse concepts and perspectives on the issue of community-based paralegalism. The first set of informants came from nongovernmental organizations (NGOs) that train, mentor, and/or deploy paralegals. Twelve organizations were selected that help to illustrate (albeit

---

[6] In the Philippines, the term *courts* is utilized to refer to dispute tribunals located within the judicial branch, while the term *quasi-judicial* agencies is usually used to refer to dispute-resolution offices located within the executive branch.

[7] Jennifer C. Franco, "Making Land Rights Accessible: Social Movements and Political-Legal Innovation in the Rural Philippines," *The Journal of Development Studies* 44, no. 7 (2008): 991–1022, doi: 10.1080/00220380802150763.

partially) the breadth of paralegal practice covering a range of issue areas, including, for example: civil and political rights; environmental protection; agrarian reform; and the rights of indigenous peoples, children, women, and migrants. Ten of the twelve organizations are members of the Alternative Law Groups (ALG), a civil society network founded in the early 1990s and anchored by lawyers dedicated to the practice of law to aid social justice. The selection of the ten ALG members (out of the total nineteen members) considered the range of paralegal practice in diverse areas such as the environment, women, and agrarian reform. The selection also took into account the representation of the various major island groups of the country, which means the locations of Luzon, Visayas, and Mindanao.

The remaining two NGOs are not ALG members, but the nature of their work qualifies them as practitioners of alternative law. Taken together, the twelve organizations constitute a critical mass of civil society groups and localized networks that engage in paralegalism and for which paralegalism is more or less institutionalized as part of their overall work.[8] For this set of participants, we conducted key interviews and focus group discussions with paralegal officers and/or trained paralegals.

All of the organizations covered in this study are specialized in one or two distinct issue areas and sets of associated law. Four of them work on agrarian issues (Balay Alternative Legal Advocates for Development in Mindanaw, Inc. [BALAOD], Solidarity toward Agrarian Reform and Rural Development [KAISAHAN], the Rural Poor Institute for Land and Human Rights Services [RIGHTS], and the Alternative Legal Assistance Center [SALIGAN]). Two work on labor issues (SALIGAN and the Center for Migrant Workers [KANLUNGAN]), with one of these specializing in migrant labor issues (KANLUNGAN). Two work on different aspects of women's rights (KANLUNGAN and the Women's Legal and Human Rights Bureau, Inc. [WLB]), and one works on children's rights issues (the Children's Legal Bureau, Inc. [CLB]). Two others work mainly on environmental issues (the Environmental Legal Assistance Center [ELAC] and Defense of Nature [TK]), and one works on the rights of indigenous persons (the Legal Assistance Center for Indigenous Filipinos [PANLIPI]). The Free Legal Assistance Group (FLAG) continues to work on civil and political rights violations, while the Ateneo Human Rights Center (AHRC), a law school–based actor, works mainly on human rights education.

Several of the civil society groups invited to participate in the study saw its potential value as a contribution to the historical record, but expressed various degrees of concern about participating in a project initiated by the World Bank. Indeed, one ALG member refused outright to participate in any World Bank–related activity, including this one. Some were particularly concerned about how the World Bank would use the data, especially on issues where the World Bank's advocacy and activities in the country were seen as deeply at odds with their own, particularly the

---

[8] A list of these twelve organizations can be found in Annex B.

promotion of large-scale mining, but also other far-reaching economic activities perceived as having intolerable negative social and environmental impacts. In the end, some of the groups that initially expressed reservations did agree to participate, in the belief that it would be important to register their experience in any study on community-based paralegals. In order to protect those informants who currently work under extremely hostile conditions in local areas adversely affected by large-scale economic activities (by trying to stop those activities), it was determined that all informants would remain anonymous.

In addition to participants from the nongovernmental sector, a second set of informants was selected that included officials from several government branches and agencies at different levels (national, regional, municipal). Those from the government sector came from the local judiciary as well as the Supreme Court, the Department of Justice, and the Public Attorney's Office. Finally, a smaller, third set of informants was drawn from the Integrated Bar of the Philippines (IBP), more specifically the director for legal aid, as well as the Asia Foundation, an important funder of paralegal programs in the Philippines historically. The IBP could be viewed as a somewhat curious institution, in that it is a professional organization of lawyers but has been created by mandate of the supervisory powers of the Supreme Court. It receives no funding from the state, only from membership contributions, giving it the character of a quasi-government institution.

All these informants were selected on the basis of the role that their institutions play in influencing and defining paralegalism in theory and in practice. In the end, a total of eighteen interviews and nineteen focus group discussions (composed of three to five individuals each) were conducted, with a fifty-fifty gender balance overall. In addition, most of the informants were from areas outside of Metropolitan Manila, namely the provinces of Zambales and Quezon on the island of Luzon, and the provinces of Cebu, Misamis Oriental, and Palawan.

B. Study Goal

The main purpose of this study was to describe the state of community-based paralegal work in the Philippines. By definition, the study was not designed to assess the impact of paralegal work in various facets of social justice, for example, the improvement of the skills of the poor over time, or the responsiveness of state institutions to paralegal engagement. The study does point out that monitoring and evaluation work in the area of paralegal work remains a substantial challenge. Thus, it is hoped that this chapter will provide the framework needed to evaluate the impact of paralegal work much more rigorously in the future.

III. BACKGROUND

Contemporary paralegal work in the Philippines is not a new phenomenon. Rather, there is precedent for paralegal work in lawyering for the poor that dates back to the early 1930s, when agrarian and labor unrest arose in response to deteriorating social and economic conditions, mainly in central and southern Luzon.[9] Demands over land tenure and labor issues both shaped and were shaped by political-legal support received from individual local lawyers who sympathized with these movements and their aspirations. The experience launched a tradition of lawyering for the poor and other marginalized groups, which continued into the ensuing decades, when new generations of workers' and peasants' organizations arose in response to still unfulfilled demands for better working terms and conditions and the recognition of land and tenure rights. When President Ferdinand Marcos imposed martial law in 1972, all opposition was suppressed, the press was muzzled, and the national legislature was shut down. Activists were rounded up by the hundreds, detained, and in many instances, tortured and summarily executed, prompting the establishment of FLAG in 1974 by the late Senator Jose W. Diokno.[10] Led by a small core of lawyers and non-lawyers, the organization pioneered a strategy of training and deploying paralegals to take up human rights cases during martial law.[11] FLAG's efforts amid repression and adversity served as a training ground for future generations of lawyers, inspiring

---

BOX 3.1: WHAT IS DEVELOPMENTAL LEGAL AID?

Jose Diokno encapsulates the concept of alternative lawyering or developmental legal aid as follows:

> Traditional legal aid is in fact the lawyer's way of giving alms to the poor. Like alms which provide temporary relief to the poor but do not touch the social structures that keep the poor poor, traditional legal aid redresses particular instances of injustice, but does not fundamentally change the structures that generate and sustain injustice . . .
>
> So development requires a different type of legal aid, one that will not supplant traditional legal aid but supplement it, concentrating on public rather than on private issues, intent on changing instead of merely upholding

---

[9] See Benedict Kkerkvliet, *The Huk Rebellion: A Study of Peasant Revolt in the Philippines* (Berkeley: University of California Press, 1977); Harlan R. Crippen, "Philippine Agrarian Unrest: Historical Backgrounds," *Science & Society* 10, no. 4 (1946): 337–60.

[10] See Box 3.1.

[11] A short description of providing free legal assistance for martial law victims can be found in Franco's *Elections and Democratization in the Philippines*. Jennifer C. Franco, *Elections and Democratization in the Philippines* (New York: Routledge, 2001), 117.

> BOX 3.1: (Cont.)
> existing law and social structures, particularly the distribution of power within society...
>
> This new type of legal aid is needed because development is more than just feeding, clothing, curing, teaching and housing people. Many prisons do as much. Development is above all the people deciding what food, clothes, medical care, education, and housing they need, and how to provide them...
>
> In ASEAN countries and, indeed, in all developing countries, then a new type of legal aid would rest on firm legal ground: the right of the people to development. Efforts to practice this new type of legal aid which for want of a better name I shall call *developmental legal aid*, have begun in ASEAN countries. Lawyers who had been imprisoned, or had practiced traditional legal aid became convinced that, under conditions in their country, something more was needed. If the rights of the poor and the oppressed were to be vindicated and just and human development achieved, the job of developmental legal aid had to be done. (Emphasis supplied)[12]

many to later set up their own institutions to expand upon its example. During this time, other similar organizations such as the Protestant Lawyers' League (PLL) and the Movement of Attorneys for Brotherhood, Integrity and Nationalism, Inc. (MABINI) also followed the FLAG model of addressing human rights abuses.

The collapse of the Marcos dictatorship in 1986 and the promulgation of a new national constitution in 1987 led to an unprecedented proliferation of "sectoral" organizations and "cause-oriented" movements, often with competing political visions and strategies for change, but similarly intent on influencing the pace and direction of national social, political, and economic reform after Marcos. This included numerous nongovernmental legal services organizations, some of which (but not all) would coalesce under the formal banner of the ALG. A new generation of activist lawyers likewise sought to take advantage of the new political space that opened up after the dictatorship, and to use the associated political-legal institutions to bring a more democratic law within the reach of everyone. The post-dictatorship constitution enshrined a whole host of new rights and provisions, positively addressing key social and political rights and justice concerns of the poor and other marginalized groups, including in relation to environmental protection and the use of natural resources. These provisions became crucial reference points for alternative law activism and paralegal efforts, partly because in the Philippines, "good" law has never by itself guaranteed "good" legal outcomes.[13] The alternative

---

[12] Jose W. Diokno, "Developmental Legal Aid in Rural ASEAN: Problems and Prospects," in *Rural Development and Human Rights in South East Asia: Report of a Seminar* (Geneva: International Commission of Jurists, Penang: Consumers' Association of Penang, 1982).

[13] Franco, "Making Land Rights Accessible," 992 (see n. 7).

law and paralegal activism approach thus gained significant new social relevance in the post-Marcos era.

Political openings at the national level, however, did not guarantee a similar change below it, and indeed since that time, subnational democratization has proceeded unevenly and in many places not at all.[14] Political structures at the local level are still largely controlled by established dynasties (whose power is rooted in control of land, labor, and other key factors of production), many of which operate in conjunction with private armies and within a strong culture of impunity. In many parts of the Philippines, journalists, activists, judges and lawyers, and others who attempt to challenge an undemocratic and repressive status quo are routinely harassed and even killed, often without any sign that justice will ever be meted out to the perpetrators. A gross example of this phenomenon was the November 2009 Maguindanao Massacre, wherein fifty-eight persons (thirty-four of them journalists) were killed by the hired assailants of a prominent local politician at the height of the political campaign for local electoral posts.

IV. PARALEGALS TODAY: DEFINITION, WORK, TOOLS, AND TRAINING

A. Definition

The word *paralegal* has been used in the legal-activism literature on development-oriented legal assistance for the past thirty years. For example, Senator Diokno wrote about "paralegals or barefoot lawyers," as he called them, in 1982.[15] In development work today, the term refers to a variety of situations, some community based, others not, but all sharing a broadly similar community-oriented, grassroots perspective. In general, paralegals are not lawyers by definition, although they do have some legal training and can include those who are the products of law schools, namely, law students or law graduates who have not yet taken or passed the bar examination. But in the Philippines, the term refers primarily to a layperson who claims some knowledge of the law and the workings of government, has had some training in these fields, and practices her/his paralegal skills *in the name of some organization*, whether state or non-state. It is important to note here the clear distinction between a paralegal and an *abogadillo* (or "little lawyer"). The term *abogadillo* refers to any layperson who offers legal advice and services in his/her own name in exchange for money – a practice considered illegitimate by alternative law activists due to a perceived lack of accountability to any greater authority. This practice is also clearly "unauthorized practice of law" and is considered illegal by the IBP and the Supreme Court. Although interesting (to the extent that it reflects a demand for such

---

[14] Franco, *Elections and Democratization* (see n. 11).
[15] Diokno, "Developmental Legal Aid in Rural ASEAN" (see n. 12). See Box 3.2.

> BOX 3.2: DIOKNO ON COMMUNITY PARALEGALS
>
> "To overcome the manpower problem, developmental legal aid groups have trained paralegals or 'barefoot lawyers' in the basic concepts of law, legal procedure, tactics and counter tactics, and in the skills needed to do routine, repetitive, or preliminary jobs and carry out simple investigations, such as interviewing witnesses, and taking down their statements, getting copies of public records, preserving physical evidence, filling out standard government forms, etc. Paralegals are chosen from among promising students of law and social sciences who agree to do field work with poor communities between school terms; representatives of depressed communities who are recommended by civic organizations working with them; and trade union members recommended by their unions. Paralegal training has produced several benefits. Lawyers have had more time to devote to the creative aspects of their job: counseling, negotiating, drafting, advocacy. Some law students were motivated by their experiences as paralegals to join legal aid groups after the bar. And paralegals have equipped the communities they live in with a knowledge of how law works and how they use law to assert or defend their rights."[16]

services), the *abogadillo* phenomenon is not the focus of the present study, nor is the type of paralegal found in mainstream law offices (e.g., those whose objective is more commercial and profit-making in nature).

B. Substance of Work and Underlying Legislation

Paralegals in the Philippines today engage in: (i) *education* on human rights, constitutional rights and provisions, and legal rights and procedures; (ii) *legal research/investigation/documentation* or casework proper; (iii) *mediation* in conflict-resolution or dispute-processing venues, especially the village-level *barangay justice system* (BJS);[17] (iv) *representation* in certain quasi-judicial dispute resolution tribunals; (v) *law enforcement* as *bantay gubat* (forest guards) and *bantay dagat* (municipal water guards); (vi) *policy advocacy* around local ordinances and national laws, policies, and programs; and (vii) *organization* and mobilization of people to more effectively address their justice concerns by making claims based on legal rights.

[16] Diokno, "Developmental Legal Aid in Rural ASEAN" (see n. 12).
[17] The *barangay justice system* (Katarungang Pambarangay) is a state-mandated mechanism that aims to complement courts in the settlement of small disputes. Under the Local Government Code, it is compulsory for disputing parties to refer petty matters to the *barangay justice system* before proceeding to courts. See Maricel Vigo and Marlon Manuel, *Katarungang Pambarangay: A Handbook* (Quezon City: SALIGAN, Pasig City: LGSP, 2004), 20–32.

As noted, a large number and wide range of new (and still evolving) legal rights became available after 1986, and in turn, have become key tools for people seeking justice. This includes new laws and policies regarding, among others: (i) land rights – the Comprehensive Agrarian Reform Program (CARP) (1980) and the Comprehensive Agrarian Reform Extension with Reforms (CARPER) (2009);[18] (ii) ancestral domain – the Indigenous Peoples Rights Act (IPRA) (1997);[19] (iii) women's rights – Violence against Women and Children Act (VAWC) (2004);[20] (iv) children's rights – Juvenile Justice and Welfare Act (JJWA) (2006);[21] (v) rights of sustenance fisher folk – the Local Government Code (LGC) (1992); (vi) coastal marine resource protection – the Philippine Fisheries Code (Fisheries Code) (1998);[22] (vii) environmental protection – the National Integrated Protected Areas System (NIPAS) Law (1991);[23] (viii) the writ of *kalikasan*[24] (2010); (ix) human rights – writ of *amparo* (2007);[25] (x) the writ of habeas data (Habeas Data) (2008);[26] and (xi) the rights of migrant workers and overseas Filipinos (Omnibus Rules and Regulations Implementing the Migrant Workers and Overseas Filipinos Act of 1995).[27]

C. Affiliation and Accountability

Examining the question of paralegal accountability is useful in making some further distinctions. Paralegals are understood in the Philippines as community based in the broad sense of being a part of or catering to a grassroots-level organization, whether from the workplace, neighborhood, parish, school, or some other basic social-

---

[18] Republic Act No. 6657; Republic Act No. 9700.   [19] Republic Act No. 8371.
[20] Republic Act No. 9262.   [21] Republic Act No. 9344.   [22] Republic Act No. 8550.
[23] Republic Act No. 7586.
[24] "The writ is a remedy available to any natural or juridical person, entity authorized by law, people's organization, NGO, or any public interest group accredited by or registered with any government agency, on behalf of persons whose constitutional right to a balanced and healthful ecology is violated or threatened with violation by an unlawful act or omission of a public official or employee, or private individual or entity, involving environmental damage of such magnitude as to prejudice to life, health or property of inhabitants in two or more cities or provinces." This remedy has been provided in the recently promulgated Rules for Environmental Courts. RULES OF PROCEDURE FOR ENVIRONMENTAL CASES, A.M. No. 09-6-8-SC, http://philja.judiciary.gov.ph/assets/files/pdf/learning_materials/A.m.No .09-6-8-SC_Rules_of_Procedure_for_Envi_Cases.pdf.
[25] "The writ is a remedy available to any person whose right to life, liberty and security is violated or threatened with violation by an unlawful act or omission of a public official or employee, or of a private individual or entity. The writ shall cover extralegal killings and enforced disappearances or threats thereof." For the full text of the procedure governing the writ of *amparo*, see Navia V. Pardico, G.R. No. 184467 (S.C., June 19, 2012) (Phil), http://hrlibrary.umn.edu/research/Philippines/The% 20Rule%20On%20The%20Writ%20Of%20Amparo.pdf.
[26] "The writ is a remedy available to any person whose right to privacy in life, liberty or security is violated or threatened by an unlawful act or omission of a public official or employee, or of a private individual or entity engaged in the gathering, collecting or storing of data or information regarding the person, family, home and correspondence of the aggrieved party." For the full text, see The Rule on the Writ of Habeas Data, A.M. No. 08-1-16 (S.C., Jan. 22, 2008).
[27] Republic Act No. 8042.

institutional setting. In practice, however, this affiliation turns out to have various meanings in terms of the paralegals' relationship with the state.

For instance, for paralegals who are strictly "PO based" – that is, embedded in a "people's organization" (PO) as a member, their accountability is to that organization.[28] Other paralegals, by contrast, are best understood as "LGU based," in that their standing as paralegals comes from being connected to and recognized by a given local government unit (LGU), usually the *barangay* (village), and their accountability is largely to the local government. Still other paralegals attempt to establish a standing in both spheres, that is, as both PO member and as member of the local development council (LDC) or *barangay* development council (BDC), for example. The study also encountered paralegals who are not based in any grassroots community-level organization, but can and do (cl)aim to serve a particular group or category of people whose justice concerns revolve around their standing as members of a particular grassroots community. This latter mode of paralegalism is more often based in an NGO (and is thus NGO based), although there are also those who are based in a government institution, such as the Department of Agrarian Reform (DAR), which launched its own paralegal program in the 1990s in order to hasten agrarian reform implementation.

In all these cases, a defining feature is that the paralegal explicitly endeavors to serve a particular group or category of people who are perceived as inadequately recognized as rights holders, and/or whose human rights are deemed insufficiently defined, guaranteed, or fulfilled by the state in practice. This should not be surprising, given that historically in the Philippines (see Section III), the main anchor of paralegalism has been the broad movement for social change, which, despite some important internal differences, reflects a basic consensus about the key problems besetting Philippine society. These include: (i) the highly skewed and uneven distribution of wealth and power, which produces chronic poverty and drives many Filipinos (including children) into precarious and unfavorable work situations at home and abroad; (ii) the continued emphasis on a development model that relies on large-scale, destructive extraction and use of natural resources (land, water, minerals, forest), which in turn intensifies conflicts over natural resource and territorial ownership and control and at the same time deepens the need for environmental protection; (iii) an entrenched sociopolitical culture that supports gender and ethnic injustice and gives rise to violence and human rights violations against women and indigenous peoples; and (iv) a deep-rooted political culture that tolerates both repression and impunity and depends on maintaining a gap between rights on paper and rights in reality, even as the number of rights available on paper continues to expand.

---

[28] The term *people's organization* refers to an association composed mainly of members of basic sectors, such as peasants, fisher folk, indigenous peoples, or slum dwellers, while *nongovernmental organization* usually refers to professionals who are working for the benefit of the basic sectors. See John Farrington and David J. Lewis, *Non-governmental Organizations and the State in Asia: Rethinking Roles in Sustainable Agricultural Development* (New York: Routledge, 1993).

D. Recognition and Training

Within the state, post-Marcos political-institutional change has unfolded only partially and unevenly, creating some openings for paralegalism in the process. Community-based paralegals are now recognized and encouraged in some quasi-judicial tribunals – for example, in the DAR Adjudication Board that handles agrarian reform–related disputes, and in the National Labor Relations Commission that handles disputes between employers and employees – but not yet formally recognized by the judiciary.[29]

Today's community-based paralegalism has also been shaped by state-led reform measures and associated peoples' initiatives. For example, when the constitution mandated the right of the people to a clean and healthy environment, this spawned various legislative proposals on the fisheries code, solid waste management, clean air, hazardous wastes disposal, the integrated protected areas system, and the like. The abundance of new environmental legislation in turn prompted the Supreme Court to designate new environmental courts with primary jurisdiction and to enhance the rules of redress in environmental cases. All of these actions have created a pressing need for specialized public information campaigns about the new legal opportunities available, both in terms of legal content and of procedures of redress. The more progressive legal provisions that are promulgated, the more there is a need for paralegal training and education. Looking back, much of the new legislation originated in the active engagement of environmental groups, rural development groups, and so on, and thus can also be seen in part as an outcome of active lobbying efforts of groups pushing for social change.

Even as alternative law organizations and paralegal programs tend to specialize and thus revolve around distinct issue areas and laws, they share a broadly similar approach in training and "forming" paralegals. This reflects the legacy they share as offspring of the earlier generation of alternative law activists. Groups such as FLAG and the PLL generated a training methodology and practical paralegal tools with enduring relevance, establishing standards adopted by later paralegal programs. The earlier wave of paralegalism created prototype modules on human rights, human rights situation analysis, and paralegal skills building and practice. As a result, standard paralegal training today includes: (i) analysis of the situation in which participants find themselves in human rights and sociopolitical terms; (ii) introduction to the philosophy of developmental legal advocacy (DLA) or legal

---

[29] Under the Law Student Practice Rule, senior law students are allowed to appear in court under the supervision of a competent lawyer. *See* Bar Matter No. 730 (June 13, 1997), www.lawphil.net/courts/bm/bm_730_1997.html. And as already mentioned, in DAR, a contractual position called paralegal has also been created, but this is purely to help the adjudicators to decide on cases and finish the backlogs, and involves non-lawyers and law graduates who have not (yet) passed the bar exam. *See* DAR Opinion No. 109-96, www.lis.dar.gov.ph/documents/998. This is paralegal work in a more restricted conventional sense (an assistant to a lawyer), but is also unique in the sense that this also indirectly contributes to the resolution of cases of farmers and landowners.

empowerment defined as the use of the law to creatively empower people, reform laws, assert rights, and hold the state or corporations accountable; and (iii) instruction in the specific human rights norms and legal principles that have application to participants' situations, in basic paralegal skills such as gathering evidence and making affidavits, and in advanced paralegal skills focusing on particular issue areas (e.g., collective bargaining, lobbying local government).[30]

V. TYPES OF PARALEGALS

This study uncovered numerous types of paralegals, which have been "captured" in the typology outlined in Box 3.3.

BOX 3.3: BASIC PARALEGAL TYPOLOGY

Type A: Grassroots Organization Paralegal. Member of a grassroots organization, usually labor (factory based) or agrarian (landholding based), who is deployed by the organization as a paralegal. Grassroots organizations are associations of the poor themselves (e.g., workers, peasants, or fisher folk) and whose members and leaders come from this sector. Grassroots organization paralegals are typically supported by a rights advocacy group, an NGO composed of professionals rendering services for the poor. Rights advocacy groups include KAISAHAN, SALIGAN, BALAOD, RIGHTS, WLB, and CLB. KAISAHAN, for example, has social science graduates and lawyers among its staff, and is dedicated to rural development, agrarian reform, and local governance issues.

Type B: Roving (Territorial) Leader-Organizer Paralegal. Member of a people's organization (PO) or network with a regional scope, for instance, an indigenous community with ancestral domain claims spread across numerous villages and municipalities, or a human rights advocate's network covering several provinces, or grassroots leaders deputized to enforce specific environmental laws, in a particular ecological zone spread across several municipalities (ELAC, PANLIPI, TK, FLAG).

Type C: Law Student Paralegal. Volunteer students who perform community legal education, election monitoring, case build-up, and legal advice and assistance (AHRC).

Type D: Office-Based/Hired Paralegal. NGO staff members who document cases, provide legal information, and assist lawyers (KANLUNGAN, PALIPI).

---

[30] See Annex A.

> BOX 3.3: (Cont.)
> **Type E: Mainstreamed Community Paralegal.** Community members who are trained by NGOs (or local officials themselves trained by NGOs) and based in a local government unit (LGU) while performing paralegal functions for the benefit of affected community members (KANLUNGAN, WLB, CLB).
> **Type F: Law Enforcement Paralegal.** Community members or members of grassroots organizations who have been entrusted by the local or the national government agencies with some form of law enforcement functions. The two most common types of these paralegals are the forest guards (*bantay gubat*) and municipal water guards (*bantay dagat*).

Among our respondents, the Type A paralegal was the most prevalent, which coincides with the availability of a state-mandated forum for the practice of paralegalism.[31]

SECTOR/ISSUE	NGO	TYPE OF PARALEGAL					
		Grassroots Leaders/ Paralegals	Roving Paralegal	Law Student Paralegal	Office Based Paralegal	Mainstreaming LGU	Law Enforcement
Agrarian Reform/ Peasants	Balaod Mindanaw						
	KAISAHAN						
	RIGHTSnet						
Children	CLB						
Environment	ELAC						
	TK						
Gender	WLB						
HRE	AHRC						
HRV	FLAG						
IP	PANLIPI						
Labor	SALIGAN						
Migrants	Kanlungan						

FIGURE 3.1 Incidence of paralegals by type of organization

---

[31] See Figure 3.1, "Incidence of Paralegals by Type of Organization."

VI. FACILITATING AND HINDERING CIRCUMSTANCES

A number of factors have helped to promote the paralegal system in the Philippines. There is a scarcity of public interest lawyers, for example, which creates a substantial need for paralegals to fill in the gap. At the same time, despite the successful emergence and development of the work of paralegals, a number of factors continue to impede their efforts (like continuity of funding). This section examines both sets of factors, those that facilitate paralegalism in the Philippines and those that often impede its effective advancement.

A. Facilitating Circumstances

1. Public Interest Lawyers

One factor identified as facilitating the emergence of paralegalism is the *scarcity of public interest lawyers*. Relatively few lawyers choose to go into public interest law in the Philippines because of a combination of low pay and potential danger. This trend resonates with the experience in the United States, where only 6.7 percent of law graduates took on public interest jobs in 2010.[32]

Entry-level positions for public interest lawyers at NGOs typically pay US$500 to US$900 per month. This is quite low, as compared to the entry-level salary of lawyers who work as public attorneys in the government service, who would earn typically US$1,400 per month, including their allowances, such as transportation. The entry-level salary of lawyers in the law firms would be similar to that of public interest lawyers; however, many lawyers are attracted to the firms because of their bonuses and profit-sharing schemes, which augment the basic salary significantly.

New lawyers often have school loans to pay off or other pressing personal financial obligations, which militates against taking such low-paying jobs. Moreover, doing public interest law in the Philippines can expose one to the same hostile forces and sociopolitical environments that confront the lawyers' clients. Lawyers are not immune from harassment or death threats, and the threat is often severe enough to keep many away. The scarcity of public interest lawyers means that it is necessary to mobilize non-lawyers to help fill the gaps.

Yet the scarcity also means that the networks of persons who do become public interest lawyers become all the more important, as they are the ones who provide the training, legal "clinic-ing," and mentoring needed to support a paralegal movement. This, then, is the second factor seen as facilitating

---

[32] Sally Kane, "Public Interest Law: A Guide to Legal Public Service Careers," *The Balance*, last modified September 15, 2016, www.thebalance.com/public-interest-law-2164664.

paralegalism, which perhaps ironically directly contradicts the first: despite their small number, a strong *network of public interest lawyers exists nonetheless, capable of anchoring and guiding paralegal programs*. The country's long tradition of public interest lawyering, reinvigorated during the dictatorship and carried on in later decades, is a contributing factor here. Some of the study's informants went further by saying that without lawyers to train and guide paralegals, there can be no paralegal movement – a stronger formulation that reflects growing concern that the traditional alternative law movement may be losing and not gaining momentum, in part because fewer lawyers are joining its ranks and in part because of the dwindling funds for existing paralegal programs and operations (a hindering factor discussed later in this chapter).

2. Institutional Support

This also points to a deeper issue: to what extent paralegal work, anchored and guided by public interest lawyers, is institutionalized within both the government and the nongovernmental spheres (for more discussion, see Section VI.C). *Institutionalization* is clearly seen as facilitating and sustaining paralegalism. The underlying assertion is that both public interest lawyers and paralegals are expanding access to justice to previously excluded groups, and thus both need to be incorporated into more formal institutional structures and in this way sustained in order for paralegal formation programs to survive. Institutionalization is not automatic or fixed over time, but must be continuously cultivated, particularly as there is concern among some informants that traditional sources of funding for paralegal programs are drying up. In practical terms, institutionalization refers to several things: (i) the existence of civil society organizations (CSOs) that can absorb and deploy public interest lawyers as paralegal program anchors; (ii) the existence of real opportunities and recognized venues for paralegals to operate and practice their skills; and (iii) the existence of what one informant called "institutional sustaining mechanisms" that can ensure the survival of paralegal programs, including (if not especially) institutional (versus piecemeal project) funds for the CSOs that host and midwife paralegal programs and work.

The institutional, programmatic, and operational sustainability of paralegal work since the collapse of the Marcos dictatorship is closely tied to *long-term donor support for the ALG network*. This refers particularly to funding from numerous foreign agencies, especially the Ford Foundation and the Asia Foundation, the Dutch funding agencies – the Catholic Organization for Relief and Development Aid (CORDAID) and the Netherlands Organization for International Assistance (NOVIB) – and the German funding agency – the German Catholic Bishops' Organisation for Development Cooperation (MISEREOR). The Paralegal Education Skills Advancement and Networking

Technology (PESANTEch) paralegal program (1994–2006), for example, an initiative of ALG members engaged in agrarian reform work, was made possible through such long-term funding. Meanwhile, the creation of a fund dedicated to legal defense work is another mechanism that serves to sustain paralegal work, as in the ALG's Environmental Defense Program or "EnDefense," which provides funds for legal defense in environmental cases.[33] The extent that paralegal work threatens to upset an unjust status quo, increase claim-making, and facilitate social justice activism often provokes legal offensives by entrenched elites (as a form of harassment), making it necessary to divert scarce financial resources away from the social change work itself and into legal defense. Having a dedicated legal defense fund can ease this problem to some extent.

In sum, the institutionalization of paralegal programs in the governmental and nongovernmental spheres could be a sustaining mechanism; however, and especially for the nongovernment sector, the process of institutionalization is dependent on whether these groups have adequate funding in the future.

3. Community Organizing

Also seen as a crucial factor facilitating paralegal programs and work is *community organizing and PO building work*. The essential notion that strong (well-organized and active) grassroots or POs facilitate community-based paralegal efforts makes sense intuitively. The very kind of paralegals this study is concerned with are those who explicitly endeavor to serve a particular group or category of people who are perceived as inadequately recognized as rights holders and/or whose human rights are deemed insufficiently defined, guaranteed, or fulfilled by the state in practice. An important political resource for people in this situation is their capacity to organize and mobilize social pressure. This is particularly critical in settings where "good law" exists, and the next challenge of making law and legal rights actually *authoritative in society* requires a struggle against powerful, entrenched interests.[34] In the Philippines, the mixed, uneven, and often hostile sociopolitical setting has given rise to community-based paralegal formation as part of a broader political strategy. The ALG network members refer to this strategy as "legal-metalegal,"[35]

---

[33] For more information about this program, see "EnDefense," Alternative Law Groups, Inc. http://alternativelawgroups.ph/index.php/projects/curent-projects/endefense.

[34] See Franco, "Making Land Rights Accessible," 998 (see n. 7).

[35] Legal-metalegal strategies involve a combination of purely legal work with actions that are lawful but not traditionally considered legal work. For example, when lawyers are debating a heated proposal in Congress, their supporters could hold a public rally or demonstration outside, or even silently drop a banner in the gallery to support a certain advocacy. Alternative Law Groups, Inc., *Final Output Report – Alternative Law Groups, Inc. National Paralegal Conference: Collecting Stories, Exchanging Models* (Quezon City: GOP-UNDP, 2006), 26.

a concept that emphasizes the limitations of a purely legal strategy and the need for organized, "metalegal" collective action as well. Other groups (such as RIGHTS) have framed this kind of strategy as "rightful resistance."[36]

Different groups have different understandings of what "strong" organization means in practice. There is likely general agreement that the ideal situation involves: (i) well-trained and accountable paralegals; (ii) well-organized and dynamic communities at the grassroots; and (iii) a mutually reinforcing relationship between the two. Beyond this there appears to be a diversity of ideas on how this ideal is to be achieved and sustained. One issue involves the question of who should do what – for example, who should do the organizing or who should do the paralegal formation and mentoring work. The theory within the ALG is that a legal NGO (that is, the member organizations of the ALG) should partner with other organizations that specialize in and can take charge of the community organizing work. The idea is to achieve a synergy and complementarity of work, for example, with one NGO partner doing the community organizing work and the other doing the legal work and paralegal formation. In practice, however, problems can arise for whatever reason; the community organizing work is not sustained and the legal NGO ends up left alone to address the legal work/paralegal formation *and* the community organizing/PO-building work. Several study informants have found themselves in such a situation, which they described as a dilemma and a source of debate within the legal NGO as well as within the ALG network more broadly (see also the discussion of decreased funding in Section VI.B.1).

4. Responsive Local Officials

A final set of facilitating factors involves *state structures and government officials*, especially at more local levels. Respondents spoke of the importance to their work of open, friendly, and approachable local government officials, especially at the *barangay* (village) level. Beyond personal politics with government officials, they placed value in *barangay*-level structures and strategies, where the paralegals trained through NGO formation programs could be embedded, such as the *barangay* development councils and the *barangay* justice system structures. These are venues where they can voice the objectives of their advocacy efforts, such as the need for a dedicated committee on violence against women, as advocated by paralegals in Marikina City on the island of Luzon. Part of the logic has to do with the fact that

---

[36] See Kevin J. O'Brien and Lianjiang Li, *Rightful Resistance in Rural China* (Cambridge: Cambridge University Press, 2006) (providing an explanation of the concept). *See* Saturnino M. Borras Jr. and Jennifer C. Franco, "Struggles for Land and Livelihood: Redistributive Reform in Agribusiness Plantations in the Philippines," *Critical Asian Studies* 37, no. 3 (2005): 331–61, doi: 10.1080/14672710500200383 (applying the concept to the Philippines' case).

barangay units, led by the *barangay* captain (the elected village head), have the authority to issue ordinances or orders to regulate everyday social relations in a village on a whole range of matters. For example, among other directives, *barangay* captains can issue a *barangay* protection order (BPO) in cases of violence against women or children, ordering the offender to desist from committing or threatening harm to the victim (woman or child). Having a good relationship with local officials enables one to have a potentially positive influence on how local officials respond to injustice.

If local officials are open and friendly, paralegals are: (i) better able to maximize localized opportunities to deepen and extend their rights education work; (ii) better able to efficiently and effectively respond to serious incidents requiring "first aid legal aid"; and (iii) potentially able to gain access to sustaining resources for their work, at least in the medium term (that is, under the current government administration), such as a physical base for their practice or financial support to cover operational expenses. Such "closeness" to a given *barangay* administration does not come without its own risks, however; most obviously, if that official does not get reelected, there is a possibility that such benefits will be lost (e.g., and transferred to someone else).

Recognition by officials in relevant government agencies and units is likewise perceived as a facilitating factor, despite potential pitfalls. An interesting distinction here can be made between official and unofficial recognition. In one case, for instance, paralegals who must frequently interact with local court employees and officials engage in what they call "alliance work" in order to befriend them and win their respect, so that even without official recognition of their work as paralegals, eventually they are given unofficial recognition as representatives of their organizations, which in their experience serves them well. In other cases, more formal types of state recognition are perceived as essential for their work, including: (i) official recognition relative to dispute tribunals under DAR and the Department of Labor and Employment (DOLE), respectively; and (ii) official deputization by law enforcement agencies such as the Bureau of Fisheries and Aquatic Resources (BFAR) and the Department of Environment and Natural Resources (DENR) for *bantay gubat* (community-based forest guards) and *bantay dagat* (community-based coast guards). These forest or coast guards deputized by the state agencies recognize the difficulty of law enforcement in very wide areas such as hard-to-reach forests and expansive coastal areas in an archipelagic country such as the Philippines. The informants expressed limited success in these areas, and more extensive cooperation between the paralegals and government law enforcement agencies is required.

For other participants, more crucial (and more acceptable) than official state recognition is unofficial but formal recognition in the form of identification cards issued by legal NGOs to those they train as paralegals.

B. Hindering Circumstances

1. Low Capacity and Declining Funding

Numerous factors were viewed as hindrances to the successful practice of paralegalism. One is the *low capacity of CSOs to absorb the public interest lawyers* needed to anchor and guide paralegal practice and programs, a problem linked to *decreased funding for public interest law work* in general. In the Philippines, CSOs primarily provide the platform upon which the public interest lawyers are able to do their work. Although there has been long-term donor support in this area, many traditional sources of funding for both alternative law activism and paralegal formation programs in the Philippines have been shifting away from such work.

This situation is further compounded by the lack of resources (time and money) legal NGOs devote to paralegal monitoring and evaluation (M&E) systems. M&E systems have been given a low priority by legal NGO leaders and paralegal program funders alike, according to study informants, who also cite limited resources as the reason for this (e.g., given limited funds, priority should be given to training over M&E). There is a basic consensus as well that M&E is unnecessary and a waste of time and resources. As one respondent said, "why devote time, effort, and funds to monitoring and evaluation, when we already know that paralegal work contributes to access to justice?" Since the paralegal work is not properly documented and evaluated, it becomes harder for the NGOs to provide evidence to funders that such types of paralegal activities work and are effective.

2. Corrupt or Indifferent Local Officials

Another hindering factor is the phenomenon of *erring local government officials*, who, instead of upholding and fulfilling state law, violate it. Seeing government officials violate the law has an immediate "chilling" effect on paralegal work. This point was emphasized by an informant who provides legal and paralegal support to impoverished and marginalized rural communities struggling against local government–sanctioned large- and small-scale mining operations that have been ravaging fragile ecosystems, livelihoods, and the health of local populations across a huge area. Such scenes are replicated in remote communities across the Philippines and are thus not rare.

Paralegals commonly encounter local officials who are not aware of certain new provisions of the law. For example, in the Fisheries Code, the local government is now in charge of declaring marine protected areas for coastal management.[37] Typically, the paralegals engage local governments and try to

---

[37] Republic Act No. 8550.

convince them to enforce this new legislation for the common good. But when the local officials themselves sanction illegal practices, such as unauthorized small-scale mining, then the local government officials themselves become hindering factors.

Less dramatic but perhaps more common are local government officials who are "unsympathetic" to a given cause in which paralegals have become active, even when the latter are "in the right" in legal terms. One example is the case of farmers who were threatened by their former landowners with dispossession despite possessing Certificate of Land Ownership Awards (CLOA) issued by the national government under the agrarian reform program.

A related hindering factor is the *lack of support in the communities for specific initiatives in paralegalism*. This point was raised especially by a group of women paralegals working at the *barangay* level on issues of violence against women, who felt that their efforts were not supported enough by the *barangay* officials. Despite the existence of a government policy mandating that 5 percent of the local government budget go toward financing gender and development work, such as local anti-VAWC efforts, the *barangay* officials in these paralegals' area of work had yet to release any funds. Unwilling or unable to force local officials to release the money, the paralegals could continue their work only by tapping into their own respective personal household finances. Although this example points specifically to the gap between official policy on paper and realities on the ground, it also may suggest a need to combine localized pressure politics with more "scaled-up" advocacy, since it is likely a problem facing paralegals who are trying to "engender *barangay* justice" elsewhere in the country.

3. Physical and Legal Threats

The phenomenon of "erring officials" reflects the partial and uneven way in which post-Marcos democratization has proceeded below the national level. In many villages, it is still regional authoritarian elites, backed by private armies and commanding extensive patronage networks, who determine which "law" rules in reality.[38] This kind of setting is behind the next factor seen as a major hindrance to paralegal work, namely, *physical and legal harassment*, which arises especially in cases where paralegals are involved in struggles against a prevailing status quo perceived as unjust, if not unlawful. Examples include: (i) cases where members of a grassroots organization – including its paralegals – get slapped with criminal charges in the course of

---

[38] See Franco, "Making Land Rights Accessible," 996 (see n. 7); Jennifer C. Franco, "Peripheral Justice? Rethinking Justice Sector in the Philippines," *World Development* 36, no. 10 (2008): 1858–73, http://dx.doi.org/10.1016/j.worlddev.2007.10.011.

trying to push forward the implementation of the government's agrarian reform law; or (ii) cases where *bantay gubat* face criminal charges after attempting to carry out their duties as government-deputized forest guards by confiscating the profits of illegal logging activity. In cases such as these, the filing of criminal charges by an entrenched power holder who feels threatened is just one side of the coin; the other side is the use of coercion and violence.[39] In some cases, the agents of such violence are neither state actors nor corporate elites, but the anti-state New People's Army.[40]

4. Skepticism of Paralegals' Abilities

In a different vein, the paralegal movement has also been hindered by the persistence of a *"lawyer-centered" legal consciousness* among ordinary citizens, including paralegals themselves, which leads them to doubt their own capacity to study and practice law. Some paralegals interviewed for the study framed the problem as: they are not lawyers but are dealing with the law, so they have to be cautious, otherwise they might find themselves in an awkward position (*ma-alanganin*). A lawyer-centered legal consciousness is prevalent among government officials as well. The strong perception that only lawyers can know and should practice law makes it difficult for paralegals to gain effective recognition, whether formally or informally, even in venues where they are officially recognized by law, such as the quasi-judicial labor tribunals. As one labor paralegal said, "The [labor] arbiters look down on paralegals" ("*Mababa ang pagtingin sa mga paralegal ng mga arbiter*"). Labor arbiters who "look down" on union and migrant labor paralegals sometimes harass them by creating technical obstacles, such as asking for additional authorization from the union or the union board. There is skepticism and suspicion of paralegals in the regular court system also, as seen in the Supreme Court's effort to limit the range of paralegal work and the prohibition against the "unauthorized practice of law" – a decision issued in the context of the Access to Justice Project funded by the European Union.[41]

---

[39] The long list of names of all those who have been killed – even just in the past five years – while trying to hold powerful elites or companies accountable by mobilizing existing state law is proof of how real this threat is.

[40] *See* Borras and Franco, "Struggles for Land and Livelihood" (see n. 36).

[41] The Access to Justice Project is a joint undertaking between the Government of the Philippines and the European Union. The Financing Agreement was signed in August 2004. The implementing agency from the Philippine government was supposed to be the Supreme Court. However, in the decision cited later, the Supreme Court has ruled that it was not the proper institution to handle the project, considering the separation of powers theory. In the course of handing out the decision, it also made a comment on the role of paralegals in the information centers as contained in the project design. A.M. No. 05-2-01-SC dated February 15, 2005. See Box 3.5.

> BOX 3.4: SUPREME COURT POSITION ON PARALEGALS
>
> A.M. No. 05-2-01-SC dated Feb. 15, 2005
> **RE: SC ACCESS TO JUSTICE FOR THE POOR PROJECT**
> **Training and Employment of Paralegals in Various Aspects of the Project Violates Existing Jurisprudence**
>
> It bears noting that the implementation of the Project relies heavily on paralegals as an essential component of the Project. Necessarily, these paralegals would engage in the practice of law which this Court in *Cayetano v. Monsod*,[14] defined as "any activity, in or out of court, which requires the application of law, legal procedure, knowledge, training and experience."[15] But the use of paralegals may be improper since under Philippine law, a person who has not been admitted as an attorney cannot practice law for the proper administration of justice cannot be hindered by the unwarranted intrusion of an unauthorized and unskilled person into the practice of law.[16] As the OCAt (Office of the Court Attorney) astutely points out:
>
> *The TAPS (Technical and Administrative Provisions) mentions the training of paralegals that shall be fielded in the implementation of the Project. Paralegals are not a common breed in this country. Although the Court has supported approval by the Commission on Higher Education of the proposal of the Manuel L. Quezon University to offer the course of Bachelor of Science in Paralegals, such support is circumscribed by the requirement that the course shall be a pre-law course. <u>Authorizing the practice of paralegals in the country is still being studied by the Committee on Legal Education and Bar Matters because of the need to regulate their practice</u> in much the same way that the practice of the members of the Integrated Bar of the Philippines is subject to the Court's rule-making authority.[17] Parenthetically, if the Project were to be properly implemented, the participation of the IBP is necessary.*
>
> The Office <u>concurs with the position of the OCAt</u> *that the Committee on Legal Education and Bar Matters (CLEBM) is still studying the prospect of certifying paralegals. Taking into account this development, the utilization of the paralegals in the <u>implementation of the Project could be held in abeyance pending proper sanction from the CLEBM</u>. We also acknowledge that the participation of the Integrated Bar of the Philippines in this Project is necessary.*[42] (Note: Emphasis and underscoring supplied, internal citations omitted.)

5. Weak Grassroots Organizations

Meanwhile, whereas strong (well-organized and active) *grassroots or POs* are seen as facilitating community-based paralegal efforts, conversely, the absence of such

---

[42] A.M. No. 05-2-01-SC dated February 15, 2005.

grassroots efforts is seen as creating sociopolitical dynamics that can undermine paralegal work. This can be from a lack of active involvement by the whole organization or community, to a lack of accountability and legitimacy on the part of the paralegal. When community organizing work and organizational strengthening efforts are not sustained in conjunction with paralegal practice, problems can result. For instance, in areas where labor unions are becoming weaker, there is increasing pressure on the legal NGOs doing paralegal formation work to do some of the organizing work also, thereby diverting attention and resources away from the paralegal formation work proper. On the agrarian reform front, a similar problem is emerging, as it is increasingly difficult to find one partner who can do the community organizing effort in conjunction with another partner doing the paralegal formation work. Stalled progress on one front can impact the other negatively, launching a downward spiral that is difficult to stop or reverse.

C. Selected Issues for Debate

In sorting through which factors facilitate and which hinder the emergence and growth of paralegalism, two issues emerged as key points of difference, disagreement, and/or debate, and therefore deserve special mention.

The first point has to do with the merits of *linking paralegal work to local government unit structures*, particularly official *barangay* structures. Two groups participating in the study, especially those addressing the rights and welfare of women or children (including migrant women and their children), have adopted a strategy of forging such linkages, framed as "mainstreaming" by one or "engendering" by another. This strategy was seen as logically flowing from the fact that when the rights of women and children are violated, the first responders tend to be *barangay* officials, who are traditionally and still oftentimes men and may not be sensitive or knowledgeable in their handling of such cases. Paralegals armed with specialized training are therefore urgently needed, both to intervene in cases arising on a day-to-day basis and to help influence and change the entrenched patriarchal culture that still largely determines local official response, especially in cases of VAWC.

In some cases, paralegal formation is oriented to lead directly into official community-based law enforcement structures (e.g., *bantay gubat, bantay dagat*) that emerged as a result of new environmental protection legislation. In the context of rampant violations of environmental protection laws and the persistence of an array of illegal economic activities harmful to local ecosystems, livelihoods, and community health, these new localized law enforcement structures were viewed as opportunities that had to be seized by people in the affected communities.

Here, it might be noted that paralegal formation can also become bound up with "unofficial" community-based law enforcement initiatives (such as *"bantay*

CADT"[43]). Such initiatives can emerge "from below" in a more spontaneous manner, often in response to those occasions when violations of environmental law are ignored (or facilitated) by local state law enforcement agents. The community-based initiatives thus operate in what might be called "the shadow of the law,"[44] that is, they are socially acceptable forms of collective regulatory action and may embody the spirit of the law, but they are not necessarily legitimate in a narrow formal-legal sense.

Unsurprisingly, many respondents expressed concerns about linking (or linking too closely) with local governments. This concern was expressed in several ways. Most common was the observation that electoral politics can "make or break" one's paralegal practice, depending on "whose side you're on" in an election. This is because in practice, local government structures themselves down to the village level are closely tied to election-fueled patronage networks. Indeed, in the Philippines, the capacity to engage with local government officials often has more to do with one's political and personal affiliations than the social relevance of the paralegal program; consequently, your strength can also become your weakness if the network you are affiliated with loses in the next election.

In sum, linking with local government units offers a lot of potential for paralegal work. The obvious advantage is the cloak of authority that the local government can provide, especially when such work (protecting women and children, environmental law enforcement) is within the remit of such local authority. But together with this advantage comes the limitations of working with such a structure, such as the change in the local officialdom every three years, and the instability that this can generate in the continuity of the work.

A second point of debate has to do with *whether and how the state should intervene and be involved in the certification and regulation of all paralegals*. This is an especially thorny issue that touches upon core elements of community-based paralegalism. Arguments in favor of state intervention through certification and regulation include: (i) the legitimizing effects that state certification can have on the activities and efforts of paralegals, especially when facing resistance from local elites; and (ii) the salutary effects that state regulation can have on paralegal practice through the setting of performance standards. Here, state intervention is seen as a potential safeguard against poor quality or corrupt practices. Arguments against state intervention include: (i) that it can also be used to filter out perceived "undesirables" based on social or political biases; and (ii) that it can end up filtering out the very kinds of people (e.g., from the poor and marginalized groups) that community-based paralegalism tries to tap and mobilize. As an alternative,

---

[43] CADT stands for Certificate of Ancestral Domain Title, which is a tenurial instrument, a land title issued by the government under the Indigenous People's Right Act (IPRA) in order to secure the land rights of indigenous peoples.

[44] Marc Galanter, "Justice in Many Rooms: Courts, Private Ordering, and Indigenous Law," *Journal of Legal Pluralism and Unofficial Law* 13, no. 19 (1981): 1–47, doi: 10.1080/07329113.1981.10756257.

some respondents suggest either relying on CSO-led certification and regulation or coursing state intervention through the governmental Commission on Human Rights.

VII. THE WORK OF PARALEGALS: THREE DIMENSIONS

The conventional notion of a paralegal in the context of Western legal practice is as an assistant to a lawyer. Even the initial discourse of Diokno on the role of the paralegal carries that sense of saving time for human rights lawyers to do more of the "creative aspects of their job."[45] But since then, in the context of developmental legal practice in contemporary times, the work that community paralegals have undertaken and continue to undertake has encompassed and moved beyond these traditional notions. The work of a paralegal today can be categorized along three dimensions: (a) building rights awareness; (b) settling private disputes; and (c) increasing state and corporate accountability.

A. Building Rights Awareness

The most elemental task of paralegals is building awareness of the rights of the poor and other marginalized groups. The term *rights* is understood in a multifaceted fashion. Prior to 1986, internationally accepted human rights standards were invoked in the Philippines to counteract the restrictive and oppressive rules laid down by the martial law regime (e.g., the issue of arrest search and seizure orders [ASSO] used against those identified as "enemies of the state"). After 1986, in the context of struggles for democratization and democratic deepening, rights awareness work could now cite the new constitution and various new laws (or their progressive provisions and elements) that ongoing social pressure helped to shape. Campaigns to make "ordinary people" more aware of their human and legal rights now increasingly include a new dimension as well: struggles to use state law to claim and enforce rights. Paralegal training today makes a clear distinction between legal literacy (know your rights) and skills training (taking action to enforce and implement your rights). A typical training for paralegals would include: (i) a "situationer" on the specific sector (or population) of concern (e.g., the national and local situation on the state of indigenous peoples); (ii) the human rights and legal rights pertinent to that sector; and (iii) the skills that may be needed in order to enforce those rights.[46]

The martial law era modules on paralegal training typically contained skills building on how to preserve evidence, how to make an affidavit based on what one has personally witnessed (e.g., very useful when someone has been arrested by the military), and which government agencies to approach in cases of human rights

---

[45] *See* Box 3.2; Diokno, "Developmental Legal Aid in Rural ASEAN," (see n. 12).   [46] *See* Annex A.

violations. Today, with the various arenas that new legislation has opened to public interest lawyers and paralegals, this aspect of training is more elaborate. Next is a sampling of the various "how to" elements (such as skills) taught in paralegal training programs today:

- How to secure a protection order from the village chieftain based on a complaint of a woman who has been abused by her husband;
- How to make a citizen's arrest of fishermen involved in dynamite or cyanide fishing;
- How to lobby the LGUs (specifically the municipal government) to declare a certain body of water as a protected area;
- How to follow through with the government for the issuance of agrarian reform land titles, from the identification of the beneficiaries and the valuation of the property to the final issuance of title;
- How to represent farmers or workers in the agrarian or labor tribunals, respectively, and argue their case to its successful conclusion; and
- How to lobby and advocate for a change in the laws and regulations at the national and local government levels.

The increased awareness of community groups and their ability to act on such awareness was noted in an evaluative study done by the Filipino NGO Social Weather Stations:

- **Knowledge of the Law.** In the battery of knowledge questions, generally, more survey respondents in the ALG target areas got the correct answers to the questions ranging from general concept of rights, to specific provisions on sectoral issues, such as women's rights, environment, labor and people living with HIV/AIDS.
- **Ability to Translate Knowledge to Action.** There is a marked difference between ALG partners and non-ALG partners' ability to assess and act on a legal problem. The ALG partners say they are fairly knowledgeable, and find it not too difficult to act. This is likely a result of education campaigns and paralegal trainings; paralegals and trainees score even higher.[47]

Although important, this first dimension of work can achieve only so much on its own, since even if paralegals are well armed with rights awareness and legal skills knowledge, *access* to justice often remains problematic. Experience suggests that gaining knowledge does not automatically lead to success; as one informant put it, "paralegal knowledge is very useful, but implementation is the problem." Among the informants there was a perception too that increased rights awareness and

---

[47] Social Weather Stations, *Research on the Poor Accessing Justice and the ALG as Justice Reform Advocate*. Inroads: ALG Study Series (Social Weather Stations, Inc., Alternative Law Groups, Inc., 2008), 82–83.

paralegal skills can lead to frustration and inaction in the absence of successful outcomes, especially the more one's understanding grows of how conflicts actually get processed. As one of our respondents said: "paralegal training is great in terms of legal literacy, but doesn't help much in achieving real results in actuality because it all gets derailed in the process; government agencies that ought to implement don't, and citizens feel that they are the ones who have to implement." As this shows, many political factors are perceived as beyond the control of paralegals, no matter how well trained. The skills training part of paralegal instruction and formation today does emphasize the need for collective action on the part of citizens in the enforcement of rights and the implementation of programs, but in the end, what matters to the affected people are the results of any legal-metalegal action. Any attempt to look more closely at whether, when, and how paralegalism is actually effective in expanding access to justice would thus have to delve into the relationship between legal and metalegal action.

Meanwhile, paralegal formation efforts, including the rights awareness–building aspect, can lead to important but unexpectedly finite results. For example, with regard to paralegal work on the agrarian reform front, one of our respondents pointed out that in her experience, once the land title is issued by DAR, there is a tendency for the community-based paralegal, who, as a member of a farmers organization is likewise a beneficiary of the agrarian reform program, to become inactive since the most immediate outcome of the farmers' campaign has been achieved. In the Philippines, land reform campaigns take more effort and time than is usually anticipated, exhausting the members of the farmers' organizations and their resources in the process, thus giving rise to a kind of "battle fatigue." When the struggle for the land has been finally "won," there may be a tendency for the farmers' organizations and their paralegals to demobilize to focus on more immediate household-level concerns, even if the next immediate challenge (such as to make the land productive) or subsequent other challenges (e.g., such as to put a stop to illegal fishing, if the agrarian reform community is also partly a fishing village) remain. Some advocates argue that this kind of situation requires creative interaction between the paralegal, the community organizers, and the legal NGO workers supporting the paralegals to devise sustaining strategies for the continued involvement of paralegals in the area. Others would say that it is up to the organizations' leaders and members to determine the next moves and whether or how paralegal work might fit in.

B. Settling Private Disputes

A second area of work is the settling of private disputes. In the Philippine context, the settlement of private disputes is not a high priority for the kind of paralegals studied here. Because paralegalism in the Philippines historically has been tied to social change-oriented, social movement actors, it tends to address issues affecting traditionally marginalized segments of the population (such as farmers, fisher folk, women, indigenous communities, political detainees), or broad public interest issues that can affect the entire population or an entire community (including environmental issues such as clean air and water and other pollution concerns, illegal logging and dynamite fishing, and so on). This is not to say that Filipino paralegals are not involved in settling private disputes at all, as they are in fact. For instance, one participant explained that due to his reputation as a paralegal and labor leader, he is often asked by people in his neighborhood, which is also home to many other members of his labor union, to mediate family disputes.

One factor that competes with paralegal intervention in private dispute settlement is the presence of formal and informal structures of mediation at the community level, which rely on customary methods of conciliation. Notable here is the BJS (*katarungang pambarangay*), which was introduced during the Marcos dictatorship in 1978 as a compulsory venue for certain kinds of disputes, and was later reiterated in the Local Government Code of 1991.[48] The BJS has reported an uptake of more than 6 million cases from 1980 to 2008, of which 79 percent were settled, 6 percent went to the courts, and the rest had varied outcomes.[49]

Many observers agree that the BJS has some advantages over the regular courts as a venue for dispute processing and that it is gaining acceptance as a dispute-resolution forum. But there are also concerns about the "double-edged" nature of the "traditions" upon which BJS is based – especially clientelist politics and gender bias.[50] In many remote rural villages and indigenous communities, village leaders often serve as conduits for mediation and conciliation even in criminal matters such as murder and rape.[51] One problem here may be competing ideas of what constitutes a just outcome in such cases; another underlying problem is power. As Nader has put it: "If there is any single generalization that has ensued from the anthropological research on disputing processes ... it is that mediation and negotiation require conditions of relatively equal power."[52] In the Philippines, as elsewhere, such conditions may hold sometimes, but certainly not always.

Another factor that can dampen demand for paralegal services is the parallel phenomenon, cited earlier, of the "privatization of paralegal services" through an

[48] See Vigo and Manuel, *Katarungang Pambarangay: A Handbook* (see n. 17), http://accessfacility.org /sites/default/files/Katarungang%20Pambarangay%20Handbook_0.pdf.
[49] Barraca, Delorino, Duman, Dumlao, Grepo, Ocampo, Reyes, and Salazar, *Understanding the Katarungang Pambarangay: Justice at the Grassroots* (Guanzon: University of the Philippines – College of Law, 2009), 11, www.slideshare.net/nehruvalera/21200493-understandingthekatarungangpam barangay.
[50] See Stephen Golub, "Non-state Justice Systems in Bangladesh and the Philippines" (paper presented for the UK Department for International Development, London, January 2003), 13–14.
[51] Franco, "Making Land Rights Accessible" (see n. 7).
[52] Laura Nader, "The Underside of Conflict Management – in Africa and Elsewhere," *IDS Bulletin* 32, no. 1 (2009): 22.

abogadillo. A Spanish term that means a "small lawyer," it is also used pejoratively to refer to persons who claim to be knowledgeable in the law and charge money for their services (often unreasonable amounts), but who produce outcomes that may or may not be legitimate. Sometimes, paralegal trainees who are the products of NGO-led paralegal formation programs end up breaking away from their base organizations to go into "practice" on their own. To illustrate, one of the paralegals from Quezon province cited an incident where an *abogadillo* was charging 5,000 pesos (roughly US$120) to secure an order from DAR that is in fact a public document and available free of charge. This phenomenon has caused concern within the alternative law movement because of the perceived lack of accountability and quality control, although there are few actual reports of this type of problem to date.

Meanwhile, what constitutes a "private dispute" may itself be a shifting, socially constructed category determined in part by the historical-institutional context and in part by the perceptions and interpretations of any number of parties. For example, some respondents identified the following as qualifying as private dispute settlement: (i) mediating farmer-to-farmer disputes over allocation of land within a certain estate or landholding; (ii) mediating land disputes using indigenous customary law systems in tribal communities; or (iii) settling family disputes between spouses and children in urban poor communities. However, at different moments and under different political conditions, each of these issues could also be conceived not as strictly private disputes, but rather as disputes that can and perhaps should be addressed as a matter of public interest as well, especially in light of the relatively new laws governing land property rights and relations and violence against women and children, for example.

Finally, some respondents from the judicial sector highlighted a need to attend to the more commonplace legal concerns of the unorganized poor, especially in far-flung communities. Because public interest law NGOs focus on organized groups and the Public Attorney's Offices (an adjunct of the Department of Justice [DOJ]) focus on indigent litigants, this leaves a gap in addressing the legal needs of the unorganized poor.[53] One trial court judge in a poor municipality in Mindanao said that she often found herself having to advise poor litigants on their legal rights and responsibilities. The unorganized poor usually have little or no access to legal services in cases such as death benefits claims, discrepancies in the records of birth, marriage, or death, and issues of registration during election time, among other matters. One top official of the DOJ recalls participating in joint legal and medical missions in rural poor

---

[53] More often than not, indigent litigants have access to legal services because they belong to organized communities and therefore know of their right to seek legal support when necessary. The unorganized poor however do not have the capacity or awareness to participate in decisions affecting them because "they are objectively and subjectively powerless." Asian Development Bank, *Law and Policy Reform at the Asian Development Bank* (Asian Development Bank, 2001), 77.

villages where the queues for those seeking legal assistance were longer than for those seeking medical assistance, indicating to him, rather unexpectedly, a real unmet need for basic legal services.

C. Increasing State and Corporate Accountability

1. State Accountability

Increasing awareness of human and legal rights is intertwined with a third dimension of paralegal work hinging on a human rights law framework. In this framework, the state is the primary "duty bearer" in relation to citizens as "rights holders," especially those who are poor, disadvantaged, and marginalized. Since states have the moral and legal responsibility to protect, defend, and fulfill the human rights of their citizens, much paralegal practice in the Philippines today revolves around working to increase state accountability, especially to poor and marginalized citizens in this sense.

Some of this state accountability work is international in character and involves mobilizing to push the Philippine government to carry out its obligations under international human rights law to protect, defend, and fulfill the human rights of its citizens. A good example is the rape case of Karen Vertido, which was brought to the attention of the Committee for the Elimination of Discrimination against Women (CEDAW) of the United Nations in 2007 and decided in July 2010.[54] In this case, CEDAW found that the trial court in the Philippines fell short of adhering to human rights principles when it dismissed the case in 1996, and recommended that the Philippine government provide "appropriate compensation commensurate with the gravity of the violations of her rights."[55] The decision also recommended that the government adopt structural changes in order to prevent rape and to improve the handling of rape cases.

By contrast, some of the state accountability work that Filipino paralegals are involved in is more national in character, revolving around the passage and meaningful implementation of national laws and associated policies and programs (e.g., the various national laws on agrarian reform and the rights of workers, women, children, migrants, indigenous peoples). In some cases, this can mean calling attention to situations in which state actors and agents of state law are involved as rights violators, such as when local officials are engaged in illegal economic activities, or the police or military units are involved in illegal detention

---

[54] Under the Optional Protocol to CEDAW, a decision of a local court could be reviewed by CEDAW if the decision fails to conform to internationally accepted principles protecting the rights of women. The case was originally brought to the attention of CEDAW by the Women's Legal Bureau, a member organization of the ALG.

[55] For the full story of this case, see Jerrie Abella, "UN Women's Committee Faults RP for Junking Rape Case," GMANews.tv, September 24, 2010, www.gmanetwork.com/news/story/201848/news/nation/un-women-s-committee-faults-rp-for-junking-rape-case.

and "salvaging,"[56] to name a few examples. Some of the legal tools that paralegals work with include the writ of *amparo*, the writ of *kalikasan*, and *barangay* protection orders, which are intended to protect a specific woman against domestic violence.[57]

A good example here is the now twenty-year-old struggle to implement the government's agrarian reform law and program. The first landmark legislation, the Comprehensive Agrarian Reform Law (CARL), was passed in 1988. Comprehensive land reform was mandated to take place within ten years, and soon after the law was passed, public interest lawyers and paralegals joined other rural reform activists as well as a broad coalition of peasant movements to work for its implementation. Intense social pressure from below was combined with pro-reform efforts from within DAR to distribute a significant amount of land and provide support services to many farmers.[58] Further mobilizations of social pressure served to ensure that the law was extended in 1998 for another ten years, and in 2008, another intensive campaign succeeded in securing a further extension of the program, this time from 2009 to 2014, or a period of five years. The work of paralegals was instrumental in providing the much-needed evidence of the weaknesses and shortcomings of the law as crafted. For example, landowners in the coconut-producing areas used criminal statutes in order to circumvent the intent of the law, and this practice was corrected in subsequent legislation. This long-standing national-level struggle for the launch and continuation of a state-led agrarian reform program and legislation can be seen as an example of paralegals' involvement in larger efforts to hold the state accountable for promises made in the constitution.

Finally, some state measures can be implemented only at the local level. For example, the declaration of marine protected areas for the regeneration of coral reefs and fish stock can be done only at the level of the municipality. Environmental NGOs and their paralegals must lobby at the local level for this safeguard, and the same is true with law enforcement in the form of *bantay gubat* and *bantay dagat*, a community-based type of paralegal mentioned earlier. Paralegals play a role in efforts to hold local officials accountable through various means, such as monitoring the utilization of the local budgets, attending the meetings of local special bodies (local development councils, peace and order councils, and so on), and if needed, filing cases with national government heads, or the Ombudsman in cases of graft and corruption or malversation. Some of our respondents report that in instances where local DENR officials are known to be involved in illegal logging, cases have to be

---

[56] *Salvaging* is a colloquial term in the Philippines that means extrajudicial killing or execution.
[57] The writ of *amparo* and the writ of *kalikasan* are explained in section 4.2. A *barangay* protection order is a preventive order issued by the village chieftain in order to protect a woman from acts of violence, usually by her husband. This order is authorized under the VAWC law.
[58] See Saturnino M. Borras Jr., *The Bibingka Strategy in Land Reform Implementation: Autonomous Peasant Movements and State Reformists in the Philippines* (Quezon City: Institute for Popular Democracy, 1998).

filed with the courts in order to hold them accountable for their misdeeds. As this suggests, working to increase state accountability at the local level is a double-edged sword for many paralegals. Sympathetic local government officials can be allies in the fight against poverty and lawlessness, but they can also be the worst of enemies if they themselves are involved in corrupt practices in their locality. Many paralegals end up adopting a strategy of "critical collaboration"; as one informant put it, "when we need to fight, we fight; when we can be friends, we are friends, but in the majority of our areas, the local governments still need to be oriented." Concretely, this means that the local officials have to be won over to the side of the paralegals, provided with the legal basis for their action, and a program for collaborative implementation has to be established with the consent of such officials.

2. Corporate Accountability

Finally, paralegals are also involved in efforts to increase corporate accountability. Here the work ranges from documenting violations and gathering evidence, to persuading victims to pursue and sustain cases, to trying to activate relevant and appropriate state bodies and agencies to mobilize and decide in favor of the groups and communities harmed by corporate activities. A good example of a major campaign in which ALG-supported paralegals have been involved is the ongoing effort to ban aerial spraying of pesticides in commercial banana plantations around Davao City. The effort has received not only broad public support but also the support of the Davao City local government. Another example is the problem of pollution through mine tailings, where some of the study's paralegal respondents have been active in gathering evidence (water samples) for examination for the presence of pollutants, in preparation for filing complaints with the DENR and its pollution adjudication board.

There are in fact numerous examples of paralegal involvement in efforts to hold large corporate entities (both foreign and domestic) accountable for either civil and political rights violations and/or social and environmental harms caused by their activities, especially mining, logging, fishing, and commercial farming, but also including illegal recruitment of migrant workers, unfair labor practices, and human trafficking. Many of the informants for this study have once been or currently are still involved in such struggles. Perhaps in part because of the difficult and sensitive nature of participating in challenges to the power of economic elites, who are often supported by powerful political elites, most participants referred to the cases in general terms and without mentioning details. Experience suggests, however, that securing accountability from corporate entities is especially difficult in the context of big power imbalances both inside and outside relevant state dispute-processing structures.

Some of the key problems and challenges for paralegal engagement on this dimension include: "window-dressing"-type official local decision-making and oversight bodies, and weak state regulatory and law enforcement functions. Even in the example of the campaign against aerial spraying (mentioned earlier), and despite solid support from local government, the legal case has been stymied in the courts, and as of this writing, there has been no final and enforceable ruling on the issue. More frequently, paralegals have to contend with uncooperative local government officials, corrupt regulatory offices, and armed resistance directed against those who try to expose and oppose their activities. As one of the paralegal informants said: "The problem is implementation at the ground level. The paralegals work hard to gather evidence, follow the law, policies, procedures etc. But the problem is in the difference between what is said at higher levels and what actually happens when you get to where we live."

VIII. CONCLUSION

The paralegal movement in the Philippines is dynamic and deeply embedded in an evolving socioeconomic and political-legal landscape. Paralegal practice was born out of the need for social mobilization of the poor and marginalized to creatively engage the state in favor of the defense and protection of their human and legal rights. Its diversity in application is partly attributable to the country's fragmented legal system, with its various segmented channels of legal entitlement, fragmented approach to dispensing justice, and multiple levels of dispute resolution. Some organs of the state have expressly recognized paralegals, including community-based paralegals, while others maintain that paralegals have to be constrained and regulated to ensure that they do not encroach upon the "real" practice of law. Despite this official skepticism and suspicion toward community-oriented paralegals, they remain a key part of the Philippines' social movement terrain, embedded in or tied to various types of grassroots organizations and supported by alternative law-oriented civil society groups, as well as in local government structures and some line agencies of the government.

The very notion of community-based paralegals is based on the hypothesis that they are an important positive factor in struggles for social justice. Therefore, whether or to what extent they actually fulfill this expectation in a given society is an important but complex empirical question. As explained at the outset of this chapter, the present study aimed more modestly to explore and examine the actually existing landscape of paralegalism in the Philippines, rather than to assess the actual impact of paralegal practice on access to justice. In leaving the systematic tracing of the outcomes and impacts of community paralegals for future study, some key issues are laid out here for consideration.

A. Issues for Consideration

1. Accountability and Sustainability: Locating Paralegals in CSOs and LGUs
In theory, paralegals embedded especially within grassroots membership organizations are subject to internal mechanisms (formal and informal) that may allow

organizational members to hold them accountable. Within legal NGOs, the system of accountability, mentoring, follow-up, and quality control may be quite robust. But civil society groups, and grassroots membership organizations especially, are often poorly financed, and it is an ongoing challenge to sustain them over time. Meanwhile, paralegal operations that are mainstreamed within LGUs – as in the case of VAWC committees within the *barangay*, or *bantay dagat* or *bantay gubat* members coming from the POs who are deputized by the local government – may gain an advantage in terms of sustainability, at least in the medium term. For example, the VAWC committees may receive some logistical support as well as office space within the *barangay* hall. However, the paralegal risks becoming primarily accountable to the local government official who supervises his or her work, such as the *barangay* captain in the case of the VAWC committees, rather than to the disadvantaged population they aim to serve. In this way, they remain vulnerable to the vagaries of patronage politics and three-year electoral cycles, and to the rent-seeking activities of some local officials. If the local government is supportive of paralegals' social justice efforts, this augurs well for a continuation of their work; if the political situation changes, their work could be severely compromised.

2. Recognition and Certification of Paralegals by the State

Another sensitive issue is the relationship of the paralegal to the state. One extreme position is that of the Supreme Court, which states that paralegals by definition are engaged in the practice of law, and therefore it is improper for them to participate in the Access to Justice Project, since the practice of law is limited to court-accredited attorneys. A middle ground of sorts is the practice of some quasi-judicial agencies to allow paralegals to appear on behalf of their fellow farmers or workers. This practice has provided a state-sanctioned venue where the paralegals can practice their craft and a built-in structure for developing their knowledge and skills in this area. On the other extreme are paralegals who are beyond the shadow of the law, so to speak, who operate below the "legal radar" within the confines of their respective organizations but who also provide essential services to their constituents, in spite of any formal recognition from the state. In the 2006 National Paralegal Conference hosted by the ALG, the 100 or so paralegal participants passed a resolution that they brought to the attention of the Court:

> *Formal recognition of the role of paralegals by the courts and quasi-judicial agencies.* Given the quantity of cases that we face and the lack of alternative lawyers that are willing to assist us, it is due time that the Supreme Court recognize our knowledge, skills, and capacity to represent ourselves and our organizations and communities.[59]

The sentiment expressed by the participants echoes the continuing problem of the shortage of public interest lawyers who defend the poor and marginalized in various

---

[59] Alternative Law Groups, Inc., *Final Output Report*, 18 (see n. 35).

tribunals, and hence the need for paralegals to act on their own, learn the law, and represent themselves. How this recognition will take place, however, is still a subject of discussion among public interest lawyers. If the state is the accrediting mechanism, which organ of the state should play this role? Should it be the Supreme Court or the specialized agencies of government like DAR or the National Labor Relations Commission (NLRC)? There is a genuine concern that even as some may pass, the accreditation process could be used to weed out the "dissenters" and the "troublemakers," making such a process discriminatory. The proponents of accreditation who participated in the study (mostly from the government sector) also talked about the need for certain standards, such as educational qualifications. But the fear is that disadvantaged groups may be further marginalized and that an elite group of paralegals may be created who will not have any organic connection to their constituencies over the long run. Should there be just one type of recognition, a "one-size-fits-all" approach? Some participants in the validation workshop argued that paralegals engaged in the enforcement of environmental laws, for example, should undergo a more stringent type of "accreditation" or "deputization," as opposed to those whose work is more about building awareness of human and legal rights.

3. Monitoring and Evaluation of the Impact of Paralegals

Despite the long history of paralegalism in the country, little has been done to measure the impact of such efforts on access to justice. The possible exception to this general statement is the evaluative study done by the Social Weather Stations.[60] The NGOs interviewed do not routinely track the outcome of the cases that have been handled by the paralegals to determine whether they have succeeded or to analyze what kinds of impacts they have made on the communities they serve. Little has also been done to track systematically the status of the many paralegals trained over the years – that is, where are they now, are they still active, how have they maintained their interest, and why did some of them become inactive? These are some of the issues that would be useful to know in order to improve the implementation of the paralegal programs. Monitoring and evaluation systems for paralegals do not seem a priority in light of the seemingly more urgent concerns of training paralegals and immediately making them work on issues facing the community. The issue of scarce resources definitely comes into play, as limited funds are used more for training and actual dispute resolution rather than for trying to monitor the outcomes of these efforts. This issue merits serious consideration. The paralegal movement cannot simply rely over the long haul on a presumption that paralegalism contributes to increased access to justice. Although this may seem obvious, more rigorous and systematic inquiry is needed to determine empirically the actual impact(s) of community-based paralegals on the lives of the poor.

[60] Social Weather Stations, *Research on the Poor* (see n. 47).

4. Funding as a Sustaining Mechanism

A few respondents emphasized that many law students have demonstrated their ability and commitment to take up a public interest law career, but that there are too few "takers" of fresh law graduates among the public interest law NGOs. The anemic "uptake" of recent law graduates by CSOs, due mainly to inadequate funds for sustaining public interest lawyers, has an impact on the quality of the training, maintenance, and monitoring of community-based paralegals. Many informants have highlighted the problem of inadequate funding for alternative lawyering as a problem for sustained paralegal formation and operation.

5. Looking at Paralegals in the Long Term

Aside from the institutional problem of financial sustainability, community-based paralegals face enormous obstacles in trying to work out legal assistance schemes at the grassroots, in the context of increased legislation and rights, as well as increased rights consciousness but weak implementation. This can be a problem especially in areas far from the reach of the central government and the national and independent media. In such settings, an inability or delay in making progress in paralegal work in specific cases can be seen as a failure to achieve success and a failure of the paralegal strategy in general. The cumulative effects can be demoralization, demobilization, or a turn toward violence. Meanwhile, poverty and impunity can make communities, grassroots organizations, and their paralegals vulnerable to adverse incorporation into the very kinds of illegal or destructive economic activities that they hope to stop. For example, they can become vulnerable to the initial enticements of mining or logging companies (in the form of local support and assistance) or to the immediate relief offered through clientelist relationships with elites, where they give up their civil and political rights and freedoms in exchange for access to social and economic benefits. In the Philippines, such responses to a very difficult situation can undermine paralegal formation, practice, and strategy.

6. Special Issues for Women and Children

As more and more paralegals become engaged in work with women and children, this sector requires a deeper understanding of the dynamics involved in order to make the work of the paralegal more effective. Experience shows that women who suffer domestic violence, for example, including rape, are unlikely to challenge their attackers without strong support from the community, and as a result, paralegals may need to engage in organizing such support as well. This could take the form of community forums on violence against women, the rights and remedies available to women, and so on. Another area that warrants close scrutiny is whether and to what extent patriarchy can interpret cases of violence against women as "petty" disputes, and push such cases into the village justice system for mediation by village leaders. While the BJS is not mandated to handle criminal cases in the first place, once there, appropriate and just outcomes for women cannot be guaranteed, and women may be forced to settle for unjust and disadvantageous results. Hence, public law work may need to give extra focus to "engendering" LGUs, most especially the people who are implementing the *barangay* justice procedures.

B. Recommendations

In spite of the challenges and obstacles, the paralegal movement in the Philippines will continue to be buoyed by factors and circumstances that heighten the urgent need of ordinary people at the grassroots to know the law and their rights and how these can be protected and promoted. Given the unlikelihood that the number of public interest lawyers will increase substantially in the future, the need for paralegals to reach out to the poorest of the poor will continue to exist. The legal opportunities created by new legislation will also continue to make paralegal services relevant in communities suffering from various kinds and degrees of social injustice. This chapter concludes with a number of recommendations for CSOs (including legal service NGOs) and state actors concerned about and involved in struggles for social justice and justice reform.

1) Locating the accountability of paralegals remains a key issue for the future. The ramifications of mainstreaming paralegals in LGUs must be carefully examined, especially its effects on both accountability and sustainability. For paralegals embedded in CSOs, accountability mechanisms must also be reviewed and strengthened to safeguard against the phenomenon of *abogadillos*.

2) The recognition of paralegals by the state is also an important area for further study and critical review. Where such recognition is deemed necessary, care should be taken that the standards imposed do not serve as a filtering or excluding mechanism, which would undermine the vibrancy and dynamism of the paralegal and alternative law movement. State recognition need not adopt a "one-size-fits-all" approach; instead, various paralegal roles (e.g., deputization of fishermen engaged in law enforcement) may merit more stringent accreditation measures than others.

3) CSOs should take a closer look at monitoring and evaluation schemes for paralegals in the future. These systems could be highly instructive for internal strengthening purposes, and also serve as a benchmark for future funding.

4) The justice concerns and legal needs of remote communities should be looked into more closely by the state and in any justice reform programming. Among other responses, a state-led paralegal program should be considered, in conjunction with the public attorney's program and the BJS. However, a state-led paralegal program should not be taken as the only solution to the justice concerns and legal needs of the poor and marginalized. Any state-led justice

reform initiatives must address their justice concerns and legal needs, and paralegals can play a key role in deepening understanding toward more relevant solutions.

5) The government as well as the donor community should put more emphasis on the funding of paralegal programs as good value for money in the crusade to improve access to justice by the poor. Partnerships between committed public interest lawyers and community-based or oriented paralegals may be one (but not the only) key to improving access to justice, and at the same time, maintaining an optimal use of scarce resources.

C. Concluding Remarks

This study has taken a historical perspective on the work of paralegals in the Philippines. It has also examined the institutional constraints and opportunities that hinder or allow paralegals to do their work productively. This chapter concludes by going back to the paralegals themselves, who were asked what it takes to be a paralegal. Numerous interesting responses from various key informants have been collated. It is hoped that this collection of responses usefully illustrates the motivations and goals of those who opt to become paralegals in the Philippines today (see Box 3.5).

BOX 3.5: WHO CAN BE A PARALEGAL?

ANYBODY CAN BE A PARALEGAL IF ...

One will take time to know and study the law (student paralegal)

One has inner strength and believes in one's ability (farmer leader and paralegal)

One has a deep understanding and knowledge of the culture and lifeways of the indigenous peoples (indigenous peoples' leader and paralegal)

One has a strong love and reverence for the sea and the environment (community based-coast guard volunteers)

One has a strong sense of service and not expecting anything in return (labor leader and paralegal)

One has the courage to defend the rights of the people (environmental paralegal)

One has a balanced perspective on the problems and legal rights (labor leader and paralegal)

One could open their eyes, their ears and their minds (student paralegal)[61]

---

[61] These quotes have been selected from the responses of informants in the focus group discussion in various places.

ANNEX A ANATOMY OF A TYPICAL PARALEGAL TRAINING

	PART 1
Module 1	**Overview** of the Human Rights Situation (sector/issue) in the country (region/area/community)
Module 2	**Basic Human Rights** Universal Declaration of Human Rights *If applicable with special attention/focus to:* • Convention of the Rights of a Child (UNCRC) • Convention on the Elimination of All forms of Discrimination against Women (CEDAW) • United Nations Declaration on the Rights of Indigenous Peoples (UNDRIP)
Module 3	Developmental Legal Framework
Module 4	The Philippine Legal System
	PART 2
Module 5	**Issue or Sector Specific Relevant Laws** **Agrarian Reform:** RA 9700 CARP Extension with Reforms • MC 15 s2004 Affirming Role of Farmer Paralegal **Children:** • RA 9344 Juvenile Justice and Welfare Act of 2006 • RA 7610 Special Protection of Children against Abuse, Exploitation and Discrimination Act **Environment:** • PD 705 Forestry Code • RA 8550 Fisheries Code • RA 7586 National Integrated Protected Areas System • RA 9003 Ecological Solid Waste Management Act • RA 8749 Clean Air Act **Human Rights Violations:** • Revised Penal Code • Writ of Amparo • Writ of Habeas Data • RA9745 Anti-Torture Law **Indigenous Peoples:** • RA 8371 Indigenous Peoples Rights Act **Labor:** • PD 442 As Amended LABOR CODE • RULE1BOOKV Labor Relations • ART. 279 Security of Tenure **Women:** • RA8353 The Anti-rape Law of 1997 • RA9262 Violence against Women & Their Children Act • RA9710 Magna Carta of Women
	PART 3
Module 5	**Basic Legal Forms**
Module 6	**Evidence Gathering** and/or **Arrest, Search, Seizure, and Detention**
Module 7	Introduction to Philippine Court System/Procedural Laws
Module 8	Metalegal Remedies

FIGURE 3.2 ANNEX A: Anatomy of a typical paralegal training

ANNEX B LIST OF ORGANIZATIONS PARTICIPATING IN THE STUDY

Ateneo Human Rights Center
Ateneo Professional Schools Building, 20 Rockwell Drive
Rockwell Center, 1200, Makati City

Balay Alternative Legal Advocates for Development in Mindanaw (BALAOD-Mindanaw)
2nd Floor, Belsar Bldg., Brgy. 19, Capistrano-Del Pilar Sts.,
9000 Cagayan de Oro City

Children's Legal Bureau
No. 10 Queen's Road, Caputhaw, 6000, Cebu City

Environmental Legal Assistance Center, Inc.
Carlos Sayang Compound, Mitra Road, Sta. Monica Puerto Preincesa, Palawan

Free Legal Assistance Group
Alumni Center, University of the Philippines, Diliman, Quezon City

KAISAHAN Tungo sa Kaunlaran ng Kanayunan at Repormang Pansakahan
No. 3 Mahabagin St., Teacher's Village West, Diliman, Quezon City

Kanlungan Center Foundation, Inc.
KANLUNGAN
No. 77-K 10th St., Kamias, 1102 Quezon City

Tanggapang Panligal ng Katutubong Pilpino PANLIPI
Unit 303 JGS Bldg., #30 Scout Tuazon cor. Dr. Lascano
Brgy. Laging Handa, Quezon City

RIGHTSNET
79C Bignay St., Brgy. Quirino 2A, Project 2, Quezon City

Sentrong Alternatibong Lingap Panligal SALIGAN
G/F Cardinal Hoffner Building, Social Development Complex,
Ateneo de Manila University, Loyola Heights Quezon City

Tanggkol Kalikasan
Room M-01, CRM Building III, 106 Kamias Road,
1102 Quezon City

Women's Legal Bureau
Room 305, CSWCD Building, Magsaysay Avenue,
U.P. Diliman, Quezon City

Program Management Office, Supreme Court of the Philippines
7th Floor, Centennial Building, Padre Faura St., Manila

Department of Justice
Padre Faura St., Manila

Public Attorney's Office
4th Floor DOJ Agencies Building, NIA Road cor. EDSA, Quezon City

Integrated Bar of the Philippines
IBP Building, Julia Vargas St., Ortigas Center,
Pasig City

The Asia Foundation
36 Lapu Lapu St. Magallanes Village, Makati, Metro Manila

FIGURE 3.3 ANNEX B: List of organizations participating in the study

REFERENCES

Abella, Jerrie. "UN Women's Committee Faults RP for Junking Rape Case." *GMANews.tv*. September 24, 2010. www.gmanetwork.com/news/story/201848/news/nation/un-women-s-committee-faults-rp-for-junking-rape-case.

Alternative Law Groups, Inc. "EnDefense." http://alternativelawgroups.ph/index.php/projects/curent-projects/endefense.

Final Output Report – Alternative Law Groups, Inc. National Paralegal Conference: Collecting Stories, Exchanging Models. Quezon City: GOP-UNDP, 2006.

Asian Development Bank. *Law and Policy Reform at the Asian Development Bank*. Pasig City: Asian Development Bank, 2001.

Barraca, Delorino, Duman, Dumlao, Grepo, Ocampo, Reyes, and Salazar. *Understanding the Katarungang Pambarangay: Justice at the Grassroots*. Guanzon: University of the Philippines – College of Law, 2009.

Borras Jr., Saturnino M. *The Bibingka Strategy in Land Reform Implementation: Autonomous Peasant Movements and State Reformists in the Philippines*. Quezon City: Institute for Popular Democracy, 1998.

Borras Jr., Saturnino M. and Jennifer C. Franco. "Struggles for Land and Livelihood: Redistributive Reform in Agribusiness Plantations in the Philippines." *Critical Asian Studies* 37, no. 3 (2005): 331–61. doi: 10.1080/14672710500200383.

Crippen, Harlan R. "Philippine Agrarian Unrest: Historical Backgrounds." *Science & Society* 10, no. 4 (1946): 337–60.

Diokno, Jose W. "Developmental Legal Aid in Rural ASEAN: Problems and Prospects." In *Rural Development and Human Rights in South East Asia: Report of a Seminar*. Geneva: International Commission of Jurists, Penang: Consumers' Association of Penang, 1982, 178–81.

Farrington, John and David J. Lewis. *Non-governmental Organizations and the State in Asia: Rethinking Roles in Sustainable Agricultural Development*. New York: Routledge, 1993.

Franco, Jennifer C. *Elections and Democratization in the Philippines*. New York: Routledge, 2001.

"Making Land Rights Accessible: Social Movements and Political-Legal Innovation in the Rural Philippines." *The Journal of Development Studies* 44, no. 7 (2008): 991–1022. doi: 10.1080/00220380802150763.

"Peripheral Justice? Rethinking Justice Sector in the Philippines." *World Development* 36, no. 10 (2008): 1858–73. http://dx.doi.org/10.1016/j.worlddev.2007.10.011.

Galanter, Marc. "Justice in Many Rooms: Courts, Private Ordering, and Indigenous Law." *Journal of Legal Pluralism and Unofficial Law* 13, no. 19 (1981): 1–47. doi: 10.1080/07329113.1981.10756257.

Golub, Stephen. "Non-state Justice Systems in Bangladesh and the Philippines." Paper presented for the UK Department for International Development, London, January 2003.

Kane, Sally. "Public Interest Law: A Guide to Legal Public Service Careers." *The Balance*. Last modified September 15, 2016. www.thebalance.com/public-interest-law-2164664.

Kkerkvliet, Benedict. *The Huk Rebellion: A Study of Peasant Revolt in the Philippines*. Berkeley: University of California Press, 1977.

Maru, Vivek and Varun Gauri. "BNPP Concept Note." World Bank Justice for the Poor Program, December 2009.

Nader, Laura. "The Underside of Conflict Management – in Africa and Elsewhere." *IDS Bulletin* 32, no. 1 (2009): 19–27.

Pardico, Navia V. G.R. No. 184467 (S.C., June 19, 2012) (Phil). http://hrlibrary.umn.edu/research/Philippines/The%20Rule%20On%20The%20Writ%20Of%20Amparo.pdf.
O'Brien, Kevin J. and Lianjiang Li. *Rightful Resistance in Rural China*. Cambridge: Cambridge University Press, 2006.
Republic Act No. 6657.
Republic Act No. 7568.
Republic Act No. 8042.
Republic Act No. 8371.
Republic Act No. 8550.
Republic Act No. 9262.
Republic Act No. 9344.
Republic Act No. 9700.
RULES OF PROCEDURE FOR ENVIRONMENTAL CASES. A.M. No. 09-6-8-SC. http://philja.judiciary.gov.ph/assets/files/pdf/learning_materials/A.m.No.09-6-8-SC_Rules_of_Procedure_for_Envi_Cases.pdf.
Rule on the Writ of Habeas Data. A.M. No. 08-1-16. S.C., January 22, 2008.
Social Weather Stations. *Research on the Poor Accessing Justice and the ALG as Justice Reform Advocate*. Inroads: ALG Study Series. Quezon City: Social Weather Stations, Inc., Alternative Law Groups, Inc., 2008.
Vigo, Maricel and Marlon Manuel. *Katarungang Pambarangay: A Handbook*. Quezon City: SALIGAN, Pasig City: LGSP, 2004.

4

Paralegalism in Indonesia

Balancing Relationships in the Shadow of the Law

Ward Berenschot and Taufik Rinaldi

1. INTRODUCTION

The fall of Suharto's New Order in 1998 inspired hope that Indonesia's fledgling legal system could be made fairer and more responsive to the interests of the poor. Decades of political meddling and institutional neglect had made the courts subservient to the privileged few, and the word *hakim* ("judge" in Indonesian) came to stand for *hubungi aku kalau ingin menang*: "contact me if you want to win." As this "contact" was out of reach for most citizens, Indonesia's legal system was seen as something to avoid rather than to invoke. In the period of *reformasi* ("reform") after 1998, legal reform became a central focus of both the Indonesian government and various development agencies.[1]

Paralegals have played a central role in these efforts. Since the foundation of Indonesia's first legal aid organization, Lembaga Bantuan Hukum (LBH), in the 1970s, paralegals had been at the forefront of the opposition against the Suharto regime as they helped local communities during the recurring conflicts about (particularly) land and natural resources.[2] Inspired by LBH's success, various groups – ranging from environmental organizations, trade unions, universities, and even political parties – started to adopt paralegal programs with the aim of helping citizens deal with a still remote and alien legal system. Foreign funding agencies have also provided support, seeing paralegals as a tool for "legal empowerment":[3] as big donors

---

The authors would like to thank the paralegals who made this project possible, particularly Subur, Agus, Ulhadi, Ibu Sisilia, Ibu Siti, Muhtarom, Mbak Sri, and Pak Delfius. Furthermore we thank the staff at UNDP and the World Bank, as well as the legal aid NGOs who worked with these paralegals: Kantor Bantuan Hukum Lampung, Gravitasi Mataram, LBH Bandung, RACA Institute, and LML Ternate. We thank the Dutch Embassy and Open Society Institute for their financial support.

[1] See Timothy Lindsey and Mas Achmad Santosa, "The Trajectory of Law Reform in Indonesia: A Short Overview of Legal Systems and Change in Indonesia," in *Indonesia: Law and Society*, ed. Timothy Lindsey (Sidney: The Federation Press, 2008), 113–30.

[2] Daniel S. Lev, *Legal Evolution and Political Authority in Indonesia: Selected Essays* (The Hague: Kluwer Law International, 2000), 283–305.

[3] *Legal empowerment* has become an umbrella term for initiatives, like paralegalism, that aim to strengthen access to legal systems for disadvantaged groups. UNDP defines legal empowerment thus: "the ability of people, particularly from poor and disadvantaged groups, to seek and obtain

like the World Bank, UNDP, and Open Society Institute increasingly felt that a focus on a "top-down" reform of legal institutions – like making the courts or the police work better – was not enough to enable common Indonesians to make use of these institutions, they have started to fund projects that train and supported paralegals.[4] In a recent count, Indonesia now has at least 622 legal aid organizations in all provinces, although two-thirds of these are based in provincial capitals.[5] A recent survey among 229 of these organizations revealed that 56 percent make use of paralegals. These legal aid organizations claim to have trained a total of 16,240 paralegals over the past decade. Yet they also report that a much smaller number of individuals remain active after such training.[6] Based on the numbers provided by the surveyed legal aid organizations, it can be estimated that there are currently between 4,000 and 6,000 active paralegals working for legal aid offices in Indonesia.[7]

Recently the Indonesian government has also stepped up its involvement. In an ambitious reform strategy called "National Strategy Access to Justice" the Indonesian government stated in 2008 its aim of enlarging the number of paralegals.[8] In 2011 the Legal Aid Bill was adopted, which provides funding to

a remedy through formal and informal justice systems, in accordance with human rights principles and standards." See UN Development Programme, *Justice for All?: An Assessment of Access to Justice in Five Provinces of Indonesia* (Jakarta: UN Development Programme, 2007); John W. Bruce, Omar Garcia-Bolivar, Tim Hanstad, Michael Roth, Robin Nielsen, Anna Knox, and Jon Schmidt, *Legal Empowerment of the Poor: From Concepts to Assessments* (Washington, DC: USAID, 2007); UN Development Programme, "Access to Justice, Practice Note" (UN Development Programme, 2004).

[4] For the need for such legal empowerment from below, see Stephen Golub, "Beyond the Rule of Law Orthodoxy: The Legal Empowerment Alternative," *Working Papers*, Rule of Law Series no. 41 (Washington, DC: Carnegie Endowment for International Peace, 2003); Benjamin van Rooij, "Bringing Justice to the Poor: Bottom-Up Legal Development Cooperation," *Hague Journal on the Rule of Law* 4, no. 2 (2012): 286–318. doi: 10.1017/S1876404512000176.

[5] The study conducted by the World Bank's Justice for the Poor program arrived at this number by combining the total number of organizations that had applied to the Ministry of Law and Human Rights to be accredited as a legal aid provider (576), with the forty-six organizations that this study identified that had not applied for accreditation. Of the 576 organizations that applied for accreditation, only 310 succeeded in receiving this accreditation. It is not unlikely that a considerable number of unsuccessful applicants were not really active. Yet it is also possible that some legal aid organizations have not been identified by this study.

[6] Justice for the Poor, World Bank and Ministry of Law and Human Rights, "Legal Aid Organizations in Indonesia: Results of Nationwide Survey of 230 Legal Aid Organizations" (unpublished report, June 2014).

[7] This number was arrived at in the following manner. The surveyed legal aid organizations provided only a range (e.g., "between one and ten") of how many paralegals they are working with, enabling only a count of how many legal aid organizations have between one and ten (or between eleven and twenty-five, etc.) paralegals. The estimate provided here is based on calculating how many paralegals that would amount to if legal aid organizations would have the exact mean value of each range (e.g., five and eighteen). This calculation suggests that the 230 surveyed organizations work with 4,000 paralegals. This number concerns only the total for the organizations included in the survey. Yet as the survey focused on accredited legal aid providers as well as legal aid organizations, the survey is likely to include the most active legal aid organizations. Hence it seems a reasonable assumption that the total number of paralegals will not exceed 6,000.

[8] See "Strategi Nasional Akses Terhadap Keadilan" (Stranas) § 3.2, available at http://perpustakaan .bappenas.go.id/lontar/file%3Ffile=digital/91553-[_Konten_]-Konten%20C6083.pdf.

expand the scope of legal aid efforts.[9] After this law became effective in 2013, 593 legal aid organizations applied in 2013 for accreditation to the Ministry of Law and Human Rights in order to be eligible for this financial support. Of these, 310 organizations have been accredited.[10] The accredited organizations can receive a maximum of US$500 as support for handling a case. In 2013, the only year for which reports are available, the Indonesian government provided funding for 194 organizations for the handling of 2,315 cases with in total Rp 5.6 billion (about US$450,000 at that time, or US$195 per case). Of this total budget, 70 percent was spent on cases involving litigation in court and only 8 percent went to training activities.[11] This suggests that paralegals have actually derived relatively little support out of the Legal Aid Bill. Yet the very mention of paralegals in this law illustrates that, after decades of being a marginal instrument of the opposition against Suharto, paralegals have now gone mainstream as an important channel to make Indonesia's legal system more accessible.[12]

This chapter discusses the impact of the presence of paralegals on processes of grievance and dispute handling in rural Indonesia, focusing on the community-based paralegals trained under programs set up by the World Bank and UNDP. Through both quantitative and qualitative material this chapter focuses on three main activities of paralegals – mediation, legal accompaniment, and community organizing[13] – to discuss how and under what circumstances these activities impact the way local disputes and grievances are addressed in villages in three Indonesian provinces: West Java, Lampung, and north Maluku. The main argument of this chapter is that in the context of a distrusted legal system, a New Order tradition of emphasizing harmony, and a rich tradition in alternative dispute resolution, the contribution of Indonesia's paralegals lies – at least in the short run – not so much in facilitating access to the formal legal system but rather in countering the impact of power imbalances on processes of grievance and dispute handling. In other words, the contribution of Indonesia's paralegals does not lie so much in facilitating the *implementation* of the law, but rather in extending the *shadow* of the law:[14] by

---

[9] Law of the Republic of Indonesia No. 16/2011 Concerning Legal Aid. The Indonesia Legal Aid Law was adopted on November 2, 2011, and has been implemented since July 1, 2013.
[10] Republic of Indonesia, Ministry of Law and Human Rights, *Laporan Tahunan: Implementasi Undang Undang Nomor 16 2011 tentang Bantuan Hukum (Annual Report of the Implementation of Legal Aid Law)*. https://sidbankum.bphn.go.id/front/download?filename=4422_laporan_tahunan_bantuan_hukum.pdf.
[11] Ministry of Law and Human Rights, *Lapora Tahunon 2013* (Jakarta, 2014), 32, available at www.kemenkumham.go.id/attachments/article/225/Laporan_Tahunan_Th_2013.pdf.
[12] *See, for example*, Ulma Haryanto, "For Indonesia's Poor, Paralegals Pave the Way to Justice," *Jakarta Globe*, January 25, 2012, http://jakartaglobe.beritasatu.com/archive/for-indonesias-poor-paralegals-pave-the-way-to-justice/.
[13] The studied paralegals also focused on legal education, which for reasons of space limitations will not be discussed here.
[14] This term was first used by Mnookin and Kornhauser describing negotiations between divorcing couples in the United States. *See* Robert H. Mnookin and Lewis Kornhauser, "Bargaining in the

inserting legal considerations more forcefully into the (often informal) process of grievance and dispute handling, paralegals can offset and sometimes neutralize the impact of power imbalances between disputants.[15]

II. APPROACHES TO STUDYING ACCESS TO JUSTICE

With these arguments we adopt a relational approach to interpreting the unequal capacity of citizens to use available legal systems to defend their interests. Surprisingly, paralegal projects rarely come with an explicit analysis of the *causes* of this unequal capacity. In Indonesian paralegal programs two main, contrasting approaches could be identified. Following Heller and Evans these approaches could be termed *residualist* and *structuralist*.[16] A *residualist* approach attributes the unequal capacity to access legal systems to the weaknesses of available legal institutions and the limited familiarity of citizens with these institutions. The inequality, in other words, is a residue of the way the state developed (or failed to develop) and the way citizens avoided interaction with this state. Such an analysis suggests that a combination of bottom-up and top-down measures could make legal institutions more accessible to poorer citizens: on the one hand policies aiming at legal reform could strengthen legal institutions, while on the other hand legal education and legal aid could boost the capacity of ordinary citizens to deal with these institutions. It could be argued that most paralegal programs, including those of the World Bank and UNDP, adopt such an analysis.[17] With their emphasis on "legal empowerment" these programs prioritize strengthening individual (legal) capacities over changing social structures.

Shadow of the Law: The Case of Divorce," *Yale Law Journal* 88, no. 5 (1979): 950–97, doi: 10.2307/795824.

[15] While articles on paralegals in Africa put more emphasis on paralegals as providing access to justice rather than as balancing unequal power relations, we regard the observations in these articles as largely comparable. See Vivek Maru, "Between Law and Society: Paralegals and Provision of Justice Services in Sierra Leone and Worldwide," *The Yale Journal of International Law* 31, no. 2 (2006): 427–76; Adam Stapleton, "Empowering the Poor to Access Criminal Justice: A Grass-Roots Perspective," in *Legal Empowerment: Practitioners' Perspectives*, ed. Stephen Golub and Thomas McInerney (Rome: International Development Law Organization, 2010), 39–62. See also Golub and McInerney, eds., *Legal Empowerment: Practitioners' Perspectives* (Rome: International Development Law Organization, 2010). By focusing on the relational underpinnings of power imbalances, we avoid interpreting these norms only as an alternative "rule system." See, *for example*, Caroline Sage, Nick Menzies, and Michael Woolcock, "Taking the Rules of the Game Seriously – Mainstreaming Justice in Development: The World Bank's Justice for the Poor Program," in *Legal Empowerment: Practitioners' Perspectives*, ed. Stephen Golub and Thomas McInerney (Rome: International Development Law Organization, 2010), 19–37.

[16] Patrick Heller and Peter Evans, "Taking Tilly South: Durable Inequalities, Democratic Contestation, and Citizenship in the Southern Metropolis," *Theory and Society* 39, no. 3 (2010): 433–50.

[17] See UNDP, *Justice for the Poor Program* (May 2008), available at http://siteresources.worldbank.org/INTJUSFORPOOR/Resources/J4POverviewMay2008.pdf; World Bank, *Forging the Middle Ground: Engaging Non-state Justice in Indonesia* (Washington, DC: World Bank, 2008); Commission on Legal Empowerment of the Poor, *Making the Law Work for Everyone*, vol. 1 (New York: Commission on Legal Empowerment of the Poor, UN Development Programme, 2008).

This is why, according to the *structuralist* approach, "residualists" fail to address the root causes of the unequal capacity to benefit from the formal legal system. The structuralist approach sees this unequal capacity as a by-product of the nature of global production and the impact of market forces on the functioning of the state. In this view, the difficulties that poorer citizens face when dealing with the formal legal system are a symptom of the way market forces are systematically disempowering poorer citizens. In this view the legal system is to be distrusted, as it often operates as a tool in the hands of (economic) elites who use the law to reduce labor costs and acquire control over natural resources.[18] The solution to unequal legal capacities does, therefore, not only lie in merely helping individuals bring their cases to court, but rather in using such cases to build up awareness and create demand for the overhaul of the legal system. These considerations led to the development in the 1980s of the concept of "Structural Legal Aid" (*bantuan hukum structural*, BHS) at LBH, which aimed to use legal cases to change the unequal distribution of power within Indonesian society.[19] In the 1990s legal aid organizations like YLBHI and HUMA further developed these ideas into a new legal aid strategy called Critical Legal Education (*Pendidikan Hukum Kritis*, PHK). PHK emphasized local customary law as an antidote to the oppressive legal system. A new type of paralegal called *pendamping hukum rakyat* (PHR, "the legal assistant of the people") was trained, whose role went beyond providing legal aid and community organizing, as PHK-paralegals are also expected to engage in critical legal analysis to challenge the domination and oppression inherent in Indonesia's laws and policies – in particular in Indonesia's laws pertaining to land and natural resources.[20]

While both types of arguments are relevant, they are of limited value to analyze the actual contribution of paralegals to addressing these inequalities. While the residualist approach overestimates the agency of justice seekers, the structuralist approach underestimates their agency. By focusing on relatively technical solutions such as (legal) training and policymaking, the residualist approach risks bracketing broader societal and economic inequalities that underlie legal inequalities. Yet the structuralist approach paints an overly deterministic picture, as it creates the impression that individual struggles cannot make a difference without a structural overhaul of the economic and legal system. Furthermore, such a broad approach is not

---

[18] Often with good reason; see the discussion of the dispossessions of poorer citizens from their land in Elizabeth Collins' *Indonesia Betrayed: How Development Fails* (Honolulu: University of Hawaii Press, 2007).

[19] As the founder of LBH, Bayung Nasution, put it, legal aid efforts should aim at "conscientization": "Cases are selected [for legal aid] which involve various kinds of conscientization efforts such as widespread publicity for those which reflect structural injustice and/or which illustrate that what would be necessary to make law effective in the interests of the poor." Bayung Nasution, "The Legal Aid Movement in Indonesia: Towards the Implementation of the Structural Legal Aid Concept," in *Access to Justice: Human Rights Struggles in South East Asia*, ed. Harry M. Scoble and Laurie S. Wiseberg (London: Zed Books, 1985), 37.

[20] Ibid.

precise enough to analyze the practical and creative ways in which justice seekers use their (limited) resources to successfully overcome injustices.

For these reasons we turned to relational sociology to discuss the impact of paralegals on processes of grievance and dispute handling. This current in modern sociology, associated with eminent social scientists like Pierre Bourdieu, Norbert Elias, and Charles Tilly, departs from the proposition that the attitudes and interests of individuals are not given units of analysis, but rather a product of the nature of the relationships in which human lives are embedded. Relational sociology thus studies social inequality not merely in terms of an uneven distribution of talents or resources between individuals, but rather in terms of the nature of interpersonal relations that enable some individuals to accumulate resources and to make this accumulation appear legitimate.[21] An unequal capacity to, say, win a dispute over landownership, is in this approach not merely the result of a lack of individual capacities to make an argument or to invoke the law, but also a product of the position of disputants within society – since it is by virtue of these positions that some disputants possess the status, knowledge, and influential connections that put them at an advantage. In other words, the strategies that people adopt to settle a dispute or address a grievance are a product not just of the normative or legal merits of their claim but also of the personal resources that come with their position within society. We will make use of the concept of "capital" to describe the content and impact of various forms of such advantages: following Bourdieu, power differentials between individuals can be described in terms of an uneven control over various forms of capital. Bourdieu distinguished four main "species of capital" to highlight existing power differentials between people: economic capital (monetary or material possessions), social capital (contacts with useful individuals), cultural capital (primarily, the possession of various forms of knowledge, including legal knowledge), and symbolic capital (prestige and social status).[22] The distribution of these forms of capital, and their perceived value, are a product of the interdependencies between people. In the words of a common analogy in relational sociology, these forms of capital are related to the social "game" in which people are involved: while a farmer in West Java might not see the importance of publishing in an obscure academic journal, a Dutch academic would not see the need for the varied levels of politeness that can be conveyed through the Javanese language.

Such a relational approach is not just useful to understand how paralegals operate at the crossroads between law, social norms, and relations of power. This approach is also helpful to understand how the paralegals' own position within the community affects their effectiveness. As community-based paralegals have long-standing

[21] *See* Mustafa Emirbayer, "Manifesto for a Relational Sociology," *American Journal of Sociology* 103, no. 2 (1997): 281–317, www.jstor.org/stable/10.1086/231209?origin=JSTOR-pdf&seq=1#page_scan_tab_contents; Norbert Elias, *What Is Sociology?* (London: Hutchinson, 1978).

[22] *See* Pierre Bourdieu and Loic J. D. Wacquant, *An Invitation to Reflexive Sociology* (Chicago: University of Chicago Press, 1992).

relationships with the people they are supposed to serve, their social background and their embeddedness in the local community have a large impact on the way they operate. Paralegals operate in villages alongside other individuals who derive status and money from solving local disputes. Various local institutions (*adat* councils, religious courts, village councils, etc.) and actors (village heads, local politicians, *preman*, etc.) are involved in dispute resolution, sometimes apply their own laws and regulations (though not always written down) that can differ from state law.[23] For this reason we have focused not only on the case handling by paralegals, but also on their role within larger struggles for status and power that mark village politics.

This chapter focuses on the paralegals trained under the World Bank's Justice for the Poor project and UNDP's Legal Empowerment and Assistance for the Disadvantaged (LEAD) project. Both programs worked with "community-based paralegals," which meant that inhabitants of designated project villages were selected as paralegals, serving only people from (or around) their village. The selected villagers received basic training on Indonesia's legal system, as well as on case handling and mediation: while "providing legal services" was the main aim, paralegals were instructed to work alongside existing (traditional) dispute resolution mechanisms.[24] The paralegal program of the World Bank – called "Revitalisation of Legal Aid" (RLA) – worked generally with village-level teams of two men and two women who worked out of a legal aid *posko* ("post"), usually the house of one of them. For the duration of the project they were supported by "*posko* facilitators" and "gender specialists" who provided assistance and who functioned as a liaison with the "community lawyers" who were involved in the project to provide paralegals with legal advice for the more complex cases. The RLA program operated in three provinces (Lampung, Nusa Tenggara Barat, and West Java) where for each province an (legal aid) NGO was involved as "implementing agency." In these three provinces the project worked with in total 120 paralegals, ninety-five village mediators, twelve *posko* facilitators, six community lawyers, and six gender specialists.[25] LEAD also worked with community-based paralegals,[26] of which some were trained

---

[23] On how this "legal pluralism" shapes everyday dispute resolution, *see* John R. Bowen, *Islam, Law and Equality in Indonesia: An Anthropology of Public Reasoning* (Cambridge: Cambridge University Press, 2003), 3–63; Keebet von Benda-Beckmann, "Forum Shopping and Shopping Forums: Dispute Processing in a Minangkabau Village in West Sumatra," *Journal of Legal Pluralism and Unofficial Law* 13, no. 19 (1981): 117–59.

[24] See the project documents: Justice for the Poor Program, *Baseline Survey: Pilot Program Revitalization of Legal Aid in Indonesia (RLA)* (Washington, DC: World Bank, 2006); Government of Indonesia, UN Development Programme, "Legal Empowerment and Assistance for the Disadvantaged (LEAD) Project" (Jakarta: Government of Indonesia, UN Development Programme, 2007).

[25] *See* "Indonesia," Justice for the Poor. http://go.worldbank.org/DH16VCUFS0.

[26] For the project description, *see* "The Legal Empowerment and Assistance for the Disadvantaged (LEAD)," UN Development Programme. www.id.undp.org/content/indonesia/en/home/operations/projects/democratic_governance/the-legal-empowerment-and-assistance-for-the-disadvantaged.html.

on specific issues (such as gender, land, and natural resources), while other paralegals were also trained as general community-based paralegals. They were selected from project villages in north Maluku, central Sulawesi, and southeast Sulawesi. UNDP also worked with local NGOs who were made responsible for the training and support of paralegals. This support was organized through "field officers" who traveled to the project villages. In total, the LEAD project claims to have trained 400 paralegals.[27]

This chapter is based on two sources of material: (a) a qualitative study on local dispute resolution in both paralegal and non-paralegal villages; (b) a quantitative analysis of a database of 338 cases that were handled and reported by the 120 paralegals supported under the World Bank's Justice for the Poor program. Our research has focused on the functioning of paralegals that were part of UNDP and World Bank paralegal programs, and in a later stage, on paralegals supported under the aegis of legal aid projects supported by Open Society Institute.[28] We documented twenty-one cases that were reported to and handled by paralegals, while also documenting ten similar cases in the same districts (but different villages) where paralegals were not involved. We focused on the functioning of paralegals in three provinces: Lampung, West Java (locations of the Justice for the Poor program), and Halmahera Timur (where UNDP financed a paralegal program).[29] The quantitative study focused on 338 cases handled by paralegals in West Java, Lampung, and West Nusa Tenggara between October 2007 and April 2009. All these paralegals were trained under the World Bank's Justice for the Poor program. As part of this project paralegals were asked to fill out basic forms about the way they handled each case reported to them. While this material needs to be treated with some caution,[30] we have used it to link our in-depth case documentation with

---

[27] Ibid.
[28] The choice for these organizations was a result of the institutional context out of which this research project grew: this research started as part of a collaborative project on access to justice in Indonesia between UNDP, the World Bank, and the Van Vollenhoven Institute, funded by the Dutch embassy in Jakarta. This project was a collaborative project between the World Bank, UNDP, VVI, and Bappenas to engage in both legal reform and legal empowerment measures, running from 2007 until 2010. Later Open Society Institute lent further support to expand our fieldwork.
[29] The choice for the research locations was shaped by our desire to study the functioning of paralegals in diverse settings: while West Java provided a more urban and affluent setting, in Lampung paralegals operated in a rural context with a less diversified economy. Halmahera Timur was selected for the relative remoteness and inaccessibility of judicial institutions and its prominence of local, customary institutions.
[30] There are three main limitations to the reliability of this data. First, we had to work with the project forms already made for the purpose of Justice for the Poor's project management, which posed limitations on the type of analysis we could do. Second, some of the forms were filled while a case was still being handled – which led to incomplete data about some of these cases. Third, some of the wording of the questionnaire was open to multiple interpretations and misunderstandings; it is quite possible that some of the paralegal-informants interpreted questions differently. Because of these limitations we discarded the data on some of the questions in the questionnaire, while we used the filled-out forms themselves to engage in an extensive checking of the given answers on, for example, the types of cases handled and the manner of case handling.

a more general overview of the types of cases received by paralegals and the manner they were dealt with.

III. MEDIATION: AN ACCIDENT IN A *KROEPOEK* FACTORY

Siswanto had been working for twenty years in the *kroepoek* factory owned by Sugiono when, on October 12, 2009, he lost two fingers in an accident with the factory's machine. After the incident Siswanto could not work for four months, and he had to spend Rp 7 million for the treatment of his hand. During this time, Siswanto tried to use the health insurance (Jamsostek) that Sugiono had arranged for him in 2005. This health insurance scheme requires the employer of more than ten employees to arrange health insurance, for which some amount can be deducted from the salary. When Siswanto contacted Jamsostek, he learned that Sugiono had paid the fee only once, in May 2005, while he had cut Siswanto's daily salary by Rp 3,000: since 2005 Siswanto had received Rp 25,000 per day (US$3) instead of Rp 28,000. Consequently Siswanto could not reclaim the costs of the treatment from Jamsostek.

Siswanto as well as his brother then approached Sugiono to ask him to pay for the incurred costs. Sugiono agreed to pay only a small amount; he said that the accident was due to negligence on Siswanto's part, so the costs would fall to him. No agreement was reached at this point and Siswanto's brother was shooed out of Sugiono's house.

This labor dispute is an example of a conflict with a marked power differential between disputing parties. Sugiono's father is a prominent member of the PDI-P, which assures him of support among the police and the village leader. He is the owner of the factory where Siswanto is employed, and is thus important for Siswanto's livelihood. Furthermore, thanks to his fancy clothes and worldly manner, he can come across as reliable and convincing when he says that Siswanto was to blame for the incident, while the uneducated Siswanto lacks any knowledge of the legal system that might enable him to invoke the law to strengthen his claim while his shyness and soft-spokenness also undermine his credibility. As a result of these disparities in terms of social, economic, cultural, and even symbolic capital, Siswanto could safely calculate that, whatever laws might exist, Sugiono would not be able to invoke them – and if he would, Sugiono's contacts and symbolic capital would ensure that his interpretation would prevail. It is thus not surprising that Sugiono at first ignored Siswanto's request for compensation. There had been two other accidents in his factory; in these cases, the workers decided to meekly accept the small compensation that Sugiono offered.

In this case, the involvement of a paralegal, Agus, had a demonstrable effect in addressing the power differentials. After Sugiono's unwillingness to pay compensation, Siswanto approached the paralegals of the BHK *posko* in Margodadi. They went over the case; Agus analyzed that available labor laws do stipulate that employers have to pay the salary of a worker when he cannot come to work due to sickness, but that as Siswanto did not have a salary slip or contract, it would be difficult to claim this money. Agus decided that it would not be helpful to bring the case to Disnaker (Dinas Tenaga Kerja, the governmental institution set up to deal with labor disputes).

Agus then went with Siswanto to negotiate with Sugiono. Now the factory owner did show some willingness to meet and discuss the claims. Agus claimed Rp 13.5 million compensation, an amount that did not include the money deducted from Siswanto's salary on the pretext of providing health insurance. During the first meeting, Sugiono refused to pay any money, stating that he had already paid Rp 1.3 million for the medical costs. A second meeting in the house of the *kepala desa* was also inconclusive, but during the third meeting, again in the house of the *kepala desa*, with the family members of both parties also present, it was agreed that Siswanto would pay Rp 4 million as compensation to Sugiono. Afterward, when Sugiono was asked why he paid this amount to Siswanto while he had refused to pay the workers who previously got injured, he said:

> Before they [the workers] understand us and we understand them, so there is not too much complaining. Now there is too much complaining and involvement of outsiders. If we bring in the law it eats time and costs. They know about the law, I don't. So I prefer to use our own way. They kept reminding me of the law and the labor rights when they proposed 13 million. I felt we should solve it *secara kekeluargaan* (i.e., informal mediation), instead of using the law. If we use the law it will increase all the cases, and all the money I have to pay to employees will increase. You cannot negotiate with the law. So we decided to accept a solution that was made through negotiation.

Similarly we asked the paralegal, Agus, why Sugiono listened to him and not to Siswanto's brother:

> If his brother came, he is just a villager and he has no power. When I came as a paralegal, the boss thought, "ok, now it's serious, now there is a legal aspect to the case." We were not a threat, but we referred to our legal analysis of the case. We said to them, we can bring this case to Disnaker. Then the company agreed to mediate; they were afraid of that.

Both Agus' and Sugiono's remarks illustrate how the impact of paralegals on local dispute resolution lies in the enlargement of the shadow of the law. It is not the facilitation of the access to the formal justice *itself* that makes a difference, it is the *threat* of starting legal proceedings that improved Siswanto's bargaining position vis-à-vis his employer. By bringing legal considerations to the table, and by conveying a credible threat that these laws might actually be invoked by going to Disnaker – the labor relations department – paralegal Agus could address the unequal bargaining position between Siswanto and Sugiono. In a well-functioning justice system,

Siswanto's interests might be better served by seeking full compensation at the labor relations court. But because of the informality of Siswanto's livelihood (as he lacks official papers), as well as an experience with a lackadaisical implementation of labor laws by Disnaker, Sugiono and Agus preferred to settle the case through negotiations:

> Our experience is that Disnaker is not neutral, that [it] will not mediate well. And then, if [it] do[es] not we woud have to go all the way to the Industrial Relations Court. That is too expensive and takes too long.

In short, in the context of an imperfect legal system, the contribution of paralegals in such conflicts often does not lie in facilitating the actual application of the law; it is by representing the *threat* that the case might indeed reach the police or the courts. The stronger party in a conflict often avails itself of various extralegal means to manipulate the outcome of a conflict; the involvement of a paralegal raises the costs of doing so – and thus improves the bargaining position of the weaker party.

This role of paralegals in extending the *shadow* of the law rather than facilitating the *application* of the law should be interpreted in the light of the necessity for most disputants to maintain good relationships within their community. As the next case study illustrates, if clients attach great importance to maintaining good relations and adhering to social norms, the legal considerations that paralegals insert into local dispute resolution can have limited impact.

IV. TAKING RESPONSIBILITY FOR CAR THEFT

Harjo, a tailor, had recently met Joni, and he had invited Joni to stay at his place. For a short vacation, Joni proposed to hire a car and go to the beach. Harjo agreed and he hired a car and a driver from the local car rental run by Pak Karyo. After driving together to the beach, Joni stole the car: under the pretext of buying a *durian*, he managed to get the keys to the car from the driver, and he drove off, leaving Harjo, his family, and the driver stranded at the beach. Neither Joni nor the car ever resurfaced. When they got back, Karyo, the owner of the rental company, demanded compensation for the loss of the car. During the first discussion he demanded Rp 65 million from both the driver and Harjo.

Harjo's income as a tailor was not sufficient to pay such an amount, and Harjo started to fear that he would have to leave his house. This was the moment he approached Subur, the local paralegal. Subur's legal analysis of the case was that Harjo was not liable for the theft; he argued that, if the police would not find Joni, only the driver and Pak Karyo should foot the bill. Harjo listened to this advice, but he did not heed it: he did not invite Subur for the next mediation session (which was led by the village head), and during this session he ignored Subur's advice – he agreed to pay Karyo the requested Rp 65 million, and a letter was written to this effect. Afterward Karyo was distraught, and started thinking about selling his house. As he later said of this mediation session: "I saw Karyo showing good will so I put aside the legal logic; it was more like we had family relations, with another sort of logic. So I did not want to insist on the legal position." A week later he approached Karyo again. During this last session, again conducted in the presence of the village head, Karyo changed his mind, and agreed to settle the issue for just Rp 10 million. Afterward he said that he changed his mind because he felt that Harjo had been reasonable, and that in any case it would be unlikely that Harjo would be able to pay more. It seemed that Karyo had pinned most of his hopes on his insurance.

Not only had Harjo ignored the advice from paralegal Subur, he also did not want him to be present. It is worth quoting his reasons to do so:

> The paralegals told me about the rule of law. We had a meeting at the *posko*. It was to prepare. Like if people go to war, you prepare your weapons. But I know that Karyo has power; I know that if I bring a paralegal, it will indicate that I prepare for conflict. I wanted to prevent him from using that power against me; I did not want him to become angry.

Harjo took into account the need to maintain a good relationship with Karyo: Karyo was from a relatively wealthy and well-respected family, and Harjo was apprehensive about starting a conflict with such a family. This family had the financial means to hire a good lawyer and win any court case, and the family had such a standing that Harjo felt many of his clients had actually stopped bringing work to him after the incident. In this case, Harjo's best option was to hope for an amicable solution, which in this situation worked out.

This case of the stolen car illustrates how paralegals operate at the crossroads between normative systems. Disputes between actors living in close proximity are shaped not only by legal provisions but also by the need to maintain good relationships within the community. That means that social norms and local (power) relations can sometimes make it impractical to take recourse to the law, as this is seen as unacceptable, unpractical, or an impolite form of addressing conflict. Some of this attitude could be traced back to the New Order period, when state propaganda regularly emphasized the need to solve conflicts in harmonious ways.[31] This stress on social harmony often favors the wealthy and the powerful, since it undermines the attempts of the less privileged to address these inequalities: when a more powerful party would be unwilling to settle an conflict *secara kekeluargaan*

---

[31] See particularly the essays in Antlöv and Cederroth's *Leadership on Java* on how (village) authority in Java was exercised through *perintah halus* ("gentle hints"). Hans Antlöv and Sven Cederroth, eds., *Leadership on Java: Gentle Hints, Authoritarian Rule* (Surrey: Curzon Press, 1994). In one of these essays, Mulder argues, for example: "Conflict or rebellious behavior that can be noted by others, that is in the open, is particularly painful. Not only because it jeopardizes a family's status, but also because it shows that people are in discord, not united and in harmony (*rukun*) as they should be." Niels Mulder, "The Ideology of Javanese-Indonesian Leadership," in *Leadership on Java: Gentle Hints, Authoritarian Rule*, ed. Hans Antlöv and Sven Cederroth (Surrey: Curzon Press, 1994), 68.

(i.e., through mediation), the importance attached to social harmony discourages a weaker party from open conflict behavior, like using the law to defend one's interests. Paralegals, through their socialization of the law, can serve to address this cultural heritage and to make legal action a more acceptable form of addressing injustices. Particularly in cases when local mediation favors the more powerful party, generating acceptance of the relevance of legal provisions can serve to support weaker parties. At the same time, Harjo's case illustrates how the strategies that disputants employ involve the weighing of legal considerations and local norms of "proper behavior," as well as assessments of the nature of social relations.

This avoidance of open conflict – whether or not a product of New Order propaganda – is one of the reasons why the studied paralegals took few cases to the police or the courts. While the facilitation of the interaction with formal legal institutions (i.e., legal accompaniment) is the activity most commonly associated with paralegals, the graph that follows shows that this activity forms a small aspect of the functioning of the studied paralegals in Indonesia.

Only in 14 percent of the 338 reported cases did paralegals help their clients report the problem to the police or a local court, with a further 5 percent of cases involving both mediation and legal accompaniment. In 20 percent of the cases clients approached the paralegal for advice, which led to no further action on the part of the paralegal. Advocacy is a rare activity for paralegals, employed in only fifteen cases (5 percent) out of the reported 338. In most cases (54 percent) paralegals deal with the issues brought to them by conducting or facilitating a mediation process between conflicting parties.

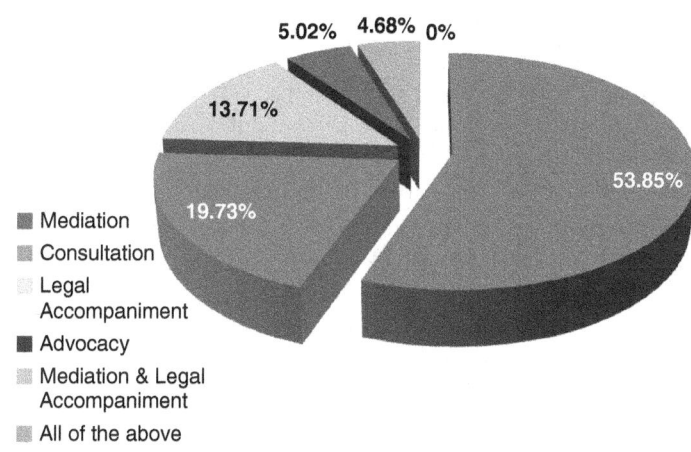

FIGURE 4.1 Case handling by paralegals

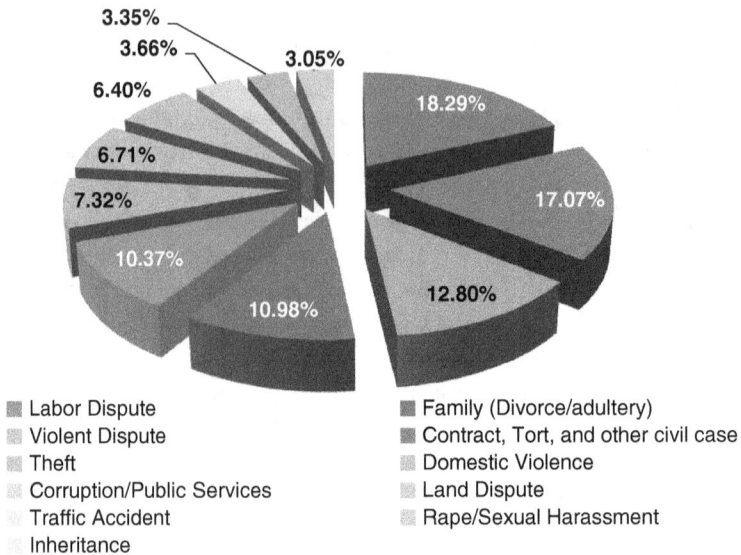

- Labor Dispute
- Violent Dispute
- Theft
- Corruption/Public Services
- Traffic Accident
- Inheritance
- Family (Divorce/adultery)
- Contract, Tort, and other civil case
- Domestic Violence
- Land Dispute
- Rape/Sexual Harassment

FIGURE 4.2 Type of case

The table that follows shows a breakdown of the types of cases paralegals are commonly involved in. The highest number of cases reported to paralegals involved family and labor disputes (17 percent and 18 percent, respectively) – types of disputes that lend themselves well to more informal dispute resolution. But also in criminal cases like theft or violent disputes paralegals rarely advise to take a case to the police or the court, only in 10 percent and 13 percent of cases, respectively – as these types of cases were also mostly dealt with through informal mediation.[32] It turns out that in cases concerning rape and labor disputes paralegals feel most confident in taking recourse to the formal justice system (30 percent and 21 percent of reported cases, respectively).

These statistics illustrate our earlier observation that the work of Indonesian paralegals only infrequently involves facilitating access to the formal justice system. While paralegals are not observed to have much impact on the actual use that people make of the formal legal system, their impact lies more in conveying a *threat* that legal procedures might be invoked. This threat not only affects the outcome of village-level mediation (as in the cases discussed earlier), but also smooths (to a certain extent) the interaction with particularly the local police. In the context of a police force that is often perceived as threatening and corrupt, paralegals can

---

[32] The "Governance and Decentralization Survey" that the World Bank conducted in 2006 reached similar conclusions; it found that villagers reported disputes most often to the village government (42 percent of informants had ever done so) and community/*adat* leaders (35 percent), and less frequently to the police (27 percent). *See* World Bank, *Forging the Middle Ground*, 17 (see n. 17).

sometimes strengthen the bargaining position of villagers vis-à-vis the police. As the next case study illustrates, this often serves to keep the police *out* – in convincing the police to have a case settled through informal mediation.

V. LEGAL ACCOMPANIMENT: A *DUKUN* FINDS A THIEF

Sulis had been working for two months at a small stationary shop, when the owner of the shop, Ruhaini, accused her of stealing Rp 2.3 million from the shop's register. There were no eyewitnesses and Sulis denied having stolen money. But as Sulis had been alone in the shop, Ruhaini felt certain that Sulis had taken the money. She consulted a local *dukun* (a healer who masters magic), whose divination also pointed to Sulis. At that point she went to the police. Ruhaini comes from a prominent family in the region and her father is the ex-head of the district police. So both the village head and the local police officers decided to take Ruhaini's word for it, and the police duly arrested Sulis. With Sulis in jail, Ruhaini went to Sulis' family together with the village head, a close friend of her father's. They told the stricken family that Sulis would be transferred to another jail if they would not sign a letter (a *surat perdamaian*), promising to repay the Rp 2.3 million. Sulis' family saw no other option but to sign the letter that the village head drafted, which admitted Sulis' guilt. With that letter, Sulis' brother went to the police – with the hope that this agreement would convince the police to release Sulis. But the letter was not enough. The police officials asked Sulis' brother for Rp 5 million. He went around his village to collect as much money as he could: in the end he paid the police Rp 2 million before they agreed to stop the case and release Sulis. A few days after Sulis was released from jail, Ruhaini sent two men to her house, who threatened to "play judge" if her family would not pay the promised Rp 2.3 million.

Sulis' parents grew sick with worry about having to pay this insurmountable amount of money. Sulis and her father decided then to visit Pak Agus. Agus is a local paralegal who has received basic legal training from KBH Lampung. The signboard in front of his house – identifying his place as a "legal aid post" – and his record as a local problem solver generate a steady stream of visitors like Sulis. He advised them not to pay the Rp 2.3 million. With a *surat kuasa* – a "letter of attorney" signifying that he was her legal representative, Pak Agus went to the village head to organize a mediation session. The meeting at the *balai desa* was tense, as Ruhaini kept insisting on the Rp 2.3 million. Sulis' family and Pak Agus told them that the letter was not valid; they argued with the village head and they stood their ground. Ruhaini threatened to get Sulis arrested again, but three months after the incident nothing more had happened. When asked about what he had learned from these experiences, Sulis' brother replied, "our neighbors were surprised that we could win against powerful people. We are an example for poor people. If we are enlightened, we do not always have to be the victim; we can fight."

Sulis' experiences illustrate two key and interrelated weaknesses associated with Indonesia's formal legal system: both the courts and the police are considered to more responsive to the wishes of more powerful sections of society, and they are prone to rent-seeking. The police officials did not really investigate whether Sulis was guilty; their standard operational procedures for such a case seemed to matter less than Ruhaini's superior status and contacts, and they demanded a very high fee for Sulis' release. The inequality between Ruhaini and Sulis in terms of their social and symbolic capital made the police more well disposed toward Ruhaini. Given such experiences, it is no surprise that surveys regularly indicate high levels of distrust toward the formal legal system. Because of the costs and the perceived corruptibility of the police, an informal settlement of a dispute or a violation is often preferred, even when it concerns criminal acts.[33] Furthermore, as one survey indicated, 50 percent of respondents felt that the formal justice system was biased toward the rich and the powerful, against only 15 percent for the informal justice system[34] – i.e., the mediation done by village heads, customary (*adat*) leaders, and other local notables. Even if no bribe is paid, taking a case to court can be expensive and time-consuming, while there is a general perception that, due to corruption, there can be no certainty about the way a law is applied in court. Police officials generally have paid a considerable amount of money to their superiors to get their jobs, which means that often they cannot avoid demanding a bribe from people like Sulis – to make good on their earlier "investment."

The capacity of paralegals to help their clients deal with the police – whether to stop a case, to report a case, or to accompany an accused – is again largely due to the threat that they represent: their presence, and their links to lawyers of legal aid associations, suggests to police officials that any misbehavior on their part might actually lead to an official complaint. While police officials can often assume that uneducated villagers will not have the skills or stamina to protest against bribe-taking or foot-dragging – the police officials in this case seemed to have few qualms about asking Sulis for Rp 2 million – the involvement of paralegals can serve to discipline individual police officials. Furthermore, this involvement seems to impart some confidence to their clients; Sulis and her family, for example, said repeatedly that they felt "less panic" and "more secure" when Pak Agus got involved. The connections that a paralegal has with outside organizations – like a legal aid association – are crucial for this interaction with the police, because these links contribute considerably to the impression that a paralegal might create problems for a misbehaving police officer.

[33] See the surveys done by Asia Foundation and UNDP. The latter found that 12 percent of respondents had used the informal justice system, against 10 percent for the formal justice system. Informants reported to be more satisfied (58 percent) with the informal justice system then with the formal system (28 percent). The Asia Foundation and ACNielsen, *Survey Report on Citizens' Perceptions of the Indonesian Justice Sector: Preliminary Findings and Recommendations* (Jakarta: Asia Foundation, 2005); UN Development Programme, *Justice for All?*, 64 (see n. 3).

[34] UN Development Programme, *Justice for All?*, 72 (see n. 3).

Paralegalism in Indonesia

In this context, it is not surprising that paralegals are reluctant to advise a client to bring a case to court. In the context of a corruptible and inaccessible formal legal system, the work of paralegals more often consists of finding alternative solutions in order to avoid or minimize and scrutinize the involvement of the police – even to victims of criminal offences.

VI. WHAT MAKES A PARALEGAL SUCCESSFUL?

Yet not every studied paralegal operated as successfully as Agus. While some of the paralegal *poskos* set up by the World Bank program reported almost no cases in more than two years, other *poskos* received more than twenty. While it has to be taken into account that many paralegals failed to report particularly the smaller cases, 338 cases is not a high number for 120 paralegals and ninety-five mediators working for two years. Furthermore, as the next graph shows, their activity was also not evenly spread in time: most of the case handling of the paralegals was concentrated in the last nine months of the project. In short, it took time before villagers trusted paralegals sufficiently to report their problems to them, and some paralegals never really managed to establish this trust.

These observations suggest that the mere fact of being a trained as a paralegal is not enough to convince villagers that he or she will indeed be of any use. In all the project areas it took considerable time before people started to trust their paralegals enough to bring their problems to them. In some areas the local community never really developed this trust. Through our fieldwork we identified a number of additional factors that influenced whether a paralegal was capable of gaining the trust of his or her community.

The World Bank's RLA project used the following criteria to select paralegals: (a) trusted by the community; (b) actively involved in community organization or

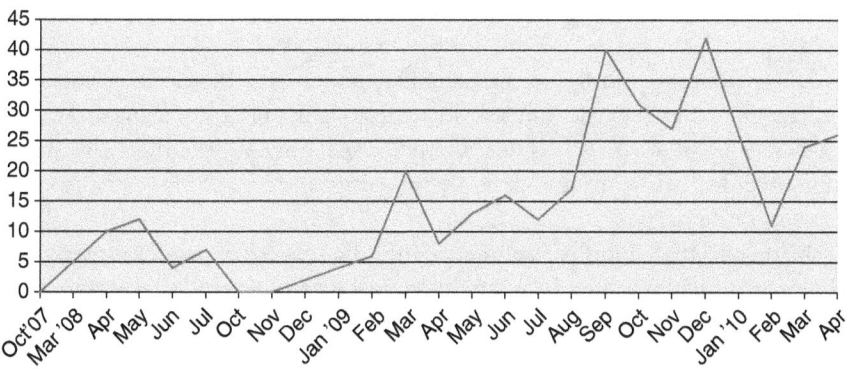

FIGURE 4.3 Cases reported by paralegals by date

activities; (c) having organizational, advocacy, or legal aid experience. UNDP's LEAD program used similar criteria. As both programs mostly operated in rural areas, most of the paralegals we encountered were farmers with limited education, aged between thirty and fifty.[35] Both UNDP and the World Bank programs worked with (relatively young) "facilitators" who were supposed to provide support to paralegals when dealing with complex cases. Yet apart from these general similarities in social background of the paralegals, there were three important differences that, in our view, accounted for the different levels of activity between paralegals.

Paralegals are not the only ones offering help to local disputants or victims of a crime. In fact, the inaccessibility of the formal legal system has engendered a whole range of "legal intermediaries" – i.e., actors involved in dispute resolution and the facilitation of interaction with the police and the courts. There are village heads, customary authorities, religious, and other local leaders offering informal justice mechanisms for dispute resolution. Since disputing parties are looking for reassurances that any agreement will be adhered to, it makes sense to involve the village head: because of his official status and his links with police and other government officials his signature on an agreement letter (*surat perjanjian*) can convince the police officers to take action. That means that often paralegals play a small role as advisors next to existing local disputing mechanisms. Furthermore, one can find various kinds of "fixers" – journalists, NGO staff members, case brokers (*makelar kasus*) and even local criminals (*preman*) – who offer to use their contacts and knowledge of procedures to report a case to the police or to bring a case to court (for a fee). Both village heads and paralegals called these fixers and their organizations "*bodrex* NGOs" or "*bodrex* journalists," referring to a medicine called Bodrex, used in Indonesia for all sorts of illnesses: these fixers jump on any kind of issue, hoping to make some money by offering their services. The presence of paralegals can be perceived as a threat for those whose local status and income depend on their facilitation of contact with the police. In this competition, skilled *makelar kasus* or *bodrex* NGOs can receive more cases than paralegals as they actively go around looking for them. The special qualities of paralegals – their legal training and their connections to supra-local (legal aid) associations and the fact that they do not ask for a fee – do not necessarily make their services superior to these various alternatives, particularly if there are locally influential leaders with the skill of brokering and enforcing a compromise between disputants.

That means that, in order to attract clients, the services of paralegals need to be perceived as superior. The following three factors seem to influence this evaluation. First, the most active and successful paralegals often already have had some

---

[35] With the exception of RLA's program in West Java, where the program worked with a local trade union and, as a consequence, most paralegals were involved in various forms of manual labor.

success in taking up community problems before becoming paralegals, often through involvement in organizing events or protests. Agus easily acquired clients because his previous activities as a local activist had given him an image of a trustworthy and effective organizer, which boosted his effectiveness as paralegal. This is also the reason why the few paralegals in the Justice for the Poor program who were also village heads received the largest number of cases: it was their position as village head that convinced villagers that he (or she) would succeed in settling their dispute.

A second, related factor is the strength of the network in which a paralegal is embedded. As contacts (with lawyers, the police, politicians, etc.) are crucial to solving issues, the development of a large network can greatly contribute to a paralegal's effectiveness. Justice for the Poor's paralegal project worked with local labor unions and agrarian organizations to select and train paralegals, and this seems to have helped paralegals to build trust and to acquire new useful contacts. Particularly the association with a local legal aid association is important for a paralegal as this constitutes his or her particular advantage over the other "legal intermediaries" mentioned earlier: this support from city-based lawyers signals to possible clients that a paralegal might actually succeed in bringing a case to court. A third factor influencing the number of cases paralegals received is their personal skills and *savoir faire*. The limited education and exposure of selected paralegals presents a great challenge to such community-based paralegal programs: while some showed extensive knowledge of the law and legal procedures and felt no hesitation about contacting power holders, there were many others who, even after being a paralegal for more than two years, lacked even basic legal knowledge and felt very shy about contacting a local police official or a village head. A self-reinforcing mechanism was at work here: because of a lack of skills and self-confidence, villagers did not ask a paralegal for help, which deprived this paralegal of the opportunity to develop the necessary self-confidence and skills.[36] This can be more difficult for women because of prevailing conservative ideas about the proper role of women in the public sphere – but this need not be an insurmountable obstacle, given the impressive female paralegals whom we encountered. The observed lack of skills and self-confidence of many paralegals points mainly to inadequacies in the training program, as the provided training seemed insufficient to turn many selected individuals into effective paralegals. In particular the training seemed inadequate to enable paralegals to engage in community organizing to address collective injustices. As we discuss in what follows, this is all the more regrettable as advocacy constitutes an area where paralegals could – compared to mediation and legal accompaniment – make a large contribution.

[36] The fact that both the Justice for the Poor project and UNDP's LEAD project worked in teams (*poskos*) did serve to address this problem, since in this way the more savvy paralegals within these teams could be an example for others to follow.

VII. ADVOCACY: A FIGHT FOR ELECTRICITY

Since March 2009 the ninety-eight families living in "Megaresidence," a housing block in Bogor for low-income groups, had not been receiving electricity. The state electricity company, PLN, had found out that the electricity for the housing block had been illegally tapped, and it demanded a fine of Rp 89 million (about US$9,000) before it would reconnect the houses. According to the inhabitants, the developer had made this illegal connection to the electricity grid while reassuring the buyers of the houses that electricity was included.

As the developer was unwilling the pay the fine imposed by PLN, the inhabitants of Megaresidence approached a group of paralegals led by Mbak Sri. The paralegals threatened the developer with a lawsuit, who subsequently sent a group of *preman* (thugs) to intimidate inhabitants. While the paralegals did manage to document the wrongdoings of the developer, they calculated that any court case would be lengthy and possibly inconclusive; they opted for a different strategy. They staged several rallies, wrote letters to several governmental agencies, arranged newspaper coverage, and, using the contacts of the labor union for which they worked, Mbak Sri and the other paralegals convinced the members of "commission C" of the local parliament (DPRD) to conduct two hearings on the case. During this formal meeting DPRD members invited the different sides to tell their story; the whole community of Megaresidence came to the DPRD building for the occasion. Sri was afterward very proud of this moment: "this was an important moment because before the people could not meet officials and did not dare to speak publicly." After the second hearing DPRD members issued (non-legally binding) advice, in which they instructed the developer to pay the fine while telling PLN to start providing electricity. At first PLN continued to press the inhabitants for payment of the fine, but after more media attention and the threat of a lawsuit the developer paid half the fine and PLN agreed to restart the provision of electricity. As Sri described her strategy: "We want to create synergy between the legal justice system and politics. We use politics to bring up the human side. We use it to touch the heart of government official. This is more effective ... If we support a winning candidate, he can support us when we are working on a case."

While strictly speaking this kind of activity might not be called "legal aid" – since it does not necessarily involve promoting access to legal systems – advocacy and community organizing is increasingly seen as an important part of the work of paralegals because these activities are often perceived (also by paralegals themselves) to be a more effective tool to address (mis)deeds by state institutions or companies than taking recourse to the formal justice system. This realization has led to calls to see legal empowerment and "social accountability" as two complementary strategies to achieve social justice.[37] In the campaign for an electricity connection, paralegals performed different roles: they offered legal advice, and they engaged in community organizing as well as lobbying. In the context of a slow and unpredictable justice system, political channels seem to offer effective alternative means to pressurize companies and state agencies. Since the fall of Suharto in 1998, local politicians have become more prominent as they are now elected and, after a decentralization process, also in control of more funds. Some of the studied paralegals – in our perception particularly the ablest ones – are seeing these increasingly prominent politicians as an effective channel to address injustices. As political parties in Indonesia generally lack a local base to facilitate interaction with citizens, paralegals are taking up this important liaising role.[38]

The involvement of politicians can serve various purposes. First, the involvement of politicians, and particularly the organization of a public hearing, can be used to put pressure on the adverse party. The coverage of such a hearing can create negative publicity that shames the other party into agreeing to a settlement – that at least seemed to have been the reasoning of PLN. Another reason to involve politicians is that they can put pressure on the bureaucracy and the judicial apparatus. While there is a long history of political meddling in the bureaucracy and the judiciary, this meddling usually favored the privileged sections of society. But, as local politicians now need to maintain electoral support, it seems that in some cases local politicians show willingness and capacity to pressurize the police and other bureaucrats to defend the interests of the less well-connected and less moneyed party.

In this case, Mbak Sri cleverly employed the electoral concerns of politicians:

> We have political contacts that we can use. We had to go almost every week to the DPRD building ... During elections there is a *"kontrak politik"* with groups: we make the candidate promise that, if I am elected, he will do this and that. So in return KBB [the labor union of which Mbak Sri is a part] organizes an [election] meeting with the candidate, where they give support.

In this case she could use this *kontrak politik* to get politicians to put pressure on the electricity company.

In all our research locations we encountered paralegals who had, like Shri, forged political links. Some had become members of the local campaign teams (*Tim Sukses desa*) of politicians, others made speeches during elections, and a third group just boasted of their friendships with politicians. Some of the paralegals said they maintained these political links because it would make them more effective paralegals – they reasoned that after elections they could ask the winning candidate for

---

[37] Vivek Maru, "Allies Unknown: Social Accountability and Legal Empowerment," in *Legal Empowerment: Practitioners' Perspectives*, ed. Stephen Golub and Thomas McInerney (Rome: International Development Law Organization, 2010).

[38] Michael Buehler and Paige Tan, "Party–Candidate Relationships in Indonesian Local Politics: A Case Study of the 2005 Regional Elections in Gowa, South Sulawesi Province," *Indonesia* 84 (2007): 41–69, www.jstor.org.proxygw.wrlc.org/stable/40376429.

favors, calling it an *investasi politik* ("political investment"). For others it was also the other way around: they believe that by working as a paralegal they could raise their public profile and thus, in a later stage, become a politician themselves.

One can evaluate this use of political contacts both positively and negatively. On the one hand Indonesia's democratization and decentralization processes have created new channels that can be used to pressurize disputing parties to reach a solution. The support from high-profile politicians is proving useful to help people to hold state institutions or companies accountable. On the other hand an increased role of political actors in dispute settlement is also creating situations where disputes are not settled on the basis of legal considerations, but on the basis of who is most capable of reciprocating (with votes or money) the support from politicians. The involvement of politicians in particular cases is not just motivated by considerations of justice; it is also motivated by a calculation about how this involvement can lead to votes and money. Compared to other Asian countries the capacity of DPRD members and other local politicians to pressurize civil servants is still limited, but there are indications that this capacity is growing[39] – where politicians can gain supporters and money by pressurizing the bureaucracy and the judiciary, they have an active interest in subverting bureaucratic procedures and, ultimately, the rule of law. These developments suggest that the prospects of improving access to justice are tied up with the way local political economies develop – particularly with the strategies that political elites are employing to hold on to power. This poses challenges for paralegal programs: while the employment of political contacts to settle issues is often very effective, it does stimulate politicians to develop their control over the bureaucracy and the judiciary – to the detriment of the rule of law. Paralegal training needs to address both the opportunities and the risks involved when associating oneself with politicians.

Given the effectiveness of paralegals in the case discussed here (as well as in other cases we studied) and given the lack of alternative actors and organizations to play such a role, advocacy played a surprisingly peripheral role in the studied paralegal programs. The number of cases involving state or corporate accountability is quite low – for example, less than 7 percent of the reported cases involved corruption and the provision of public services – and it seems that advocacy skills were not sufficiently trained – interviewed paralegals state that they hardly received training on political lobbying, organizing rallies, getting media attention, etc. Furthermore, the design of the World Bank and UNDP projects influenced the number of advocacy cases paralegals receive: by choosing to train villagers to work as paralegals *within* their community, it remains accidental whether they run into cases involving state or

---

[39] Particularly India has been called a "patronage democracy" because of the discretionary power that politicians have over the everyday functioning of the bureaucracy, which enables them to manipulate the execution of public policies as well as the functioning of the police and the courts. See Ward Berenschot, "Everyday Mediation: The Politics of Public Service Delivery in Gujarat, India," *Development and Change* 41, no. 5 (2010): 883–905, doi: 10.1111/j.1467-7660.2010.01660.x.

corporate accountability. It depends on whether such a case happens to present itself. In most villages there are only small village-level disputes to work on – which are also dealt with by local mechanisms. This is a drawback of working with community-based paralegals in this way: by selecting project areas that are known to be involved in supra-local disputes with companies or state agencies, or by training paralegals to move around and work in different villages, paralegals could become more regularly involved in such supra-local disputes and advocacy campaigns against corporate or governmental malpractices. This could improve the overall contribution of paralegal projects.

VIII. CONCLUSION

In this chapter we discussed the impact of the presence of paralegals on grievance and dispute handling in rural Indonesia. Focusing on the paralegal projects supported by UNDP and the World Bank, we discussed the three main spheres of activities of paralegals: mediation, legal accompaniment, and advocacy. Deriving inspiration from relational sociology, we argued that the impact of the presence of paralegals does not lie so much in improving the access to the formal legal system, but rather in countering the impact of power imbalances between disputing parties on the outcome of processes of grievance and dispute handling. The presence of paralegals does not necessarily lead to a large number of cases being referred to the formal legal system – the widespread distrust of the formal legal system combined with the availability of local mechanisms also often discourages paralegals themselves to advise such legal action. This might be different in the long run: although difficult to substantiate, we found some indications that the way paralegals familiarize their fellow villagers with Indonesian law could in the long run serve to overcome this avoidance of the Indonesian legal system. But in the short run the impact of paralegals lies mainly in enlarging the shadow of the law as they do insert legal considerations more forcefully into mediation (and advocacy) processes, and in this manner paralegals strengthen the bargaining position of their clients.

Not every paralegal has the capacity to do so, however. Paralegals compete with other local actors for the status (and money) involved in solving disputes and addressing grievances, as various actors and local institutions can be found who perform similar tasks. We observed that the role of paralegals during mediation processes is often modest, as these sessions are usually led by village heads or customary leaders with paralegals in an advisory role. Various "legal intermediaries" – ranging from village heads to case brokers, *bodrex* NGOs, and local *preman* – could be identified who are also engaged in dispute settlement and in the facilitation of the interaction with the police and the courts. The competition with these various other legal intermediaries can limit the effectiveness of paralegals and forms an obstacle for gaining trust among the local population.

It is unfortunate that one area of work where paralegals do offer unique skills – advocacy – plays a marginal role in the studied programs. Those paralegals who possessed advocacy skills proved highly effective in helping communities deal with government or corporate malpractices. As political parties in Indonesia's young democracy are generally very weakly institutionalized, paralegals are playing an important role as liaisons between local communities and politicians. Since decentralization and the institution of local elections are making local politicians more prominent, many paralegals now feel that a strong political lobby can be more effective than legal action. For this reason some paralegals are carefully nurturing their political contacts, which often stimulates them to campaign for candidates during elections. While this capacity to engage with politics boosts the effectiveness of paralegals, this engagement also carries risks – particularly that this engagement can go against the stated aim of paralegal projects to strengthen the rule of law.

Paralegalism in Indonesia is as yet still weakly institutionalized. The paralegal programs currently operative in Indonesia are set up by a limited group of universities, Indonesian legal aid organizations, and international donors. Efforts to institutionalize the accreditation of paralegals are still in its infancy. Unfortunately the recently adopted Legal Aid Bill did little to change that, as its efforts as well as funding have largely concentrated on supporting representation in court. Yet the need for legal aid beyond the courts is as big as ever. Conflicts arising out of, for example, the relentless expansion of palm oil companies and Indonesia's vague land regime, as well as the recent empowerment of village heads (through the new village law), are having a big impact on people's livelihoods. Many more paralegals are needed to address such conflicts and find fairer outcomes as they can help to tackle the impact of social inequalities within Indonesian society on processes of dispute resolution. Operating at the crossroads between law, social norms, and power relations, paralegals can contribute to making the outcomes of these processes more equitable.

REFERENCES

Antlöv, Hans and Sven Cederroth, editors. *Leadership on Java: Gentle Hints, Authoritarian Rule*. Surrey: Curzon Press, 1994.

Asia Foundation and ACNielsen. *Survey Report on Citizens' Perceptions of the Indonesian Justice Sector: Preliminary Findings and Recommendations*. Jakarta: Asia Foundation, 2005.

Berenschot, Ward. "Everyday Mediation: The Politics of Public Service Delivery in Gujarat, India." *Development and Change* 41, no. 5 (2010): 883–905. doi: 10.1111/j.1467-7660.2010.01660.x.

Bourdieu, Pierre and Loic J. D. Wacquant. *An Invitation to Reflexive Sociology*. Chicago: University of Chicago Press, 1992.

Bowen, John R. *Islam, Law and Equality in Indonesia: An Anthropology of Public Reasoning*. Cambridge: Cambridge University Press, 2003.

Bruce, John W., Omar Garcia-Bolivar, Tim Hanstad, Michael Roth, Robin Nielson, Anna Knox, and Jon Schmidt. *Legal Empowerment of the Poor: From Concepts to Assessments*. Washington, DC: USAID, 2007.
Buehler, Michael and Paige Tan. "Party–Candidate Relationships in Indonesian Local Politics: A Case Study of the 2005 Regional Elections in Gowa, South Sulawesi Province." *Indonesia* 84 (2007). www.jstor.org.proxygw.wrlc.org/stable/40376429.
Collins, Elizabeth F. *Indonesia Betrayed: How Development Fails*. Honolulu: University of Hawaii Press, 2007.
Commission on Legal Empowerment of the Poor. *Making the Law Work for Everyone*, vol. 1. New York: Commission on Legal Empowerment of the Poor, UNDP, 2008.
Elias, Norbert. *What Is Sociology?* London: Hutchinson, 1978.
Emirbayer. Mustafa. "Manifesto for a Relational Sociology." *American Journal of Sociology* 103, no. 2 (1997): 281–317. http://www.jstor.org/stable/10.1086/231209?origin=JSTOR-pdf&seq=1#page_scan_tab_contents.
Golub, Stephen. "Beyond the Rule of Law Orthodoxy: The Legal Empowerment Alternative." *Working Papers*, Rule of Law Series, no. 41. Washington, DC: Carnegie Endowment for International Peace, 2003.
Government of Indonesia, UN Development Programme. "Legal Empowerment and Assistance for the Disadvantaged (LEAD) Project." Jakarta: Government of Indonesia, UN Development Programme, 2007.
Haryanto, Ulma. "For Indonesia's Poor, Paralegals Pave the Way to Justice." *Jakarta Globe*. January 25, 2012. http://jakartaglobe.beritasatu.com/archive/for-indonesias-poor-paralegals-pave-the-way-to-justice/.
Heller, Patrick and Peter Evans. "Taking Tilly South: Durable Inequalities, Democratic Contestation, and Citizenship in the Southern Metropolis." *Theory and Society* 39, no. 3 (2010).
"Indonesia." Justice for the Poor. http://go.worldbank.org/DH16VCUFS0.
Justice for the Poor Program. *Baseline Survey: Pilot Program Revitalization of Legal Aid in Indonesia (RLA)*. Washington, DC: World Bank 2006.
Justice for the Poor, World Bank and Ministry of Law and Human Rights. "Legal Aid Organizations in Indonesia: Results of Nationwide Survey of 230 Legal Aid Organizations." Unpublished report, June 2014.
Law of the Republic of Indonesia No. 16/2011 Concerning Legal Aid.
Lev, Daniel S. *Legal Evolution and Political Authority in Indonesia: Selected Essays*. The Hague: Kluwer Law International, 2000.
Lindsey, Timothy and Mas Achmad Santosa. "The Trajectory of Law Reform in Indonesia: A Short Overview of Legal Systems and Change in Indonesia." In *Indonesia: Law and Society*, edited by Tim Lindsey. Sydney: The Federation Press, 2008, 2–22.
Maru, Vivek. "Allies Unknown: Social Accountability and Legal Empowerment." In *Legal Empowerment: Practitioners' Perspectives*, edited by Stephen Golub and Thomas McInerney. Rome: International Development Law Organization, 2010, 81–93.
"Between Law and Society: Paralegals and Provision of Justice Services in Sierra Leone and Worldwide." *The Yale Journal of International Law* 31, no. 2 (2006): 427–76.
Mnookin, Robert H, and Lewis Kornhauser. "Bargaining in the Shadow of the Law: The Case of Divorce." *Yale Law Journal* 88, no. 5 (1979): 950–97. doi: 10.2307/795824.
Mulder, Niels. "The Ideology of Javanese-Indonesian Leadership." In *Leadership on Java: Gentle Hints, Authoritarian Rule*, edited by Hans Antlöv and Sven Cederroth. Surrey: Curzon Press, 1994, 57–73.

Nasution, Buyung. "The Legal Aid Movement in Indonesia: Towards the Implementation of the Structural Legal Aid Concept." In *Access to Justice: Human Rights Struggles in South East Asia*, edited by Harry M. Scoble and Laurie S. Wiseberg. London: Zed Books, 1985, 30–45.

Republic of Indonesia, Ministry of Law and Human Rights. *Laporan Tahunan: Implementasi Undang Undang Nomor 16 2011 tentang Bantuan Hukum* (Annual Report of The Implementation of Legal Aid Law). https://sidbankum.bphn.go.id/front/down load?filename=4422_laporan_tahunan_bantuan_hukum.pdf.

Sage, Caroline, Nick Menzies, and Michael Woolcock. "Taking the Rules of the Game Seriously – Mainstreaming Justice in Development: The World Bank's Justice for the Poor Program." In *Legal Empowerment: Practitioners' Perspectives*, edited by Stephen Golub and Thomas McInerney. Rome: International Development Law Organization, 2010, 19–39.

Simarmata, R. "Negara & Kekuasaan." *Pusat Studi Hukum & Kebijakan Indonesia* 8, no. 3, 2003.

Stapleton, Adam. "Empowering the Poor to Access Criminal Justice: A Grass-Roots Perspective." In *Legal Empowerment: Practitioners' Perspectives*, edited by Stephen Golub and Thomas McInerney. Rome: International Development Law Organization, 2010: 39–63.

"Strategi Nasional Akses Terhadap Keadilan" (Stranas) § 3.2, available at http://perpustakaan .bappenas.go.id/lontar/file%3Ffile=digital/91553-[_Konten_]-Konten%20C6083.pdf.

UN Development Programme. "Access to Justice, Practice Note." UN Development Programme, 2004.

Justice for All?: An Assessment of Access to Justice in Five Provinces of Indonesia. Jakarta: United Nations Development Programme, 2007.

"The Legal Empowerment and Assistance for the Disadvantaged (LEAD)." www.id .undp.org/content/indonesia/en/home/operations/projects/democratic_governance/ the-legal-empowerment-and-assistance-for-the-disadvantaged.html.

Van Rooij, Benjamin. "Bringing Justice to the Poor: Bottom-Up Legal Development Cooperation." *Hague Journal on the Rule of Law* 4, no. 2 (2012): 286–318. doi: 10.1017/ S1876404512000176.

Von Benda-Beckmann, Keebet. "Forum Shopping and Shopping Forums: Dispute Processing in a Minangkabau Village in West Sumatra." *Journal of Legal Pluralism and Unofficial Law* 13, no. 19 (1981): 117–60.

World Bank. *Forging the Middle Ground: Engaging Non-state Justice in Indonesia*. Washington, DC: World Bank, 2008.

5

Kenya's Community-Based Paralegals

A Tradition of Grassroots Legal Activism

H. Abigail Moy

1. INTRODUCTION

Last month, around the 26th of September, a big fight broke out among boys living in the dam site, who collect wares and sell them. The police came. Three people were killed by police officers – one child was shot in the neck.

Our office is within the community, in the center of the slum. As a paralegal, I am a trained human rights activist. Earlier, we had raised awareness about what paralegals do in the community. So everyone knows that there is a center where you can run and report your problems. People don't distinguish between criminal and civil problems. Whenever there is any problem, they rush to the center.

They began calling me at midnight. I woke up to ten text messages: "People are being killed, people will be lynched, you are a leader, come and speak to us, give us direction on what we can do."

First thing, I rushed to the center. I found seven people waiting by the office. Each and every one had a problem to tell. Some were robbed at night, during the fight. Some women were raped, some were beaten. Some of them just ran away from the scene because they feared for their lives.

A Catholic priest called me and told me about the child who was shot. "The child is still lying outside, with parents beside him," he said. "The police shot the child in the crossfire, but they will not come to collect the body."

---

* Special thanks to Mary Amuyunzu-Nyamongo, Monica Wabuke-Lutta, and the staff of the African Institute for Health and Development for organizing field research and gathering data for this chapter. We are grateful to the research partners who worked tirelessly on this project: Kituo Cha Sheria, International Commission of Jurists–Kenya Chapter, International Federation of Women Lawyers–Kenya Chapter, Legal Resources Foundation, Muslims for Human Rights, and Plan International. We are particularly indebted to the members of the research teams, who braved great distances and personal hardship in the course of their work: Robert Rapando, Winnie Wanjugu, Mildred Arum, Hillary Apollo, James Murage, Nahashon Kipruto, Michael Kadima, Esther Makona, Allan Nyange, Fredrick Odanga, Barlet Jaji, Stephen Mkangi, and George Biruri. Many thanks to Christina Williams for analyzing and drafting case studies, to Madhu Ramankutty for her research support, and to Alice Goldenberg and Anisa Rahaman for their editorial assistance. This chapter is dedicated to the many paralegals and human rights leaders who shared their time and stories with us. I hope that in some small way, these pages honor the many sacrifices they have made in the name of justice.

They told me that when they called the police, the police told them, "we cannot go to the slums because you people are fighting us back." Really, the police don't want to come between the people and the boys. They actually protect the boys because they give them money.

So I started reacting. I started trying to reach people. That whole day I was trying to organize assistance. I called Kituo Cha Sheria. I took cases: there was an old woman of sixty-five years, I documented evidence of her rape. Another woman of fifty years was shot in the arm, another boy was shot in the cheek. I called referral systems to get them help – they know me because I have been working with them. I'd say, "I have someone here, can you come?" I sent the lady to MSF [Medicins sans Frontieres]. They brought a vehicle and picked her up. I put the boy on a motorbike; he was rushed to the hospital.

Then I called the OCS [Officer Commanding Police Station]. I told him to send officers to retrieve the body of the boy. Leaving him on the street was a violation of the rights of the child. The OCS was not ready to accept. He told me, "you never went to training, why are you telling me what to do?" But I kept trying.

The police finally came the following day. I was with the parents, on the side of the community. But I was not inciting – I was there to bring peace. I talked to the parents and said this is a legal issue, and law must take due course. When the people of the community realized that I was there, they silenced to listen to what I was trying to advise them. I was trying to tell them to stop fighting. The police officers took the child at last, because I was there. Even the police agreed that I played a part in this.

I went with the police and personally saw the case recorded in the Occurrence Book. The child was taken to the mortuary. We talked to the OCS. He was very hostile; he was opposed to starting an investigation. But I myself will push. I intend to go farther than that because it's the truth.

The role of the paralegal is not only to see that people whose rights are violated get some reprieve, but also to ensure that there is peace and tranquility where we stay. Most of these informal settlements are very sensitive and emotive. A small thing can erupt into a very big conflict. We are not only paralegals, but also peace ambassadors. Our main issue in terms of peace is mitigation of conflict.

– As told by Michael, a community paralegal in Korogocho, Nairobi

For most Kenyans, the formal justice system is an inhospitable place for resolving conflicts or seeking remedies. The national police force is understaffed and ill-equipped;[1] lawyers are scarce and costly;[2] the courts are backlogged and often

---

[1] Patricia K. Mbote and Migai Akech, *Kenya Justice Sector and the Rule of Law: A Review by AfriMAP and the Open Society Initiative for Eastern Africa* (Nairobi: Open Society Foundation, 2011), 11; Human Rights Watch, *High Stakes: Political Violence and the 2013 Elections in Kenya* (Nairobi: Human Rights Watch, 2013).

[2] Currently fewer than 8,000 advocates serve Kenya's population of nearly 40 million. A majority of these lawyers are based in major cities, despite the fact that 78 percent of the population lives in rural areas. Although typical legal fees are beyond the ability of the average Kenyan to afford, most advocates outside of NGOs do not feel compelled to engage in pro bono work or reduce fees for the indigent. Human Rights Watch, *High Stakes*, 114, 158–59 (see n. 1); UN Office on Drugs and Crime (UNODC), *Access to Legal Aid in Criminal Justice Systems in Africa: Survey Report* (Vienna: United Nations, 2011), 12.

geographically inaccessible;³ procedures are inefficient and complicated; and corruption famously plagues the judiciary.⁴ Consequently, formal courts handle only 4 percent of disputes in Kenya, according to a household survey undertaken by the Governance, Justice, Law and Order Sector (GJLOS) Reform Programme.⁵ Meanwhile, 67 percent of disputes are handled by chiefs and traditional elders⁶ – members of their respective communities who in turn rely on local justice systems to maintain order.⁷

In many ways, customary local systems are more accessible, affordable, and attuned to cultural expectations of fairness than their formal counterparts.⁸ However, even they are not immune to abuse or manipulation by local elites, whose influence perpetuates social dynamics that consistently disempower the poor and marginalized.⁹

Community paralegals bridge the gap between these two worlds. Kenya's Paralegal Support Network (PASUNE) defines a paralegal as "a community based individual, who is not a lawyer but who has basic legal knowledge and skills. Paralegals are therefore development workers and community members who educate people about the law or offer basic legal services."¹⁰

Paralegals in Kenya are familiar with local power dynamics and customs, on the one hand, and aware of modern law and formal institutions, on the other. They are able to devise flexible, innovative solutions to justice problems for their communities. Their ability to translate complex legal concepts into more accessible local languages has made paralegals particularly effective in raising awareness of rights and laws. Because paralegals are often trained by, and connected to, pro bono lawyers and other referral services, they can pursue cases further than clients may be able to on their own. Paralegals' training and connections also enable them to more readily challenge adverse local practices or powerful elites.

---

³ For citizens in Lodwar County, for example, the nearest court is 400 km away. Shermit Lamba, *A Topographical Analysis of the Law Courts of Kenya* (Nairobi: Mazingira Institute, 2011), 8.
⁴ Mbote and Akech, *Kenya Justice Sector*, 7 (see n. 1) (citing Republic of Kenya, *Final Report of the Task Force on Judicial Reforms* (Nairobi: Government Printer, 2010), 20); Makau W. Mutua, "Justice under Siege: The Rule of Law and Judicial Subservience in Kenya," *Human Rights Quarterly* 23, no. 1 (2001).
⁵ Republic of Kenya, Governance, Justice, Law and Order Sector (GJLOS) Reform Programme, *National Integrated Household Baseline Survey Report* (Nairobi: World Bank, 2006), 33.
⁶ Ibid.
⁷ Tanja Chopra, *Reconciling Society and the Judiciary in Northern Kenya* (Nairobi: Legal Resources Foundation Trust, 2008).
⁸ *Balancing the Scales: A Report on Seeking Access to Justice in Kenya* (Nairobi: Legal Resource Foundation Trust, 2004), 17, cited in Connie Ngondi-Houghton, *Access to Justice and Rule of Law in Kenya* (UN Development Programme Initiative on Legal Empowerment for the Poor, 2006), 43.
⁹ Andrew Harrington and Tanja Chopra, "Arguing Traditions: Denying Kenya's Women Access to Land Rights," *Justice for the Poor Research Report* 2, no. 52674 (2010), 1–2.
¹⁰ Paralegal Support Network (PASUNE), *Handbook for Paralegals* (Kenya: PASUNE, 2005), 4.

The paralegal movement is growing rapidly across Kenya. Today, more than thirty organizations are deploying paralegals across all seven provinces. Yet little research exists into the impact, methods, and historical role of paralegals in the Kenyan context. To learn more about the impact of community paralegals and the circumstances that influence their effectiveness, we undertook a mapping and assessment of sixteen major paralegal organizations, in-depth interviews with experts and paralegal program staff, a review of literature and program documentation, and extensive case tracking.[11]

The case tracking involved a series of semi-structured interviews with paralegals, local chiefs, clients, respondents, and third parties involved in 120 randomly selected cases.[12] We sampled the cases from twelve sites across six of Kenya's eight provinces: Nairobi, Coast, Eastern, Western, Central, and Rift Valley Provinces. For every province, we investigated ten cases in each of two separate communities: one with an active paralegal presence and another with no access to paralegals. In the "paralegal sites," we tracked cases from paralegals' files.[13] In the "non-paralegal sites," we asked local and assistant chiefs to recall cases they had handled and we selected randomly from that list. Community opinion leaders at paralegal sites were also interviewed to ascertain the effect of paralegal programs on local dispute resolution processes and governance.[14] Paralegals who participated in our study had been trained by six different organizations: International Commission of Jurists–Kenya Chapter (ICJ), Kituo Cha Sheria, International Federation of Women Lawyers–Kenya Chapter (FIDA), Legal Resources Foundation Trust (LRF), Muslims for Human Rights (MUHURI), and Plan International.[15]

Drawing from all of these, this chapter strives to accomplish the following: (1) describe the history of the community paralegal movement; (2) provide an overview of the paralegal sector as it exists today; and (3) analyze the institutional, organizational, and cultural determinants that facilitate or hinder paralegal effectiveness.

---

[11] We undertook this research in two stages. In the first, the African Institute for Health and Development (AIHD) conducted the case tracking, institutional mapping, and initial literature review. In the second stage, I analyzed the data for gaps and supplemented it with interviews with experts, program staff, and paralegals, as well as with a more in-depth review of documents and literature.

[12] At a minimum, the complainant, the respondent, and the paralegal or dispute resolver were interviewed for each case. Depending on availability, witnesses and third parties were also interviewed.

[13] Researchers reviewed case files at paralegal offices and assigned each case a number. They wrote the numbers on slips of paper and blindly selected cases from the pile of slips. Parties were tracked down using contact information contained in case files. Case files missing contact information were excluded from the pool. Some offices had to be replaced in the study because of the poor condition of case files.

[14] Opinion leaders included local chiefs, market chairladies, youth leaders, clan elders, imams, pastors, district officers, and local magistrates, among others.

[15] A representative from each of these organizations worked with an independent AIHD researcher to contact paralegals and community leaders, gather and identify a random selection of case files, and conduct interviews.

II. HISTORICAL OVERVIEW

The community paralegal approach in Kenya grows out of a long tradition of legal activism, galvanized into action during the presidency of Daniel Arap Moi. Prior to Moi's regime, Kenya's underdeveloped legal profession served principally as an administrative apparatus in service to the colonial state.

A. Colonial Kenya

Through a series of regulations passed from 1897 to 1930, the British established a dual legal system that applied different rules to British colonial settlers and indigenous Kenyans.[16] The former enjoyed access to a formal legal system based on judicial principles, protections, and due process. The latter were subject to an informal legal system based on administrative, rather than judicial, principles.[17] In accordance with the philosophy of "indirect rule," the resolution of matters between African Kenyans was left to "native courts": local tribunals overseen by the state but operating under customary or religious laws.[18]

For years, the British excluded indigenous Kenyans from the legal profession.[19] In native courts, though, judicial officers could license Africans to deliver limited legal services. These individuals were known as *vakeels*, or "local persons knowledgeable in basic court procedures, although possessed of no legal qualifications."[20] However, the Legal Practitioners Act of 1906 barred *vakeels* and clerks from the formal practice of law.[21]

Even after the legal profession formally opened up to non-Europeans in 1949, not a single African lawyer joined its ranks until the late 1960s.[22] This was due to hostility from the profession, combined with a long-standing colonial policy that denied government bursaries to African students aspiring to study law. At the time, the cost

---

[16] Maureen Catherine Feeley, "Transnational Movements, Human Rights and Democracy: Legal Mobilization Strategies and Majoritarian Constraints in Kenya 1982–2002" (PhD diss., University of California, San Diego, 2006), 234, eScholarship (b6635496).

[17] Ibid.

[18] Jackton Boma Ojwang and D. R. Salter, "The Legal Profession in Kenya," *Journal of African Law* 34, no. 1 (1990), 11, doi: 128.112.200.107.

[19] Yash P. Ghai, "Legal Profession: Themes and Issues," in *The Legal Profession and the New Constitutional Order in Kenya*, ed. Yash P. Ghai and Jill C. Ghai (Nairobi: Strathmore University Press, 2014), 13.

[20] East Africa Protectorate High Court, "East Africa Legal Practitioners' Rules 1901," in *East Africa Protectorate: Law Reports Containing Cases Determined by the High Court of Mombasa, and by the Appeal Court at Zanzibar, and by the Judicial Committee of the Privy Council, on Appeal from that Court*, ed. Robert W. Hamilton (London: Stevens and Sons, Ltd., 1906), 121–25.

[21] Amos O. Odenyo, "Professionalization amidst Change: The Case of the Emerging Legal Profession in Kenya," *African Studies Review* 22, no. 3 (1979), 34, doi: 128.112.200.107.

[22] Kivutha Kibwana, ed., *International Commission of Jurists, Law and the Administration of Justice in Kenya* (Nairobi: International Commission of Jurists, Kenya Section, 1992), 3.

of a legal education was otherwise beyond the means of most African families. As Yash Ghai explains:

> The [British colonial government] was obsessed with fear that lawyers would promote political difficulties for it. Indigenous lawyers were regarded with extreme distrust. This attitude stemmed in part from British experience in India, where lawyers like Gandhi and the Nehrus led the struggle for independence, and partly from West Africa, where African lawyers were already agitating for the safeguarding of the rights of Africans.[23]

As a result of Kenya's dual legal structure and the exclusion of African lawyers, the Law Society of Kenya (LSK) – the nation's premier bar association, with compulsory membership for all Kenyan lawyers – rarely came into contact or concerned itself with the problems of ordinary African Kenyans.[24] This remained the case through the early years of independence.[25]

Instead, African Kenyans primarily interacted with the colonial state through public assemblies or outdoor meetings known as *barazas*, which continue to be held to this day. Administrative officials, often chiefs, typically convened *barazas* to inform the public about government programs and policies. *Barazas* ranged in size from smaller gatherings of 50 to 100 individuals to rallies of several thousand. At times, *barazas* provided African Kenyans with a forum to debate social issues, resolve disputes, or raise concerns and complaints. People known as opinion leaders often had a voice in these proceedings. By and large, however, *barazas*, like the courts, served as an instrument of the state to disseminate and enforce colonial policies.

B. Early Independence

These exclusionary dynamics began to shift, although marginally, during the regime of Kenya's first president, Jomo Kenyatta (1963–78), and the early years of the Moi regime (1978–82).

Around this time, the first trickle of African lawyers began joining the LSK. In 1960, on a recommendation made at Kenya's first constitutional conference, a committee formed to investigate and improve legal education in Africa. Its recommendations led to the founding of the first legal education programs for African students, and the establishment of the Faculty of Law at the University of

---

[23] Yash P. Ghai, "Law and Lawyers in Kenya and Tanzania: Some Political Economy Considerations," in *Lawyers in the Third World: Comparative and Developmental Perspectives*, ed. Clarence J. Dias, R. Luckham, D. O. Lynch, and J. Paul (New York: International Center for Law in Development, 1981), 148–49, quoted in Feeley, *Transnational Movements*, 232 (see n. 16).

[24] Feeley, *Transnational Movements*, 235 (see n. 16).

[25] African Institute for Health and Development (AIHD), "Kenya Draft Report: Multi-country Study on the Impact of Paralegals" (draft report, African Institute for Health and Development, May 10, 2012), 4.

Nairobi. The Nairobi Law Faculty accepted its first class of students in 1970, and graduated its first class in 1972.[26]

In 1973, a small group of young African lecturers and students from the university founded Kenya's first nongovernmental legal aid organization.[27] They named it Kituo Cha Mashauri, literally "assistance with law" in Kiswahili (later changed to Kituo Cha Sheria, or "Legal Advice Center" in 1989).[28] The founders, many of whom are now notable figures in the Kenyan judiciary, came together because they recognized a dire need among the Kenyan poor for legal aid services that they could not afford.[29] In its early days, Kituo largely dealt with the legal problems of slum dwellers, manual laborers, and domestic workers, who were vulnerable to forced evictions, poor or abusive working conditions, or exorbitant rent increases.[30]

Over the next decade, as the number of African lawyers in Kenya grew, so too did the number of lawyers and law students who volunteered through Kituo to supply pro bono legal aid. Yet their numbers remained far too few when faced with the scale of the demand. To keep pace, Kituo began training opinion leaders and community members in basic law so that they could assist with cases. These people came to be known as Kenya's first paralegals.[31]

By the mid-1980s, African Kenyans would finally constitute the majority of the legal profession. But even as the LSK's constituency grew more progressive in nature, it kept relatively silent in the face of systematic human rights violations and repression under Kenyatta and Moi. The LSK maintained a low profile "out of necessity, for any public comment critical of government action would be quickly seized upon as evidence that the Bar was not loyal to the new state of Kenya, since similar comment had not been forthcoming in the colonial era."[32]

---

[26] "Brief History: Introduction," Patricia Kameri-Mbote, University of Nairobi-School of Law. http://law-school.uonbi.ac.ke/node/1569; University of Nairobi, *The 3rd Congregation for the Conferment and Presentation of Degrees and Diplomas at the Great Court* (Nairobi: University of Nairobi, 1972).

[27] Charles Olungah, "The Role of Academia in Democratization in Kenya," in *Discourses on Civil Society in Kenya*, ed. P. Wanyande and M. A. Okebe (Nairobi: African Research and Resource Forum, 2009), 34; Caroline Amondi, "Legal Aid in Kenya: Building a Fort for Wanjiku," in *The Legal Profession and the New Constitutional Order in Kenya*, ed. Yash P. Ghai and Jill C. Ghai (Nairobi: Strathmore University Press, 2014), 205.

[28] Gertrude Angote, interview by Abigail Moy (Namati), November 2013.

[29] These included Justice Vitalis Juma, Chief Justice Willy Mutunga, Justice Mary Ang'awa, and respected legal figures Murtaza Jaffer, Stehen Andere, and Pheroze Nowrojee. Kituo Cha Sheria, *Annual Report 2010* (Nairobi: Kituo Cha Sheria, 2010).

[30] Kituo Cha Sheria, *Kituo Cha Sheria Strategic Plan 2009–2013* (Nairobi: Kituo Cha Sheria, 2008); Ripoca Project, *Organizational Study: Kituo Cha Sheria*.

[31] Angote, interview (see n. 28); AIHD, "Kenya Draft Report," 4 (see n. 25).

[32] Yash P. Ghai and J. P. W. B. McAuslan, *Public Law and Political Change in Kenya: A Study of the Legal Framework of Government from Colonial Times to the Present* (New York: Oxford Press, 1970), 138, quoted in Feeley, *Transnational Movements*, 235 (see n. 16).

C. The Moi Regime

The silence broke in 1982. In June, the Moi government, having already banned groups potentially harboring opposition viewpoints, declared Kenya a *de jure* one-party state. The National Assembly, under strict control, amended the constitution accordingly.[33] Two months later, the Moi government undertook massive arrests and detentions in response to an attempted coup. Thousands of military personnel, followed soon after by university professors and student leaders, were detained.[34]

A group of African LSK members spoke up in criticism of these acts, framing them as violations of domestic and international law.[35] As repression intensified over the ensuing years, a pattern of open solidarity began to emerge among activist lawyers and sympathetic LSK members.[36] Members of the legal profession began founding or allying with various human rights organizations. Their efforts ultimately fed into a broader popular movement for democracy.[37] Without formal political organizations to counterbalance the Moi Regime, the resulting web of non-state actors served as some of the few opposition voices during the 1980s[38] – and they drew heavily on legal tactics to achieve their aims. In addition to providing legal representation to victims of unlawful detention and torture and challenging laws they deemed unconstitutional, they mobilized citizens around laws and constitutional principles.[39]

During this time, Kituo began to transform from a purely charitable legal aid organization into an agent for social change. The organization started its "Taking the Law to the People" program at the University of Nairobi's law school, which encouraged young lawyers to apply their skills toward empowering and promoting the rights of the poor. The program sought to change the perception of lawyers as elitist and make their work relevant to the everyday lives of Kenyans. As it grew, Kituo teamed up with the LSK and strengthened its relationship with dominant church organizations, including the National Council of Churches of Kenya (NCCK). The latter affiliation improved Kituo's populist appeal and legitimacy, particularly in rural areas. This enabled Kituo to engage and empower community members on a larger scale.

[33] "Kenya Profile: Timeline," *BBC*, July 30, 2015.
[34] Feeley, *Transnational Movements*, 186 (see n. 16).
[35] Martha Karau, interview by Robert M. Press, August 15, 2002.
[36] Robert M. Press, *Peaceful Resistance: Advancing Human Rights and Democratic Freedoms* (Aldershot: Ashgate, 2006), 112.
[37] Feeley, *Transnational Movements*, 336–49 (see n. 16).
[38] Frank K. Matanga, "Civil Society and Politics in Africa: The Case of Kenya," in *The Third Sector: For What and for Whom?* (paper presented at the Fourth International Conference of ISTR, Dublin, Ireland, July 5–8, 2000), 12–14.
[39] Jennifer Widner, *The Rise of a Party-State in Kenya: From "Harambee!" to "Nyayo!"* (Berkeley: University of California, 1992), 188–90; Feeley, *Transnational Movements*, 239–42 (see n. 16); Pheroze Nowrojee, "The Legal Profession 1963–2013: All This Can Happen Again – Soon," in *The Legal Profession and the New Constitutional Order in Kenya*, ed. Yash P. Ghai and Jill C. Ghai (Nairobi: Strathmore University Press, 2014), 35.

In 1983, the NCCK worked with the LSK to launch the Public Law Institute (PLI).[40] PLI primarily focused on public interest litigation and policy issues, but it also established legal aid clinics staffed by volunteer advocates, law students, and community paralegals. These centers fielded legal aid requests touching on labor rights, the role of the police, women's rights, landlord–tenant issues, consumer protection, and the relationship between customary and state laws.[41] Meanwhile, ICJ began exploring how to expand legal services in rural areas, in relation to family matters, child support, labor issues, pensions, rents, and consumer exploitation.[42] ICJ programming, which spanned multiple African countries, drew from experiments in the use of community paralegals and "barefoot lawyers" throughout Asia and Latin America.[43]

Resistance efforts against the Moi administration came to a head in the early 1990s. The increasingly politicized LSK ended its long-standing internal debate over its neutrality with the election of activist Paul Muite as chair, alongside a council that included former detainees, human rights advocates, and other activists.[44] With a number of leaders in the legal community in exile, Kenya's human rights situation caught the attention of the global community. The Catholic Church and international press vocally criticized the regime. Kenya's major donors condemned the regime's arrests and violence and refused to renew Kenya's aid allocations without evidence of democratic reform. The combination of international and domestic pressure ultimately forced Moi to relent and permit multiparty elections in December 1992.

D. Multiparty Elections

The return of multiparty politics "created an atmosphere in which human rights monitoring groups could safely operate."[45] During and after the 1992 elections, a handful of civil society and religious organizations – many of whom would become key actors in the modern paralegal movement – rose to prominence. In addition to those already mentioned – Kituo, PLI, ICJ, and the NCCK – these groups included the Kenya Human Rights Commission (KHRC), FIDA, the Legal Education Aid Programme (LEAP), and the Catholic Justice and Peace

---

[40] Oki Ooko-Ombaka, "Education for Alternative Development: The Role of the Public Law Institute, Kenya," *Third World Legal Studies* 4, art. 11 (1985): 171, http://scholar.valpo.edu/twls/vol4/iss1/11.

[41] Ibid. At this time, representatives from PLI, the LSK, and the Legal Advisory Committee participated in an international seminar on training paralegals, based on experiences across Asia, Africa, and Latin America. International Commission of Jurists, African Bar Association, and All-Africa Conference of Churches, *Legal Services in Rural Africa: Report of a Seminar Held at Limuru, Near Nairobi, 1 to 4 October 1984* (Geneva: International Commission of Jurists, 1985).

[42] Amy S. Tsanga and Olatokunbo Ige, *A Paralegal Trainer's Manual for Africa* (Geneva: International Commission of Jurists, 1994), 15.

[43] Ibid., 9–10.   [44] Press, *Peaceful Resistance*, 113 (see n. 36).

[45] Willy Mutunga, interview by Maureen C. Feeley, Nairobi, May 15, 1998, quoted by Feeley, *Transnational Movements*, 344 (see n. 16).

Commission (CJPC).[46] LSK members led the majority of these organizations. They existed in leaner form for some time, but flourished after Kenya's political opening, in large part due to increasing support from international donors.[47]

In the lead-up to the elections, many organizations conducted civic education outreach programs on voting rights. Kituo, for instance, launched an extensive information campaign, issuing booklets, posters, and video- and audiocassettes that played on *matatus* (popular public transport) throughout the country.[48] LEAP organized legal education and training programs for the Kenyan poor in Rift Valley Province.[49]

ICJ and FIDA, both volunteer organizations for lawyers, were particularly active in promoting free and fair elections. The two formed an "Election Monitoring Unit," in which election monitors publicized human rights violations and educated Kenyans on how to recognize and report them. As with Kituo's early alliances, FIDA and ICJ joined forces with the respected rural leadership of the Catholic Church, a move that granted them access to extensive grassroots organizational networks.[50]

E. The 1990s: The Rise of the Paralegal

After the elections, organizations that had rallied around voting rights began applying their expertise in grassroots legal mobilization to a broader spectrum of social issues.[51] Their principal causes included: advancing the agenda for constitutional reform, addressing critically neglected women's and children's rights, securing land rights of poor urban and rural communities, and demanding greater accountability of local government, among others.[52] Over the ensuing decade, newcomers to the legal empowerment arena emerged, including LRF, Center for Legal Education and Aid Networks (CLEAN),[53] Widows' and Orphans' Welfare Society of Kenya (WOWESOK),[54] and

---

[46] Feeley, *Transnational Movements*, 486–87 (see n. 16); Amondi, "Legal Aid in Kenya," 205 (see n. 27).
[47] Jereon de Zeeuw, *Project Report Assessing Democracy Assistance: Kenya* (United Kingdom: FRIDE, 2010), 2; Feeley, *Transnational Movements*, 427 (see n. 16).
[48] Feeley, *Transnational Movements*, 359 (see n. 16).   [49] Ibid., 360.   [50] Ibid., 349–52.
[51] But they would continue to fulfill their historical roles, as well. During the presidential and parliamentary elections of 2007, paralegals were called upon to observe the electioneering process. African Institute of Health and Development, "Kenya Paralegal Study: Literature Review on Paralegalism in Kenya" (draft for discussion, February 2012), 16 (citing Legal Resource Foundation Trust, *Opinion Brief on Paralegal Support Network* [May 11, 2011], 2).
[52] Particularly with regard to specific problematic legislation, for example: (1) the Societies Act; (2) the Public Order Act; (3) the Chiefs' Authority Act; (4) the Outlying Districts Act and the Special Districts (Administration) Act; (5) the Preservation of Public Security Act; and (6) the Public Collections Act. Angote, interview (see n. 28).
[53] Godwin R. Murunga and Shadrack W. Nasong'o, *Kenya: The Struggle for Democracy* (London: Zed Books, 2007), 36.
[54] Marjolein Benschop, *Rights and Reality: Are Women's Equal Rights to Land, Housing and Property Implemented in East Africa?* (Nairobi: UN Human Settlements Programme, 2002), 176.

later, CRADLE (The Children's Foundation)[55] and the Education Centre for Women in Democracy (ECWD).[56]

Each of these organizations began strategically deploying paralegals in programs promoting legal awareness, rights promotion, and conflict resolution.[57] For some, paralegals took on the form of "human rights defenders" or "monitors."[58] KHRC widely deployed monitors for its programs against torture and police brutality, for example, and FIDA trained "community-based monitors," who collected data on gender-based violence cases and reported them back to FIDA headquarters.[59] For both organizations, public interest lawyers would take up serious cases reported by monitors. In general, case intake and referral to lawyers for pro bono assistance was the most basic of paralegal functions.

Paralegals were also responsible for enhancing legal literacy and awareness. Groups like LRF, ICJ, FIDA, and Kituo worked through community church organizations to identify "opinion leaders" or individuals who were respected within their communities.[60] These people were then trained to facilitate rights awareness, to promote basic legal education in their communities, and to advise community members on remedies if rights were violated.[61] Similarly, ECWD's paralegals conducted regular civic workshops for citizens on their legal and political rights, with a focus on women's and widows' property and inheritance rights.[62]

The most skilled paralegals took on the challenge of solving justice problems themselves. They mediated interpersonal conflicts or interceded on behalf of clients, often by challenging authorities or assisting with customary or formal legal

---

[55] Mbote and Akech, *Kenya Justice Sector*, 162–63 (see n. 1).

[56] Other organizations offering a range of legal aid services included: Children Legal Action Network, Christian Legal Education and Research, Independent Medico-Legal Unit, Coalition on Violence against Women, Center for Human Rights and Awareness. Amondi, "Legal Aid in Kenya," 205 (see n. 27).

[57] During this era, practitioners of legal aid and community development began convening internationally to discuss and refine paralegal methodologies. International Commission of Jurists, *Legal Services for Rural and Urban Poor and the Legal Status of Rural Women in Anglophone West Africa, Report of a Seminar, 19–23 July 1993, Accra, Ghana* (Geneva: International Commission of Jurists, 1995).

[58] Jedidah W. Waruhiu and John J. O. Otieno, "Access to Justice: The Paralegal Approach," in *The Legal Profession and the New Constitutional Order in Kenya*, ed. Yash P. Ghai and Jill C. Ghai (Nairobi: Strathmore University Press, 2014), 190.

[59] See results of the reports in FIDA's annual report, e.g., Federation of Women Lawyers Kenya (FIDA Kenya), *So Far, How Far?: 2007 Annual Report* (Kenya: Federation of Women Lawyers Kenya, 2008), 43–51.

[60] Kituo initiated paralegal training in the slum communities of Nairobi such as Korogocho, Kibera, and Mathare. It worked closely with Catholic churches based in the slums to identify trainees. AIHD, "Kenya Draft Report," 4–5 (see n. 25).

[61] Feeley, *Transnational Movements*, 315–16, 20 (see n. 16).

[62] Amanda Ellis, Jozefina Cutura, Nouma Dione, Ian Gillson, Clare Manuel, and Judy Thongori, *Gender and Economic Growth in Kenya: Unleashing the Power of Women* (Washington, DC: World Bank, 2007), 70.

proceedings. Indeed, while paralegals took on many roles, Stephen Orvis observes that "[t]he greatest political effect of paralegals' work might well come from cases that directly involved assisting citizens facing harassment from local authorities."[63] In rural Kenya in particular, where local accountability is weak, "confronting the state at the local level and forcing it to fulfill its legal obligations is an important form of civic education, both asserting citizens' rights and teaching them how to do the same in the future."[64] In Orvis' study of four organizations conducting civic education and paralegal programs in rural Kenya, 50 percent of paralegals reported having taken on at least one case requiring engagement with local authorities. Eighty-four percent of paralegals reported resolving such cases successfully in favor of their clients.[65]

F. Consolidation of the Paralegal Movement

In 2000, twenty-six paralegal organizations came together to form the Paralegal Support Network (PASUNE). They aimed to create a forum for paralegal programs to share their experiences and discuss possibilities of working together to advance the paralegal movement in Kenya. Members also expressed interest in coordinating geographically to avoid duplication and to maximize the coverage of paralegals across the country.[66]

After a number of meetings, PASUNE members undertook three primary initiatives: (1) identifying commonalities in curricula and training methodologies among paralegal programs; (2) developing and adopting a common minimum standard in the training of paralegals; and (3) advocating for the formal recognition of paralegals within the justice system.[67]

In 2002, PASUNE harmonized paralegal training materials into a single curriculum, complemented in 2006 by a handbook, training guide, user-friendly brochures, posters, and other training materials for use by all members.[68] These materials were disseminated to nonmembers as well, including the Kenya School of Law (KSL), where they supported the development of a draft curriculum for paralegal training to be introduced at a diploma level. On the advocacy front, PASUNE actively campaigned around a legal aid bill that formally recognizes paralegals as justice service providers. PASUNE also worked closely with the Kenya Law Reform Commission (KLRC) on the establishment of small claims courts, in hopes that they would provide another avenue for paralegal services.

---

[63] Stephen Orvis, "Kenyan Civil Society. Bridging the Urban–Rural Divide?" *Journal of Modern African Studies* 41, no. 2 (2003), 261.
[64] Ibid.
[65] Interestingly, paralegals who were opposition activists or campaigners were almost twice as likely as paralegals with no political experience to take on cases directly challenging local authorities. Ibid.
[66] AIHD, "Kenya Draft Report," 2 (see n. 25).   [67] Ibid.   [68] PASUNE, *Handbook*, 4 (see n. 10).

G. A Shift in Government: From Opponent to Ally

In 2005, the Kenyan government launched the Government Justice Law and Governance Programme (GJLOS) in a bid to more holistically address problems spanning three target sectors: "governance," "justice," and "law and order."[69] In total, more than thirty government institutions and ministries were involved in this ambitious program.[70] The program created a basket fund for international donors, which has presented additional opportunities for financing the paralegal sector.[71]

In 2007, drawing on allocations from the basket fund, the Department of Justice in the Office of the Attorney General (at the time known as the Ministry of Justice, National Cohesion and Constitutional Affairs), established the National Legal Aid and Awareness Programme (NALEAP) and its National Steering Committee.[72] The Committee's primary functions were to advise on national legal aid policy and to oversee pilot projects testing various methods of enhancing justice for all.[73]

After the first national coordinator of the program came on board in 2008, the Committee set up six pilots across six thematic areas. One of these projects, based in Kisumu, explored the use of paralegals in the provision of basic justice services. Based on positive experiences with the Kisumu pilot and extensive consultation with civil society, NALEAP became a strong proponent of establishing a national system for recognizing and accrediting paralegals. It adopted as one of its key goals the passage of a legal aid policy and legal aid law that accounts for the role of paralegals in enhancing access to justice.[74]

---

[69] GJLOS, *Survey Report*, 2 (see n. 5). The vision of GJLOS aligned with the Kenyan government's growing acknowledgment of access to justice as critical to economic development and poverty reduction. This recognition was articulated in the National Poverty Eradication Plan 1999–2015, Poverty Reduction Strategy Paper (PRSP) of 2001–04, and the Investment Programme for Economic Recovery Strategy for Wealth and Employment Creation (ERS) 2003–07. Amondi, "Legal Aid in Kenya," 206 (see n. 27).

[70] GJLOS, *Survey Report*, 2 (see n. 5).

[71] For instance, when GJLOS identified prison congestion as one of the major challenges facing prisons in Kenya, Kituo began training prisoners on law to build their capacity for self-representation. To date, paralegals have helped prisoners in Shimo La Tewa prison to draft 400 applications and letters to the Chief Magistrates' Courts; 80 applications, 260 appeals, and 150 letters to the High Court in Malindi; and 125 applications, 400 appeals, and 200 letters to the High Court in Mombasa. Mary Amuyunzo-Nyamongo, "Kenya Paralegal Study Preliminary Report" (preliminary report, AIHD, submitted to World Bank Justice for the Poor, Nairobi, September 2011), 7.

[72] *Kenya Gazette* Notice No. 11598.

[73] The pilots had initially been proposed in a 2001 report commissioned by the Legal Aid Steering Committee, a body set up by the attorney general in 1998 that sought to explore suitable models for a national legal aid scheme. However, the government did not act upon the proposals until many years later, after a change in administration. Amondi, "Legal Aid in Kenya," 207 (see n. 27).

[74] Caroline Amondi (national coordinator for NALEAP), interview by Abigail Moy (Namati), November 2013.

In August 2010, Kenya adopted a new constitution, Article 48 of which states: "The State shall ensure access to justice for all persons and if any fee is required, it shall be reasonable and shall not impede access to justice."[75] That year, KSL underwent a restructuring based on the recommendations of the Ministerial Task Force on the Development of Policy Legal Framework and Education in Kenya. KSL established a two-year paralegal training program, drawing heavily from PASUNE's curriculum, with a Diploma of Law (Paralegal Studies) awarded upon completion. KSL would become the first public institution in Kenya to offer paralegal training.

In the ensuing years, due in part to NALEAP's and PASUNE's advocacy, government support for a cohesive national approach to enhancing access to justice mounted. A taskforce on judicial reforms recommended that the Kenyan government establish a national legal aid system and adopt a corresponding policy and legislative framework.[76] Reports commissioned by the Ministry of Justice urged the enactment of a legal aid scheme that promoted paralegals, greater public education, and legal literacy campaigns to address the needs of vulnerable citizens.[77] The Truth and Reconciliation Commission, noting a concentration of paralegals in Nairobi, recommended expanding the presence of community paralegals in rural, arid, or semiarid regions of the country.[78] Vision 2030, Kenya's national development plan, endorsed the policy, legal, and institutional reforms necessary to achieve access to justice.[79]

These contributions laid the groundwork for the ultimate passage of Kenya's 2016 Legal Aid Law. The events that led to the law's adoption, and its many implications, are described in greater detail later in this chapter (*see* Institutional Factors).

III. CONTEMPORARY PARALEGALS IN KENYA: A SNAPSHOT

A. *Placement and Specialization*

The vast majority of paralegals in Kenya today are recruited, trained, and deployed by civil society, which in turn relies heavily on international donors for support.[80]

---

[75] The Constitution of Kenya (2010), art. 48. Other relevant constitutional articles include: art. 49(1)(c) (an arrested person has the right "to communicate with an advocate, and *other persons whose assistance is necessary*") and art. 50(7) ("in the interest of justice, a court may *allow an intermediary to assist* a complainant or an accused person to communicate with the court").

[76] Amondi, "Legal Aid in Kenya," 207 (see n. 27). [77] Ibid., 207–8. [78] Ibid., 208. [79] Ibid.

[80] Key donors supporting the promotion of access to justice in Kenya include the European Union, the Open Society Initiative of Eastern Africa (OSIEA), The Deutsche Gesellschaftfür Internationale Zusammenarbeith (GiZ), UN Women, UNICEF, Department for International Development (DfID) UK, Canadian International Development Agency (CIDA), and others. Ibid., 206.

Paralegals operate in a wide variety of informal and institutional settings, on a diversity of issues.

Many paralegals work out of their homes or are based in modest local offices maintained by civil society or community-based organizations. Of these community-based paralegals, some are trained to take a generalist approach; they aim to respond to any problem that affects a given community. Paralegal programs that adopt this approach rely on petitions or walk-ins to learn about grievances, or they may send staff on fact-finding missions to investigate major needs. They then train their paralegals in the thematic areas identified.

Most paralegal programs, however, focus on specific thematic areas or marginalized groups. For example, Bar Hostess trains paralegals from within the sex worker community; they address security issues, police abuse, and access to HIV/AIDS treatment. Nubian Rights Forum, Haki Centre, and Wajir Human Rights Network help minority communities overcome discriminatory practices and obtain legal identity documents or proof of citizenship. Muslims for Human Rights (MUHURI) aids remandees and accused persons who encounter problems with the criminal justice system. Frontier Indigenous Network trains paralegals in northern Kenya to restore women's right to inheritance and to fight genital mutilation. Paralegals working with KELIN and Nyeri Hospice help patients with terminal illnesses to make end-of-life legal arrangements, including the drafting of wills and the assignment of power of attorney. Kenya Land Alliance, Ogiek People's Development Program, and Kivulini Trust support communities in leveraging national land laws to protect customary land claims. Their paralegals, often called community mobilizers, spearhead processes for documenting and registering lands, while strengthening mechanisms for accountable and participatory management of land and natural resources.

While the majority of paralegals in Kenya are community based, a fair number of paralegals are based within state institutions and integrated into state services. Paralegals in this category include those stationed in prisons and remand homes. LRF paralegals, for instance, visit prisons every weekday to offer legal advice to inmates, hold educational legal clinics, train prison liaison officers on human rights standards, and monitor prison conditions.[81] They participate in the Parole Board of the Kenya Prisons Service and serve on the Case Management and Anti-Corruption Committees of the Probation and Aftercare Department.[82] Meanwhile, Kituo trains

---

[81] Mbote and Akech, *Kenya Justice Sector*, 152 (see n. 1).
[82] Waruhiu and Otieno, "Access to Justice," 185 (see n. 58); UN Office on Drugs and Crime (UNODC), *Handbook on Improving Access to Legal Aid in Africa*, Criminal Justice Handbook Series (Vienna: United Nations, 2011), 25.

prisoners as paralegals who can represent themselves and other detainees in appeals and bail proceedings.

Paralegals who focus on monitoring courts also fall into this category. They take part in Court Users Committees and can be found staffing judicial-paralegal customer care desks, where they advise the general public on court procedure.[83] State agencies have also identified paralegals as volunteer child officers, who monitor and assist with child protection cases. PLAN International's paralegals, for example, work with the Children's Department, police, and the provincial administration to address cases of violence against children.

B. Skill Level

In addition to operating in a variety of settings, paralegals demonstrate differing levels of skill depending on need and context. Contemporary paralegals now specialize in any combination of the following tasks:

1. Basic Skills

- **Improving Rights Consciousness.** Educating others in basic law and rights; conveying complex legal-judicial processes in a language that the community can understand; disseminating educational materials and content such as handbooks and brochures to the general public.
  - This includes efforts targeting specific populations or clients, e.g., explaining criminal procedure to suspects, or describing the process of lodging reports with the police to victims of crime.
- **Making Referrals.** Referring clients to others, including pro bono lawyers, police, local administrative agencies, and other authorities, depending on the nature of the case. Prior to doing so, paralegals will investigate the facts of a case as necessary.
- **Monitoring.** Monitoring government performance in the management of public affairs and resources; documenting cases of abuse and human rights violations; reporting to civil society organizations who in turn publicize or act on the data.

2. Intermediate Skills

- **Offering Legal Advice.** Offering basic legal advice on seeking remedies or resolving disputes in specific cases. Prior to doing so, paralegals will investigate the facts of a case and apply the law as necessary.

---

[83] The judiciary has sought the assistance of paralegals in reaching the general public during marches and open days. Paralegals work through Court User Committees to share public feedback, offer their own observations on bottlenecks in the administration of justice, and report abuses. Paralegal contributions at customer care desks has improved judiciary–public relations, reduced registry bureaucracy, the number of "lost" users, and the effect of conmen posing as judicial officers who prey on court users. Waruhiu and Otieno, "Access to Justice," 194–95 (see n. 58).

- **Dispute Resolution/Reconciliation.** Mediating conflicts, usually with regard to land boundary matters, contract and labor relations, or family disputes. Prior to doing so, paralegals will investigate the facts of a case and help parties reach a satisfactory outcome.
- **Accompaniment.** Accompanying the clients in accessing justice, e.g., at a court, administrative office, or service provider.
- **Document Support.** Drafting simple legal documents, e.g., applications for bail.

3. Advanced Skills

- **Advocacy.** Lobbying government (local or otherwise) and public officials for action on reforms to policy or practice; persuading local authorities to act to address a client's case, or challenging them to cease illicit practices; participating in stakeholder meetings relating to the betterment of the community.
- **Community Mobilization.** Organizing the community around common issues of concern; sensitizing the community about the need for positive change.

Kenya's paralegal movement is still young. It is constantly diversifying and honing its methodologies. But even at this early stage, we have been able to identify institutional, organizational, and cultural factors that influence paralegal success across a range of operating environments.

IV. DETERMINANTS OF EFFECTIVENESS

We interviewed parties involved in 120 randomly selected cases to learn more about the impact of community paralegals and the circumstances that influence their effectiveness. Our researchers sampled cases from paralegals working in six of Kenya's eight provinces: Nairobi, Coast, Eastern, Western, Central, and Rift Valley Provinces. Community opinion leaders were also interviewed to ascertain the effect of paralegal programs on local dispute resolution processes and governance.

Overall, we were struck by the variance in the case types handled by paralegals, and the differing degrees to which they affected outcomes of disputes in their communities. The most accomplished paralegals could resolve justice challenges requiring management of emotionally tense situations, engagement with a range of authorities and institutions, and mastery of skills in mediation, mobilization, and advocacy, as in the case examined next.

> CASE 1: "NOW, THERE IS ENOUGH WATER"
>
> *Location*: Eastern Province
> *Type of Dispute*: State and Corporate Accountability
> *Issue*: Natural Resource Rights
> *Tools Used*: Advocacy, Organizing, Information Provision
> *Other Institutions Used*: Before Paralegal Involved: Chief, Police, District Officer; After Paralegal Involved: Chief, Assistant Chief, District Officer, National Environmental Management Authority, Parent Organization, Provincial Administration
>
> The clients were leaders of a community that relied on natural sources of water. All water catchment areas for the local river fell within private land. One landowner was harvesting sand heavily from the catchment area, which dried up the only source of water in the community. The community leaders asked the landowner to stop, to no avail. They approached the police, district officer, and chief, all of whom claimed they could not stop the company, as it was beyond their mandate. The community leaders suspected that the chief and assistant chief received money from the sand sales.
>
> The community leaders approached two paralegals who worked together in an office. The paralegals called two community meetings, which were attended by 400 people, and educated the community on natural and community resource management. Because a mob had previously arisen, resulting in the burning of a lorry and the arrest of two community members, the paralegals sought to keep the meetings calm and convinced the community to take legal action instead. The chief and assistant chief expressed unhappiness with the paralegals mobilizing the community, but the paralegals urged the community not to be afraid and to fight for their rights.
>
> On the advice of the paralegals, the community held two demonstrations and chased away lorries arriving to collect sand. The paralegal and the community also wrote a petition describing the community's grievances and proposing solutions. It was sent to the District Office, National Environmental Management Authority (NEMA), LRF (the parent organization for the paralegals), and the police.
>
> NEMA responded by outlawing sand harvesting in the area – confirming that it was the only catchment area for the river in the region. The provincial administration was copied and ordered to enforce sanctions. The sand harvesting has since ceased. The company owner issued a public apology, as he did not want to be shunned by the community. However, he maintains that the sand harvesting was good for the

> CASE 1: (Cont.)
> community because it provided a source of employment for youth. Community members say that people are now afraid to harvest sand because they are "wary the paralegals will stop them." One client emphasized, "The paralegal cooled tempers, educated us and even told the accused the legal provisions on sand harvesting ... The law says water catchment areas belong to the community and there is need to conserve the environment for future generations."

Indeed, many interviewees were quick to cite positive impacts arising from the presence of effective paralegals. Clients reported that, through paralegals, they were able to access remedies denied to them in other venues. Community leaders credited paralegals for reducing disputes and incidents of violence, as well as raising rights awareness among the public.

> *The paralegals have helped here so much. This is because the paralegals help parties to a suit, not only to solve their disputes but also to ensure that the parties can still relate with each other without any hard feelings held against each other.* – Community Leader, Rift Valley Province
>
> *Now, we have very few cases of family violence, child abuse and neglect as more people have been educated on their rights and they understand consequences for crimes committed and this has given me room to do other things. More people understand their rights in marriage, issues of succession and how to take care of children. Referral cases to the District Children's Offices have really decreased.* – Community Leader, Western Province
>
> *Before paralegals were trained here, it was really bad, especially in Soweto. But now at least there is security. Instead of people taking up matters in their own hands, they now report to paralegals who then try to resolve disputes or refer.* – Community Leader, Nairobi Province
>
> *They help a lot to reduce the bulk log of cases in the judicial system; this is because the cases that can be handled by the paralegals are handled with them without necessarily going to court. Hence this saves the time of the parties involved in the case and this also helps the government to save the resources and time [for cases] that would have been easily solved by the paralegals.* – Community Leader, Central Province

At the same time, other interviewees voiced concerns about inconsistencies in the quality of paralegal services. They challenged paralegals' capacity to tackle complex issues or to take on the volume of cases in need of resolution. They expressed concern over a lack of clarity regarding the role of paralegals.

> *Paralegals are limited in their knowledge of the law and at times when acting in good faith, they end up misleading their clients. This is a very serious challenge.* – Resident Magistrate, Central Province
>
> *Not everyone accepts what a paralegal does. This is because their interactions with people are misinterpreted, thus risking their lives. All trained paralegals should be introduced to all communities, in churches and chiefs' barazas and even in schools, where they clearly state their role in the community.* – Community Leader, Eastern Province
>
> *[Paralegals] have to deal with the challenge of giving legal advice in a small way yet the issues they deal with are very complex. Thus there's need for upgrading on their capacity building. The training they receive is far too little for the complex matters they do handle.* – Community Leader, Western Province
>
> *Paralegals should be increased in number. The few paralegals we have here cannot manage to cover each village. They ought to be going to churches, chiefs' barazas, and all other public events.* – Community Leader, Eastern Province

Our research reveals that the effectiveness of paralegals, as perceived by themselves, their clients, and their communities, hinged on a handful of institutional, organizational, and cultural factors. We analyze these determinants of success in turn.

A. Institutional Factors

1. Relationships with Local Authorities

The success of paralegals' efforts often depended on the quality of their relationships with principal institutional actors and local leaders, including police, local administrative and other government officials, prison authorities, councilors, and chiefs.

> *The fact that the [paralegal] office is next to mine should tell you more about our relationship. Us delegating peace and reconciliation to them speaks volumes. It is the biggest resource center in the district ... They have the legal knowledge while we have the administrative capability. We even seek advice there. We cannot give them minor cases, we give them cases of weight.* – Community Leader, Eastern Province

Where relationships were collaborative, paralegals enjoyed greater recognition and respect in their communities. In Rift Valley Province, for example, paralegal offices that worked closely with authorities transformed their communities and contributed extensively to resolving disputes. Community members and leaders alike would seek out paralegals, whose services were integrated into customary and formal dispute resolution processes. Paralegals' ability to traverse both customary and formal institutions empowered them to take on more complex, multidimensional cases.

CASE 2: WORKING TOGETHER

Location: Rift Valley Province
Type of Dispute: State Accountability
Issue: Water
Tools Used: Advocacy, Organization
Other Institutions Used: After Paralegal Involved: Elders, Church, Ministry of Water, CDTF (Community Development Trust Fund)

A lack of water in a community was causing tension between farmers – who comprised the majority of the community and needed the water for irrigation – and herders, who needed water for livestock. A severe shortage of water from 2009 to 2010 "was so bad that it almost started tribal clashes."

Community leaders worked together with a paralegal to devise a solution. The paralegal was consulted because he had a good reputation for settling problems within the community and he was known for teaching people at *barazas* about human rights issues. The paralegal met with community leaders and elders. Together, they decided to request funds to drill a bore hole from the Ministry of Water and the Community Development Trust Fund (CDTF).

The paralegal wrote a proposal to the two offices. The Ministry of Water responded that it had some funds earmarked for drilling bore holes in the community's district. It agreed to do water prospecting in their division. A month later, paralegal and community members showed prospecting officials around the area. A suitable place in the water table was found underneath a nursery school and church compound. The Ministry of Water asked the delegation to speak with the landowners about drilling a bore hole on their plot.

The paralegal "took the challenge" and went to meet the *wazees* (elders) and representatives from the church and nursery. They worked out an agreement permitting a bore hole on the land. The paralegal recorded minutes to the meeting, which he delivered alongside the agreement to the Ministry of Water. A 700 meter-deep water bore was constructed a few months later.

CASE 3: "WE KNEW HIM AS A DISPUTE RESOLVER"

Location: Rift Valley Province
Type of Dispute: State Accountability, Private Dispute
Issue: Property
Tools Used: Advocacy, Organizing
Other Institutions Used: Before Paralegal Involved: Chief, Police, Community Leaders; After Paralegal Involved: Ministry of Lands

> **CASE 3: (Cont.)**
>
> During the 1980s, land where water collected during the rains was designated "public utility land" for use by the community. The community had plans to build a dam on the site. In 2010, a person came forward with a title deed and fenced off the land, claiming it for himself. This upset the community. The youth in the community threatened to take action and destroy the fence as men were putting it up. The police were called in to defuse a confrontation.
>
> The community leaders, including the chief, met to decide a course of action. After meeting, they approached a paralegal, "who we knew as a dispute resolver." The paralegal went with the chief to speak with the youths, asking them to be tolerant as they sorted out the problem.
>
> The paralegal arranged to speak to representatives from district headquarters and the Ministry of Lands. He made the trip together with the chief and the chairman of the *wazee*. Initially, the district lands officer confirmed that his records indicated that the land belonged to the individual. Dissatisfied, the group went to the district commissioner, who agreed to look into the issue. The paralegal followed up with the commissioner a number of times. During the course of the case, the community pooled money to pay for the paralegal's travel expenses.
>
> After an investigation and several meetings, the district commissioner determined that someone had forged the land deed. The fence was taken down and the property was restored to the community.

In contrast, where relationships between paralegals and institutions were contentious, the reputation and effectiveness of paralegals appeared to suffer. In one Coast Province site, for example, paralegals reported that the area councilor and area chief were "not on good terms with paralegals," and therefore did not cooperate on land issues. This led to stalled cases. Paralegals confronting such constraints were still able to prevail, but at times met with mixed results.

> *The police are complaining about paralegals educating the masses on their rights. It is bringing friction between them.* – Community Leader, Coast Province
>
> *The police frustrate the complainant and use delaying tactics, which leads to spending a lot of money and delay in justice delivery ... What police embrace is what we hate ... They are trained that the first enemy is "mwananchi," meaning the first enemy is the citizen. There is no good relationship between us and the police.* – Paralegal, Coast Province

> CASE 4: THE DAM COMMITTEE
>
> *Location*: Eastern Province
> *Type of Dispute*: State Accountability
> *Issue*: Water
> *Tools Used*: Advocacy, Organizing, Information Provision
> *Other Institutions Used*: Before Paralegal Involved: Chief; After Paralegal Involved: District Officer
>
> A community elected a dam committee to oversee the provision of water. After some time, the committee stopped providing monthly statements on how it was spending money to operate the water kiosks and resisted efforts to hold it accountable. Two community members went to a paralegal for help.
>
> The dam stopped working two weeks later, after which the community did not want to pay the committee for the water. The paralegal asked the assistant chief, who was also the chair of the dam committee, to call a public *baraza* (meeting) on the issue. The chief refused. The paralegal called a community meeting anyway, at the chief's office. Around 200 people attended. The chief came with men and threatened to have the paralegal arrested for inciting the public and calling an illegal meeting. The chief felt that the issue should only be addressed in the Water Appeals Court.
>
> The paralegal then worked with community members to find a way for people to draw water directly from the dam without having to pay the committee, since the dam still didn't work. The dam committee was dissolved. The district officer has begun educating the community how to create a new one. Clients felt that the paralegal helped the situation, but they wanted more; they wanted help to get the dam running again and wanted the committee members to be held publicly accountable for mismanaging funds.
>
> The assistant chief felt that the case was handled poorly, warning: "If the paralegals are not checked, they will soon start mobilizing people for regime change. Even community workers operate under guidelines, not just haphazardly. I tell you they will cause problems in the country. The chief and district officer were with us but changed their tune after something happened. They might have been silenced by the NGO supporting the paralegals." The paralegal recounts, "People have a colonial legacy of not questioning the chief ... Initially I was alone with a handful of people, but now the whole community has audacity to question without fear."

In areas where paralegals had not forged open relationships with institutional actors, our interviews recorded fewer instances of paralegals undertaking significant roles in resolving complex cases. Instead, paralegals more often relied on referrals to police, chiefs, or government authorities.

> **CASE 5: NEW ELECTIONS**
>
> *Location*: Coast Province
> *Type of Dispute*: State Accountability
> *Issue*: Police
> *Tools Used*: Organizing, Information Provision
> *Other Institutions Used*: Before Paralegal Involved: District Office, Police, Chief; After Paralegal Involved: District Government, Police
>
> A community donated money to build an office for community policing. The chairman, who was elected to the Community Policing Office, became corrupt. Several community members approached the paralegal for help after they failed to get any results through the chief. The paralegal guided members in writing district government officials about the situation. Once informed, the district government banned the Office and held new elections. The clients were satisfied with the fact that new elections were called, but the community continues to disagree on aspects of community policing.

Where local institutions were corrupt, dysfunctional, discriminatory, or otherwise an unsuitable destination for referrals, paralegals could often only prevail when they bypassed local authorities. In these cases, paralegals typically engaged higher levels of government or relied on sheer adversarial persistence.

> **CASE 6: GOING HIGHER**
>
> *Location*: Central Province
> *Type of Dispute*: Private
> *Issue*: Family/Property, Gender-based Violence
> *Tools Used*: Information Provision, Referral
> *Institutions Involved*: Before Paralegal Involved: Police; After Paralegal Involved: Hospital, District Officer
>
> The client and her husband bought a parcel of land together. The husband wanted to sell the land, but she refused and the husband beat her. The paralegal, having been sought out by the wife, was unable to raise the police and suspected that the husband had bribed them.
>
> After lending the client money to visit the hospital, the paralegal sent the client to the district officer (DO) to lodge a complaint. The DO warned the husband against further violence and issued an injunction that prevented him from selling the land. The couple separated and the client found another place to live with her daughters.

> ### CASE 7: PUSHING THE POLICE
>
> *Location*: Nairobi Province
> *Type of Dispute*: Private, State Accountability
> *Issue*: Theft
> *Tools Used*: Advocacy
> *Other Institutions Used*: Before and after Paralegal Involved: Police
>
> A reverend reported the theft of his church's medical equipment. When the police were slow to investigate the robbery, the reverend enlisted the help of a paralegal. Police response picked up after the paralegal intervened. Due to pressure applied by the paralegal, the police arrested three church staff members and retrieved the medical equipment. The paralegal also worked to secure the release of the accused after they cooperated with the investigation. The police admitted that the paralegal's presence "simplified" their investigation, but also expressed that they were annoyed by how "pushy" the paralegal was in urging them to move more quickly.

Regardless of the talent or craftiness of a given paralegal, there are limits to what one can achieve when institutions simply do not perform their core functions well. While paralegals can, on occasion, overcome failed institutions to achieve satisfactory remedies, partial victories are sometimes the best they can accomplish.

> ### CASE 8: "I NO LONGER TRUST AUTHORITIES"
>
> *Location*: Central Province
> *Type of Dispute*: Private
> *Issue*: Gender-based Violence
> *Tools Used*: Information Provision, Advocacy
> *Other Institutions Used*: Before Paralegal Involved: Police, Hospital; After Paralegal Involved: NGO, Counselor
>
> The client, a young woman, tried to bring rape charges against her neighbor. The police refused to help her. After being examined at the hospital, she was told to go home. After her mother was told about a paralegal's office, she approached a paralegal, who took the young woman to the Nairobi office of CLAN, an organization that works on children's cases. The paralegal noted, "We went there but nothing seemed to be coming out of our visits so while we were still waiting for CLAN, I advised her to seek counseling."

> CASE 8: (Cont.)
> The paralegal tried to follow up with the police, but they insisted that they would not interfere in a disagreement between neighbors. The paralegal believed that the police had been bribed, as the client's written statement had mysteriously disappeared from the station. Ultimately, the only reprieve the paralegal could obtain was arranging for a counselor for the client, for which the young woman was grateful. However, the client stated that she did not feel empowered to take on injustices in the future because she "no longer trusts authorities."

Clearly, the ideal operating environment for a paralegal is one in which institutional actors are functional and cooperative, or at least permissive, of legal empowerment efforts. This tends to happen where local authorities view paralegals as supportive, rather than threatening, to their work. Chiefs in particular resolve many of the kinds of disputes that paralegals do – and derive income or prestige from doing so. Often, clients approach chiefs and other local authorities first, turning to paralegals only when they are dissatisfied with the results or treatment they receive. As such, paralegals offer an additional layer of accountability for local leaders.

Where paralegals are perceived as a force for facilitating or enhancing the work of institutional actors, amity and even collaboration have ensued. In some communities, chiefs have invited paralegals to participate in the dispute resolution activities of their council of elders, for instance. But where paralegals are seen to infringe on the domain of local authorities, relations suffer.[84]

How, then, have some paralegals forged strong relationships with authorities? Local institutions tend to be friendlier to paralegals' efforts when they are proactively informed about what paralegals are doing, routinely consulted on important issues, involved in relevant activities, and in regular contact with paralegals.[85] This helps authorities to feel like they have input and insight into how paralegals operate. It casts paralegals as colleagues, as opposed to competitors.

> *At their inception, I had a very rough time with [paralegals] since I felt they were overstepping their mandate. We had to agree on some fundamentals of law – where my powers end and how they can enter into the system. Right away, I can tell you that there are some cases I refer back to them and they forward cases to my office. So we help each other and my work now is very easy.* – Community Elder, Rift Valley Province

---

[84] Waruhiu and Otieno, "Access to Justice," 192 (see n. 58).
[85] Aimee Ongeso, interview by Abigail Moy (Namati), February 2016. Kituo Cha Sheria finds it helpful to formally introduce local authorities to paralegals prior to setting up an office; involve authorities in training, community outreach, and awareness sessions; develop joint actions wherever possible; and hold periodic briefing meetings with chiefs and police every few months to allow for complaints and encouragement, or to identify issue areas that need addressing.

Moreover, the paralegal movement has long argued that local, ad hoc arrangements would be significantly bolstered by nationwide laws or policies that recognize the role and authority of community paralegals.

2. Formal Recognition: Kenya's 2016 Legal Aid Law

Nearly every paralegal and community leader we interviewed identified the lack of formal recognition as one of the most serious challenges facing paralegals. Paralegals frequently referred to instances when authorities rebuffed them for lack of legitimacy. Meanwhile, community leaders wanted a clearer sense of what defines a paralegal, the type of training required, and what paralegals are authorized to do and not do.

> *It would be a good idea if we can be recognized by the Kenyan government. For example, when a young man lost his phone and we took him to the police station, the officers told him to forget about us [female paralegals]. They despised us. But when I produced my identification the police started to cooperate and talked nicely. It shows how the work of paralegals is breaking ground and shaking barriers of impunity.* – Paralegal, Coast Province

For years, the laws of Kenya prohibited anyone who was not an admitted lawyer (or working under the supervision of an attorney) from providing legal advice. This has complicated paralegals' efforts to advise clients on specific cases. Paralegals reported instances when judicial personnel prevented them from supporting their clients in court because they lacked credentials. But paralegals require access to courts to accompany clients at hearings, investigate and pursue "forgotten" cases, and monitor court proceedings to correct errors in the administration of a case.

Formal recognition, paralegals argued, would help them to more effectively challenge local authorities – particularly in cases of corruption and abuse – and to more effectively interact with the court systems. Community leaders agreed that recognition might also alleviate general public confusion around the role and capacities of paralegals. Interviewees speculated that a system of accreditation might further clarify matters by standardizing training for paralegals, at a time when the length, recurrence, and quality of paralegal training varies widely across the country.

In 2016, after a broad stakeholder consultative process and many years of advocacy by members of PASUNE, the Kenyan government adopted the Legal Aid Act, which recognizes paralegals so long as they are supervised by an accredited legal aid organization or advocate.[86] The move followed a flurry of activity arising out of an unprecedented multi-stakeholder meeting in April 2015. The meeting convened civil society, the LSK, the Kenyan Parliamentary Human Rights Association, the attorney general, the chief justice, and the Human Rights Commission. Their purpose: to discuss how to address Kenya's critical justice issues in light of the pending UN Agenda 2030 for Sustainable Development – which featured access

---

[86] The Legal Aid Act No. 6 (2016), *Kenya Gazette* Supplement No. 56 § 68(1).

to justice in Goal 16 – as well as Kenya's constitution and the national development plan, Vision 2030, which also prioritized justice.[87]

The meeting participants agreed upon a strategy to advance legislation key to enhancing access to justice across Kenya, including the then languishing 2013 Legal Aid Bill, 2013 Access to Information Bill, 2014 Community Land Bill, and Kenya's National Human Rights Policy and Action Plan. Immediately after the close of the meeting, members of the Kenyan Parliamentary Human Rights Association introduced the Legal Aid Bill afresh to Parliament. The bill was passed into law by the end of the session.[88]

The Legal Aid Law embodies a number of victories for Kenya's paralegal movement. First, it grants "accredited paralegals" the authority to provide legal advice and assistance; previously, only licensed attorneys could do so.[89] Under the law, paralegals can be accredited by the National Legal Aid Service (the successor to NALEAP) or by association with a civil society organization accredited as a legal aid provider.[90] While paralegals are prohibited from requesting or receiving payments from clients who qualify for legal aid,[91] the law establishes the Legal Aid Fund, which leaves the door open for public financing for paralegals.[92] The law does not proscribe remuneration of paralegals by training or parent organizations.

Second, the law defines legal aid as including the larger scope of activities typically undertaken by community paralegals: raising awareness of laws, out-of-court alternative dispute resolution, and advocacy on behalf of the community.[93] This broader scope empowers paralegals in all aspects of their work, rather than merely those that relate to courts and forums more traditionally associated with legal aid.

Third, the law tasks the National Legal Aid Service with developing "programs for legal aid education and the training and certification of paralegals."[94] This mandate could contribute to the development of more comprehensive and accessible learning infrastructure for paralegals seeking to advance their skills. Stakeholders from both civil society and government, including the National Land Commission, also see this as an opportunity to develop curricula for paralegals specializing in priority issue areas.

Finally, the National Legal Aid Service will be governed by a board upon which a civil society representative will serve, to represent "Public Benefit Organizations offering legal aid to the public, including women, youth and children."[95] Preserving a role for civil society in the governance and accreditation of paralegals is appropriate and necessary, given the history and nature of the paralegal movement in Kenya.

A number of outstanding issues need resolution before moving ahead, however. The division of labor and the allocation of responsibility among the many stakeholders across government, the private sector, and civil society remain unclear. How

---

[87] Jedidah Waruhiu, interview by Abigail Moy (Namati), November 2013.
[88] While the session should have ended in 2015, it was extended into 2016. Oliver Mathenge, "Kenya: MPs to Miss August Deadline for Bills," *The Star*, August 5, 2015, http://allafrica.com/stories/201508050140.html.
[89] The Legal Aid Act No. 6 (2016), *Kenya Gazette* Supplement No. 56 § 68(1).   [90] Ibid., § 59.
[91] Ibid., § 68(2).   [92] Ibid., §§ 29, 30.   [93] Ibid., § 2.   [94] Ibid., § 7(1)(h).   [95] Ibid., § 9(1)(j).

the new law interacts with or supersedes existing legal aid programming is yet to be determined. Mechanisms for coordination among all actors have not been established.

Financing presents another critical challenge. The Legal Aid Act establishes the Legal Aid Fund to "defray the expenses incurred by the representation of persons," "pay remuneration of legal aid providers,"[96] or "meet the expenses incurred by legal aid providers."[97] However, details on how the fund will work in practice are still being negotiated. To ensure adequate financial support for community paralegals throughout the country, civil society has submitted recommendations to the Kenyan government suggesting avenues for interagency coordination around legal aid implementation and financing. These recommendations emphasize sustainable measures, as well as systems for assessing community needs and monitoring progress toward the Act's goals. Planning is underway for multi-stakeholder meetings on these issues, bringing together civil society, multiple government agencies, members of Parliament, the Human Rights Commission, the private sector, and international and donor agencies.

Meanwhile, civil society continues to advocate for paralegal recognition in other areas. The draft National Human Rights Policy and Action Plan, which has been revised to integrate justice components into its objectives, is presently on the agenda for consideration before Parliament. In the new draft, paralegal presence and impact is being tracked in three outcome indicators relating to access to justice goals. The Kenyan government's statistical division is incorporating a legal needs survey into its household survey. Civil society is also working to include references to the role of paralegals and other intermediaries in the draft of the Access to Information Bill.

For now, the 2016 Legal Aid Act opens up a number of potential opportunities for Kenya's paralegal movement. Community paralegals finally won formal acknowledgment for their services enhancing public participation and providing legal information, awareness, and assistance. Adoption of the law may accelerate the presence and establishment of paralegals in communities, courts, and police stations. These measures may ultimately lead to new synergies between paralegals and other justice service providers across the sector.

B. Organizational Factors

Organizational factors – different ways in which civil society organizations train, manage, monitor, and support paralegals – also influence the effectiveness of community paralegals.

1. Support Structures

Paralegal networks relate to their parent civil society organizations in diverse ways. Their relationships can be roughly classified according to levels of support that

[96] Ibid., § 30(a).   [97] Ibid., § 30(c).

paralegals receive from an NGO: (a) training and access to pro bono referral contacts only; (b) training, referral contacts, and ongoing logistical support/guidance; and (c) training, referral contacts, ongoing logistical support/guidance, and monetary support. While an exceptional, deeply motivated paralegal can succeed without an extensive support structure, we have found that greater levels of support will on the whole strengthen the long-term morale, commitment, and performance of paralegals.

2. Training Only

Community paralegals in the first category typically receive an initial training,[98] and occasionally a refresher training, by a given NGO.[99] Training may combine legal instruction with coaching in practical skills and site visits to communities, courts, prisons, police stations, or legal aid clinics. A graduation ceremony is commonly held within the communities to build awareness of the paralegals' services.[100] New paralegals are equipped with basic resources, including a book of basic statutes, a t-shirt, a paralegal identification badge and jacket, a journal for documentation, and a carrier bag.[101] They are then encouraged to voluntarily support their communities with their newly gained knowledge. From then on, these paralegals operate more or less independently. When they cannot resolve a case alone, they refer clients to the parent NGO or other authorities.

Enhanced legal knowledge and established connections to attorneys are powerful tools. Indeed, due in large part to their training, some paralegals have gone on to earn places on chiefs' councils of elders or have even served as chiefs.[102] After witnessing the accomplishments of paralegals in their communities, public administrators have sought out paralegal training themselves.

Still, lack of coordination, oversight, and systems for accountability for paralegals can lead to problems. While paralegals are preselected on the basis of their reputation for integrity, this is not a guarantee against unethical or self-interested behavior. NGOs recount instances of paralegals charging for legal advice when the policy of the parent NGO is to provide free services. In other instances, a paralegal may charge for services on behalf of the parent NGO, but pocket the money rather than forwarding it to the organization as represented. Communities can fall victim to such misrepresentation because of uncertainty as to the precise duties and qualifications of community paralegals.

---

[98] LAN is one organization that provides training to paralegals without follow-up logistical support. AIHD, "Kenya Draft Report," 9 n. 24 (see n. 25).
[99] As of 2011, FIDA Kenya trained for two weeks, LRF for one year, Kituo Cha Sheria for two weeks with refresher courses conducted on a quarterly basis, and some organizations held one-day trainings for paralegals. Mary Amuyunzu-Nyamongo, "Kenya Paralegal Study," 19–20 (see n. 71). Other training programs may last up to six to seven weeks. Waruhiu and Otieno, "Access to Justice," 187 (see n. 58).
[100] Waruhiu and Otieno, "Access to Justice," 187 (see n. 58).
[101] A practice taken up by ICJ, LRF, Kituo, CJPC, and the Anglican Church. Ibid., 187, n. 14.
[102] Ibid., 185.

> CASE 9: THE ROGUE PARALEGAL
>
> **Location**: Eastern Province
> **Type of Dispute**: Private
> **Issue**: Theft
> **Tools Used**: Mediation
> **Other Institutions Used**: After Paralegal Involved: Chiefs, Police, Parent Organization
>
> The client came to a paralegal office during a "Legal Aid Day" to speak to an attorney about a land dispute. The paralegal acted as translator during the meeting. The paralegal later approached the client, bearing a number of forms that he falsely claimed had been sent to him by the attorney. The paralegal convinced the client to give him money, which he would hold on the client's behalf to pay for the case.
>
> The client raised and delivered the money, then requested to meet with the attorney. The paralegal began to make excuses and the client went to another paralegal office to complain. The other paralegal uncovered the deception and tried to get the accused paralegal to refund client's money, without success. The second paralegal recounted, "we called our mother organization and they said that these are our issues and as an organization they could not interfere."
>
> The case was taken to a series of chiefs and finally, the police. The accused paralegal was arrested and summoned to appear before court the next day. However, the next morning, the accused paralegal returned all of the client's money and ultimately did not have to go to court.
>
> Despite this setback, the client's original land case prevailed under the management of the second paralegal and the pro bono attorney. The satisfied client stated that others in the community are increasingly using paralegals because they "refuse to be misused after they saw me succeed. You know I am a person of no status in the community. People are wondering how I won the case against the rich man [with whom I had the land dispute]."
>
> The accused man is no longer able to practice as a paralegal, having been stripped of his title by the parent organization.

Another drawback of the "training only" model is unpredictable length of service. Paralegals serve clients for as long as they wish, but for many, pressing livelihood needs impede their ability to remain active over a long stretch of time. A significant number of these paralegals eventually fall dormant and do not take up paralegal duties again.

> *This is purely volunteer work and it becomes hard ... our [geographic] area is very expansive. I serve two villages, yet I am only given a T-shirt and IEC [information, education, and communication] materials. How do I reach out to the communities?"* – Paralegal, Eastern Province
>
> *Most of our paralegals come from afar. Z----- [a fellow paralegal] uses a motorcycle, [for] which she pays 400 Kenyan shillings and also uses a boat to cross to the other side. Some have to sacrifice and there is nothing they get for resolving cases. When victims have to be taken to hospital, it becomes hard, especially sourcing for means of transport. We have to sacrifice because we have families that depend on us.* – Paralegal, Coast Province

Some organizations have countered this problem by training paralegals who already have access to funding from other sources. Typically, NGOs will consult with community leaders, chiefs, and other provincial administration officers in order to identify individuals respected by their community. But some NGOs target officials, such as chiefs and assistant chiefs, as well as religious leaders, police officers, and others for paralegal training. Not only do individuals in power positions have the capacity to effect change, but they also can use the resources or prestige of their office for paralegal activities that align with their existing duties. This approach carries risks, however. Since paralegals serve as a backstop for ensuring the accountability of other authorities, combining these roles may present fundamental conflicts of interest. As such, local authorities with paralegal training should be considered a supplement to community paralegals who are capable of operating independently of government influence.

CASE 10: A PASTOR'S INFLUENCE

Location: Rift Valley Province
Type of Dispute: Private
Issue: Theft
Tools Used: Information Provision, Mediation
Other Institutions Used: After Paralegal Involved: Phone Company, Police, Formal Court

After noticing several thousand Kenyan shillings missing from his Mpesa (mobile banking) account, the client sought help from a paralegal, who was also his pastor. The paralegal advised him to call the phone company to ascertain precisely what happened. The phone company confirmed that a transfer had been made from the client's Mpesa account to the account of a friend. Three days earlier, the client had lent his phone to the same friend,

CASE 10: (Cont.)
who secretly accessed his Mpesa account and made the transfer. The client reported the theft to the police and the friend was detained.

After the paralegal ascertained that the client wanted nothing more than the return of the money, he worked with the accused man's mother to explore ways of meeting the payment. The paralegal discovered that the accused man was recently married and possessed only two sheep, and that his grandfather was ill. Rather than deprive the young family of its sole property in a time of need, the paralegal attempted to negotiate a better solution for the parties. The client, who wanted to avoid hefty court fees, assented to mediation and agreed to give the accused man's family time to raise and repay the money in full after seeing to the grandfather's health.

When the parties went to inform the police that they had settled the matter outside of court, the police refused to release the accused without a court order. The parties were unable to proceed until the paralegal intervened again by approaching the court. The court staff, upon recognizing him as both a pastor and a paralegal, "softened their stance." The court permitted the client to drop the case, upon swearing to the court clerk that the case would not be brought to court again. The accused man was set free. The stolen amount was repaid and both parties expressed satisfaction with the outcome of the case.

In cases involving institutions, a paralegal's political background may factor into his or her ultimate success. Orvis' research found that paralegals who were opposition activists or campaigners were almost twice as likely as paralegals with no political experience to take on cases directly challenging local authorities.[103] Yet recruitment of politically active paralegals has its risks. In one area of Kenya covered by Orvis' study, all paralegals were supporters of a specific member of Parliament and used their services as a platform to support him.

In other cases, national NGOs will identify an existing community-based organization (CBO) or help an individual to establish a CBO or network that can serve as a local framework for the activities of paralegals in the absence of the NGO.[104] The national NGO thereafter connects the CBO to pro bono lawyers and advises them on matters of law or organizational development, but encourages the CBO to raise its own funds. However, this is no easy task; the majority of the CBOs approached during this study struggled to access financing.

---

[103] Stephen Orvis, "Kenyan Civil Society," 247–68 (see n. 63).
[104] Examples of CBOs include LLF, KICODI, BUDAPAN. Mary Amuyunzu-Nyamongo, "Kenya Paralegal Study," 19 (see n. 71).

3. Training and Logistical Support

Paralegals in the second category receive ongoing logistical support from their parent organizations, in addition to training and referral contacts. NGOs may secure paralegals an office that serves as their base of operations, and may donate books, materials, computers, and other resources to the office. ICJ, for instance, provides motorcycles to paralegal office station coordinators, which are used for travel during the discharging of their duties.[105] In-kind benefits make it easier for paralegals to stay active, although challenges remain without additional financing.

NGOs may also provide support through regular supervisory visits, oversight and guidance over case management systems, and the provision of legal advice. Interviewees observed that close mentorship and supervision increase paralegals' effectiveness and empowers them to take on tougher cases. Paralegals especially find it helpful when they can call lawyers or experts at their parent NGO with day-to-day questions, or ask for assistance in formulating strategy or editing demand letters. For their part, NGOs have found that maintaining a supervisory relationship allows them to better monitor the quality of services provided by their paralegal corps.[106]

When support from a parent organization is consistent and dependable, its presence can help not only in the resolution of cases but also in the enforcement of agreements afterward.

> *For example if a man impregnates a schoolgirl, like the one we had some time back, the Laikipia Legal Forum (LLF) helps the mother of the child to pressure the husband/father of the child for upkeep and maintenance.* – Community Leader, Rift Valley Province

However, when contact with NGOs is irregular or unreliable, this can prove a source of frustration for paralegals.

> *Documentation and reporting on what we do is very weak partly because what we report to our parent organizations is not properly acted upon.* – Paralegal, Eastern Province

NGOs currently do not provide substantial assistance with security, although the issue arose in many conversations with paralegals. Interviewees described paralegal work as dangerous and life-threatening. Community leaders speculated that paralegal turnover rates could be attributed to the risks they take on. Paralegals surmised that stronger security measures would help them feel less vulnerable, thus enabling them to be more productive and bold.

---

[105] Organizations such as LRF and FIDA also provide this kind of support to their paralegals. AIHD, "Kenya Draft Report," 9 (see n. 25).
[106] Ongeso, interview (see n. 85).

> *Security is the main challenge. Most of the paralegals receive deadly threats during the course of their work. If the accused is confronted, sometimes he can physically harm the paralegal. One paralegal in the Soweto area, when pursuing a rape case, was told, "Leave that case or you will find your head in Ruai" (a nearby area known for crimes). Insecurity makes paralegals fear to operate at night. Threatening messages and phone calls make them immediately refer cases to the police instead of trying to deal with disputes.* – Community Leader, Nairobi Province
>
> *As a paralegal, when I find something touching on the provincial administration, I will conflict with them. When I interfere with matters that touch on the government, I risk my life.* – Paralegal, Eastern Province

4. Training, Logistical Support, Funding

The third category of paralegals is the least common. These paralegals receive direct monetary support from their parent NGOs, usually by way of allowances to meet day-to-day expenses.[107] The issue of paralegal salaries in Kenya is hotly debated within the movement. Some argue that paralegalism was founded on the spirit of volunteerism, altruism, and service to the community; to remunerate paralegals would warp their motives and lead to the commercialization of their services. Others see remuneration as a solution to the common problem of paralegals abandoning their posts for livelihood reasons.

> *I paid money at the police and courts for photocopies. The paralegal never asked for money but I would have given it to him. He really helped in seeing that [the accused] paid me back for the damage.* – Client, Eastern Province

Paralegals interviewed for this study consistently cited lack of funds as one of the main impediments to improving the effectiveness of their work. Most indicated that small allowances would be sufficient to cover costs. Several referred to instances when they could not afford to transport themselves or their clients to courts, hospitals, or other sites as needed to resolve or follow up on cases. Others cited an inability to afford basic office supplies. Given the many burdens shouldered by paralegals, most interviewees felt that truly effective and sustainable paralegal work requires financial support in some form.[108]

---

[107] CARE International is one such organization that at one point paid its paralegals as employees. AIHD, "Kenya Draft Report," 9, n. 23 (see n. 25). Other civil society organizations issue allowances that range from KES 4,000 and 30,000 per month. Waruhiu and Otieno, "Access to Justice," 192 (see n. 58).

[108] The sentiment is shared by other researchers, as well. "The inadequate pay or voluntary services have had negative impact in the quality and consistency of paralegal services in the community." Waruhiu and Otieno, "Access to Justice," 192 (see n. 58).

C. Cultural Factors

Finally, our research revealed a few cultural factors that shaped the nature of the roles in which paralegals proved most effective.

1. Clans and Tribes

Interviewees identified clan and tribal loyalties as a source of potential tension and conflict of interest for paralegals. Where a paralegal office did not reflect the ethnic composition of a diverse area, the public easily mistook it for serving only one tribe. Other paralegal offices offered themselves up as neutral ground for disputes between people hailing from different ethnic groups. This proved appealing for clients who remained uncertain as to the proper forum for their grievances.

CASE 11: MEDIATING BETWEEN MEMBERS OF DIFFERENT TRIBES

Location: Nairobi Province
Type of Dispute: Private
Issue: Property
Tools Used: Mediation
Other Institutions Used: Before and after Paralegal Involved: Police

A driver and a customer were involved in a dispute about the car fare the driver was charging. After the customer left, the window of the car shattered. Both parties were aware that customary law wouldn't apply to their case; a chief could not preside over it since the driver and customer were from different tribes.

The driver reported the damage to the police and named the customer as the cause. The police locked the customer in a cell; the customer's cousin asked the paralegal to assist. The paralegal mediated a deal between the two parties to split the cost of the broken window and free the customer. Though both parties wished they could have received more from the settlement, both felt it was fair and were satisfied they didn't have to go to court.

---

2. Power Dynamics

Women now know their rights and understand that they can contribute to the community's well-being by educating themselves on economic as well as cultural and political rights. The paralegals have encouraged them to embrace and live these rights. There are harsh cultural practices which are a giant against the advancement of women's rights. The paralegals are trying to break these barriers: women's inheritance, polygamy, girl child disadvantages in education. All this dispute resolution has a great impact on the community's way of life.

– Community Leader, Western Province

Paralegals often find themselves challenging entrenched power dynamics within their communities. They commonly represent women attempting to assert their rights in marriage, childcare, inheritance, or property ownership, as well as poor clients in grievances against the wealthy. Their ability to do so makes them an appealing alternative to, or source of pressure on, established authorities.

CASE 12: INHERITANCE

Location: Nairobi Province
Type of Dispute: Private
Issue: Theft
Tools Used: Information Provision
Other Institutions Used: After Paralegal Involved: Lawyers, Paralegals, Police

The client was a recent widow and the other party was her brother-in-law. After the death of the client's husband, the brother-in-law was tasked with collecting money for the burial. When the client asked for the money, the brother-in-law wouldn't release it. He said that unless "she decided to be inherited by him nothing will take place, the deceased will stay in the mortuary, dependents of the deceased will suffer." The client involved a paralegal, who requested the help of other paralegals and lawyers. As a group, they visited the brother-in-law at the police post (he was a police officer). With the help of other police in the office, they forced him to hand over the client's money.

CASE 13: SAYING "NO" TO DISCRIMINATION

Location: Eastern Province
Type of Dispute: Private
Issue: Business
Tools Used: Information Provision, Organizing
Other Institutions Used: Before Paralegal Involved: Assistant Chief; After Paralegal Involved: Community Development Assistant (CDA)

The client was a member of a welfare committee organized by the community to help each other pay for funeral expenses. Each member paid monthly contributions of 200 shillings per household. The client approached the paralegal because the committee had come under the influence of wealthy administrators who overlooked the needs of the poor.

CASE 13: (Cont.)

When the client lost his son, the committee refused to help. Only after three days did the committee reluctantly facilitate some burial expenses. Soon after, the committee shouldered all funeral expenses for a wealthy community member. When questioned about this, the committee said that the poor were not prompt with their payments, which excused the committee from helping. The client said that sometimes the poor have troubles for two to three months, but when they recover, they always pay the full amount in arrears, so that should not stop them from being helped. Moreover, the welfare committee discriminated against girls, youth, and unmarried women – girls under the age of twenty-five, for example, were not permitted to join.

After the paralegal helped raised money to bury the client's son, he told mourners "it was time they said no to discrimination by the rich." He advised people to stop making monthly contributions to the committee. After organizing a meeting and hearing everyone's views, they informed the paralegal that they wanted to start their own committee. The paralegal registered a new committee, open to all. The new committee now has more members than the old committee, as a number of people defected from the old committee to join the new one. The contribution is a more affordable 50 shillings. The client is content with this, although he wished the paralegal had helped him get their money back from the old committee.

CASE 14: CHILDCARE

Location: Rift Valley Province
Type of Dispute: Private
Issue: Family
Tools Used: Information Provision, Mediation
Other Institutions Used: After Paralegal Involved: NGO

The client became pregnant by a friend, who married her neighbor two months before the baby was due and refused to provide child support. The client approached a paralegal who, after hearing her case, took her to a legal NGO that issued a summons to the father. The father brought relatives and friends to the first meeting but relaxed after realizing the paralegal was a neutral party. The paralegal made sure the father read the national law on children himself and impressed on the man that the matter could be referred to the Children's Court. After two meetings, the respondent agreed to pay a monthly sum, which the complainant would collect from the office.

Because of a strong cultural preference for keeping marriages intact, gender-based violence presents a special challenge for paralegals. In such cases, paralegals tend to focus on the resolution of visible conflict and reconciliation between the couple, even when the long-term safety of the woman might be in question. It is difficult to alter the course of abusive relationships caught in a pattern of violence with a single intervention. Where reconciliation is appropriate, paralegals must tread carefully; mediation works best when the power dynamics between the participants are not vastly unbalanced, as they tend to be in cases involving domestic violence. Mediating under these circumstances requires tailored considerations and a plan for continued monitoring of the situation. In cases unfit for mediation, a willingness to consider alternatives, such as separation of the couple, could bear longer-term effects on the health and safety of the woman.

CASE 15: "WHERE THERE IS LIGHT"

Location: Coast Province
Type of Dispute: Private
Issue: Family, Gender-based Violence
Tools Used: Mediation, Information Provision
Other Institutions Used: Before Paralegal Involved: Village Elder; After Paralegal Involved: Community Police

The parties to the dispute were a married couple and the complainant alleged that her husband had assaulted her and threatened to take their money and leave. The complainant originally brought the case to the village elder, who referred it to the paralegal. The village elder and paralegal discussed whether to report the case to the police or to mediate; the chief favored the former option. The paralegal opted to mediate the dispute with a community policing member present. Before the mediation, the husband wanted to divorce his wife, but afterward, he agreed to return the money and stay. When interviewed a year after the incident, the wife reported, "for now, everything is all right. But if it happens again I will go back to the paralegal office where there is light." Meanwhile, the husband stated, "the paralegal acted fairly, because the village elders had called the paralegal to take me to Nyai police station, but the paralegal refused and requested the village elder to let the case be resolved by the paralegal."

CASE 16: "PARALEGALS ARE EVERYWHERE"

Location: Nairobi Province
Type of Dispute: Private
Issue: Family, Gender-based Violence
Tools Used: Mediation, Information Provision
Other Institutions Used: N/A

After a year of marriage, the husband began beating his wife daily. At first, he would beat her for the way she opened the door: a second too early and he would beat her for opening the door for an "expected lover," a second too late and he would beat her for taking her time. Then he would beat her for any number of reasons. The husband stepped on her stomach, chest, and legs, and ignored her pleas for mercy. One day the husband slapped his wife across the face, leaving her with a swollen left eye. "It got to the point where I did not want anyone who knew me to meet me or even greet me. I lived in isolation."

A neighbor observed what was happening and advised the wife to seek help from a paralegal. The wife met with the paralegal and felt "relieved I have a fellow woman who has a lot of strength and advice for me. I learnt about violence against women, and its implications, both social and legal."

The paralegal summoned the husband to the office. The paralegal did not want to separate the couple "because it will be unfair for young couples who are starting marriage life." But the paralegal recognized that the husband had to answer for his actions, so she "made him aware."

The husband stated, "I can't really understand why and how I used to beat my wife. The day I received a phone call from [the paralegal] is the day I felt something was not right with me ... Now I was being searched by the police. To tell the truth, I had lost a job and wanted my wife to go. After talking to both my wife and [the paralegal], I realized I was wrong." The husband apologized to his wife, who accepted. For six months at least, there has been no further violence.

The wife was satisfied with the outcome, although she said "the paralegal could have cautioned the man and brought more witnesses." The neighbor wanted the paralegal to go further: "Her approach was good but at least a court warning would have been better. What if the couple moves to another place where no one can help [the wife]? You see a court warning and follow-ups from time to time will be much better." For his part, the husband observed, "I know men beat their wives, but not to a bigger magnitude anymore. Paralegals are everywhere."

3. Reconciliation

In general, community leaders from every region considered paralegals' reconciliation and peacemaking activities among their most valuable contributions to society. They praised paralegals' ability to reach an outcome in which both parties bore no ill will toward each other far more than they noted paralegals' ability to achieve remedies or resolve injustices for clients. This may reflect a cultural preference for reconciliation over redress, or at least an overriding concern for peace.

> *Most of the impact is felt on the issue of reconciliation. The paralegals have help[ed] here so much. The paralegals help the parties to a suit let go [of] the bitterness they had against each other.* – Magistrate, Central Province
>
> *Yes, I think the outcome was fair, as I said there is now peace between the two families, they have gone back to being very good friends.* – Community Leader, Rift Valley Province

---

CASE 17: SCHOOL UNIFORMS

Location: Nairobi Province
Type of Dispute: Private
Issue: State Services, Education
Tools Used: Mediation, Arbitration, Information Provision
Other Institutions Used: N/A

The client was an internally displaced person and father of three children who brought a case against the headmaster of a primary school. The client sought the paralegal's help after the headmaster refused to let the children attend school because they didn't have uniforms. The paralegal mediated a compromise that enabled the children to attend school on the client's promise that he would buy school uniforms within two months. Both parties felt the resolution was fair. The client reiterated throughout this interview that he was most happy about the fact that, after reaching the compromise, he is now friends with the headmaster. Months later, the paralegal confirmed that "the children are now attending school."

> **CASE 18: MIDDLE GROUND**
>
> *Location:* Central Province
> *Type of Dispute:* Private
> *Issue:* Business
> *Tools Used:* Mediation
> *Other Institutions Used:* N/A
>
> The client bought a phone from his neighbor. Two weeks later, the client tried to return the phone because it was defective and the neighbor refused to take it back. The client asked the paralegal to resolve the dispute. The paralegal listened to both parties and advised the client to take the phone to a repair shop. The parties were reported to be on good terms. Though the complainant did not get what he wanted (he wanted the neighbor to fix the phone), both parties thought the paralegal acted fairly in this case and would seek out the paralegal again if another similar dispute occurred.

V. CONCLUSION

In a few short decades, Kenyan paralegalism has grown from modest roots into a vibrant nationwide movement, with institutional, legislative, and policy backing. Today, paralegals are expanding in number, diversifying their skill sets and methodologies, developing specializations in priority issues, and strengthening collaborative and innovative relationships with state and customary authorities.

The movement nevertheless faces many challenges. Paralegal programs continue to seek a sustainable model that can provide paralegals with the logistical, financial, and capacity-building support they need to take on ever more complex cases. The solution must satisfy the need for scale, given the gaps in justice services that persist throughout the country. Dysfunction in formal and customary institutions responsible for the administration and enforcement of justice must be rooted out. Working relationships between these institutions and paralegals must be defined, acknowledged, and respected.

With the adoption of the 2016 Legal Aid Act, all involved in the effort to achieve universal access to justice in Kenya – civil society, the legal community, government, communities, and citizens – now have a platform to make progress on these fronts. Given the success paralegals have experienced in helping people to understand, use, and shape the law throughout Kenyan history, they will undoubtedly play a critical role in continuing efforts to deepen democracy and empower citizens across the nation.

REFERENCES

African Institute of Health and Development (AIHD), "Kenya Paralegal Study: Literature Review on Paralegalism in Kenya" (draft for discussion, February 2012).
African Institute for Health and Development (AIHD). "Kenya Draft Report: Multi-country Study on the Impact of Paralegals." Draft report, African Institute for Health and Development, May 10, 2012.
Aimee Ongeso, interview by Abigail Moy (Namati), February 2016.
Amondi, Caroline. "Legal Aid in Kenya: Building a Fort for Wanjiku." In *The Legal Profession and the New Constitutional Order in Kenya*, edited by Yash P. Ghai and Jill C. Ghai, 201–20. Nairobi: Strathmore University Press, 2014.
(National coordinator for NALEAP), interview by Abigail Moy (Namati), November 2013.
Amuyunzo-Nyamongo, Mary. "Kenya Paralegal Study Preliminary Report." Preliminary report, African Institute for Health and Development (AIHD), submitted to the World Bank Justice for the Poor Program, Nairobi, September 22, 2011.
Angote, Gertrude. Interview by Abigail Moy (Namati). November 2013.
Balancing the Scales: A Report on Seeking Access to Justice in Kenya. Nairobi: Legal Resource Foundation Trust, 2004.
BBC. "Kenya Profile: Timeline." July 30, 2015.
Benschop, Marjolein. *Rights and Reality: Are Women's Equal Rights to Land, Housing and Property Implemented in East Africa?* France: United Nations Human Settlements Programme, 2002.
Chopra, Tanja. *Reconciling Society and the Judiciary in Northern Kenya*. Nairobi: Legal Resources Foundation Trust, 2008.
The Constitution of Kenya (2010).
de Zeeuw, Jereon. *Project Report Assessing Democracy Assistance: Kenya*. United Kingdom: FRIDE, 2010.
East Africa Protectorate High Court. "East Africa Legal Practitioners' Rules 1901." In *East Africa Protectorate: Law Reports Containing Cases Determined by the High Court of Mombasa, and by the Appeal Court at Zanzibar, and by the Judicial Committee of the Privy Council, on Appeal from that Court*, edited by Robert W. Hamilton, 121–25. London: Stevens and Sons, Ltd., 1906.
Ellis, Amanda, Jozefina Cutura, Nouma Dione, Ian Gillson, Clare Manuel, and Judy Thongori. *Gender and Economic Growth in Kenya: Unleashing the Power of Women*. Washington, DC: World Bank, 2007.
Federation of Women Lawyers Kenya (FIDA Kenya). *So Far, How Far?: 2007 Annual Report*. Kenya: Federation of Women Lawyers Kenya, 2008.
Feeley, Maureen C. "Transnational Movements, Human Rights and Democracy: Legal Mobilization Strategies and Majoritarian Constraints in Kenya 1982–2002." PhD diss., University of California, San Diego, 2006. eScholarship (b6635496).
Ghai, Yash P. "Law and Lawyers in Kenya and Tanzania: Some Political Economy Considerations." In *Lawyers in the Third World: Comparative and Developmental Perspectives*, edited by Clarence J. Dias, Robin Luckham, D. O. Lynch, and J. Paul. New York: International Center for Law in Development, 1981, 144–76.
"Legal Profession: Themes and Issues." In *The Legal Profession and the New Constitutional Order in Kenya*, edited by Yash P. Ghai and Jill C. Ghai, 1–32. Nairobi: Strathmore University Press, 2014.

Ghai, Yash P. and J. P. W. B. McAuslan. *Public Law and Political Change in Kenya: A Study of the Legal Framework of Government From Colonial Times to the Present.* New York: Oxford Press, 1970.
Harrington, Andrew and Tanja Chopra. "Arguing Traditions: Denying Kenya's Women Access to Land Rights." *Justice for the Poor Research Report* 2, no. 52674 (2010).
Human Rights Watch. *High Stakes: Political Violence and the 2013 Elections in Kenya.* Human Rights Watch, 2013.
International Commission of Jurists. *Law and the Administration of Justice in Kenya*, edited by Kivutha Kibwana. Nairobi: International Commission of Jurists, Kenya Section, 1992.
  Legal Services for Rural and Urban Poor and the Legal Status of Rural Women in Anglophone West Africa: Report of a Seminar, 19–23 July 1993, Accra, Ghana. Geneva: International Commission of Jurists, 1995.
International Commission of Jurists, African Bar Association, and All-Africa Conference of Churches. *Legal Services in Rural Africa: Report of a Seminar Held at Limuru, Near Nairobi, 1 to 4 October 1984.* Geneva: International Commission of Jurists, 1985.
Jedidah Waruhiu, interview by Abigail Moy (Namati), November 2013.
Kameri-Mbote, Patricia. "Brief History: Introduction." University of Nairobi School of Law. http://law-school.uonbi.ac.ke/node/1569.
Karau, Martha. Interview by Robert M. Press. August 15, 2002.
Kenya Gazette Notice No. 11598.
Kituo Cha Sheria. *Annual Report 2010.* Nairobi: Kituo Cha Sheria, 2010.
  Kituo Cha Sheria Strategic Plan 2009–2013. Nairobi: Kituo Cha Sheria, 2008.
Lamba, Shermit. *A Topographical Analysis of the Law Courts of Kenya.* Nairobi: Mazingira Institute, 2011.
Legal Aid Act No. 6 (2016), *Kenya Gazette* Supplement No. 56.
Matanga, Frank K. "Civil Society and Politics in Africa: The Case of Kenya." In *The Third Sector: For What and for Whom?* Paper presented at the Fourth International Conference of ISTR, Dublin, Ireland, July 5–8, 2000.
Mathenge, Oliver. "Kenya: MPs to Miss August Deadline for Bills." *The Star*, August 5, 2015.
Mbote, Patricia K. and Migai Akech. *Kenya Justice Sector and the Rule of Law: A Review by AfriMAP and the Open Society Initiative for Eastern Africa.* Nairobi: Open Society Foundation, 2011.
Murunga, Goodwin R. and Shadrack W Nasong'o. *Kenya: The Struggle for Democracy.* London: Zed Books, 2007.
Mutua, Makau W. "Justice under Siege: The Rule of Law and Judicial Subservience in Kenya." *Human Rights Quarterly* 23, no. 1 (2001): 96–118.
Mutunga, Willy. Interview by Maureen C. Feeley. Nairobi, May 15, 1998.
Ngondi-Houghton, Connie. *Access to Justice and Rule of Law in Kenya.* UN Development Programme Initiative on Legal Empowerment for the Poor, 2006.
Nowrojee, Pheroze. "The Legal Profession 1963–2013: All This Can Happen Again – Soon." In *The Legal Profession and the New Constitutional Order in Kenya*, edited by Yash P. Ghai and Jill Co. Ghai, 33–58. Nairobi: Strathmore University Press, 2014.
Odenyo, Amos O. "Professionalization amidst Change: The Case of the Emerging Legal Profession in Kenya." *African Studies Review* 22, no. 3 (1979): 33–44. doi: 128.112.200.107.
Ojwang, J. B. and D. R. Salter. "The Legal Profession in Kenya." *Journal of African Law* 34, no. 1 (1990): 9–26. doi: 128.112.200.107.
Olungah, Charles. "The Role of Academia in Democratization in Kenya." In *Discourses on Civil Society in Kenya*, edited by P. Wanyande and M. A. Okebe, 31–39. Nairobi: African Research and Resource Forum, 2009.

Ongeso, Aimee. Interview by Abigail Moy (Namati). February 2016.
Ooko-Ombaka, Oki. "Education for Alternative Development: The Role of the Public Law Institute, Kenya." *Third World Legal Studies* 4, art. 11 (1985): 171–77.
Opinion Brief on Paralegal Support Network (Legal Resource Foundation, 2011), 2.
Orvis, Stephen. "Kenyan Civil Society. Bridging the Urban–Rural Divide?" *Journal of Modern African Studies* 41, no. 2 (2003): 247–83.
Paralegal Support Network (PASUNE). *Handbook for Paralegals*. Kenya: PASUNE, 2005.
Press, Robert M. *Peaceful Resistance: Advancing Human Rights and Civil Liberties*. Aldershot: Ashgate, 2006.
Republic of Kenya. *Final Report of the Task Force on Judicial Reforms*. Nairobi: Government Printer, 2010.
Republic of Kenya, Governance, Justice, Law and Order Sector (GJLOS) Reform Programme. *National Integrated Household Baseline Survey Report*. Nairobi: World Bank, 2006.
Ripoca Project. *Organisational Study: Kituo Cha Sheria*.
Tsanga, Amy S. and Olatokunbo Ige. *A Paralegal Trainer's Manual for Africa*. Geneva: International Commission of Jurists, 1994.
UN Office on Drugs and Crime (UNODC). *Access to Legal Aid in Criminal Justice Systems in Africa: Survey Report*. Vienna: United Nations, 2011.
   Handbook on Improving Access to Legal Aid in Africa. Criminal Justice Handbook Series. Vienna: United Nations, 2011.
University of Nairobi. The 3rd Congregation for the Conferment and Presentation of Degrees and Diplomas at the Great Court. Nairobi: University of Nairobi, 1972.
Waruhiu, Jedidah W. and John J. O. Otieno. "Access to Justice: The Paralegal Approach." In *The Legal Profession and the New Constitutional Order in Kenya*, edited by Yash P. Ghai and Jill C. Ghai. Nairobi: Strathmore University Press, 2014.
Widner, Jennifer. *The Rise of a Party-State in Kenya: From "Harambee!" to "Nyayo!"* Berkeley: University of California, 1992.

6

Squeezing Justice Out of a Broken System

Community Paralegals in Sierra Leone

Vivek Maru, Lyttelton Braima, and Gibrill Jalloh[1]

1. INTRODUCTION: A GOLD MINE OWNS UP AT LAST

In Valunia chiefdom, in southern Sierra Leone, Cluff Gold Company mined for fifteen years without paying rent or compensation to the communities whose land it was using. Every time people complained, company officials claimed they were "only doing mineral exploration, not actively mining gold." The paramount chief and a few elders visited the mining ministry office in Bo, the district capital, several times, but they were always told to go and come back.

When a paralegal named Prince Wudie began to work in Valunia, residents asked if he could help them take on Cluff Gold. Prince explained that Sierra Leone's mining law was consistent with what the community knew intuitively: a mining company must pay surface rent to its hosts. Prince and chiefdom leaders initially tried to reach out to the company directly, but company officials refused to meet.

Prince and several community representatives also returned to the mining authority in Bo, but they too were told to go and come back. They then took a trip to Freetown and, with the help of the director of Prince's organization, presented their case at the national directorate of the Ministry. The official in Freetown responded that the company was clearly in breach. He wrote to the firm, stating that its mining license was at risk if it could not come to an agreement with the people of Valunia.

---

[1] This chapter was a team effort. We are grateful to the organizations whose work we studied: Timap for Justice, Network Movement for Justice and Development, and Methodist Church Sierra Leone. These groups accommodated the burden that research imposes because they believe in learning. We hope the findings are useful in their ongoing work. We collaborated with a crew of intrepid field researchers: Mohamed Bangura, David K. Conteh, Mohamed C. Bah, Josephine K. Turay, Edith Konneh, and Khadijatu Shaw. They overcame many obstacles, from seemingly unpassable roads and rivers to malaria. Varun Gauri was a powerful and generous force throughout: he helped design the research, pilot the questionnaires, craft the coding system, and analyze the data. When an earlier draft failed to engage the data adequately, he pushed us to rewrite. We received invaluable research assistance from Burke Butler, Abigail Moy, and Donald Beaudette. Alice Goldenberg played a clutch role, redoing the analyses when we'd lost our way. Sonkita Conteh read multiple drafts and taught us important lessons, as he always does. Jinyoung Lee tracked down citations and got us across the finish line. We are grateful to all the people who shared their stories with us. We honor their struggles for justice.

Staff from the company told Prince they were willing to talk. The negotiation involved meetings with large numbers of community members, to hear their grievances and desires, as well as smaller discussions between company officials and Valunia's chiefdom administration. The process took eight months. Ultimately, all sides agreed to a written agreement that stipulated, among other things:

- An annual payment of surface rent to landowning families of up to 150,000,000 SLL (US$46,875) with a 3 percent increase every year during the life of the lease.
- Backlog payment of surface rent for the previous eight years.
- The construction of water wells and latrines for communities in the mining lease area.
- Improvement on the main road linking the chiefdom headquarter town and other major towns.
- Preference for employment of local youths in both skilled and unskilled jobs.

This was not a perfect solution. The company committed to paying eight years of back rent, for example, rather than the fifteen it owed. And the agreement did not include environmental protections. But after years of impunity, it was a meaningful step toward justice. The communities asked Prince to help monitor implementation of the agreement going forward. An elder who was active throughout the process said, in Sierra Leonean Krio:

> If den man yah nor bin put wi en di company pipul den togeda, wi nor bin fo get dis wan word, en wi nor bin for benefit tay di company comot na yah.
>
> If the paralegals did not bring us and the company management together, we would never have found this common ground, and the company would have finished mining and left this place without us benefiting.

Community paralegals emerged in Sierra Leone after the end of an eleven-year civil war as a way of providing basic access to justice and repairing the ties between citizens and state. The first paralegal organization, Timap for Justice, was founded in 2003, drawing explicitly on the long experience of community paralegals in South Africa. Since then, several groups have deployed paralegals, together serving as much as 40 percent of the population. In 2012 the government adopted a legal aid law that recognizes the role paralegals play in delivering justice services and calls for a paralegal in every chiefdom of the country.

This chapter aims to illuminate the experience of paralegals to date and the outlook for their work going forward. We start with a brief history of paralegal efforts in the country. Next, we present data from case-tracking research we conducted with three organizations deploying paralegals. We then draw on that data, as well as interviews with key actors, to explore the nature of paralegal efforts in Sierra Leone.

We discuss the kinds of cases paralegals take on, how paralegals work, how they interact with the state, and how they're funded. We close with a reflection on the role of paralegals in deepening Sierra Leonean democracy.

11. PARALEGALS IN SIERRA LEONE, FROM POST-CONFLICT TO POST-EBOLA

Between 1991 and 2002 some 50,000 people – 1 out of every 100 Sierra Leoneans, most of them civilians – were killed in a brutal civil war. A rebel faction called the Revolutionary United Front (RUF) started the conflict by challenging Sierra Leone's weak army in the east. Eventually the RUF captured the capital Freetown in 1997 in partnership with a group of disgruntled army officers called the Armed Forces Revolutionary Council. The war was characterized more by attacks on civilians than by conflict between combatants. West African regional forces, the United Nations, and the British military all intervened over the next several years, finally leading to peace under a civilian government in 2002.

Among the root causes of the conflict were arbitrariness in government and maladministration of justice.[2] The Special Court for Sierra Leone was established in 2002 for retrospective accountability – to try those most responsible for crimes against humanity during the war. At the same time several civil society groups expressed a desire to improve accountability going forward, by helping people who face injustice in their daily lives.

A coalition called the National Forum for Human Rights received seed funding for this purpose from an international organization, the Open Society Justice Initiative. A young Sierra Leonean lawyer, Simeon Koroma, and one of us, Vivek Maru, served as founding directors.

It was an open question what legal aid would look like. Sierra Leone has a dualist legal system. The formal system based on British law is concentrated in the capital. In 2003 there were 100 lawyers in the country total, and more than ninety of those lived in Freetown. A "customary" system, including "local courts" in each chiefdom, and lower chiefs' courts that operate illegally, handle the majority of disputes. These institutions apply customary law, which varies by region and tribe and is uncodified. Lawyers have no standing in customary courts.[3]

---

[2] According to the Truth and Reconciliation Commission, for example, "the war in Sierra Leone was largely the result of failures in governance and institutional processes in the country." Sierra Leone Truth and Reconciliation Commission, *Witness to Truth: Report of the Sierra Leone Truth and Reconciliation Commission*, vol. 2 (2004) 7, par. 16. See also Paul Richards, *Fighting for the Rain Forest: War, Youth & Resources in Sierra Leone* (London: International African Institute, 1996), 60.

[3] See, for example, Ryann E. Manning, "Landscape of Local Authority in Sierra Leone: How 'Traditional' and 'Modern' Justice and Governance Systems Interact," in *Decentralization, Democracy, and Development: Recent Experience from Sierra Leone*, ed. Yongmei Zhou (Washington, DC: World Bank, 2009), 114. See also Richards, *Fighting for the Rain Forest: War, Youth & Resources in Sierra Leone*, 46 (see n. 2); Owen Alterman, Aneta Binienda, Sophie Rodella, and

So a lawyer-based model of legal aid would have been unworkable. Instead, drawing on the experience in South Africa, the coalition proposed to experiment with a paralegal approach. It was thought that paralegals could work closely with communities, and engage customary and formal institutions alike. At the outset Koroma and Maru recruited thirteen paralegals – two in Freetown, and the others from five out of Sierra Leone's 149 chiefdoms. Initial training focused on basic Sierra Leonean law, the structure and procedures of Sierra Leonean institutions, and skills like fact-finding, mediation, organizing, and advocacy.[4]

In contrast to the way lawyers typically treat clients – as victims requiring a technical service – the paralegals sought to advance "legal empowerment": to bolster the knowledge and agency of the people with whom they work. Not "I'll solve it for you," but "we'll solve it together."[5]

In 2005, this effort became an independent Sierra Leonean organization called Timap for Justice. *Timap* means "stand up" in Krio. According to Daniel Sesay, one of the original paralegals, "When we began, we had no recipe for ... how paralegals could address any of the myriad and complex injustices that Sierra Leoneans face."[6] Paralegals developed methods through trial and error, by taking on real cases. Over time, they built relationships with local leaders and government officials. In a small number of severe cases, Simeon Koroma took formal action in the courts. Sesay writes, "We made this road by walking."[7]

In the years after the war several other groups besides Timap began to deploy community paralegals. The Catholic Church founded the Access to Justice Project in the Northern Province in 2005, for example, with a focus on survivors of sexual violence.[8] Another group, Advocaid, started in 2006; its paralegals and lawyers assist women in prison. In 2007, Timap itself doubled in size, growing to serve ten chiefdoms in the North and South.

A team from the World Bank led by Pamela Dale completed a study of Timap in 2009. Researchers randomly selected cases from three of Timap's offices, and interviewed all the parties involved. An imam in Bo District said to the researchers, "Before Timap, people who didn't have money to sue to the chiefs or court resorted to either fighting or swearing or sorcery as a way of investigating or satisfying their desire to seek

---

Kimyia Varzi, *The Law People See: The Status of Dispute Resolution in the Provinces of Sierra Leone in 2002* (Freetown: National Forum for Human Rights, 2002).

[4] For a detailed account of Timap's experience, including how Timap paralegals aimed to respond to their context, see Vivek Maru, "Between Law and Society: Paralegals and the Provision of Justice Services in Sierra Leone and Worldwide," *Yale Journal of International Law* 31, 2 (2006): 427–76.

[5] See, for example, Maru, "Between Law and Society: Paralegals and the Provision of Justice Services in Sierra Leone and Worldwide," 458 (see n. 4). See also Daniel Sesay, *Community-Based Paralegals in Sierra Leone: Case Studies and Stories* (Namati, 2014), 20–22.

[6] Sesay, *Community-Based Paralegals in Sierra Leone: Case Studies and Stories*, 4 (see n. 5).

[7] Sesay, *Community-based Paralegals in Sierra Leone: Case Studies and Stories*, 4 (see n. 5).

[8] Amnesty International, *Sierra Leone – No One to Turn To: Women's Lack of Access to Justice in Sierra Leone* (London: Amnesty International, 2005), 7.

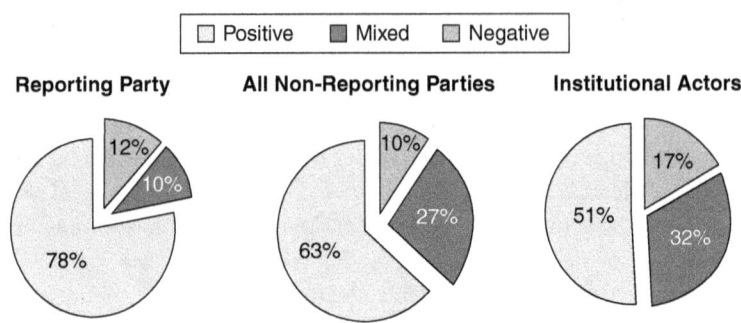

FIGURE 6.1 Satisfaction with Timap, reporting versus non-reporting parties
Source: Dale, *Delivering Justice to Sierra Leone's Poor*, 45.

justice." The study found that clients were attracted to Timap because its service was "free, fast, and fair," and "associated in many respondents' minds with fair solutions."[9]

Fifty-five percent of cases sampled in the World Bank study involved family law – issues like alimony and child custody – though paralegals addressed many other kinds of problems as well: violations of labor rights, disputes over land and debt, and assault. In addition to the random sample, researchers asked paralegals to identify a few "high impact" collective cases in each site – these included supporting workers at a sugar factory to seek compliance with a collective wage agreement, and supporting several villages to advocate with the Sierra Leone Roads Authority for repair of a broken bridge on the main road connecting them to the provincial capital.

Dale found that a large percentage of reporting (i.e., those who brought cases to paralegals) and non-reporting parties, and even a narrow majority of institutional actors – whom paralegals sought to hold accountable – spoke positively of their experience working with Timap.

Clients – especially women and young people – reported that "Timap's presence and advocacy ... encouraged them to demand rights that may otherwise have gone unrecognized." Many informants perceived that "police, chiefs, and courts ... were more thorough, fair, and fast in their dispute resolution" as a result of monitoring and advocacy by the paralegals.[10]

Dale identified several areas for improvement. A few respondents indicated that paralegals had taken on cases involving family members and friends. Dale recommended better enforcement of Timap's conflict of interest policy, which would require paralegals to recuse themselves from those cases. Dale also found that many clients could not describe Timap's work in detail beyond their own

---

[9] Pamela Dale, *Delivering Justice to Sierra Leone's Poor: An Analysis of the Work of Timap for Justice*, Justice for the Poor Research Report, no. 1 (Washington, DC: World Bank, 2009), 12–13. Two of us, Lyttelton Braima and Gibrill Jalloh, were part of the research team for this study.

[10] Dale, *Delivering Justice to Sierra Leone's Poor*, 33, 38 (see n. 9).

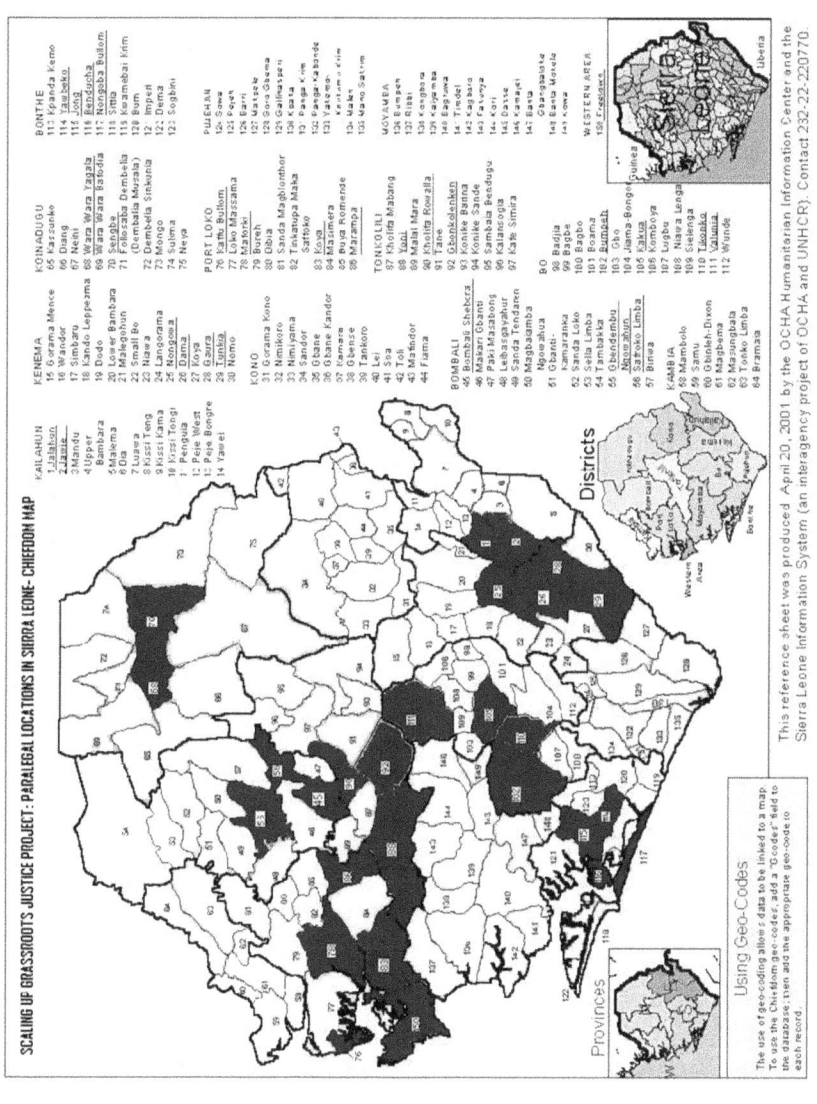

FIGURE 6.2 Scaling up grassroots justice: Chiefdoms served by paralegals as of 2011
Source: Open Society Justice Initiative.

cases; she recommended clear, consistent communication on the role Timap plays in the community. She also noted that some case files were missing or incomplete, and emphasized the importance of more rigorous management of case information.[11]

In 2010, President Koroma and the Open Society Foundation agreed to support a further scale-up of community paralegals. Timap, the Catholic Access to Justice Project, two other faith-based groups – the Methodist Church and the Catholic Justice and Peace Commission – and the Bangladeshi NGO BRAC all agreed to apply the Timap model with common systems for training, data collection, and paralegal supervision. A small team from the Open Society Justice Initiative coordinated the coalition and supported new partners to adapt Timap's methodology.

Together, by the end of 2010, the organizations deployed more than seventy paralegals in eight out of Sierra Leone's twelve districts, and served an estimated 38 percent of the population in the country.

In 2013, paralegals from the five organizations collectively opened 6,031 new cases and resolved 4,306. The cases were diverse – they included abuse of power by local authorities, accident compensation, unpaid wages, and breaches in the delivery of basic services like water and health care. The following tables show the most prominent case types and the kinds of actions paralegals took to address them.

FIGURE 6.3 Common case types (2013)

Case Type	Number of Cases	Percentage
Larceny	729	17%
Land/Property Dispute	569	13%
Debt	516	12%
Domestic Violence	495	11%
Marital Problems	412	9%
Child Neglect	411	9%
Breach of Contract	226	5%
Child–Parent Conflict	220	5%
Unpaid Wages	212	5%
Family Disputes	204	5%
Health	180	4%
Wounding	174	4%
Wife Neglect	59	1%

Source: Namati Sierra Leone.
Note: Some cases involve more than one issue. This table is based on the most prominent issue per case.

[11] Dale, *Delivering Justice to Sierra Leone's Poor*, 41 (see n. 9).

FIGURE 6.4 Primary action taken by paralegals to resolve cases (2013)

Tool Used	Number of Cases	Percentage
Gave Information	3,068	47%
Mediation	1,487	23%
Advocacy	628	10%
Helped Navigate Authority	523	8%
Community Education	301	5%
Organized Collective Action	270	4%
Lead Paralegal Involved	234	3%
Litigation	23	<1%
COB Involved	16	<1%
Other	5	<1%

Source: Namati Sierra Leone.
Note: Paralegals take more than one type of action in many cases. This table is based on the one approach to which paralegals gave the greatest emphasis in any given case.

Starting in 2010, this group of organizations began to advocate for formal recognition from government for the role paralegals play. In 2012, Sierra Leone passed the Legal Aid Law that establishes a national Legal Aid Board and, among other things, calls for a paralegal in every chiefdom. Government has been slow to implement this law, and many government functions were interrupted during the Ebola epidemic. But the Legal Aid Board was constituted, and a director appointed, in 2015. As of this writing in 2018, the Board has begun to support some paralegals assisting pretrial detainees, but it has not certified or funded paralegals serving communities on a wider range of justice issues.

In the meantime, some paralegals have honed their focus on cases involving the greatest imbalances of power, like conflicts between rural communities and mining or agriculture companies.

To offer a closer look at how paralegals work, we turn now to present data from our case-tracking research.

III. CASE TRACKING OF A REPRESENTATIVE SAMPLE OF PARALEGAL AND NON-PARALEGAL CASES

A. Methods

We collaborated with a team of field researchers to study in detail the work of three organizations – Timap for Justice, the Network Movement for Justice and Development, and the Methodist Church of Sierra Leone – across five chiefdoms. We chose cases at random from the dockets of these organizations.[12]

If clients from selected cases consented to take part in the study, researchers reviewed the case file. They then interviewed clients, paralegals, and all other major actors in the case, including officials and parties against whom complaints were brought. These interviews were semi-structured; based on each interview the researchers filled out standard data collection instruments.

To create a basis for comparison, we conducted similar case tracking in five chiefdoms where paralegals were not operating. There, we generated "dockets" by asking people involved in dispute resolution – chiefs, elders, religious leaders – about cases they had handled. We selected cases at random from that list, and then followed a similar process, interviewing all parties involved in each case, and filling out the same standard data collection instruments.

In all, a team of five researchers, under the close supervision of two of us, Lyttelton Braima and Gibrill Jalloh, conducted a total of 460 interviews to track 127 cases. The table that follows shows the distribution of cases tracked across location and paralegal organization.

FIGURE 6.5 Distribution of cases tracked

Province	District	Chiefdom	Paralegal organization or non-paralegal site	No. of cases tracked
North	Bombali	Gbendembu Nguwahun	Timap	15
		Sanda Loko	Non-paralegal	14
South	Bo	Bumpe Ngao	Timap	15
		Bargbo	Non-paralegal	14
		Valunya	Timap	15
		Komboya	Non-paralegal	14
	Bonthe	Nongoba Bullom	MCSL	10
		Sittia	Non-paralegal	10
East	Kono	Nimikoro	NMJD	10
		Sandoh	Non-paralegal	10
Total Cases Tracked				127

---

[12] Collective cases are fewer in number than individual cases, but tend to represent a larger proportion of paralegal effort per case. So we segmented our sampling: we chose 70 percent of our sample at random from the case docket as a whole, and the remaining 30 percent at random from among the collective cases within the case docket.

B. Results

The following tables summarize results across paralegal and non-paralegal sites on questions like who initiated cases, what issues were involved, and how fair the parties perceived the outcomes to be. Several of the differences between paralegal and non-paralegal organizations are statistically significant, but we omit formal tests because of possible bias in the selection of non-paralegal cases – we discuss this under "perceptions of fairness" later in this chapter. The number of respondents varies from table to table because not all interviewees answered all questions.

FIGURE 6.6 Who brought complaints?

	Non-paralegal sites	Paralegal sites (all organizations)	TIMAP	NMJD	MCSL
Total number of people either initiating dispute (non-paralegal sites) or approaching paralegal	76	89	62	10	17
Female	25%	41.6%	43.5%	50%	29.4%
Male	75%	58.4%	56.5%	50%	70.6%
Median age	45	40	43.5	39	36
Percent who can read	32.9%	43.2%	47.5%	20%	41.2%

FIGURE 6.7 Why did they choose the institution or organization they approached?

	Non-paralegal sites	Paralegals (all organizations)	TIMAP	NMJD	MCSL
Total number of people either initiating dispute (non-paralegal sites) or approaching paralegal	64	65	45	10	10
Low cost/free	1.6%	24.6%	31.1%	10%	20%
No delay/ speedy handling	0%	3.1%	4.4%	0%	0%
Effective dispute resolver	7.8%	16.9%	15.6%	20%	0%
Recognized authority	43.8%	9.2%	6.7%	10%	20%
Perceived to be fair	4.7%	10.8%	11.1%	20%	0%
Personal/family connection	21.9%	3.1%	0%	10%	10%
Other	39.1%	40%	37.8%	30%	60%

Note: Respondents could identify more than one reason for choosing their forum, so percentages in most columns total more than 100 percent.

FIGURE 6.8 What kinds of cases?

	Non-paralegal sites	Paralegal sites (all organizations)	TIMAP	NMJD	MCSL
Total number of cases tracked	62	65	45	10	10
Child Support and/or Alimony	8.1%	40%	35.6%	20%	80%
Child Abuse/Child–Parent Conflict	0%	7.7%	6.7%	20%	0%
Domestic Violence	4.8%	3.1%	2.2%	10%	0%
Family Dispute and Marital Problems	27.4%	21.5%	15.6%	50%	20%
Inheritance	4.8%	1.5%	2.2%	0%	0%
Assault	1.6%	0%	0%	0%	0%
Rape/Sexual Abuse	1.6%	3.1%	2.2%	10%	0%
Abuse by Formal Government	1.6%	0%	0%	0%	0%
Breach of Contract	12.9%	12.3%	13.3%	10%	10%
Debt	14.5%	12.3%	17.8%	0%	0%
Housing	0%	4.6%	4.4%	10%	0%
Land/Property Dispute	22.6%	1.5%	2.2%	0%	0%
Animal Dispute	1.6%	3.1%	4.4%	0%	0%
Larceny/Conversion/Theft	3.2%	1.5%	2.2%	0%	0%
Employment	0%	1.5%	2.2%	0%	0%
Education	0%	6.2%	8.9%	0%	0%
Health	1.6%	0%	0%	0%	0%
Roads	0%	3.1%	2.2%	0%	10%
Water/Sanitation	3.2%	0%	0%	0%	0%
Agriculture Development	0%	1.5%	2.2%	0%	0%
Mining	0%	1.5%	2.2%	0%	0%
Market/Commerce Development	1.6%	1.5%	2.2%	0%	0%
Support Community Institutions	1.6%	3.1%	0%	0%	20%
Harboring	1.6%	0%	0%	0%	0%
Group Conflict	0%	3.1%	4.4%	0%	0%
Religious Dispute	4.8%	0%	0%	0%	0%
Other	3.2%	9.2%	8.9%	20%	0%

Note: Cases can involve more than one issue, so percentages in each column total more than 100 percent.

FIGURE 6.9 What methods were used in addressing the case?

	Non-paralegal sites	Paralegals (all organizations)	TIMAP	NMJD	MCSL
Total number of cases tracked	40	63	43	10	10
Information provision	0%	12.7%	13.9%	0%	20%
Mediation	62.5%	79.4%	76.7%	100%	70%
Advocacy	0%	22.2%	23.3%	0%	40%
Organizing	0%	1.6%	2.3%	0%	0%
Lawyer consulted/involved	0%	1.6%	2.3%	0%	0%
Community oversight board consulted/involved	0%	1.6%	2.3%	0%	0%
Adjudication	50%	0%	0%	0%	0%
Arbitration	5%	3.1%	2.3%	10%	0%

Note: Paralegals and dispute handlers in non-paralegal sites sometimes employ multiple strategies in a single case, so percentages in most columns total more than 100 percent.

FIGURE 6.10 How did parties perceive the outcomes? (all interviewees)

	Non-paralegal sites	Paralegals (all organizations)	TIMAP	NMJD	MCSL
Total number of respondents	146	119	80	20	19
Outcome was not fair	34.9%	31.1%	31.3%	20%	42.1%
Outcome was partly fair	5.5%	2.5%	2.5%	0%	5.3%
Outcome was fair	59.6%	66.4%	66.3%	80%	52.6%

FIGURE 6.11 Were participants aware of relevant law?

	Non-paralegals	Paralegals (all organizations)	TIMAP	NMJD	MCSL
Total number of interviewees assessed	221	176	120	30	26
Percent of clients with at least partial knowledge of relevant national law	22.8%	50.6%	50%	43.3%	61.5%
Percent of clients with at least partial knowledge of relevant customary law	78.3%	63.2%	67.5%	53.3%	54.2%

Note: These data are based on assessments by the interviewing researchers.

We completed the case tracking in 2011. In addition, we interviewed paralegals, lawyers, and government officials – that research continued into 2018. We now draw on both the case-tracking data and the stakeholder interviews to explore the institutional, cultural, and organizational factors that shape the work of paralegals in Sierra Leone.

IV. DISCUSSION

A. Compared with Traditional Institutions, Paralegals Focus More on the Rights of Women and on State and Corporate Accountability

We found significant differences between, on the one hand, the types of cases people brought to paralegals and, on the other hand, the types of cases handled by dispute-resolving institutions in the sites where paralegals were not active. Together, child support, alimony, and rape/sexual abuse made up 43 percent of all cases handled by paralegals, for example, but less than 10 percent of the cases we encountered in non-paralegal sites.

All of these cases involved complaints by women against men. We infer that women are bringing these cases more often to paralegals and less often to local authorities because of the bias of existing institutions. Customary and formal institutions alike offer weak protection for the rights of mothers, wives, and survivors of sexual violence.[13]

Legal empowerment organizations prioritize gender equity. Paralegals receive training on, for example, three 2007 laws that expanded the legal rights of women and girls – the Domestic Violence Act, the Devolution of Estates Act, and the Child Rights Act.[14] Women see the paralegals as a source of help with problems that they would otherwise find difficult to resolve.

Forty-two percent of all clients approaching paralegals were women; in contrast 25 percent of the people initiating disputes in non-paralegal sites were women. One client, a mother of two children from Gbap village in Nongoba Bullom chiefdom, described the work of paralegals this way (translated from Krio):

> Since the human rights [paralegals] came here, any time our men forsake us or beat us, the human rights people talk for us women. Like this my own case, if the human rights people weren't here to talk for me, I would have been taking care of myself and my child alone, my man wouldn't have lifted his hand to help.[15]

Two other categories made up a significant proportion of the cases of one of the paralegal organizations, Timap for Justice, but were comparatively rare in non-

---

[13] *See, for example,* Lisa Denney and Aisha F. Ibrahim, *Violence against Women in Sierra Leone: How Women Seek Redress* (London: Overseas Development Institute, 2012), 10–17.

[14] The Domestic Violence Act No. 20 (2007) (Sierra Leone); The Devolution of Estates Act No. 21 (2007) (Sierra Leone); The Child Right Act No. 7 (2007), SUPPLEMENT TO THE SIERRA LEONE GAZETTE EXTRAORDINARY Vol. CXXVIII, No. 43.

[15] The quote speaks to the value many women see in paralegals. But most paralegals would be disappointed to hear this endorsement, because the aim of legal empowerment is not to "talk for" clients but rather to equip people to advocate for themselves.

paralegal sites. Grievances with respect to public services and infrastructure – education, health care, housing, roads, water, and sanitation – made up 15.5 percent of Timap's cases, but less than 5 percent of the cases in non-paralegal sites. Grievances with respect to livelihood development and/or the private sector – agriculture, mining, employment, market development – made up another 8.8 percent of Timap's cases but only 1.6 percent of the cases in the non-paralegal sites.

Here too, we attribute the differences at least in part to the nature of existing institutions. The local authorities we approached in non-paralegal sites – chiefs, chiefdom administrators, religious leaders – tend to have little power or inclination to challenge corporations or the administrative state.[16] As a result their constituents often do not bother to bring those kinds of grievances to them. Moreover, failed public services are so much the norm that many Sierra Leoneans would not think to complain about them at all.[17]

Timap paralegals, in contrast, proactively encourage communities to take action on exactly these kinds of issues. The paralegals conduct community meetings on topics like education and agriculture policy. The discussions often reveal that a specific state failure or a corporate abuse is not only a moral wrong – it's a violation of law. Paralegals then suggest channels by which communities can pursue redress. Paralegals support clients to go beyond local authorities – to engage district councils, line ministry officials, and company managers.

The other two organizations in our study were relatively new and had provided less training to their paralegals at the time of the research. Our findings were consistent with what those organizations told us – that their paralegals were as yet focused primarily on intra-community disputes rather than problems involving the state or private firms.

B. In Intra-community Disputes, Paralegals Advocate for a Fair Solution if Mediation Does Not Result in One

When paralegals help people take on intra-community disputes, they play a different role from traditional dispute resolvers. Chiefs in Sierra Leone are technically barred from adjudication, but in practice they run their own courts.[18] Indeed half the cases we observed in non-paralegal sites involved adjudication. Other dispute resolvers – religious leaders, elders, youth leaders – engage in either mediation (63 percent of cases in non-paralegal sites) or arbitration (5 percent of cases in non-paralegal sites).[19]

---

[16] See, for example, World Bank, *Sierra Leone: Strategic Options for Public Sector Reform*, AFTPT, African Region Report 2511-SL (Washington, DC: World Bank, 2003), 24–27; see also Manning, "Landscape of Local Authority," 110–27 (see n. 3).

[17] See, for example, Vivek Srivastava and Marco Larizza, "Working with the Grain for Reforming the Public Service: A Live Example from Sierra Leone," *International Review of Administrative Sciences* 79, 3 (2013): 466.

[18] Manning, "Landscape of Local Authority," 115 (see n. 3).

[19] The percentages exceed 100 because many cases involve multiple methods. See Figure 6.9.

Paralegals mediate in intra-community disputes as well – they did so in 79 percent of the cases in our sample – but in a different way. Paralegals prioritize educating people about national law, and they attempt to mediate in its shadow. We found that paralegal clients were more than twice as likely to have at least partial knowledge of relevant national law than parties to disputes in non-paralegal sites.[20]

If mediation does not result in an agreement that paralegals and clients consider reasonably just, paralegals help clients to advocate with authorities for a remedy. Paralegals engaged in advocacy in 22 percent of their cases; dispute resolvers in non-paralegal sites did not engage in advocacy at all.

These differences between paralegals and existing dispute resolvers are reflected in the reasons people cited for choosing to approach them. Compared with people in non-paralegal sites, paralegal clients were more than twice as likely to cite "perceived to be fair." Clients also chose paralegals to avoid what are often described as abusive fees charged by chiefs – 25 percent of paralegal clients cited "low cost/ free," as compared with 2 percent of parties in non-paralegal sites.

In contrast, people in non-paralegal sites were more likely to choose their resolution forum because it was a "recognized authority" or a "personal or family connection" (44 percent and 22 percent, respectively, as compared with 9 percent and 3 percent among paralegal clients). People approach paralegals, in sum, because paralegals do not charge fees and because they will advocate for a solution that is fair to the weaker party.

C. Mr. Bona, from Bumpeh Ngao Chiefdom, and His Land Dispute

The case of Mr. Bona,[21] from Bumpe Ngao chiefdom, illustrates how paralegals engage in mediation to assist parties whose rights are being abused. Mr. Bona supported a family of eighteen by cultivating a parcel of land near Fulaninahun village. He said the land has been in his family for generations, and that he had tilled it himself for more than a decade without dispute. But in 2010 Mr. Kapuwa, from a neighboring village, claimed the land belonged to his family instead. This sparked a bitter dispute.

Local chiefs barred both families from the land until the matter was resolved. Mr. Bona pleaded with the chiefs not to impose the ban until he harvested cassava he had already planted for that season. The chiefs refused; instead, they promised swift resolution of the matter.

Mr. Bona obeyed the ban. But the chiefs' inquiry dragged on, and Mr. Bona struggled to feed his family while the crops he'd planted began to rot on the ground. Mr. Bona's nephew (a junior high school pupil and one of his dependents) took part in a legal awareness session organized by paralegals in another village. The nephew

---

[20] The discrepancy is consistent with, but does not by itself prove, causation. It could be that people who approach paralegals are more likely to know of national law already. Paralegal clients were, to this point, slightly more likely to be literate than parties to disputes in the non-paralegal sites (43 percent as compared with 34 percent).

[21] Names of clients have been abbreviated or changed.

suspected collusion between the chiefs and Mr. Kapuwa to confiscate his uncle's land. He advised his uncle to approach the paralegals.

On receiving the complaint, paralegal Joseph Sawyer went to the two villages and first met with the chiefs, then with Mr. Kapuwa. After gathering facts and viewpoints from both sides, Sawyer initiated a mediation including the disputing parties and traditional leaders.

The first stage of mediation resulted in the relaxing of the ban on the farm, allowing Mr. Bona to harvest his cassava while the mediation continued. Ultimately seven witnesses addressed the group, and all but one confirmed that Mr. Bona's family had farmed the land since the founding of the village. Mr. Kapuwa agreed to abandon his claim on the condition that Mr. Bona perform a swearing ritual in which he would affirm his true ownership of the land. Mr. Bona accepted, and swore in the presence of the paralegal Joseph Sawyer and the chiefs.

Mr. Bona told researchers that Sawyer "restored the lifeline of my family," something he attributed to Sawyer's skill in mediation. Bona's nephew said Sawyer "demonstrated inclusiveness and fairness in handling the matter."

Sawyer did not invoke a specific national law in this case, but he said his association with law in general – and a lawyer who could litigate in select cases – served as a check on abusive behavior by chiefs. The solution itself – the swearing ritual – was based on custom. An advantage of the paralegal approach in Sierra Leone is its ability to straddle the customary and formal systems.

D. Increasing Focus on Land and Environmental Justice

Our case-tracking research was completed in 2011. Since then, some paralegals have shifted focus away from intra-community disputes and toward cases involving state institutions and private firms, on the view that the imbalances of power are greater and the added value of paralegals is higher. In those kinds of cases – like the one involving Cluff Gold Company, with which we opened the chapter – paralegals do not engage in mediation at all; instead they help communities to advocate with authorities and negotiate with firms.

In particular, there is an acute need to protect community rights to land and environment. In the past decade government has aggressively courted large-scale agriculture and mining investments. The government has doubled down on this strategy as a way of restarting the economy after the Ebola epidemic.[22] Most land is held by communities and families under customary tenure, without recognized

---

[22] See, for example, Ernest Bai Koroma, "A Post-Ebola Plan for Sierra Leone," *Wall Street Journal*, November, 26, 2015.

maps or clear processes for decision-making. The combination of weak land rights and increased investment interest has led to inequitable, environmentally irresponsible deals and sometimes outright theft.[23]

Institutional context shapes the way paralegals support communities in relation to these threats. Namati, an international legal empowerment group, works with paralegals focused on land and environmental justice in both India and Sierra Leone.[24] In India, the paralegals help communities pursue remedies from administrative institutions, including pollution control boards, coastal zone management authorities, and district governments.

Many communities there have lived near industry for decades. They have often attempted on their own to request relief from firms, with little success. The contribution of paralegals is to help people invoke law and the regulatory authority of the state instead.[25]

In Sierra Leone, in contrast, large-scale development projects are relatively new, environmental law is nascent, land law is outdated,[26] and regulatory institutions are very weak. Paralegals and communities in Sierra Leone have tried repeatedly but never succeeded in persuading the Environmental Protection Agency to take enforcement action, for example. They have had greater – though still modest – success negotiating directly with firms.[27]

Even when those negotiations result in a partial remedy, they do not strengthen the regulatory function of the state. Namati Sierra Leone advocates for better rules and stronger institutions based on its case experience, but the state's fundamental lack of capacity is a major limitation.

Paralegal efforts in relation to land and environment are also shaped by the place of chiefs in Sierra Leonean society. Under customary law no one owns land per se – it belongs to the ancestors and the descendants who are not yet born. Chiefs are stewards, not owners. Families have strong use rights, and in principle decisions

---

[23] *See, for example,* The Oakland Institute, *Understanding Land Investment Deals in Africa – Country Report: Sierra Leone* (Oakland, CA: The Oakland Institute, 2011), 11–20.

[24] One of us, Vivek, started Namati in 2011.

[25] *See, for example, Paralegals for Environmental Justice,* a practice guide describing how paralegals and communities can seek enforcement of environmental regulation. The guide is based on the experience of a team of paralegals in India working with Namati and Delhi-based Centre for Policy Research. Manju Menon, Meenakshi Kapoor, Vivek Maru, and Kanchi Kohli, *Paralegals for Environmental Justice* (New Delhi: Center for Policy Research – Namati Environmental Justice Program, 2017), https://namati.org/wp-content/uploads/2017/12/Practice-Guide-for-Environmental-Justice-Paralegals.pdf.

[26] *See* Ade Renner-Thomas, *Land Tenure in Sierra Leone: The Law, Dualism and the Making of a Land Policy* (Bloomington: Authorhouse, 2010).

[27] *See, for example,* "London Mining and Manonkoh Community Sign MOU," *Awoko,* December 18, 2012. http://awoko.org/2012/12/18/london-mining-and-manonkoh-community-sign-mou/; "Masethele Village in Important Land Renegotiation with Addax Bioenergy Sierra Leone Limited," *Sierra Express Media,* March 14, 2013. www.sierraleonenews.net/article/213188649/masethele-village-in-important-land-renegotiation-with-addax-bioenergy-sierra-leone-limited.

about land can only happen with their consent.[28] But in practice many chiefs make decisions on their own.[29] As a result collective cases are often vulnerable to elite capture.

E. Securing Partial Redress from the Sierra Leone Diamond Corporation

A case from Bumpeh chiefdom illustrates both of these trends: the tendency to negotiate directly with firms for remedies rather than engage the state, and the risk of chiefs undermining collective action. The case involved what was then called Sierra Leone Diamond Corporation (SLDC), now called African Minerals Limited.

SLDC made grand promises – cash payments to landowning families, jobs for youths, a school, roads – in exchange for the chance to mine on what was previously farmland across six villages. The company mined for several years while fulfilling almost none of those promises. Then it closed its operations without notice. The company left behind several unfilled pits that were each one to two stories deep and about the length of an Olympic swimming pool.

SLDC had dammed the river Kpejeh, which caused flooding on people's farms, and its trucks had broken the single bridge that connected the six villages to the main road. Several community members visited the office of SLDC in Bo Town, the capital of the southern province, to complain. They were ejected from the premises by security guards.

The communities then approached paralegal Marian Tebbi, who was based in Kaniya, one of the six affected villages. Marian worked with farmers to document the damage and record what if any compensation had been paid. For a large case like this, she invoked her vertical network – lead paralegal Daniel Sesay and directors Vivek Maru and Simeon Koroma.

Together they researched mining law. Substantively, the firm's actions constituted clear legal violations.[30] But procedurally, at the time in 2006, there was no administrative process or institution through which communities could seek redress for grievances against mining companies.

The courts might have been an option, but Timap and other legal empowerment groups treat litigation as a last resort. Courts are expensive, slow, and sometimes subservient to the executive branch. Moreover, the process of litigation is so technical and removed that it's difficult to fulfill the legal empowerment ideal of placing

---

[28] See Renner-Thomas, *Land Tenure in Sierra Leone: The Law, Dualism, and the Making of a Land Policy*, 141–49 (see n. 26).

[29] See, *for example*, the story from Nimiyama Chiefdom, in Eastern Sierra Leone, described in Chapter 1 of this book. In that case, a paramount chief sold 1,400 acres to a Chinese rubber company without asking the seventy families who had customary rights to the land.

[30] See, *for example*, Sierra Leone Mines and Minerals Decree No. 5 (1994), Section 26, requiring that the holder of a mineral right provide "fair and reasonable compensation" for any disturbance of the rights of the owner or lawful occupier of any land on which mining is carried out.

clients in the driver's seat. Litigation can easily become "I'll solve this for you" rather than "we'll solve it together."

Instead Timap and the communities decided to petition SLDC directly. They wrote a letter outlining the harms and specifying the violations of law. Even without court or administrative action, the invocation of law can have some sway.[31] The firm was initially responsive and expressed a willingness to remedy the damages.

But after about a month company officials stopped answering calls or taking meetings. Timap tried extending the vertical network one more notch, by contacting Clare Manuel, a lawyer in the United Kingdom who engaged in pro bono work related to corporate accountability. Ms. Manuel wrote to SLDC's office in London, asking for remedial action in Bumpeh and threatening a complaint to the ombudsman of the Organization for Economic Cooperation and Development.

Almost immediately, the Timap team started receiving calls from SLDC officials in Freetown. "Our bosses in London want this resolved. How can we solve this problem?" After a meeting with Timap staff, including paralegal Marian, and representatives from the six villages, the company took several concrete steps. It removed the debris blocking the river Kpejeh, it repaired the bridge, and it paid community members to fill the pits.

The negotiations stalled, however, on the point of compensation. Timap and the communities requested monetary damages for the loss of crops and fruit and palm trees. Marian created a detailed docket on the specific claims of each farmer.

On a day when Marian had left her village to attend a training in Freetown, SLDC's public relations officer visited Kaniya. He offered free mobile phones and the equivalent of about US$2,000 in cash to chiefs of the six villages. He asked the chiefs to put their thumbprints on an agreement that settled all claims. Timap had requested that the communities not interact with SLDC without contacting Marian, and had made the same request to SLDC in writing.

This was during what Sierra Leoneans call "hungry season" – the months before the annual harvest, when crops from the previous year are running low. The chiefs took the money and phones, and offered their thumbs. Timap found out when Marian returned. Many of the affected farmers were furious. The chiefs had distributed much of the cash among village residents, but the sums were paltry compared with what the farmers felt they were owed.

At a long community meeting several weeks later, the chiefs apologized to their own citizens and to Timap. The chief of Kaniya said, "the hunger and the cash made us blind." Timap leadership said it would be difficult to pursue the case further, and indeed SLDC never returned and never paid another Leone.

[31] See Maru, "Between Law and Society: Paralegals and the Provision of Justice Services in Sierra Leone and Worldwide," 451–52 (see n. 5) for a discussion of how "the color of law" helps paralegals and communities to achieve remedies despite institutional dysfunction.

F. Advocating for Effective Regulation: Collaborating when Possible and Crossing the Line between Law and Politics

International lawyers like Ms. Manuel can be helpful in cases involving multinational firms. But they are no substitute for a functioning regulatory regime. In 2013, the Environment Protection (Mines and Minerals) Regulation laid out clearer procedures for addressing community grievances,[32] but those procedures have not been implemented as of this writing.

To pursue remedies from the state, communities need to have access to the regulatory conditions under which firms operate. In India, when community members approach a paralegal with a complaint about a company – air emissions are causing sickness, say, or water pollution is killing fish – the paralegals' first move is to obtain the firm's regulatory clearances and permits.

Those typically include an environmental clearance from the ministry of environment, a consent to operate from the pollution control board, and sometimes, depending on the location, a forest clearance or a coastal clearance. Paralegals translate those documents into the local language and explain in simple terms the conditions contained in them.

A factory might be required to use a specific air filtration system, for example, or run its effluents through a treatment plant, or mitigate dust pollution with a boundary wall of a specific height. Paralegals and communities can then compare what's in the conditions with reality, and use the discrepancies to file an administrative complaint.[33]

In Sierra Leone, similar regulatory permits exist in principle. Most industrial and agricultural projects need an environmental license, for example, which should contain binding conditions growing out of the environmental impact assessment process.[34]

But Namati Sierra Leone, which focuses exclusively on land and environmental issues, has not been able to access a single environmental license. Paralegals have filed requests using Sierra Leone's Right to Information law; those requests have been ignored. As of this writing, Namati is considering litigation under the Right to Information Act to obtain licenses and other project documents. Legal empowerment is difficult if people are not allowed to see what the law requires.

The opacity may stem from an even deeper problem: corruption.[35] In one case involving a Chinese iron ore mine in the north of the country, where poisonous

---

[32] Environmental and Social Regulations for the Minerals Sector (2012) (Sierra Leone) § 76.
[33] Menon et al., *Paralegals for Environmental Justice* (New Delhi: Center for Policy Research – Namati Environmental Justice Program, 2017), https://namati.org/wp-content/uploads/2017/12/Practice-Guide-for-Environmental-Justice-Paralegals.pdf, 30 (*see* n. 25).
[34] Environmental Protection Agency Act, Supplement to the Sierra Leone Gazette Vol. CXXXIX, No. 44 (2008) (Sierra Leone), art. 23(1), 30(d).
[35] In *Why Nations Fail*, Acemoglu and Robinson argue that Sierra Leone has had extractive political and economic institutions from the colonial period through to the present. Daron Acemoglu and James A. Robinson, *Why Nations Fail: The Origins of Power, Prosperity, and Poverty* (New York: Currency, 2012), 335–44, 401–02.

tailings were flowing openly onto farmland, and drinking water was severely contaminated, an officer of the Environmental Protection Agency said to Namati paralegals: "We're glad you're working on this. We're not going to be able to do much about it though, because the President is personally interested in the project."[36]

Legal empowerment groups try to help build the state their clients need. Namati offered extensive suggestions for Sierra Leone's 2015 Land Policy, for example, based on challenges and patterns that emerged from case experience. The parliamentary committee overseeing the policy insisted that Namati's inputs be incorporated. Namati is now partnering with the Ministry of Lands to pilot provisions in the policy that would allow communities to receive formal tenure over their customary lands.

In a similar spirit, the director of Timap for Justice, Simeon Koroma, represents civil society on the governing body of the Legal Aid Board. Koroma aims to help the board fulfill the progressive potential of the 2012 Legal Aid Law.

But legal empowerment groups sometimes conclude that collaborative engagement is not enough. Faced with many environmental justice cases in which firms are intransigent and government is unresponsive, Namati Sierra Leone joined with others to launch a public pledge, "Our Land Our Future," in advance of Sierra Leone's 2018 national election. The pledge asks candidates to commit to a set of reforms. These are measures that communities and paralegals identified as most important based on their attempts to seek justice.

There are eleven measures in all; here are two: "Establish accessible grievance redress mechanisms that provide real remedies for social and environmental violations by corporations" and "Ensure the public, and in particular the communities directly affected, have full access to key information related to mining or agriculture projects. This includes environmental licenses, land lease agreements, community development action plans, and any private financial interest in companies held by politicians or public officials."[37]

As of this writing, ten local organizations, a private university, and several thousand citizens, many of whom come from communities where Namati paralegals work, have endorsed the pledge. The pledge represents an acknowledgment that an effective state can't be built without politics.

---

[36] Interview with Sonkita Conteh, Director of Namati Sierra Leone, July 2017. Having exhausted all options, communities and Namati sued the mine, run by Shandong Limited, in February 2018. See "Namati, 9 Villages Sue AML for Pollution and Other Legal Violations," *Concord Times*, February 14, 2018, http://slconcordtimes.com/namati-9-villages-sue-aml-for-pollution-and-other-legal-violations/.

[37] "Our Land Our Future: A Pledge," https://ourlandourfuture.com. Namati's international entity is registered as a 501(c)(3) nonprofit in the United States and is prohibited from "electioneering," including the promotion of candidate pledges. Namati Sierra Leone is a company registered in Sierra Leone and not subject to a similar limitation. Namati Sierra Leone worked on the pledge without the involvement of its international counterpart, using revenue Namati Sierra Leone had earned independently.

This move from a legal frame to an openly political one poses risks. If one major party adopts the pledge and another doesn't, paralegals could be seen as partisan. Depending on who wins the election, paralegals might experience less cooperation and greater retaliation from government.

The popular nature of the pledge – it is a consensus position by many organizations and citizens – may mitigate that danger. And work on land and environmental justice is risky no matter what.[38] Namati team members felt they would not be faithful to their mission if they did not evolve their work in this way. The goal of legal empowerment is to equip people to understand, use, and, when necessary, shape the law. The third of these, the shaping dimension, is ultimately and unavoidably political.

G. Organizing to Prevent Elite Capture

Alongside organizing for national change, paralegals organize locally to prevent elite capture.[39] When communities request support, Namati paralegals help them to select committees who will lead the effort to seek a solution. Paralegals ask that the committees include not just chiefs but women, young people, and what are called "strangers," non-indigenes living in the affected community.

Paralegals also ask that any communication or information from the other party – usually mining or agricultural companies – be shared with all committee members and the paralegals, and that no decision be taken without consulting the affected population as a whole. Hassan Sesay, a former Timap paralegal who now works with Namati, says he spends a good deal of his time supporting these committees to function in an equitable and accountable way.

H. Financing and Recognition

In Sierra Leone, as in all the countries featured in this volume, paralegal groups grapple with the question of how to source sustainable and resilient revenue. The costs are relatively low. According to one estimate, paralegals could serve the entire country for US$2 million per year, or $0.34 per capita,[40] which is, by way of

---

[38] See, for example, Global Witness (2017), *Defenders of the Earth: Global Killings of Land and Environmental Defenders in 2016*, documenting 200 people murdered for attempting to exercise rights to land and environment.

[39] We only noted explicit organizing in 1.6 percent of paralegal cases in our sample (as compared with 0 percent of cases in non-paralegal sites). This low figure may have been due to a misunderstanding about the meaning of "organizing." Also, percentage of cases is not a good indicator for proportion of effort. There were many more individual cases in the paralegal dockets than collective cases, but the collective cases take up more of a paralegal's time per case. Namati paralegals work on collective cases exclusively, and organizing is involved in all of them.

[40] Law and Development Partnership, *Developing a Portfolio of Financially Sustainable, Scalable Basic Legal Services Models*, Briefing Paper (London: Law and Development Partnership, 2016), 8.

comparison, 3 percent of what the government allocated to health care in 2013.[41] But it is not clear where the money should come from over the long term.

The faith-based groups do draw on the considerable infrastructure of their sponsors, the Catholic and Methodist Churches. BRAC is the largest development NGO in the world, with more than US$600 million in annual revenue. In Bangladesh BRAC gives some support to its paralegal program from its wider operations, and to some extent the same is true in Sierra Leone.

But despite this institutional backing, those paralegal efforts and all the others in the country are presently funded largely by external donors – bilateral institutions like the British Department for International Development or Ireland's Troicare, philanthropic groups like the Open Society Foundation, and multilaterals like the UN Development Program.

Reliance on foreign donors can be hazardous. The resources are time-bound and subject to factors unrelated to the work. For example, legal empowerment organizations successfully advocated that a British-sponsored justice sector reform project dedicate a portion of funds – about £2 million out of £25 million GBP over 2012–17 – to support community paralegals. The groups saw this as a chance to sustain paralegal efforts that grew with the help of the commitment from Open Society Foundations from 2009 to 2013.

But in the end a large portion of the funds allocated for paralegals under the UK project was spent on foreign consultants, and the remainder was pegged to specific project districts. As a result some existing paralegal efforts in districts not chosen by the project were forced to scale down, while in some districts that were chosen, the project struggled to find effective grantees.

Reliance on foreign donors also makes legal empowerment groups vulnerable to the charge of foreign interference. When governments seek to weaken domestic civil society, they often exploit the fact of foreign funding – by revoking permission to receive funds from abroad, for example, or by restricting the activities of foreign-funded NGOs.[42] The Sierra Leone government has not pursued a systematic policy of this kind as of this writing, but this is a risk to consider, especially as paralegals challenge larger-scale corruption.

---

[41] Government of Sierra Leone, Ministry of Finance and Economics Development, *Budget Profile for FY 2011–2015*, annex I.

[42] *See, for example*, Mark Tran, "Ethiopia Curb on Charities Alarms Human Rights Activists," *The Guardian*, January 25, 2009, www.theguardian.com/world/2009/jan/26/ethiopia-charities-human-rights; Gaurav Vivek Bhatnagar, "Home Ministry Cancels FCRA Licences of 20,000 NGOs," *The Wire*, December 27, 2016, https://thewire.in/89933/home-ministry-cancels-fcra-licences-20000-ngos/; Ellen Barry, "As 'Foreign Agent' Law Takes Effect in Russia, Human Rights Groups Vow to Defy It," *New York Times*, November 21, 2012, www.nytimes.com/2012/11/22/world/europe/rights-groups-in-russia-reject-foreign-agent-label.html?mtrref=www.google.com&mtrref=www.nytimes.com&gwh=CBB552E22AACB3750594FF04473C2C1B&gwt=pay. *See also* "Summary of Strategies and Tactics," *Defending Dissent: Civil Society and Human Rights in the Global Crackdown*, Bernstein Institute Annual Conference (2017), 3.

One way to diversify from dependence on international donors is to pursue public funding. Legal empowerment groups advocated strenuously, over several years, for the 2012 Legal Aid Law and in particular the provisions recognizing the role of paralegals as legal aid providers. They saw statutory recognition as a source of legitimacy and a pathway to government revenue. In advocating for the law the organizations had to overcome opposition from Sierra Leone's small private bar.

Sonkita Conteh began "10 Misconceptions about Paralegals in Sierra Leone," an op-ed that ran in several Sierra Leonean papers in 2010, with this:

> A few among the many lawyers I have had the opportunity to discuss the subject of "paralegals" with initially seemed to have deep suspicion of paralegals and their activities. Minutes into our conversation they realise that there is really no firm evidential basis to warrant a conviction so they drop all charges. Since I may not be able to talk to every individual lawyer or person who might have an unflattering opinion about the work of paralegals, I thought it prudent to ... correct some of the most common misconceptions of paralegals.

The top four misconceptions in his list are "paralegals will impersonate lawyers," "paralegals will charge fees," "paralegals will want to appear in court," and "paralegals are not properly trained."[43] Conteh argues that there is little to no overlap between the clients paralegals serve and the ones who can pay for services from private lawyers. And just as microfinance initiatives have ultimately brought more people into the formal banking system, paralegals may ultimately increase business for lawyers, as a small percentage of their clients will require litigation.

A joint statement endorsed by twelve civil society groups argued:

> Community-based paralegals can provide approachable, culturally acceptable, quick, inexpensive and effective ways to access justice. A legal aid framework that combines the proven utility of community based paralegal interventions with the representational role of legal practitioners has a more significant chance of making a dent in the huge access to justice deficit that the government seeks to reverse.[44]

The 2012 law was a significant normative victory for the legal empowerment movement, and it has been cited in legislative debates elsewhere.[45] But with the exception of a small pilot focused on pretrial detainees, the law has not yet led to public financial support for paralegals.

In the meantime, some groups have explored the possibility of sector-specific solutions to the problem of sustainable revenue. Namati and others successfully argued, for example, that Sierra Leone's 2015 Land Policy should require firms interested in land to contribute to an independent basket fund that will in turn

---

[43] Sonkita Conteh, "10 Misconceptions about Paralegals in Sierra Leone," *Sierra Express Media*, April 9, 2010.
[44] "Joint Statement on the Draft Legal Aid Bill 2010," *Sierra Express Media*, April 13, 2010.
[45] *See, for example,* David McQuoid Mason, "Access to Justice in South Africa: Are There Enough Lawyers?" *Onati Socio-legal Series* 3, 3 (2013): 573.

support legal empowerment via paralegals for landowning communities.[46] The provision has not been implemented as of this writing, but in principle it could provide funding for paralegal efforts to address one set of problems for which they are needed.[47]

If substantial funding does eventually flow from either the Legal Aid Board or the proposed land-focused legal aid fund, legal empowerment organizations will need to manage the risk of state interference in their work. The Legal Aid Board and the land-focused fund are both meant to be independent from the executive. But the Sierra Leonean government has arguably grown more authoritarian in recent years, and authoritarian regimes often find ways to steer ostensibly independent institutions.[48]

Just as governments can restrict the activities of groups receiving foreign funds, similarly they can limit the activities or organizations to which domestic public funding is dedicated. Governments in general are often disinclined to pay for work that holds them accountable.[49]

---

[46] Government of Sierra Leone, Ministry of Lands, Country Planning and the Environment, *National Land Policy of Sierra Leone* (2015), 67.

[47] Several large-scale agricultural investors had adopted a practice of directly hiring private law firms to represent communities from whom they intended to lease land. In a number of cases those communities later asked legal empowerment groups to help in seeking redress for abuses committed by the company, or to renegotiate the terms of the land lease. Landowning communities reported that at the time of the initial deal they hardly saw the lawyers engaged by the investor on their behalf; that if anything those lawyers were among the ones cajoling them to place their thumbprints on an agreement they did not understand. Namati proposed this policy as a way of ensuring that communities have independent legal assistance from the outset.

[48] See, for example, Cooper Inveen, "President's Iron-Fist Methods Raise Fears for Future of Democracy in Sierra Leone," *The Guardian*, October 20, 2017, www.theguardian.com/global-development/2017/oct/20/president-ernest-bai-koroma-iron-fist-methods-raise-fears-for-future-of-democracy-in-sierra-leone-march-election. The publicly funded Anti-Corruption Commission could be offered as a counterexample, in that it has indicted more than one sitting minister. But some argue that it too has been guided by the president's wishes. According to *The Economist*, "The commission's recent actions suggest it may not be as well insulated from political interference as it might be. Last year it settled a major case involving Sierra Leone's social security agency, NASSIT, out of court, rather than seeking prosecutions. It has never achieved a custodial sentence for graft; and the current head, Joseph Kamara, was appointed after his predecessor ruffled too many official feathers." "Presidential Calculations," *The Economist*, October 5, 2012.

[49] The history of legal aid funding in the United States is instructive. The US government began investing significantly in civil legal aid during Lyndon Johnson's War on Poverty; financial support grew steadily through the 1970s. These legal services programs often took on systemic problems. Legal aid lawyers translated the experiences of their clients into reforms by bringing impact cases, including class actions, and by lobbying legislatures. Ronald Reagan first attacked legal services as governor of California and continued to do so as president. Republicans were disturbed that federal money was going toward changing government policies according to the interests of poor people. Legislation passed in 1996, during Newt Gingrich's "Republican Revolution," gutted what was left of legal services funding and placed crippling restrictions on legal aid lawyers: no class actions, no lobbying legislatures, no representing prisoners or illegal aliens, etc. See William P. Quigley, *The Demise of Law Reform and the Triumph of Legal Aid: Congress and the Legal Services Corporation from the 1960's to the 1990's*, 17 ST. Louis U. PUB. L. REV. 241,260–61 (1998). (This footnote is adapted from footnote 113 in Maru, "Between Law and Society: Paralegals and the Provision of Justice Services in Sierra Leone and Worldwide," 474 [*see* n. 4]).

Even if public funding does go to some case-specific work that challenges abuses or failures by the state, it's unlikely that government funds would support the systemic change campaign on land justice described in an earlier section. Those more explicitly political efforts would need to be financed independently.[50] So sole reliance on public revenue would also put the mission of legal empowerment at risk.

Another way to diversify revenue is to look to clients themselves. People are drawn to paralegals in part because they do not demand payment, and indeed the Legal Aid Act prohibits paralegals from charging for their services.[51] But it is possible for clients and communities to make voluntary contributions, in kind or otherwise. All the chiefdoms where Timap works have offered land on which Timap can build permanent offices, for example. And communities who have achieved remedies in large-scale land cases have sometimes contributed chickens, bags of rice, and money out of gratitude.

To date programs have not requested these donations, and the amounts do not defray a significant proportion of program cost.[52] It may be worth exploring whether programs can encourage community contributions without deterring those who cannot pay or damaging the reputation of paralegals for integrity. In principle community support can decrease the dependence of paralegals on outsiders and deepen the connection between paralegals and the people they serve.

Every source of funding has risks. For legal empowerment groups to be active in Sierra Leone for decades to come, they will need to find diverse enough revenue to weather the vicissitudes.

I. Perceptions of Fairness, Vertical Networks, and the Role of Case Data

At the outset of our research, we hypothesized that clients who worked with paralegals might express greater satisfaction with the way their cases were resolved as compared with cases in non-paralegal sites. That turned out to be true, but only by a narrow margin. Sixty-six point four percent of all interviewees in paralegal sites

---

[50] In the United States, after government severely restricted the mandate of federal legal aid funding in 1996, many legal aid organizations opened two parallel entities, one that receives federal funds and focuses on individual cases, and another which receives private funding and engages in policy advocacy, class actions, and other systemic change efforts. *See, for example*, Catherine R. Albiston and Laura Nielsen, "Funding the Cause: How Public Interest Organizations Fund Their Activities and Why It Matters for Social Change," *Law and Social Inquiry* 39 (2014): 82–83, n. 46. If public funding becomes a reality in Sierra Leone, organizations may need to do something similar.

[51] The Legal Aid Act (2012), SUPPLEMENT TO THE SIERRA LEONE GAZETTE Vol. CXLIII, No. 42, § 37.

[52] Sierra Leone has a higher rate of charitable giving than most countries in the world – it's ranked 54 out of 145 countries in the 2015 World Giving Index. *World Giving Index 2015: A Global View of Giving Trends* (November 2015), 8–9. But generosity tends to focus on the provision of basic services like health care and education rather than justice or rights.

thought the outcome of their case was fair, as compared with 59.6 percent of interviewees in non-paralegal sites.

Three factors may have contributed to such a modest result. First, as we described earlier, paralegals were taking on different kinds of disputes from the ones we found in non-paralegal sites. Paralegals were more likely to be working on cases involving women's rights and corporate or state accountability. In those areas, the institutional and cultural norms are particularly inequitable. So comparing the uphill battles in paralegal dockets with the more routine cases in non-paralegal sites may be like asking why a dozen pieces of cassava aren't sweeter than a dozen mangoes.

Second, there was a difference in sampling methods between paralegal and non-paralegal sites. Where there were paralegals, we were able to take a random sample from case records. In non-paralegal sites, we relied on dispute resolvers to provide us with a list of cases from which we then selected a sample. Our field researchers felt chiefs and other dispute resolvers may have tended to share more successful and harmonious cases, and omit ones that involved abuse or exploitation. If true, this sampling bias in the non-paralegal sites would dilute any "fairness advantage" in paralegal cases.[53]

Third, we observed variation in effectiveness, among individual paralegals and also among organizations. For three of the ten paralegals whose work we studied, 100 percent of the parties interviewed from their cases said the outcome of the case was fair; for three other paralegals, the average was below 60 percent. Of interviewees in cases handled by NMJD, 80 percent thought the outcome was fair; the proportion was 66.3 percent for Timap and 52.6 percent for the Methodist Church. So the variation across individual paralegals and across organizations was greater than the difference between paralegal and non-paralegal sites.

What causes this variation in paralegal effectiveness? Our qualitative findings suggest that the biggest factor is ongoing support and supervision. Where paralegals were part of a vertical network – they had a "lead paralegal" visiting them regularly and watching their performance, they had a lawyer whose help they could seek out in difficult cases – we saw paralegals handling cases well.

The SLDC and Cluff Gold cases described earlier are examples of the vertical network responding to tough problems. Paralegals Marian and Prince were able to

[53] The Liberia evaluation by Sandefur and Siddiqui avoids both of these problems – differences between the kinds of cases paralegals take on and the kinds of cases that come to existing local authorities, and inability to sample randomly from the case dockets of existing authorities – because in Liberia "treatment" and "control" subjects were all people who brought cases to paralegals during legal awareness sessions. The control subjects were randomly chosen to receive help from the paralegals a few months later than the treatment subjects, after the evaluation was complete. Justin Sandefur and Bilal Siddiqi, "Delivering Justice to the Poor: Theory and Experimental Evidence from Liberia" (paper presented at the World Bank Workshop on African Political Economy, Washington, DC, May 2013), 4, 29–30. This Sierra Leone study focuses less on evaluating impact and more on understanding how paralegals work. Our "control" sites helped us to compare the dynamics in cases handled by paralegals with the dynamics of conflicts that occur in places where paralegals are not present.

make progress because of the help they had from lead paralegals and lawyers. Where paralegals were trained initially but then left largely on their own, as was the case with the one paralegal whose work we studied from the Methodist Church, we saw serious lapses, including disorganization and poor follow-up.[54]

A rigorous system for tracking case information makes supervision and support possible. If there is a clear record of what has happened in every case, a supervisor can easily review strategy and progress during a visit. Better still, if those data are analyzed in aggregate, the organization can observe trends across paralegals and identify both common problems and useful innovations.

Rigorous data collection is crucial for a second reason. Data from across cases create a picture of how laws and systems are working in practice, something often no one else has. Organizations and the communities they serve can use that information to identify and advocate for positive systemic reforms. Tracking, aggregating, and analyzing data is time-consuming and difficult, especially because of Sierra Leone's poor internet connectivity. But the returns in program quality and evidence-based advocacy seem worth the investment.

V. CONCLUSION: CAN PARALEGALS DEEPEN DEMOCRACY?

Sierra Leone found peace after war. It regularly holds relatively free and fair elections. And it managed to extinguish Ebola. But from the perspective of many Sierra Leoneans, government steals from its people rather than serving them. The singer Emerson chants this, in his 2016 hit "Munku boss pa matches."

> *Adebayor ein just dae buy/*
> *All de land na de city /*
> *e jus dae buy/*
> *Shares na de company/*
> *E just dae buy/*
> *Contri dae poor/*
> *In just dae buy/*
> *People dae suffer*
> *in just dae buy/*
>
> Adebayor just buys/
> All the land in the city/
> He just buys/
> Shares in the company/
> He just buys/
> The country is poor/
> He just buys/

---

[54] Our case-tracking research took place before the Methodist Church worked with Timap, the Open Society Justice Initiative, and a coalition of groups to scale paralegal efforts and improve standards. Part of that effort involved strengthening systems for supervision and support.

People are suffering/
He just buys.

Emerson doesn't specify the identity of Adebayor, but it's clear that he's pointing at the state.[55]

By equipping ordinary people to understand, use, and shape the law, community paralegals are attempting to deepen Sierra Leonean democracy. They are fighting to replace kleptocracy, authoritarianism, and impunity with a society in which rules and institutions work for everyone, including the least powerful.

It's a bold vision. The cases paralegals and their clients manage to win make it tangible. But the opposing forces are strong. At best, it's a long journey ahead.

REFERENCES

Acemoglu, Daron and James A. Robinson. *Why Nations Fail: The Origins of Power, Prosperity, and Poverty*. New York: Currency, 2012.

Albiston, Catherine R. and Laura Nielsen, "Funding the Cause: How Public Interest Organizations Fund Their Activities and Why It Matters for Social Change," *Law and Social Inquiry* 39 (2014).

Alterman, Owen, Aneta Binienda, Sophie Rodella, and Kimyia Varzi. *The Law People See: The Status of Dispute Resolution in the Provinces of Sierra Leone in 2002*. Freetown: National Forum for Human Rights, 2002.

Amnesty International. *Sierra Leone – No One to Turn To: Women's Lack of Access to Justice in Sierra Leone*. London: Amnesty International, 2005. AI Index: AFR 51/011/2005. www.amnesty.org/download/Documents/80000/afr510112005en.pdf.

Awoko. "London Mining and Manonkoh Community Sign MOU." December 18, 2012. http://awoko.org/2012/12/18/london-mining-and-manonkoh-community-sign-mou/.

Barry, Ellen. "As 'Foreign Agent' Law Takes Effect in Russia, Human Rights Groups Vow to Defy It. *New York Times*. November 21, 2012. www.nytimes.com/2012/11/22/world/europe/rights-groups-in-russia-reject-foreign-agent-label.html?mtrref=www.google.com&mtrref=www.nytimes.com&gwh=CBB552E22AACB3750594FF04473C2C1B&gwt=pay.

Bhatnagar, Gaurav Vivek. "Home Ministry Cancels FCRA Licences of 20,000 NGOs." *The Wire*. December 27, 2016. https://thewire.in/89933/home-ministry-cancels-fcra-licences-20000-ngos.

Charities Aid Foundation. *World Giving Index 2015: A Global View of Giving Trends*. November 2015. www.cafonline.org/docs/default-source/about-us-publications/caf_worldgivingindex2015_report.pdf?sfvrsn=2.

Child Right Act, The No. 7 (2007), Supplement to the Sierra Leone Gazette Extraordinary Vol. CXXVIII, No. 43.

Conteh, Sonkita. "10 Misconceptions about Paralegals in Sierra Leone." *Sierra Express Media*, April 9, 2010. www.sierraexpressmedia.com/?p=7206.

"Joint Statement on the Draft Legal Aid Bill 2010." *Sierra Express Media*, April 13, 2010. www.sierraexpressmedia.com/?p=7281.

Dale, Pamela. *Delivering Justice to Sierra Leone's Poor: An Analysis of the Work of Timap for Justice*. Justice for the Poor Research Report, no. 1. Washington, DC: World Bank, 2009.

---

[55] There was a Togolese football player named Adebayor. Emerson may have used the name because it sounds similar to *Ar-dae-buy-all*, which means I buy everything.

The Economist. "Presidential Calculations." October 5, 2012. www.economist.com/blogs/baobab/2012/10/sierra-leone.
Environmental and Social Regulations for the Minerals Sector (2012) (Sierra Leone).
Denney, Lisa and Aisha F. Ibrahim. *Violence against Women in Sierra Leone: How Women Seek Redress*. London: Overseas Development Institute, 2012.
Devolution of Estates, The Act No. 21 (2007) (Sierra Leone).
Domestic Violence Act, The No. 20 (2007) (Sierra Leone).
Environmental Protection Agency Act, Supplement to the Sierra Leone Gazette Vol. CXXXIX, No. 44 (2008) (Sierra Leone).
Global Witness (2017), Defenders of the Earth: Global Killings of Land and Environmental Defenders in 2016.
Government of Sierra Leone, Ministry of Finance and Economic Development. *Budget Profile for FY 2011–2015*, annex I. http://mofed.gov.sl/speeches/profile%202013-15.pdf.
Government of Sierra Leone, Ministry of Lands, Country Planning and the Environment. *National Land Policy of Sierra Leone* (2015).
Interview with Sonkita Conteh, Director of Namati Sierra Leone, July 2017.
Inveen, Cooper. "President's Iron-Fist Methods Raise Fears for Future of Democracy in Sierra Leone," The Guardian, October 20, 2017, www.theguardian.com/global-development/2017/oct/20/president-ernest-bai-koroma-iron-fist-methods-raise-fears-for-future-of-democracy-in-sierraleone-march-election.
Koroma, Ernest Bai. "A Post-Ebola Plan for Sierra Leone," Wall Street Journal, November, 26, 2015.
Law and Development Partnership. *Developing a Portfolio of Financially Sustainable, Scalable Basic Legal Service Models*. Briefing Paper. London: Law and Development Partnership, 2016.
The Legal Aid Act (2012), Supplement to the Sierra Leone Gazette Vol. CXLIII No. 42.
Manning, Ryann E. "Landscape of Local Authority in Sierra Leone: How 'Tradit ional' and 'Modern' Justice and Governance Systems Interact." In *Decentralization, Democracy, and Development: Recent Experience from Sierra Leone*, edited by Yongmei Zhou, 110–37. Washington, DC: World Bank, 2009.
Maru, Vivek. "Between Law and Society: Paralegals and the Provision of Justice Services in Sierra Leone and Worldwide." *Yale Journal of International Law* 31, no. 2 (2006): 427–76. http://digitalcommons.law.yale.edu/yjil/vol31/iss2/5.
McQuoid Mason, David. "Access to Justice in South Africa: Are There Enough Lawyers?" *Onati Socio-legal Series* 3, no. 3 (2013): 561–79.
Menon, Menon, and Meenakshi Kapoor, Vivek Maru, and Kanchi Kohli, *Paralegals for Environmental Justice* (New Delhi: Center for Policy Research – Namati Environmental Justice Program, 2017), https://namati.org/wp-content/uploads/2017/12/Practice-Guide-for-Environmental-Justice-Paralegals.pdf.
"Namati, 9 Villages Sue AML for Pollution and Other Legal Violations." *Concord Times*. February 14, 2018. http://slconcordtimes.com/namati-9-villages-sue-aml-for-pollution-and-other-legal-violations.
Oakland Institute. *Understanding Land Investment Deals in Africa – Country Report: Sierra Leone*. Oakland, CA: The Oakland Institute, 2011.
"Our Land Our Future: A Pledge," https://ourlandourfuture.com.
Quigley, William P. The Demise of Law Reform and the Triumph of Legal Aid: Congress and the Legal Services Corporation from the 1960's to the 1990's, 17 ST. Louis U. PUB. L. REV. 241, 260–61 (1998).

Renner-Thomas, Ade. *Land Tenure in Sierra Leone: The Law, Dualism and the Making of a Land Policy*. Bloomington, IN: Authorhouse, 2010.

Richards, Paul. *Fighting for the Rain Forest: War, Youth & Resources in Sierra Leone*. London: International African Institute, 1996.

Sandefur, Justin and Bilal Siddiqi. "Delivering Justice to the Poor: Theory and Experimental Evidence from Liberia" (paper presented at the World Bank Workshop on African Political Economy, Washington, DC, May 2013).

Sesay, Daniel. *Community-Based Paralegals in Sierra Leone: Case Studies and Stories*. Namati, 2014.

Sierra Express Media. "Masethele Village in Important Land Renegotiation with Addax Bioenergy Sierra Leone Limited." March 14, 2013. www.sierraleonenews.net/article/213188649/masethele-village-in-important-land-renegotiation-with-addax-bioenergy-sierra-leone-limited.

Sierra Leone Mines and Minerals Decree No. 5 (1994), Section 26.

Sierra Leone Truth and Reconciliation Commission. *Witness to Truth: Report of the Sierra Leone Truth and Reconciliation Commission*, vol. 2. Accra: Graphic Packing Ltd., 2004.

Srivastava, Vivek and Marco Larizza. "Working with the Grain for Reforming the Public Service: A Live Example from Sierra Leone." *International Review of Administrative Sciences* 79, no. 3 (2013): 458–85.

"Summary of Strategies and Tactics." *Defending Dissent: Civil Society and Human Rights in the Global Crackdown*. Bernstein Institute Annual Conference (2017).

Tran, Mark "Ethiopia Curb on Charities Alarms Human Rights Activists." *The Guardian*. January 25, 2009. www.theguardian.com/world/2009/jan/26/ethiopia-charities-human-rights.

World Bank. *Sierra Leone: Strategic Options for Public Sector Reform*. AFTPT, African Region Report 25110-SL. Washington, DC: World Bank, 2003.

7

The Contributions of Community-Based Paralegals in Delivering Access to Justice in Postwar Liberia

Peter Chapman and Chelsea Payne

I. INTRODUCTION

After decades of instability in Liberia, the Accra Peace Accords brought an end to civil conflict in August 2003. Liberia's postwar transitional government faced enormous challenges and several postwar assessments revealed the arduous task ahead for strengthening access to justice and the rule of law. An evaluation of the justice sector by the International Legal Assistance Consortium, in 2003, revealed "an almost unanimous distrust of Liberia's courts, and a corresponding collapse in the rule of law."[1] A 2006 report by the International Crisis Group (ICG) found institutional dysfunction and serious infrastructure constraints in the justice sector in particular; more than half of the justices of the peace, the lowest level of the statutory legal system, were estimated to be illiterate. Of the 130 Magistrate's Judges identified by ICG, only three were trained as lawyers.[2] Nearly all formal court buildings were destroyed during the conflict. With this baseline, the Government of Liberia and its international partners began the task of supporting the emergence of accountable and representative public institutions.

Much of the post-conflict development in the justice sector concentrated on formal institutions. Western donors and the Liberian elite, who predominantly managed these reforms, set about reconstructing a formal justice system modeled largely on the United States. As these efforts were ongoing, however, a smaller set of Liberian civil society activists, Western donors, and Liberian government officials embraced community-based paralegals as a complementary, and at times

---

We would like to express our appreciation to current and former Carter Center program staff, including Tom Crick, Pewee Flomoku, Cllr. Lemuel Reeves, Robert Pitman, Amanda Rawls, Johnny Ndebe, David Kortee, and the staff of the Catholic Justice and Peace Commission. We would also like to thank researchers Justin Sandefur and Bilal Siddiqi for their work researching and evaluating the Community Justice Advisor program. The views expressed herein are those of the authors and do not necessarily reflect the views of the United Nations.

[1] International Legal Assistance Consortium, *ILAC Report: Liberia* (Stockholm: International Legal Assistance Consortium, 2003), vii.

[2] International Crisis Group, *Liberia: Resurrecting the Justice System* (Brussels: International Crisis Group, 2006), 1.

alternative, model of legal development. These non-lawyer paralegals came to be a front line of legal assistance for many Liberians.

The cases of Hauwa, a rural Liberian mother of four children, and of a community in River Gee County are illustrative of the diverse roles community paralegals play in Liberia.[3] When Hauwa's husband stopped supporting his children, she found herself unable to cover the cost of living. Hauwa considered taking her partner to court to compel him to support his children, but with uncertainty about her legal position and the fear of high court fees, Hauwa instead approached a paralegal from a Liberian civil society organization, the Catholic Justice and Peace Commission (JPC). The community paralegal counseled Hauwa and began by describing the options available to her under Liberia's dual legal framework, from pursuing a case in court, mediation by a civil society organization, to appealing to traditional leadership. Hauwa weighed these options and eventually asked the paralegal to mediate between her and her husband. The paralegal explained to Hauwa's partner his legal responsibilities concerning child support and the seriousness of a charge of "persistent non-support" under the Domestic Relations Law and Penal Law. With this information, and with the engagement of the JPC paralegal, the husband agreed to resume support for his children and Hauwa received the support she needed: Hauwa reports that her husband now provides "food [and] the children are going to school."[4] Her life and the lives of her four children changed for the better.

In a community in River Gee County, the Sustainable Development Institute (SDI), another Liberian civil society organization, trained two community members as paralegals (called "community animators"). These animators were trained to help strengthen the community's governance of its land and natural resources, document property boundaries, and assist with pursuing formal registration of the community's land with the Land Commission. The community paralegals worked with existing community leadership as well as other community members to develop and refine bylaws for governing land and natural resources. Each step of the way the paralegals worked to ensure widespread participation, including of vulnerable groups within the community, through mobilization and outreach.[5] Over time, and with the paralegals' assistance, the community advanced through multiple revisions of the community bylaws with the regulations becoming more inclusive of different community members. One community member reported real change in the way decisions are made: "In the past elders and our big people made all the decisions. Now we call meetings for everyone to take part."[6]

---

[3] All client names have been changed for confidentiality.   [4] JPC client, interview, 2013.
[5] Rachael Knight, Silas Kpanan'Ayoung Siakor, and Ali Kaba, *Protecting Community Lands and Resources: Evidence From Liberia* (Rome: International Development Law Organization, Washington, DC: Namati, 2012), 11.
[6] Rachael Knight, Marena Brinkhurst, and Jaron Vogelsang, *Community Land Protection: Facilitators Guide* (Washington, DC: Namati, 2016), 30.

This chapter describes and analyzes the use of community-based paralegals in post-conflict Liberia. This chapter begins by discussing the Liberian justice system, then reviews paralegal models in Liberia, particularly the approach of JPC, and finally uses a recent working paper to analyze the impact of JPC paralegals across three domains: rights consciousness, private disputes, and state or corporate accountability cases.[7] The conclusion discusses the determinants of success and the future of the paralegal movement in Liberia.

II. LIBERIA'S JUSTICE SYSTEM

Following the conflict, as Liberian and international policymakers began to address the severe capacity and infrastructure constraints throughout Liberia, Liberia's dual justice system posed a particular paradox.[8] The origins of Liberia's legal dualism trace back to the founding of the modern Liberian state. The Liberian state was founded by freed American slaves who, with the support of the American Colonization Society, "returned" to a part of Africa from which few had originally come. As the new government of Liberia began to consolidate power, first in Monrovia and then outside of the capital in what came to be known as the "hinterland," it established a dual legal system whereby a settler elite were deemed "civilized" and subject to Western law, whereas "uncivilized natives" were subject to customary law. Natives could not use the Western system and, similarly, chiefs could not preside over disputes that included a civilized party.[9]

This dual approach was further refined and institutionalized in 1949 through the Rules and Regulations Governing the Hinterland of Liberia (the "Hinterland Regulations").[10] The Hinterland Regulations, as in the British colonial administration next door in Sierra Leone, reinforced a codified system of indirect rule over rural Liberia, grounded in the legal dualism harnessed by governing elites in many colonial states.[11] The Hinterland Regulations sanctioned the executive branch of government, through the Ministry of Internal Affairs (MIA) rather than an

---

[7] Justin Sandefur and Bilal Siddiqi, "Delivering Justice to the Poor: Theory and Experimental Evidence from Liberia" (paper presented at the World Bank Workshop on African Political Economy, Washington, DC, May 2013), https://editorialexpress.com/cgi-bin/conference/download.cgi?db_name=CSAE2013&paper_id=1014.

[8] For further discussion, see Stephen Lubkemann, Deborah Isser, and Peter Chapman, "Neither State nor Custom – Justice Naked Power: The Consequences of Ideals-Oriented Rule of Law Policy-Making in Liberia," *Journal of Legal Pluralism and Unofficial Law* 43, no. 63 (2011): 73–109, doi: 10.1080/07329113.2011.10756658.

[9] International Crisis Group, *Liberia: Resurrecting the Justice System*, 7 (see n. 2).

[10] Republic of Liberia, Rules and Regulations Governing the Hinterland of Liberia (1949) (amended January 7, 2001). The legal status of the Hinterland Regulations is subject to much debate and even today there are disagreements as to whether the MIA under President Charles Taylor reauthorized the regulations in 2001.

[11] See Mahmood Mamdani, *Citizen and Subject: Contemporary Africa and the Legacy of Late Colonialism* (Princeton, NJ: Princeton University Press, 1996), 87 (discussing the introduction of "[i]ndirect rule institutions" in Liberia through the "implementation of the Barclay Plan in 1904").

independent judiciary, to have general oversight over a nationwide system of dispute resolution managed by government-recognized chiefs. Under this system, dispute resolution was not required to comply with principles of due process or equal protection codified under the Liberian constitution. The MIA could license ordeal doctors who could use trial by ordeal[12] "of a minor nature and which do not endanger the life of the individual" to ascertain the guilt of parties.[13] Cases in this chieftaincy system would be appealed to the president of Liberia, not the Supreme Court. This system of governance and dispute resolution was valuable in extending state control over rural areas while simultaneously avoiding the need for a large government footprint outside Monrovia.

The dual system of dispute resolution and governance helped to promote the government's core pursuit of extractive economic development. The government advanced a strategy of enclave investment that enriched a small elite. Private corporations and individuals were encouraged to lease large tracts of state "public land." Indeed, by the 1960s, one-fourth of Liberia's total land area was under concession, including rubber, iron, and timber.[14] The settler-dominated government closely guarded benefit flows. However, competing claims between private interests, public interests, and local communities were facilitated and exacerbated by the dual justice system. Competition over revenues and sharing of environmental and social costs was a major source of grievance. The 1980 coup d'état by indigenous

---

[12] See Deborah H. Isser, Stephen C. Lubkemann, and Saah N'Tow, "Looking for Justice: Liberian Experiences and Perceptions of Local Justice Options," *Peaceworks* 63 (2009): 58. Isser, Lubkemann, and N'Tow discuss numerous forms of trial by ordeal (TBO) and distinguish between those that are harmful prima facie and other forms that do not necessarily result in harm to the participants:

> It is equally important to distinguish between different types of methods of TBO and the logic behind their use. Thus, one set of methods involves practices that are physically harmful prima facie – meaning that they would be expected to cause physical harm if applied in any normal situation out-side of the ritual context of TBO. Examples of such forms include the ingestion of poison, the application of hot metal to the skin (usually described as a "cutlass"), and the immersion of one's hand in a pot of boiling oil. The logic of TBO in this form is that the supernatural power of the ritual will protect the innocent from harm (by not burning the skin, or by forcing the innocent to vomit ingested poison), but not the guilty, who will suffer physical harm or even death. This form is generally used to identify a guilty party.
>
> A categorically different set of TBO methods involve activities that are not physically harmful prima facie – such as eating a small clot of dirt, taking an oath, or trying to separate two brooms after these have been lain on top of each other (there are many more specific variations in this category). The logic of the TBO ritual in this form is that the supernatural power of the ritual will identify the one who is guilty and/or who does not tell the truth, and punish them by ensuring that the guilty or untruthful person will (eventually) suffer malaise if they perform a mundane and harmless act within a defined ritual context. In another version of this method, a guilty person will supposedly be incapable of doing a mundane and harmless task that others who are innocent can do with ease (such as uncrossing two brooms when one is laid on top of the other). This form may be used for any of the three purposes described earlier.

[13] Republic of Liberia, Rules and Regulations Governing the Hinterland of Liberia, art. 73 (see n. 10).

[14] See Robert W. Clower et al., *Growth without Development: An Economic Survey of Liberia* (Evanston, IL: Northwestern University Press, 1966), 127.

military officer Samuel Doe was motivated, at least in part, by a desire to gain control over the valuable resource rents the Monrovia government controlled. The Doe (1980–90) and the Taylor governments (1997–2003) both used land and resource access and revenues to solidify constituencies at the local and national levels. Such a policy did little to build institutional coherence and continued to maintain the historical system of indirect rule and parallel governance.[15]

A. The Preeminence of Local Dispute Resolution

Despite the discriminatory history surrounding the codification of Liberia's dual justice system, and years of civil conflict, local systems continue to serve as the dominant form of dispute resolution and are generally an accepted part of Liberian communities. The community-based or traditional system is made up of family heads, elders, a range of customary authorities, and officials in secret societies. Some of these institutions are recognized and codified by Liberian law; other elements are not. Many Liberians view these different local institutions – even after they were coopted and shaped by the dual system – as more accessible than the formal justice system and report that they are more directly responsive to their normative preferences. A US Institute of Peace (USIP) study in 2009 found that Liberians viewed physical accessibility, cost, comprehensibility (both in terms of languages used and terminology) and transparency as some of the most important features of a functional justice system.[16] The USIP study found that the chieftaincy system regulated by the MIA, while not without flaws, was largely seen to better respond to these preferences.

Average Liberians know much more about how to access community-based systems and are often unfamiliar with formal court processes. A 2011 national household survey found that 91 percent of respondents said they had little or no knowledge of the formal court system.[17]

While customary systems are viewed as more accessible and locally relevant, they are also at times in conflict with human rights and the Liberian constitution. Vulnerable groups, including women, children, and those foreign to local communities (called "strangers" by Liberians), suffer through these systems. Indeed critics contend that customary forums are, in particular, susceptible to

---

[15] See generally Stephen Ellis, *The Mask of Anarchy: The Destruction of Liberia and the Religious Dimension of an African Civil War* (New York: New York University Press, 2007); Philip A. Z. Banks III, "Forward," in *Strategic Plan 2009–2012* (Monrovia: Ministry of Justice of the Government of Liberia, 2008) (noting "the failings of the nation's justice system have been cited as one of the prime factors that caused, generated or attributed either to the turmoil or to the prolongation of the chaos that consumed the society").

[16] Isser, Lubkemann, and N'Tow, "Looking for Justice" (see n. 12).

[17] Patrick Vinck, Phuong Pham, and Tino Kreutzer, *Talking Peace: A Population-Based Survey on Attitudes about Security, Dispute Resolution, and Post-conflict Reconstruction in Liberia* (Berkeley: Human Rights Center, University of California, Berkley, 2011), 4.

elite capture.[18] A University of California, Berkeley population-based survey from 2011 also elucidated widespread mistrust of the formal system; less than 20 percent of survey respondents who reported being victims of a crime said they reported it to the police. Of the 19 percent who reported the crimes, more than half reported paying for the service.[19] Another survey found that 43 percent of respondents believe the Liberian National Police (LNP) is corrupt, 40 percent of respondents believe courts are corrupt, and nearly two-thirds of respondents said that they believe they would have to pay for the police to investigate a crime.[20] One in four Liberians reported feeling unsafe or not very safe,[21] and nearly one in seven households had a member who was a victim of crime or violence.[22]

The challenge for Liberian and international policymakers working in the justice sector in this immediate postwar period was to put aside preconceptions of what Liberian institutions should look like and try to find ways to provide immediate and effective means of dispute resolution for the multitude of grievances present in Liberian society – from large-scale land and resource conflict to petty crime or corruption. Paralegal organizations have sought to bridge this divide and lay a foundation for a more equitable justice system.

III. BUILDING ON COMMUNITY CAPACITIES WITH COMMUNITY-BASED PARALEGALS

Peace came to Liberia at the same time as a growing movement of community paralegals was gaining traction across Africa. The 2008 Commission on Legal Empowerment documented such programs in other developing and post-conflict countries – for example, Kenya, Malawi, and Sierra Leone. Drawing on inspiration from these experiences, a handful of individuals within the Liberian government, civil society, and international development organizations in Liberia began to explore the role non-lawyer, community paralegals might play in Liberia. These groups theorized that given weak state capacity, the historically discriminatory role justice institutions played in Liberia and the widespread distrust of state institutions paralegals might help expand rights consciousness and resolve disputes – both

---

[18] See, for example, Janine Ubink and Benjamin van Rooij, "Towards Customary Legal Empowerment: An Introduction," in *Customary Justice: Perspectives on Legal Empowerment*, ed. Janine Ubink and Thomas McInerney (Rome: International Development Law Organization, 2011), 9.

[19] Vinck, Pham, and Kreutzer, *Talking Peace*, 65 n. 57 (see n. 17).

[20] Robert Blair, Christopher Blattman, and Alexandra Hartman, *Patterns of Conflict and Cooperation in Liberia (Part 1): Results from a Longitudinal Study* (New Haven, CT: Yale University, Innovations for Poverty Action, 2012), 12–13.

[21] Vinck, Pham, and Kreutzer, *Talking Peace*, 40–41 (see n. 17). Furthermore, four out of five Liberians considered themselves a victim of the civil war, including displacement (77 percent), destruction of property (61 percent), and destruction of farms (60 percent).

[22] Small Arms Survey, "Reading between the Lines: Crime and Victimization in Liberia," *Small Arms Survey Issue Brief*, no. 2 (Geneva: Small Arms Survey, 2011), 1.

private disputes at the community level and disputes with government or corporate interests. Multiple paralegal models have subsequently emerged in Liberia over the past ten years. This section discusses several of these paralegal models before focusing on the JPC.

A. Prison Fellowship Liberia (PFL)

Prison Fellowship Liberia (PFL),[23] founded in 1989, uses paralegals to improve accountability in Liberian detention and correctional facilities. In Monrovia, Buchanan, and Gbarnga, PFL paralegals promote rights consciousness among detainees and prison staff and respond to specific allegations of abuse. Beginning in 2009, PFL began working in partnership with Open Society Foundations, JPC, and the American Bar Association to implement a project aimed at reducing prolonged pretrial detention at Monrovia Central Prison (MCP). The project supported efforts by the judiciary and the Ministry of Justice to establish a mechanism for regular review of detainee status. The Liberian government, in partnership with PFL and others, established the Magistrate's Sitting Program, which consisted of rotational meetings of magisterial courts at MCP for preliminary examination. PFL paralegals played an important role in this project by working inside MCP, eventually with the support of the Ministry of Justice, to assist with organization, record management, and monitoring of prison conditions. PFL's organization and monitoring component linked to attorneys from JPC who provided free legal assistance to detainees. PFL has sourced funding from a variety of sources, including international donors such as Prison Fellowship International, the East-West Management Institute, Open Society Foundations and UN agencies.

B. The Sustainable Development Institute (SDI)

The Sustainable Development Institute (SDI) is a Liberian civil society organization that works to improve natural resource governance.[24] Beginning in 2009, SDI partnered with the International Development Law Organization (IDLO),[25] and now Namati, to explore the use of paralegals, along with other approaches, in demarcating and securing community land. The joint effort focused on (1) advancing community land titling in accordance with procedures agreed upon with Liberia's Land Commission; (2) improving understanding of the most effective modalities of supporting communities to pursue community land titling; and (3)

---

[23] For more information, see "EWMI Awards Grant to Support Access to Justice in Liberia," East-West Management Institute, last modified February 2009, www.ewmi.org./CDRILLFebruary2009.

[24] For an in-depth discussion of the community land titling initiative, please see Knight et al., *Protecting Community Lands and Resources* (see n. 5).

[25] IDLO implemented the project in three countries: Mozambique, Uganda, and Liberia.

developing and testing approaches to improve intra-community land and resource governance through these processes.[26]

The SDI project tested four different levels of assistance: monthly legal education, paralegal assistance, direct assistance of lawyers and other technical professionals, and a control group that received only hard copies of relevant information. A core objective was to understand how to best support communities to establish intra-community mechanisms to protect the land rights of women and other vulnerable groups. In communities selected for paralegal support, SDI conducted monthly training sessions for community members over the course of fourteen months. These training sessions lasted approximately three hours and included advice from legal and technical professionals on subjects including the statutory provisions for community land titling, advice on the legal framework on customary tenure, practical techniques to document community land, how to engage relevant government authorities, and effective strategies to deliberate intra-community land administration and governance. In addition to this support from SDI, two community-based paralegals were elected in each selected community. These two community members elected to serve as paralegals – typically one man and one woman – received an intensive two-day introductory training and then had monthly meetings and trainings with SDI over the course of the project. While these paralegals were not formally certified by the government, they helped supervise and implement the community titling processes within their community on a day-to-day and week-to-week basis.[27]

An evaluation of the SDI program revealed that the paralegal treatment group was most effective in helping communities meet the requirements of the community land documentation process. The study authors suggested that paralegals were effective in three areas:

- The success of paralegal communities in completing the land registration process seems to suggest that paralegal assistance was flexible enough to ensure that communities took ownership over the registration process.[28]
- Paralegals seemed to be particularly effective in helping communities "navigate through intra-community tensions or obstacles that a full-services team of outside professionals may either inadequately address, fail to perceive, or accidentally exacerbate."[29]
- The authors also contend that there were spillover effects associated with community-based paralegals. The control groups and education-only communities that bordered paralegal communities were more successful than similarly situated communities that did not border paralegal treatment areas, which led the authors to suggest that "well-trained and rigorously supervised paralegals may not only help their own

[26] Knight et al., *Protecting Community Lands and Resources*, 12 (see n. 5). [27] Ibid., 36.
[28] Ibid., 17–18. [29] Ibid., 18.

communities, but may also have spillover impacts throughout the region in which they are based."[30]

C. Norwegian Refugee Council (NRC)

From 2006 to 2014, the Norwegian Refugee Council (NRC) supported a paralegal program focused on resolving land disputes.[31] Through its Information, Counseling and Legal Assistance (ICLA) program, NRC paralegals used mediation and "facilitated negotiation" to resolve land disputes, particularly related to the "return and reintegration of refugees and internally displaced persons.[32] Over the course of this program, NRC paralegals resolved thousands of land dispute cases.

D. The Catholic Justice and Peace Commission (JPC)

Beginning in 2007, The Carter Center partnered with the Catholic Justice and Peace Commission (JPC) to implement a paralegal program in southeast Liberia. The JPC is one of the largest human rights organizations in Liberia and former executive directors of the organization have recently served as the solicitor general, minister of labor, minister of public works, and vice president of the Liberian Bar Association. JPC was founded in 1991 as an interfaith effort supported by the Catholic Church's global network to promote social justice, human rights, and accountability in Liberia.[33]

1. Establishment and Funding

The Carter Center has worked on access to justice issues in Liberia since 2006. In partnership with the Ministry of Justice, JPC and The Carter Center began by training ten paralegals to operate in five southeastern counties. This area continues to be plagued with some of Liberia's worst development indicators, including poor access to basic services and information and extremely limited infrastructure. During the rainy season, whole counties are, at times, inaccessible by road from the Liberian capital.

The ten paralegals, initially called community legal advisors, were trained to provide practical advice and support to citizens and communities in resolving their justice issues. Building on this approach, in 2008 the UN Peacebuilding Fund, through the UN High Commissioner for Refugees, expanded the program into

---

[30] Ibid.
[31] See "Leaving Liberia," Norwegian Refugee Council. www.nrc.no/news/2015/july/leaving-liberia/.
[32] Norwegian Refugee Council, *Searching for Soap Trees: Norwegian Refugee Council's Land Dispute Resolution Process in Liberia* (Oslo: Norwegian Refugee Council, 2011), 13. Norwegian Refugee Council, "Liberia Fact Sheet" (2014). www.nrc.no/arch/_img/9182931.pdf.
[33] "JPC Liberia," Justice and Peace Commission, Liberia. http://jpcliberia.org/.

central Liberia. Over the years, additional donors have assisted the program including Humanity United, a California-based foundation, and the US Agency for International Development. The Carter Center has also regularly contributed institutional funding to bridge gaps between donor assistance cycles.

By 2013, the program supported forty-five paralegals in seven counties, including Montserrado containing the Liberian capital of Monrovia. The title of "paralegals" was eventually changed in 2012 due to concerns raised by members of the Liberian legal community over the ability of non-lawyers to provide legal advice (evidencing how narrowly the formal legal professional views the justice system), and paralegals are now known as community justice advisors (CJAs).[34] CJAs typically possess secondary school or college education and many are recruited from the counties in which they work.

2. JPC Organizational Structure and Management

Following the end of the civil conflict in Liberia, JPC extended a nationwide network of staff and volunteers. Unlike many organizations in Liberia that keep offices only in the capital, Monrovia, JPC has a decentralized structure with three regional offices supporting activities in counties across the country. In addition to staff and volunteers at these central offices, JPC maintains a network of parish-based committees at the county and district levels where local volunteers work on the organization's human rights mission.

The JPC aims to support individuals and deliver justice for marginalized communities through a mixture of front-line paralegals, lead paralegals, JPC regional coordinators, attorneys, and Carter Center staff. Paralegals are based in offices throughout their counties and are recognizable from their JPC-branded vests, motorbikes, and offices. In each county, paralegals are supported and mentored by staff from various levels. At the county level, lead JPC CJA paralegals are responsible for regularly working directly with the other paralegals in the county, ranging from four to six paralegals per county.

Paralegals are backstopped by trained attorneys who assist them through regular training, mentoring, and case-specific assistance. Paralegals are tasked with helping clients navigate complicated legal and administrative issues that sometimes require additional legal assistance. Even what might seem to be a simple case at the community level invariably will confront complex power relationships. JPC is directed by a Liberian attorney in the national office. The Carter Center also provides support to the program through a senior Liberian councilor-at-law, based in the Monrovia office, Liberian attorneys based in the regional offices, and a network of program staff to assist with general program and financial management. The Carter Center has also employed several foreign-educated lawyers in management and capacity-building roles.

---

[34] For the purposes of continuity, this chapter will use the term *community justice advisor* (CJA) to describe the paralegal program from 2007 onward.

JPC uses several tools to document and track case progress, including a client agreement form, a case record form, and a case options log. The case record form is filled out in triplicate and regularly sent to the JPC regional office to be included in its case database. This information is transmitted to The Carter Center head office in Monrovia, which maintains a master database. This database is used to track outcomes across the program and to refine training and program designs.

Every six months, the JPC secretary at each regional office will select twenty cases for every paralegal. Ten of these case records are transferred to the lead paralegal at the county level, and ten case records are given to The Carter Center's regional office. The lead paralegals and The Carter Center review all of the case materials with each paralegal to ensure that the case records are complete and to talk through the legal ramifications of the case and potential strategy. Attorneys also review paralegal case files at quarterly trainings to strategize about opportunities for resolution. There are also regular evaluations of specific cases, involving direct meetings with clients and affected parties.

3. Tools

CJAs employ a range of tools to assist clients, including education, negotiation, organization, advocacy, and mediation. Empowerment of clients is stressed across the program and paralegals are encouraged to strategize about how each tool can be deployed in a way that ensures client ownership, direction, and control.

In nearly all cases, CJA engagement begins by counseling the client or clients on the relevant legal provisions and principles of equity. CJAs are trained to present all options to the clients and encouraged to seek advice from the lawyers on staff to ensure the accuracy of information and provide context-specific, flexible solutions. In addition to the relevant legal standards, CJAs explain to the clients the various steps required through different courses of action and what the clients can expect. The clients control case decisions.

Beyond giving information, advocacy and mediation are two of the most commonly used paralegal tools. CJAs advocate with government and disputing parties to address issues of injustice. Across a variety of case types, CJAs regularly find themselves forced to confront abuses of power: a local magistrate detains someone for the invented charge of "eye rape"; a county official takes it upon himself to help mediate a divorce while insisting that he should keep the family's small generator as his "fee"; a chief issues a crippling fine for violating an unknown village ordinance. In each of these cases, CJAs have advocated on behalf of the less powerful and vulnerable parties to ensure that injustices are remedied. Often through an implicit or nuanced threat of escalating the case to more senior authorities, CJAs help local clients combat abuses of authority and advocate for more equitable outcomes.

Mediation is one of the most commonly used tools employed by CJAs. CJAs are not an independent mediator, which you would find in some legal traditions; instead CJAs actively inform both parties about governing law, discuss principles of equity,

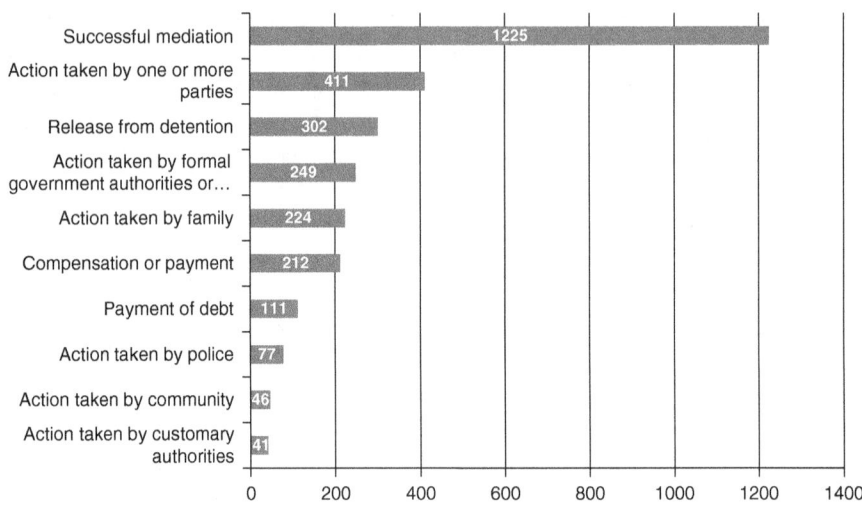

FIGURE 7.1 Successfully resolved cases: 2007–September 2012
Source: The Carter Center, 2013.

and work for empowerment of the vulnerable and aggrieved party. In this sense, CJAs work toward a facilitated negotiation as opposed to a pure, impartial mediation. The program adopts this approach in an effort to even power asymmetries and promote more just and equitable outcomes. More than 40 percent of the CJA cases that have been "successfully resolved" (cases to which a resolution is found and the case is closed) since 2007 involved CJA mediation.

For JPC, a case is "successfully resolved" when its client can address a legal issue or dispute in accordance with the law *and* in a way that advances principles of fairness and equity. If a CJA is approached by an abusive spouse or partner asking advice on his or her rights, the CJA will provide information on what the law says and whether the individual is in violation of the law. The CJA would also seek to work with the other party to ensure that he or she is capable of exercising his or her rights. Where Liberian law itself is insufficient or discriminatory, JPC, The Carter Center, and partners will work toward reform.

Over the years, CJAs have engaged in a wide variety of disputes. As indicated in Figure 7.2, CJAs regularly assist with family issues (34 percent of cases), economic injustice (31 percent of cases), private violence (15 percent of cases), abuse by authorities (11 percent of cases), and social infrastructure and development cases (2 percent of cases). Women bring approximately half of cases to the JPC, including 90 percent of child abandonment cases, 84 percent of domestic violence matters, and 81 percent of rape and sexual violence complaints.

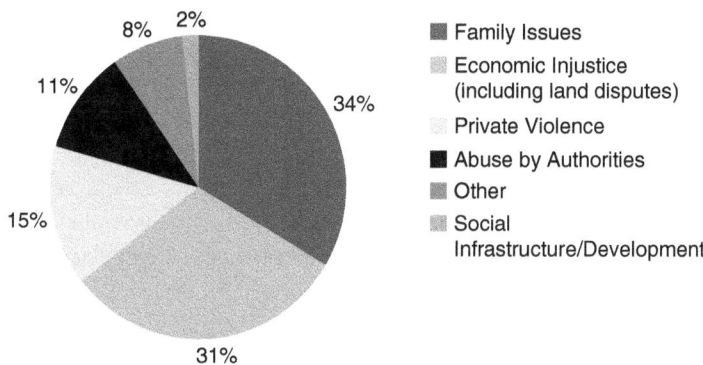

FIGURE 7.2 Percentage of case type categories: 2007–September 2012
Source: The Carter Center, 2013.

IV. AN EVALUATION OF THE CATHOLIC JUSTICE AND PEACE COMMISSION PROGRAM

Starting in 2008, The Carter Center and JPC agreed to work with researchers Justin Sandefur and Bilal Siddiqi to use a randomized controlled trial to evaluate the effectiveness of the paralegal program. The study had two components, both of which are relevant to addressing the impact of community-based paralegals in Liberia: an initial household survey to document justice experiences of Liberians, and a specific focus on JPC's model of paralegal assistance.

A. Forum Shopping and a Role for Community Paralegals

Sandefur and Siddiqi's evaluation began with a household survey across more than 2,000 households spread across 176 communities in five Liberian counties. This survey identified, through self-reporting, some 4,500 separate disputes. Details were then collected for each dispute reported within the past year, covering the forums visited, time and costs incurred, and satisfaction with the outcome reported. Limited socioeconomic and demographic information was obtained about each disputant.

This initial analysis of household dispute data established a number of tendencies in the use of the forums that were of interest for the paralegal intervention. There was a clear tendency for violent crimes to be taken to the formal system (namely, justices of the peace, magistrates, police, and other military/government officials), while the civil cases that dominated the sample were likely to be taken to the customary system (including town, clan, and paramount chiefs, as well as elders, family leaders, and secret societies). The study found that the socially disadvantaged are on average significantly more likely to take their cases to the customary system.[35] The analysis concluded that, overall, the subjective satisfaction of this more "restorative" customary system, which is focused on redistributing loss from defendant to plaintiff, is far higher than that of the "punitive" formal, with a focus on remedies that "harm" defendants more than they benefit plaintiffs.[36]

The discussion of the findings raises a core question leading Sandefur and Siddiqi to look at the role of legal assistance services in the Liberian context. The authors note the *prima facie* tension that exists between what appeared to be a documented bias in Liberian customary law against the less powerful party (women and marginalized), and the empirical fact that these disadvantaged plaintiffs choose to take most of their disputes to customary forums. They ask: "Why would marginalized groups choose to bring cases to customary courts that systematically repress them?"

A likely reason, as previously explored, is that despite the presence of bias, the formal justice system is viewed as more out of reach and even less responsive for many Liberians. Sandefur and Siddiqi suggest that the barriers to accessing justice through the formal system in Liberia are significant, ranging from prohibitive travel costs, to corrupt officials, to formidable formal legal procedures. The study posits that flexible, locally oriented legal assistance can offer the poor access to low-cost, remedial justice using quasi-formal alternative dispute resolution mechanisms, by way of pro bono mediation and advocacy services. These are the services provided by JPC's community paralegal program.

B. *Exploring the Impact of the CJAs*

Within this institutional environment, the study sought to track the effects of paralegal services on clients through an evaluation launched in July 2011 that extended through December 2011. Paralegals conducted civic education sessions and then met with potential clients. Each client was surveyed and then randomly assigned to a treatment group, to be assisted with their dispute right away, and a control group, to receive assistance three months after first contact. The control group was encouraged in the meantime to pursue the matter using other available forums and resources, the vast majority of whom did. In November 2011, follow-up surveys were administered to the clients. The cases themselves spanned a wide range of cases and case types, from commercial debt disputes to marital infidelity.

The engagement and findings of the evaluation cover the three domains associated with the JPC program as well as the other chapters of this volume: rights consciousness, private disputes, and corporate accountability cases.

---

[35] The socially disadvantaged were defined as including women more so than men, non-farmers more so than farmers, and the "powerless" in society more so than the "powerful."

[36] This includes after controlling for demographic characteristics and the nature of the dispute. While plaintiffs who win favorable verdicts in the customary system exhibit higher satisfaction than those who do not, no such pattern exists in the formal system.

C. Rights Consciousness

The JPC CJA program focuses on improving community awareness through civic education and outreach as well as through handling cases, helping clients directly claim entitlements. In their work plan each month, CJAs are expected to expand awareness of rights in their communities. The Carter Center has historically supported additional local civil society organizations to conduct awareness sessions, often through drama and question and answer sessions designed to directly engage community members. These groups were encouraged to refer specific cases or disputes to the JPC CJAs for resolution.

The study found that treatment of a case by the community paralegal strongly impacted the legal knowledge of the respondents over the three months of interaction with the CJA. This included knowledge of such topics as women's rights to inheritance, domestic violence, and corruption.[37]

Such knowledge of how the system *should* work has real, individual impacts. In a small village outside of Fishtown, in the southeast, for example, an old woman was accused of being a "witch" after a young boy fell from a palm tree. Community members accused her of casting a spell that caused the child to fall, injuring him badly. Following the accusations, the old woman was beaten and jailed in the bathroom of the paramount chief's house. After managing to escape she fled to town to find the county attorney, who acknowledged that the treatment was wrong, but was not confident in resolving such an issue where the "formal" and "local" laws conflicted. Recognizing the flexible services offered by the CJAs, the county attorney referred her to the JPC. The local CJAs contacted the county inspector, an MIA official who is often responsible for these types of "mysterious" cases, who accompanied them to the village. At first the townspeople threatened to expel the CJAs and the inspector, but the CJAs talked with the townspeople and the paramount chief and advocated on the woman's behalf. The CJAs explained the necessary formal legal process if they believed the woman had caused someone harm. The community eventually agreed that there was no proof the woman had caused the child to fall from the tree and trust was built. Today the CJAs report that "the people who wanted to [expel] us are now bringing cases to us."

The authors also found that the paralegal intervention positively impacted justice-seeking behavior: paralegal intervention "increases the number of reported disputes by providing an outlet for grievances that otherwise would have gone nowhere."[38]

---

[37] Interestingly, there was no impact found on measures of attitudes (the evaluation measured trust, subjective happiness, and attitudes toward gender-based violence) nor was there any impact found on behavior related to protect property rights (land titling and demarcation) or engaged in credit market activity (lending and borrowing).

[38] Sandefur and Siddiqi, "Delivering Justice to the Poor," 32 (see n. 7).

D. Private Disputes

A predominance of CJA cases are private disputes. As indicated, between 2007 and 2012, approximately a third of all cases were family issues and another third were economic injustice cases. Women, who bring approximately half of cases to the JPC, account for 90 percent of child abandonment cases. Indeed, in the evaluation, a high proportion of cases concerned child support. These private disputes all cover areas where there is potentially significant impact on issues such as food security, economic well-being, and social cohesion.

The research found that CJA work improved household food security, child food security, and the proportion of households with single mothers receiving child support payments from absentee fathers. The study found that "clients were 22.8% more likely to receive child support payments, and reported large increases in household and child food security."[39] This finding suggests that CJAs were playing an important role in securing child support and that these funds were translating directly into improved child and household food security.

Like the case of Hauwa, who we met in the introduction, the case of Nandi and her child illustrates the individual impact of the CJA intervention. Nandi and her partner, John, lived together in central Liberia and, in 2011, they had a child. Soon after the birth, John abandoned Nandi and his child, telling her to stop breastfeeding and not to ask him for any assistance. Nandi approached a JPC CJA for advice. The CJA helped Nandi understand John's legal obligations – from child support to the implications of his demand for her to stop breastfeeding. Nandi was fearful of pursuing a remedy through Liberia's court system and instead asked the CJA to assist with mediation. During this process John learned that if Nandi decided to take him to court, a judge might decide whether and how much he should provide to Nandi and their child. Nandi and John eventually agreed to terms of support, and the CJA drafted the agreement detailing a monthly payment of Liberian dollars as well as twenty-five kilograms of rice. The CJA monitored this agreement for three months to make sure the terms were being upheld, which they were. A year after this initial agreement a Carter Center staff member, as a component of their evaluation process, followed up with Nandi and found that John had not missed a monthly payment.

While the study was able to confirm that these client-level impacts positively affected child and household food security, the study did not find that the work of the CJAs impacted some of the other household well-being indicators that were measured, such as the amount of farming land and the incidence of gender-based violence.

E. State and Corporate Accountability

The Sandefur and Siddiqi study showed that clients who had seen paralegals improved their relationships with aggrieving parties and that there was a decrease

---

[39] Ibid., 33–34.

in having to pay a bribe to a police officer or a public official, suggesting that paralegal involvement may lower the corruption costs of access to justice through the formal system.[40]

Such cases are common challenges for many Liberians. One instance is a case of an elderly beverage seller in River Gee County who was left virtually penniless when someone stole 875 Liberian dollars from his backpack. The perpetrator was apprehended, taken to the police, and imprisoned by the local magistrate until he could pay back the money. Seeing the man soon free in the town, the beverage dealer was upset, and heard rumors that the magistrate had stolen the money repaid by the perpetrator's family. The beverage seller called the CJA, and the CJA was able to assist his client in meeting with the magistrate – who had in fact wrongfully retained the money – recovering the old man's savings, and extracting a public apology from the justice official. Without the CJA, the man likely would have had nowhere to turn to enforce his rights. Instead, this case provided an important example of accountability for the community.

Musu's case presents another example of accountability and assistance in navigating the formal justice system: her life was almost destroyed by domestic violence when her boyfriend threw acid over her, burning her face and upper torso. The perpetrator was arrested and charged, but due to a lengthy pretrial wait and an incomplete case file, he was eventually released back into the community. Musu feared for her life and brought the case to the JPC. A CJA used her psychosocial skills to counsel Musu, explained how the criminal justice system operates, and assisted her in meeting with the county attorney and agreeing to act as a witness. Her former partner was re-apprehended and successfully convicted. Through the CJA's assistance, Musu utilized the formal court system to obtain justice. Without the CJA's intervention, the case would likely have been forgotten, Musu's justice denied.

Overall, Sandefur and Siddiqi show that paralegals improved client satisfaction, fairness, perceptions of well-being, and relationships with other parties. The study concluded that legal empowerment interventions aimed at improving access to justice and bringing to life otherwise "dead letter" laws can produce large socioeconomic benefits.

V. THE DETERMINANTS OF SUCCESS

Paralegalism and legal empowerment programming in Liberia are at a crossroads. On the one hand, studies like Knight et al and Sandefur and Siddiqi's have shown client-level impacts. Program evaluations of people engaging with the CJA program report satisfaction and positive experiences from engaging with paralegals. Evidence of institutional impacts is beginning to emerge as well. But the policy and fiscal environment has not seen a similar improvement over the past ten years. Paralegal

---

[40] The research did not, however, find an impact on harassment by public officials.

programs in Liberia remain reliant on externally sourced donor funding, which is not surprising given Liberia's current budget, but implicit and explicit reticence on the part of Liberia's legal community is hampering longer-term sustainable impacts.

What makes for success in paralegal organizations in Liberia? There are both organizational and institutional factors.

A. Organizational Determinants

The effectiveness of paralegals in Liberia is significantly impacted by the organizational effectiveness of the managing organization. Within the JPC program, effective supervision and support of paralegals from both JPC and The Carter Center has proven critical in ensuring high-quality service delivery for clients. Liberia lacks infrastructure and travel between regions is challenging for many Liberians. JPC and The Carter Center's program infrastructure and management play important roles in bridging this gap.

As the Liberian legal community opens space for paralegals to operate, managers of paralegal programs and Liberian policymakers should further professionalize paralegal services. While specific projects have implemented their own standards, with degrees of success, paralegals are emerging as a dedicated class of professionals who have the responsibility to provide accurate and accountable advice to communities and individuals. Here the government and academia can play an important role by strengthening the programmatic approach. There are numerous contexts where governments and universities work collaboratively and proactively with frontline civil society legal aid providers to expand access to practical legal advice and assistance. In South Africa, for example, there are university courses in paralegal studies, and law students working in law clinics partner with the community advice offices described elsewhere in this volume. As discussed in Chapter 6, a legal aid bill sets the parameters for paralegal engagement at the local level, including minimum standards and required training.

What might this look like in the Liberian context? A key goal should be to maintain the programmatic flexibility and independence of civil society justice programs while simultaneously ensuring they have the organizational support required for effective and accountable service delivery. Liberian paralegal organizations, and those supporting these efforts, should come together to establish minimum standards for training, supervision, and support. An umbrella association bringing together paralegal providers across sectors might help to promote learning, maintain quality across programs and strengthen the voice of paralegal organizations more generally.

B. Institutional Determinants

The institutional environment has significant impacts on the paralegal sector in Liberia. Mistrust from the legal community is particularly inhibiting. In part due to the influence of the Liberian legal establishment, the Liberian government has allocated neither fiscal nor political support to the majority of paralegal efforts. There has been some progress engaging various government commissions, including the Land and Governance Commissions, as well as in MCP, but central state agencies have historically been wary to support or institutionalize independent paralegals. While the international community has been supportive at times, much of the large-scale support to the justice system is directed to the highest levels of the state justice and security system. The budget for the UN Peacebuilding Fund's "quick start" justice and security hub initiative, for example, prioritized infrastructure support and capacity building for formal sector personnel as opposed to community-based assistance.[41]

Some in the Liberian legal and political establishment have, however, moved closer to embracing a role for non-lawyers in the justice system. Indeed, in 2008 it appeared as if paralegals and community-based justice programming might be incorporated into the legal framework. Discussion around the applicability of paralegals in Liberia intensified following a visit to Malawi by a delegation of senior members of the Liberian legal establishment. These officials visited the Malawian government and paralegal organizations to see how the programs worked in practice and to explore opportunities for similar programming in Liberia. The lessons from this trip played an important role in helping some members of the judiciary temper their resistance toward non-lawyers operating in the justice sector. Many of these officials now agree that paralegals and other non-lawyers have an important role to play in improving the accountability and efficiency of the justice system.

Following the Malawi trip, the Taskforce on Non-Lawyers was launched in 2008. The Taskforce was jointly organized by the judiciary and the executive to explore appropriate areas for paralegals to operate. Despite some initial progress by the Taskforce, in the end there was significant bureaucratic resistance to any reforms. By 2013, the Taskforce had been unable to approve its own terms of reference.

This may be unsurprising, given the history of efforts to diversify the legal profession in Liberia. In the immediate postwar period, for example, the Liberian National Bar Association fought off attempts by international development partners to explore the admission of foreign trained lawyers in an effort to expand the pool of qualified lawyers and improve the efficiency and accountability of the legal profession.[42]

---

[41] The "hub and corrections infrastructure and equipment" budget is US$2,390,000 compared to US$610,000 for "public outreach, tracking system, logistics and training." UN Office for Project Services, UN Development Programme, "Peacebuilding Fund: Quick Start for Liberia Priority Plan II (2011–13)" (UNDP, 2011). www.undp.org/content/dam/undp/documents/projects/LBR/00061292_PBF%20Quick_Start_Project.pdf.

[42] Several international donors and organizations proposed that the Governance and Economic Management Assistance Program (GEMAP), a partnership between the government and the international community to build accountability in economic governance, allows for the admission of foreign lawyers. These efforts were ultimately rebuffed. See, for example, International Crisis Group, Liberia: Resurrecting the Justice System, 2 (see n. 2).

Liberia continues to have only one law school at the University of Liberia and entry into the Bar remains tightly controlled by law school administrators and senior members of the Bar Association. Despite some progress in reform, civil and criminal procedure remains extremely formalized and there are regular complaints that the system is essentially unintelligible for much of the population.

Opponents of Liberian paralegal programs typically argue that non-lawyers will provide misinformation to communities. One senior member of the legal establishment explained to us that paralegals carry a far greater risk than so-called barefoot doctors or primary healthcare professionals who work in local communities, providing information and helping refer serious medical cases to hospitals. According to this attorney, if a health worker provides misinformation, only the sick patient might die. If a paralegal, on the other hand, provides misinformation to a community on law and rights, the official suggested that the whole community would suffer irreparable harm (or "die" in his words).

Such views are commonly expressed in policy circles and many believe that paralegals should not be able to provide guidance on legal issues to communities and individuals. Liberian media reported, for example, that several members of the Liberian legal community attending the April 2013 National Criminal Justice Conference suggested that it was essential to avoid "non-lawyers posing as lawyers to exploit the common people who are already crying for justice."[43] Lawyers also worry that paralegals will provide misinformation and prey upon the local population by demanding fees. Such positions overlook the reality that at this time the vast majority of Liberian paralegals provide services free of charge, or subject to a small fee.

While it is certainly important to raise questions of the cost and reliability of legal services, objections from many members of the Bar miss a fundamental reality confronting many in Liberia: most individuals simply cannot engage lawyers for advice or assistance or access formal courts with legal and administrative issues. The fees and geographic factors are prohibitive. The legal community is overwhelmingly based in Monrovia and, even there, it does not provide the types of services most people need: advice on rights, entitlements, and managing community-level disputes. Paralegal programs are instead working to respond to the actual needs and experiences of most Liberians in ways that are accessible.

Active obstruction by some in the legal establishment, compounded by a complex and slow-moving regulatory environment, has also limited international investment in paralegal programs and hampered efforts to diversify funding. For paralegal programs like the JPC's CJA program to become sustainably successful in Liberia, they need to move from being exclusively externally funded to a central component of Liberia's justice strategy. Rhetorically, there has been some support by senior

---

[43] Winston W. Parley, "Fears over Justice Program," *New Dawn*, April 1, 2013. http://allafrica.com/stories/201304010955.html.

officials, but policymakers, both Liberian and international, need to move away from short-term and iterant support to the sector. As several other chapters of this volume make clear, governments around the world are productively grappling with questions of how to integrate the paralegal model into state justice service delivery. Much as medical doctors work with a frontline of primary health care officials, the Liberian legal system might be strengthened through a broadening of avenues for legal information and assistance. A move away from a justice system that privileges legalistic approaches, and prioritizes the role of lawyers in formulaic proceedings, would respond to a call for just outcomes for the poor. Such efforts would be in line with the values of the majority of Liberians.

Developing ways to ensure the relative independence of paralegals while simultaneously providing sufficient funding will be a challenging task in the Liberian context. The availability of autonomous funding from government would require a reprioritization of justice sector activities and expenditure over a longer period of time. The international community should support such efforts to ensure the justice system is able to more holistically respond to the challenges most Liberians face.

VI. CONCLUSION

Liberia's 2008 Poverty Reduction Strategy argues that a "culture of participation by all citizens and partnership with government is critical to increasing transparency and accountability, reducing corruption and improving governance."[44] Community paralegals in Liberia play an important role in bringing this culture of participation to life. Beyond a focus on regulation, professionalization, and the perennial sustainability challenge of financing, a commitment by the Liberian government to focus on just outcomes, and strengthening the rule of law from a Liberian community and individual perspective, would be a necessary step in the right direction. The past ten years of experimentation with and rigorous evaluation of community-based paralegal models in Liberia has demonstrated quantifiable and positive results, in terms of both client satisfaction in the immediate case and broader socioeconomic benefits. There is a gradual realization in Liberia that rule of law reform that focuses predominantly on a foreign formal legal system is neither the only nor the best option for Liberians. Flexible, locally oriented legal assistance benefits the lived experience of the justice system and must factor in Liberian rule of law reform. This alternative path prioritizes engagement at the community level and empowers individuals and communities to navigate the administrative and bureaucratic structures that govern their lives, demand appropriate reform, and access a holistic justice system that can provide redress for wrongs and the peaceful and productive resolution of disputes.

[44] International Monetary Fund, *Liberia: Poverty Reduction Strategy Paper*. IMF Country Report no. 08/219 (Washington, DC: International Monetary Fund, 2008), 85.

REFERENCES

Banks III, Philip A. Z. "Forward." In *Strategic Plan 2009–2012*. Monrovia: Ministry of Justice of the Government of Liberia, 2008.

Blair, Robert, Christopher Blattman, and Alexandra Hartman. *Patterns of Conflict and Cooperation in Liberia (Part 1): Results from a Longitudinal Study*. New Haven, CT: Yale University, Innovations for Poverty Action, 2012.

Clower, Robert W., George Dalton, Mitchell Harwitz, and A. A. Walters. *Growth without Development: An Economic Survey of Liberia*. Evanston, IL: Northwestern University Press, 1966.

East-West Management Institute. "EWMI Awards Grant to Support Access to Justice in Liberia." Last modified February 2009. www.ewmi.org./CDRILLFebruary2009.

International Monetary Fund. *Liberia: Poverty Reduction Strategy Paper*. IMF Country Report no. 08/219. Washington, DC: International Monetary Fund, 2008.

International Crisis Group. *Liberia: Resurrecting the Justice System*. Brussels: International Crisis Group, 2006.

International Legal Assistance Consortium. *ILAC Report: Liberia*. Stockholm: International Legal Assistance Consortium, 2003.

Isser, Deborah H., Stephen C. Lubkemann, and Saah N'Tow. "Looking for Justice: Liberian Experiences and Perceptions of Local Justice Options." *Peaceworks* 63 (2009).

JPC client, interview, 2013.

"JPC Liberia." Justice and Peace Commission, Liberia. http://jpcliberia.org/.

Knight, Rachel, Judy Adoko, Teresa Auma, Ali Kaba, Alda Salomao, Silas Siakor, and Issufo Tankar. *Protecting Community Lands and Resources: Evidence from Liberia*. Rome: International Development Law Organization; Washington, DC: Namati, 2012.

Knight, Rachel, Marena Brinkhurst, and Jaron Vogelsang. *Community Land Protection: Facilitators Guide*. Washington, DC: Namati, 2016.

Lubkemann, Stephen, Deborah Isser, and Peter Chapman. "Neither State nor Custom – Justice Naked Power: The Consequences of Ideals-Oriented Rule of Law Policy-Making in Liberia." *Journal of Legal Pluralism and Unofficial Law* 43, no. 63 (2011): 73–109. doi: 10.1080/07329113.2011.10756658.

Mamdani, Mahmood. *Citizen and Subject: Contemporary Africa and the Legacy of Late Colonialism*. Princeton, NJ: Princeton University Press, 1996.

Norwegian Refugee Council. "Leaving Liberia." www.nrc.no/news/2015/july/leaving-liberia/.

Searching for Soap Trees: Norwegian Refugee Council's Land Dispute Resolution Process in Liberia. Oslo: Norwegian Refugee Council, 2011.

Parley, Winston W. "Fears over Justice Program." *New Dawn*. April 1, 2013. http://allafrica.com/stories/201304010955.html.

Republic of Liberia. Rules and Regulations Governing the Hinterland of Liberia. 1949 amended January 7, 2001.

Sandefur, Justin and Bilal Siddiqi. "Delivering Justice to the Poor: Theory and Experimental Evidence from Liberia." Paper presented at the World Bank Workshop on African Political Economy, Washington, DC, May 2013. https://editorialexpress.com/cgi-bin/conference/download.cgi?db_name=CSAE2013&paper_id=1014.

Small Arms Survey. "Reading between the Lines: Crime and Victimization in Liberia." *Small Arms Survey Issue Brief*, no. 2. Geneva: Small Arms Survey, 2011.

Ubink, Janine and Benjamin van Rooij. "Towards Customary Legal Empowerment: An Introduction." In *Customary Justice: Perspectives on Legal Empowerment*, edited by

Janine Ubink and Thomas McInerney. Rome: International Development Law Organization, 2011.

UN Office for Project Services, UN Development Programme. "Peacebuilding Fund: Quick Start for Liberia Priority Plan II (2011–13)" (UNDP, 2011). www.undp.org/content/dam/undp/documents/projects/LBR/00061292_PBF%20Quick_Start_Project.pdf.

Vinck, Patrick, Phuong Pham, and Tino Kreutzer. *Talking Peace: A Population-Based Survey on Attitudes about Security, Dispute Resolution, and Post-conflict Reconstruction in Liberia*. Berkeley: Human Rights Center, University of California, Berkley, 2011.

Index

Abahlali base Mjondolo, 53
Access to Justice Cluster Program (AJC), 70–71
Accountability
 and post-conflict development, 212
 community oversight (accountability of paralegals to communities), 33–34, 194–95
 corporate accountability, 128
 local accountability, 190
 state accountability, 15–17, 126–27, 185–88, 189, 257
Advocacy, 60, 151, 158–62, 176, 181, 224
 advocating to translate grassroots experience into systemic change, 18–19
 and organizing, 12, 158
 political, 162
African Minerals Limited. See Sierra Leone Diamond Corporation (SLDC)
African National Congress, 15, 47, 50, 52, 53
Alternative dispute resolution, 55
Alternative Law Groups (ALG), 12, 16, 99, 102, 112
Alternative Legal Assistance Center (SALIGAN), 16, 33, 99
Anti-Privatisation Forum (South Africa), 53
Apartheid, 14, 46–47
 antiapartheid movement and transition to democracy, 28
 dom pass, 46
 influx control, 46
 pass laws, 15, 46
ASEAN countries, 102
Asia Foundation, 100, 111
Association of University Legal Advice Institutions (AULAI) Trust, 64, 65, 70–71
Ateneo Human Rights Center (AHRC), 99, 108
Atlantic Philanthropies, 24, 59, 64, 69
Authoritarianism. See also Democracy
 responses against, 15, 35

Balay Alternative Legal Advocates for Development in Mindanaw (BALAOD), 99
Bantay dagat, 104, 109, 114, 127, 130
Bantay gubat, 104, 109, 114, 117, 127, 130
Barangay justice system, 16, 113, 124, 132
 Barangay captain, 114, 130
 Barangay development council (BDC), 106, 113
 Barangay protection order (BPO), 114
Barazas, 170, 184, 185, 187
Barefoot lawyers. See Community paralegals
Berenschot, Ward, 12, 27, 29, 139
Billings, Lucy, 19 n. 42
Black Sash, 4, 15, 48, 50, 59–62, 71
 Black Sash Trust, 64
 Grahamstown Regional Office, 61
 Johannesburg Regional Office, 59, 62
Bourdieu, Pierre, 144
BRAC, 5, 25, 216, 232
Braima, Lyttelton, 210
British Department for International Development (DFID), 232

Case management
 case data, 32–33, 235–37
 case forms, 71, 251
 case logs, 60, 71, 93
 case management systems, 93, 198
 case tracking, 10, 168, 211, 217–22
 interviews, 72, 218
 Monitoring and evaluation (M&E), 115, 131
Catholic Access to Justice Project (Sierra Leone), 213, 216
Catholic Justice and Peace Commission (JPC), 33, 174, 216, 242, 249, 253
Catholic Organization for Relief and Development Aid (CORDAID), 111
Center for Legal Education and Aid Networks (CLEAN), 174

Center for Migrant Workers (KANLUNGAN), 99, 108
Centre for Applied Legal Studies (CALS) (South Africa), 48
Centre for Criminal Justice (South Africa), 44, 50, 54, 68–70, 78, 82, 92
Certificate of Land Ownership Awards (CLOA), 116
Chapman, Peter, 17, 19, 241
Children's Legal Bureau (CLB), 99
Cisnero, Maria Roda, 18, 96
Citizen vs. Citizen disputes. *See* Intra-community disputes
Citizens Advice Forum, 50
Civil society organizations (CSOs). *See* Organizations
Clarke, Thomas, 8
Cluff Gold Company, 210–12, 236
Community Advice Offices (CAOs), 11, 20, 22, 28, 33, 34
Community health workers, 3
Community Justice Advisors (CJAs), 250–58
Community Law and Rural Development Centre (CLRDC), 49, 51, 68–70, 73–74
Community Monitoring and Advocacy Programme (CMAP), 60
Community paralegals
  advantages of, 5, 167
  definition of, 2–3, 103–4
  formal recognition of, 19–23, 114, 131, 133, 191, 217
  impact of, 18, 121–23
  limitations of, 5–6
  payment of, 31–32, 192, 197
  problem solving of, 10–13
  recruitment of, 31, 59, 197
  specialization of, 35, 113, 119, 180
  supervision of, 33, 198, 236, 237
  training of, 57, 70, 92, 104, 107, 121, 135, 157, 176, 194–96
  types of, 108–9
Conteh, Sonkita, 13 n. 32, 230 n. 36, 233
Contractual disputes, 79
Convention for a Democratic South Africa, 50
Corruption, 229–31
  in court, 154, 166, 167, 227, 246
  in local government, 190, 229
  in paralegals, 28
  paralegals fighting corruption, 257
Courts
  access to courts, 52, 89, 260
  and corruption. *See* Corruption in court
  distrust toward, 154, 161

formal court, 167
native court, 169
relationship with paralegals, 91
tribal court, 83
Criminal justice. *See* Justice
Culture
  cultural factors, 26–28, 36–37, 200
  customary local systems, 167
  tribal authority, 200

Dale, Pamela, 7, 213–16
Debt claims, 79, 81
Defense of Nature (TK), 99, 108
Democracy
  and repressive regimes, 14–16, 35, 172
  democratic reform, 51
  role of paralegals in deepening democracy, 37, 93, 162, 237, 261
Diokno, Jose W., 101–3, 121
Disputes with firms, 3, 17, 18, 161, 201, 225, *See also* corporate accountability
  and power imbalance, 36, 128
  and protection of community lands, 182, 225
Disputes with states, 3, 17, 18, 93, 126, 161, 185, 187, 188, 225, *See also* state accountability
  and power imbalance, 36
DPRD (Indonesia), 158, 159
Drage, Katherine, 20, 27, 28, 32, 34, 43
Dugard, Jackie, 20, 27, 28, 32, 34, 43
Duterte, Rodrigo, 16

Education, 70, 76, 205
Elections, 159–60, 173–74
Elias, Norbert, 144
Environmental justice, 225, 229–30
Environmental laws, 107, 119, 131
Environmental Legal Assistance Center (ELAC), 99, 108
Erasmus, Greg, 28, 55, 65, 87

Familial disputes, 74, 75, 201, 202, 256, *See also* Intra-community disputes
Financing. *See also* Legal aid funding
  challenges obtaining, 85, 193
  client contributions, 235
  community fundraisers, 26
  development assistance, 24
  efforts to diversify, 25–26, 36
  international, 36, 232
  public, 19, 192, 233
  risks to paralegal independence, 25, 234
Ford Foundation, 6, 69, 111
Foundation for Human Rights, 59
Franco, Jennifer, 18, 96

Free Legal Assistance Group (FLAG), 15, 99, 101, 107, 108
Funding. *See* Financing

Gauri, Varun, 1, 2, 210 n. 1
Gender
  domestic violence, 36, 132, 203, 204, 257
  gender-based violence, 52, 188, 203
  sexual violence, 43–44, 69, 189
  women's rights, 17, 200, 222
George Civic Association, 49
German Catholic Bishops' Organisation for Development Cooperation (MISEREOR), 111
Golub, Stephen, 3, 6
Governance, Justice, Law and Governance Programme (GJLOS), 167, 177
Grassroots organizations. *See* Organizations

Haki Centre, 179
Harding, Joanne, 86, 92
HIV/AIDS, 67
Housing
  access to state-sponsored housing, 77
  forced evictions, 8
  lawsuits related to, 158

Identity documents, 77
Indonesia
  Ministry of Law and Human Rights, 20, 141
Indonesian laws
  Law on Legal Assistance (2011), 20
  Legal Aid Bill (2011), 140, 162
Inequality
  in access to justice, 142
  under relational sociology, 144
Informal Settlements Network (South Africa), 53
Infrastructure
  grievances in relation to, 223, 249
  infrastructure constraints in the justice sector, 241
Institutions
  institutional factors, 17, 36, 97, 111–12, 184, 190, 226, 258
  intermediary, 2
  judicial institutions, 76, 96
  legal institutions, 142
  local government units, 109, 119, 120
  local institutions, 245
  paralegals' relationship with local institutions, 29
  regulatory/administrative institutions, 229–31
  state institutions, 2, 81–83, 246

Integrated Bar of the Philippines (IBP), 100, 103, 118
International Commission of Jurists – Kenya Chapter (ICJ), 168, 173–74, 198
International Development Law Organization (IDLO), 247
International Federation of Women Lawyers – Kenya Chapter (FIDA), 168, 173–76
Intra-community disputes, 3, 6, 11, 16–18, 141, 181, 205, 206, 223
  and effectiveness of mediation, 90
  and relationship to cultural and social norms, 150, 200
  and relationship to local institutions, 36, 123–24, 145, 190
  debt claims, 79
  methods of resolution in, 152, 253

Jalloh, Gibrill, 210
Joseph Rowntree Charitable Trust, 64, 69
Justice
  criminal, 82
  reform, 133–34
  social, 45, 66, 112, 133–34

Kampala Declaration on Community Paralegals (2012), 2
Kenya
  Ministry of Justice, 178
  Ministry of Lands, 186
  Ministry of Water, 185
  National Human Rights Policy and Action Plan, 193
  Water Appeals Court, 187
Kenya Human Rights Commission (KHRC), 173, 175
Kenya Law Reform Commission (KLRC), 176
Kenyan laws
  Access to Information Bill, 193
  Legal Aid Act (2016), 20, 178, 191–93, 206
  Legal Practitioners Act of 1906, 169
Kituo Cha Mashauri. *See* Kituo Cha Sheria
Kituo Cha Sheria, 166, 168, 171–74, 179
Knight, Rachael, 7, 257
Koroma, Ernest Bai, 216
Koroma, Simeon, 212, 230
Kubayi, Winnie, 69
Kumar, Sunil, 7

Labor disputes
  and power imbalance, 147
Landless People's Movement (South Africa), 53

Law
  and politics, 120, 160, 162, 172, 229–31
  common, 51, 83
  customary, 83, 212, 226
  customary law, 169, 225
  enforcement, 119–20
  firms, 56, 88, 110
  legislation, 20, 48, 107, 192
  litigation, 227–28
  policies, 98, 126
  school, 103, 260
Law Society of Kenya (LSK), 170–73
Lawyers
  bar associations, 170, 259
  difficulties accessing, 5, 19, 44, 212, 260
  litigation, 44, 88, 227, 233
  pro bono, 88, 171, 180
  public interest, 2, 110–11, 130, 132
  relationship to paralegals, 19
Lawyers for Human Rights (LHR) (South Africa), 48
Legal aid
  board, 20, 22, 217, 234
  civil, 58
  developmental, 97, 101–2, 104
  funding, 36, 234 n. 49, 235 n. 50
  legislation, 9, 20, 26, 140, 162, 191–93, 206, 211, 217, 233, 258
  systems, 21–23
Legal Aid South Africa (LASA), 47, 57–59, 85
  call center, 62
  justice center, 89
Legal Assistance Center for Indigenous Filipinos (PANLIPI), 99, 108
Legal awareness, 10–12, 121, 175
Legal clinic
  walk-in clients, 58, 179
Legal dualism, 243
Legal Education Aid Programme (LEAP), 173, 174
Legal empowerment, 2, 25, 96, 108, 213, 222 n. 15, 227–28
  and social accountability, 158–59
Legal intermediaries, 34, 156, 157, 161
  abogadillo, 34, 103, 125
  blackman lawya, 34
  makelar kasus, 34, 156
Legal literacy. *See* Legal awareness
Legal Resources Centre (LRC) (South Africa), 48, 57
  Grahamstown LRC, 50
Legal Resources Foundation Trust (LRF), 168, 174, 179
Legislation. *See* Law
LegiWatch, 51

Lembaga Bantuan Hukum (LBH), 139
Liberia
  Liberian National Police (LNP), 246
  Ministry of Internal Affairs (MIA), 243
Liberian laws
  Domestic Relations Law and Penal Law, 242
Litigation. *See* Law
Lobbying, 15, 107, 159, 181
Local dispute resolution, 11–12, 16–19, 148, 186, 245–46
  and customary courts, 212
  as shaped by political contexts, 160
  other actors in (aside from paralegals), 156
  state-judicial dispute tribunals, 98
Local government units. *See* Institutions

Maguindanao Massacre, 103
Mansuri, Ghazala, 34 n. 76
Manuel, Clare, 228
Manuel, Marlon, 16
Marcos, Ferdinand, 15, 101, 102, 124
Martial law (Philippines), 101, 121
Maru, Vivek, 1, 55, 87, 210, 212
McQuoid-Mason, David, 85
Mediation, 11–12, 17, 55, 80, 90–91, 124, 147–55, 200, 203, 224–25, 251
Meinzen-Dick, Ruth, 19 n. 42
Methodist Church of Sierra Leone, 216, 217, 237
Mining, 115, 210–12, 227–28
  impact on water supply, 1, 12, 128, 182–83
  sand-mining, 1
Moi, Daniel Arap, 169, 172–73
Monitoring, 48, 60, 127, 173–74, 175, 179, 180, 247
Monitoring and evaluation (M&E). *See* Case management
Monrovia Central Prison (MCP), 247
Mott Foundation, 59, 64, 71
Movement of Attorneys for Brotherhood, Integrity and Nationalism (MABINI), 102
Moy, H. Abigail, 29, 32, 33, 165
Mtshali, Langa, 85, 92
Mueller, Valerie, 19 n. 42
Muslims for Human Rights (MUHURI), 168, 179

National Alliance for the Development of Community Advice Offices (NADCAO), 20, 28, 63–66, 87, 93
National Community Based Paralegal Association (NCBPA), 54, 64, 65
National Council of Churches of Kenya (NCCK), 172–73
National Forum for Human Rights, 212
National Legal Aid and Awareness Programme (NALEAP), 177–78

National Legal Aid Service (Kenya), 20, 192–93
National Welfare Forum (South Africa), 62
Natural resources, 106, 139, 242
  water, 185–87
Negotiation, 55, 148–49, 197, 211, 226, 252
Netherlands Organization for International Assistance (NOVIB), 111
Network
  coordination, 35, 193
  umbrella clusters, 79, 89
  vertical networks, 30–31, 228, 236
Network Movement for Justice and Development (Sierra Leone), 217
Norwegian Refugee Council (NRC), 249
Nubian Rights Forum, 179

Omnibus Rules and Regulations Implementing the Migrant Workers and Overseas Filipinos Act (1995), 105
Open Society Foundation, 24, 140, 146, 216, 232, 247
Open Society Institute. *See* Open Society Foundation
Open Society Justice Initiative (OSJI), 212, 216
Organization for Economic Cooperation and Development (OECD), 228
Organizations
  civil society organizations (CSOs), 50, 53, 63, 193
  community-based organizations, 197
  effective organizational choices, 31–35
  grassroots organizations, 33, 108, 109, 118
  organizational factors, 89–93, 193–94, 258
Organizing, 12, 112–13, 119, 181, 231
Our Land Our Future Public Pledge (Sierra Leone, 2018), 230

Paralegal Education Skills Advancement and Networking Technology (PESANTEch), 112
Paralegal Support Network (PASUNE), 167, 176–78, 191
Payne, Chelsea, 17, 19, 241
Pensions, 71, 73
Philippine laws
  Comprehensive Agrarian Reform Extension with Reforms (CARPER) (2009), 105
  Comprehensive Agrarian Reform Program (CARP) (1980), 105
  Indigenous Peoples Rights Act (IPRA) (1997), 105
  Juvenile Justice and Welfare Act (JJWA) (2006), 105
  Local Government Code (1991), 105, 124

National Integrated Protected Areas System (NIPAS) Law (1991), 105
Philippine Fisheries Code (1998), 105, 115
Violence against Women and Children Act (VAWC) (2004), 105
Philippines
  Bureau of Fisheries and Aquatic Resources (BFAR), 114
  Department of Agrarian Reform (DAR), 21, 106, 107
  Department of Environment and Natural Resources (DENR), 21, 114, 127
  Department of Labor and Employment (DOLE), 114
  National Labor Relations Commission, 21, 107
  Office of the Court Attorney (OCAt), 118
  Public Attorney's Office, 125
  Supreme Court of, 21, 100, 103, 107, 117–18, 130
Pitkin, Hannah, 2
Plan International, 168, 180
Policies. *See* Law
Poverty
  and impact on paralegal work, 132
  poverty alleviation and legal empowerment, 25, 261
Power
  imbalance of, 8, 35, 128, 141, 161, 201, 225
Prison Fellowship Liberia (PFL), 247
Protestant Lawyers' League (PLL), 102, 107
Protests, 48
Public Law Institute (PLI), 173

Rallies. *See* Protests
Rao, Vijayendra, 34 n. 76
Referral system, 55, 89–90
Regulatory/administrative institutions. *See* institutions
Revitalisation of Legal Aid (RLA), 145, 155
Revolutionary United Front (RUF), 212
Rights
  consciousness, 180, 255
  consumer, 60
  land, 7, 105, 225
Rinaldi, Taufik, 12, 27, 29, 139
Ringold, Dena, 15
Rules and Regulations Governing the Hinterland of Liberia (the "Hinterland Regulations"), 243
Rural Poor Institute for Land and Human Rights Services (RIGHTS), 99

Sandefur, Justin, 8, 10, 253–54, 256, 257
Sandefur, Rebecca, 8
Service delivery, 60, 82, 261

Siddiqui, Bilal, 8, 10
Sierra Leone
  Environmental Protection Agency, 230
  Ministry of Lands, 230
  Special Court for Sierra Leone, 212
  Sierra Leone Diamond Corporation (SLDC), 227–28, 236
Sierra Leonean laws
  Child Rights Act (2007), 222
  Devolution of Estates Act (2007), 222
  Domestic Violence Act (2007), 222
  Environment Protection (Mines and Minerals) Regulation (2013), 229
  Land Policy (2015), 230
  Legal Aid Law (2012), 20, 211, 217, 233
  Right to Information Act, 229
Social Change Assistance Trust (SCAT), 26, 34, 50, 54, 60, 66–68, 86
  Fund-Raising Incentive Scheme (FRIS), 67
Social embeddedness, 37, 90–91, 155, 157
Social movements
  and paralegals, 27–28, 33, 123, 129
Social security, 52, 62, 76, 77
  social grants, 50, 56, 61
Socio-Economic Rights Institute of South Africa (SERI), 85, 91
Solidarity toward Agrarian Reform and Rural Development (KAISAHAN), 33, 99
Soliman, Hector, 18, 96
South Africa
  Constitution of, 51, 89
  Department of Home Affairs, 60, 77
  Department of Judicial Affairs and Constitutional Development (DJCD), 83
  Police Service, 54, 69, 82
South African Defence and Aid Fund, 47
South African Human Rights Commission (SAHRC), 83
South African laws
  Bill of Rights, 44, 53, 83
  Consumer Protection Act (2011), 60
  Legal Aid Act (1969), 47
  Legal Practice Act (2014), 84
  Legal Practice Bill (2002), 20, 65, 84
  National Credit Act (2005), 60
  Social Assistance Act (1992), 61
South African National Civic Organisation (SANCO), 49
South African Social Security Agency (SASSA), 60, 77

Sustainable Development Institute (SDI), 242, 247–49
Systemic change, 37, 235 n. 50
  challenge of funding, 235
  through network collaboration, 31
  translating grassroots experience into systemic change, 18–19, 33

Talbot, Colin, 8
Taskforce on Non-Lawyers, 259
The Carter Center, 249–53
The Children's Foundation (CRADLE). See Widows' and Orphans' Welfare Society of Kenya (WOWESOK)
The Society for Elimination of Rural Poverty (India), 7
Tilly, Charles, 144
Timap for Justice, 6, 7, 211, 213–16, 217, 222, 227–28
Troicare, 232
Trust (from communities). See social embeddedness
Truth and Reconciliation Commission (TRC), 178

UN Commission on Legal Empowerment, 1, 5
UN Peacebuilding Fund, 249, 259
Unemployment, 56
  unemployment benefit claim, 74
Unions, 30, 56, 117, 157
United Democratic Front (UDF), 49
United Nations Development Programme (UNDP), 140, 141, 145, 156, 160, 232

Varvaloucas, Alaina, 8

Wajir Human Rights Network, 179
Widows' and Orphans' Welfare Society of Kenya (WOWESOK), 174
Wiggan, Jay, 8
Women's Legal and Human Rights Bureau (WLB), 99, 109
Women's rights. See Gender
World Bank, 99, 140, 141, 145, 155, 160, 213
  Justice for the Poor Project, 145, 146, 157
Writ of amparo, 105, 127
Writ of habeas data, 105
Writ of kalikasan, 105, 127

Zulu, Thandiwe, 59

For EU product safety concerns, contact us at Calle de José Abascal, 56–1°, 28003 Madrid, Spain or eugpsr@cambridge.org.

www.ingramcontent.com/pod-product-compliance
Lightning Source LLC
LaVergne TN
LVHW021654060526
838200LV00050B/2344